WENDY DOBSON
and
PIERRE JACQUET

Financial Services Liberalization in the WTO

INSTITUTE FOR INTERNATIONAL ECONOMICS
Washington, DC
June 1998

Wendy Dobson, *Visiting Fellow* (1990–91, 1998), is Professor and Director, Centre for International Business, at the Rotman School of Management at the University of Toronto. She served as Associate Deputy Minister of Finance in the Canadian government and Canada's G-7 Deputy (1987–89). She was president of the C. D. Howe Institute (1981–87) and has written on Canadian issues in macroeconomic and trade policy and on international economic relations, including *Economic Policy Coordination: Requiem or Prologue?* (1991). *Multinationals and East Asian Integration* (1997, coedited with Chia Siow Yue) won the Ohira Prize

Pierre Jacquet is Deputy Director of the Paris-based French Institute of International Relations (IFRI) and chief editor of the French quarterly review *Politique étrangère*. He is also head of the department of economics and social sciences and professor of international economics at the Ecole Nationale des Ponts et Chaussées. He belongs to the Conseil d'Analyse Economique, an independent advisory panel created by the French prime minister in July 1997. He coedits IFRI's annual *RAMSES* report on the world economy and publishes articles on international economic relations and European and international monetary issues.

INSTITUTE FOR INTERNATIONAL ECONOMICS
11 Dupont Circle, NW
Washington, DC 20036-1207
(202) 328-9000   FAX: (202) 328-5432

C. Fred Bergsten, *Director*
Christine F. Lowry, *Director of Publications*

Printing by Kirby Lithographic
Typesetting by Sandra F. Watts

Printed in the United States of America
00   5 4 3 2

Library of Congress Cataloging-in-Publication Data

Dobson, Wendy.
  Financial services liberalization in the World Trade Organization / by Wendy Dobson and Pierre Jacquet.
     p. cm.
  Includes bibliographical references and index.
  1. Financial services industry—OECD countries. 2. World Trade Organization.
  I. Jacquet, Pierre.
  HG173.D57   1997
  332.1—dc21   97-39379
                                              CIP
  ISBN 0-88132-254-7

Contents

Preface   **ix**

Acknowledgments   **xiii**

1 Introduction and Overview   **1**
   The Benefits of Financial Reform   5
   Objections to Deregulation and Market Opening   8
   The Organization of This Book   12
   Conclusions and Recommendations   12

2 The Benefits of Financial Reform   **15**
   Benefits to Users   16
   Economywide Benefits of Financial Reform: A Review
      of the Literature   24
   Conclusion   29

3 The Pitfalls of Reform and Transitional Issues   **31**
   Three Common Concerns   32
   Policy Implications and the Management of the Transition   47
   Conclusion   65

**4 Setting the Context: Toward the WTO Financial
   Services Agreement**   **69**
   Services in the Uruguay Round   70
   Overview of the GATS   72

Objectives, Stances, and Strategies 75
The Financial Services Negotiations: A Brief History
of WTO Discussions 80

5 The FSA and Beyond: Financial Reform and the WTO 87
Assessing the FSA 89
The Role of GATS and the WTO in Promoting Financial
Opening 95
The Task Ahead: A Strategic Note 99
Concluding Remarks 101

**Appendix A Accelerating Change: The Global
Financial Services Sector 107**

Appendix B Case Studies 126

References 327

Index 335

Tables

Table 1.1 Estimated benefits to users of phasing in
financial services reform by 2010 7
Table 2.1 Performance indicators for East Asian banks,
various years 21
Table 3.1 Openness of financial markets, 1997 35
Table 3.2 Selected economic indicators: Asian economies,
1993-97 49
Table 3.3 Characteristics of the financial sector, 1997 54
Table 5.1 Market access in financial services: Status quo
versus WTO commitments, 1997 91
Table 5.2 World Trade Organization financial services
agreement: market access in selected countries, 1997 93
Table A.1 Banking industry indicators in selected
developing and industrial countries, 1994 110
Table A.2 Net financing in international markets, 1994-96 113
Table A.3 Net private capital flows to developing countries,
1990-96 118
Table B.1 Argentina: Assets of financial institutions, 1994
and 1997 132
Table B.2 Chile: Assets of financial institutions, 1996 157
Table B.3 Indonesia: Assets of financial institutions,
1969, 1982, 1988, and 1991 204
Table B.4 Japan: Assets of financial institutions, 1970,
1980, 1989, and 1993 220

Table B.5   South Korea: Assets of financial institutions,
            1970, 1980, and 1995   242
Table B.6   Malaysia: Assets of financial institutions, 1987
            and 1993   258
Table B.7   Singapore: Assets of financial institutions, 1987
            and 1993   293
Table B.8   Taiwan: Assets of financial institutions, 1970,
            1980, and 1990   302
Table B.9   Thailand: Assets of financial institutions, 1983,
            1989, and 1992   313

Figure
Figure A.1 Activity in international financial markets   114

Box
Box 5.1   Financing Growth in APEC   88

Preface

This study evaluates the financial services agreement (FSA) that was reached in the World Trade Organization in December 1997 and is to be implemented in early 1999. Financial services are one of three major sectors, along with telecommunications services and information technology products, where multilateral liberalization agreements were reached in the WTO during the past two years. The Institute has already published a similar study of the telecommunications agreement (*Unfinished Business: Telecommunications after the Uruguay Round*, edited by Gary Clyde Hufbauer and Erika Wada) and has analyzed the Information Technology Agreement in several of its releases on the trading system.

In this study, authors Wendy Dobson and Pierre Jacquet analyze the basic rationale for the FSA: efficient financial sectors are important contributors to economic growth and stability. Their focus is underscored by the pivotal role that weak financial sectors played in triggering the Asian financial crisis. Financial market development, in turn, depends on deregulation and other domestic measures to strengthen financial systems. However, market opening and foreign investment, which are the focus of the FSA, are also important contributors because foreign institutions bring new skills and products and promote competition and efficiency. Global success in delivering financial services is of course associated with capital account convertability; however, it is efficient financial systems, rather than totally free capital investments, that are key to growth and development.

The authors recognize that the benefits of financial liberalization can be offset by risks and costs: possible financial crises, loss of national control of a "strategic sector," and political backlash from those who lose from sectoral reforms. They stress the importance of responding to these concerns, primarily by strengthening the financial system's ability to evaluate and manage risk. Internationalization of the sector, far from exacerbating these problems, can contribute to their solution because of the positive role that foreign financial institutions can play.

Dobson and Jacquet conclude that the FSA largely formalizes the status quo. It makes a modest contribution to growth-promoting financial-market development by enabling most of the main players to bind existing practices in an international agreement and by providing a mechanism for settling disputes. But the agreement entails little new liberalization. Individual OECD countries did not do much to open their markets further. The main emerging market economies, with some exceptions, offered little new access to their banking sectors, which often dominate their financial industries, though they did offer more new access to their insurance sectors. Given these results, the authors characterize the FSA as "a first, insufficient yet useful, step toward more open and efficient financial systems."

Governments should therefore go beyond the modest commitments in the FSA that are currently slated to be implemented in 1999. The gains from full liberalization of the financial sector are potentially huge. A more ambitious FSA, perhaps included in comprehensive new WTO trade negotiations beginning in 2000, should be folded into a wider set of negotiations that address competition policy and foreign direct investment. A new FSA should:

- Secure the right of financial services firms to establish and operate freely in all participating countries;

- Provide national treatment for these firms once established;

- Free cross-border trade in financial services and movements in personnel; and

- Provide limited and transparent exemptions and MFN-compatible grandfathering of existing investments.

This study began as an effort by Professor Dobson to address the issue of financial services liberalization solely in the Asia Pacific region, as part of the Institute's program on trade liberalization and facilitation in the Asia Pacific Economic Cooperation (APEC) forum. Its scope was broadened in late 1996, to cover the full range of the WTO negotiations, when it became clear that global talks in the WTO would supersede APEC's regional deliberations. The initial emphasis on Asian countries turned out to be fortuitous, however, because much of the WTO focus, in the final stages of its negotiation, was on countries in that region. Nevertheless, the Institute owes a special debt of gratitude to both authors: to Professor Dobson, for her willingness to shift (and substantially enlarge) the extent of her research in the midst of the project, and to Professor Jacquet, for making a full contribution to completing the study despite joining it only in midstream.

The Institute for International Economics is a private nonprofit institution for the study and discussion of international economic policy. Its purpose is to analyze important issues in that area and to develop and communicate practical new approaches for dealing with them. The Institute is completely nonpartisan.

The Institute is funded largely by philanthropic foundations. Major institutional grants are now being received from The German Marshall Fund of the United States, which created the Institute with a generous commitment of funds in 1981, and from The William M. Keck, Jr. Foundation, The Andrew W. Mellon Foundation, and The Starr Foundation. A number of other foundations and private corporations also contribute to the highly diversified financial resources of the Institute. About 12 percent of the Institute's resources in our latest fiscal year were provided by contributors outside the United States, including about 6 percent from Japan.

The Board of Directors bears overall responsibility for the Institute and gives general guidance and approval to its research program—including identification of topics that are likely to become important to international economic policymakers over the medium run (generally, one to three years), and which thus should be addressed by the Institute. The Director, working closely with the staff and outside Advisory Committee, is responsible for the development of particular projects and makes the final decision to publish an individual study.

The Institute hopes that its studies and other activities will contribute to building a stronger foundation for international economic policy around the world. We invite readers of these publications to let us know how they think we can best accomplish this objective.

C. FRED BERGSTEN
Director
May 1998

Acknowledgments

We would like to acknowledge the contributions of the many who shared their time and expertise during the course of the study. Responsibility for the conclusions, of course, rests with us alone. First and foremost, C. Fred Bergsten and Gary Hufbauer organized two projects on which this study is based, and were constant sources of encouragement and assistance. We benefited from discussions with colleagues at IFRI and at the Institute for International Economics, from Institute-organized study group meetings in September and December 1996 and October 1997, from participants in two meetings of the Financial Leaders Group in December 1996, in Washington, and in Geneva in June 1997, and from financial sector participants and users in Seoul in December 1996 at a meeting organized by the Korean Institute for International Economic Policy (KIEP). Bob Vastine of the Financial Leaders Group and Patrick Lefas of the Fédération Française des Sociétés d'Assurances also provided constant encouragement. Manulife Financial was supportive in important ways in Toronto. Michael Aho and Kwon Jae Jong (of KIEP) contributed to early stages of the study.

Particular mention must be made of unstinting critical assistance from Pierre Sauvé, who read various drafts, and from Sir Nicholas Bayne, Tom Bernes, Joshua Dolten, Stijn Claessens, Richard Cooper, Brant Free, Harry L. Freeman, Monty Graham, Carl J. Green, Bill Hawley, Oakley Johnson, Charles Levy, Neal Luna, Scott Pardee, Adam Posen, Mary Podesta, Christian Weller, and John Williamson, who read one of the drafts and provided valuable comments.

Finally, we are grateful to our research assistants, Stefanie Fischel and Birgitta Weitz (who prepared appendix B), and Eddy Fougier, who assembled and treated a considerable amount of relevant material. Stefanie Fischel also played a key role in coordinating electronic interchange among authors in three rather far-flung locations. We are most grateful to David Krzywda, editor, for his patience and expert editing of the manuscript.

Introduction and Overview

The World Trade Organization (WTO) financial services agreement (FSA), completed on 13 December 1997, included market-opening commitments by 102 WTO members, which will take effect early in 1999. The FSA is a milestone for the WTO because a significant number of WTO members agreed to a legal framework for cross-border trade and market access in financial services and to a mechanism for dispute settlement. It extends the General Agreement on Trade in Services (GATS), negotiated within the Uruguay Round agreement to bring services trade broadly within the purview of WTO disciplines, to financial services, adding to existing agreements in the telecommunications and information technology industries.[1] The FSA was concluded in spite of unprecedented turmoil in Asian financial markets, perhaps because authorities hoped that their offers would signal their determination to undertake reforms that would help to restore credibility and stability.

Yet, in an important sense, the FSA is less than meets the eye, and our evaluation suggests that there is a significant agenda of market-

---

1. The FSA replaces an interim agreement concluded in 1995 at the initiative of the European Union. In that agreement, the United States withdrew most favored nation (MFN) treatment in financial services and committed itself only to granting market access and national treatment (that is, the same legal and regulatory treatment as for domestic firms) to the existing operations of foreign service providers. The United States and other industrial-country members of the Organization for Economic Cooperation and Development, faced with the reluctance of governments in some important emerging-market economies to provide reciprocal access, feared the latter would become free riders on a global agreement. A July 1997 US offer of unrestricted access to its market is conditioned on such reciprocal market access.

opening measures still to be taken. For the most part, the FSA simply formalizes the status quo. Commitments made by countries that are members of the Organization for Economic Cooperation and Development (OECD) do little to further open the market. The United States will provide access to its markets on a reciprocal basis, whereas most OECD countries already have such access and developing countries, with less-mature financial institutions, find it of little interest. With a few important exceptions, the significant emerging-market economies offer little new access to their often-underdeveloped banking sectors, while they offer significant new access to their insurance sectors.

There may be good reasons that there was so little movement beyond the status quo. Developing countries must decide how quickly they will integrate their economies with the rest of the world and determine the role that they wish foreign institutions to play in that process and in the domestic economy. They encourage foreign savings to accelerate growth above the level determined exclusively by domestic savings. However, as the Asian financial and economic crisis of 1997-98 (and the experiences of the southern-cone countries in Latin America in the 1980s) demonstrates, such integration holds dangers if the process is not planned and managed with great care. Indeed, an exclusive focus on attracting foreign capital could mean that a country overlooks a significant ingredient of financial system development, namely, the role of foreign financial firms in improving efficiency.

Central to the evaluation in this book is the proposition that financial-market development is a potentially fundamental factor in an economy's long-term growth and development. Financial-market development is fundamental in two ways: it changes the speed at which capital accumulates, and it influences the efficiency of production in an economy. Financial institutions not only mobilize an economy's resources and facilitate the transactions necessary to carry on economic exchange but also play a critical role in managing risks and closing information gaps.[2] These institutions lessen the risks faced by investors by pooling investor's savings and distributing them among many users. They also collect and evaluate the information necessary to make prudent and productive investment decisions. And they participate in corporate governance by evaluating the performance of corporate borrowers and,

---

2. One of the central problems that financial systems address is that of information asymmetry between the providers and users of funds. On the asset side, financial institutions take on risk in valuing projects and funding borrowers whose ability to repay is uncertain. On the liability side, creditors and depositors have imperfect information on the actual position of the financial institution and must have confidence in those institutions. When these institutions are highly leveraged, lack liquidity, or provide little information on their assets, they are vulnerable to losses in confidence, and depositors have an incentive to flee when confidence erodes (Lindgren, Garcia, and Saal 1996).

when necessary, compelling them to act in the best interests of the corporation—and, therefore, of its providers of funds (Levine 1996). Traditional analysis has tended to portray finance as an auxiliary factor in growth and development. More recently, however, as financial crises have occurred with increasing frequency (and most recently in the east Asian economies discussed below)—disrupting growth and other aspects of real economic activity—interest in financial reform has grown, and with it the realization of the potentially central role in economic growth. It is apparent, however, that financial institutions in the east Asian economies that are experiencing crisis have not carried out the functions outlined above or have failed to carry them out properly.

Therefore, how does the FSA contribute to financial-market development and to a country's long-term growth and development? OECD governments seek market access through the FSA for their large financial firms, which face maturing markets at home and possess technologies that have reduced transactions costs, to take advantage of business opportunities and higher rates of return in the dynamic offshore economies. The goals of developing-country governments differ. The governments are more interested in foreign capital flows (and, to a lesser extent, in foreign institutions) to accelerate growth and less interested in access to OECD-country financial markets. Capital inflows take several forms, including short-term debt and equity (portfolio) flows, commercial bank lending, and bonds. These instruments are subject to volatility if investors flee at signs of uncertainty or trouble. Of more value is long-term foreign direct investment (FDI), which brings foreign ownership or control but also the transfer of more sophisticated technologies. The FSA promotes a country's growth and welfare by providing a legal framework that reassures foreign institutions with long-term investments. It also provides external pressure for changes that promote sound financial institutions, which domestic groups often resist to protect their own interests.

This discussion has included many terms that will be used throughout this study. These terms require careful distinction at the outset. "Liberalization" in the context of financial services often refers to both domestic financial deregulation and the opening of the economy to international trade and capital flows. In this study, however, for the sake of clarity, we reserve liberalization specifically for opening domestic markets to cross-border trade, allowing entry by foreign firms, and opening the capital account (easing restrictions on capital flows in and out of the economy). This process is also called "internationalization." We refer to the process of deregulation and strengthening domestic financial institutions as "domestic financial reform" and to the broad process of domestic reform and internationalization as "financial reform." Domestic deregulation of financial services does not mean the wholesale elimination of prudential regulation (which, instead, needs to be strengthened), but the withdrawal of government intervention through, for example, privatizing state-owned banks, freeing key prices such as interest rates to be determined in the market, and easing restrictions on cross-sectoral activities to allow banks, insurance companies, finance companies, and securities firms to enter each others' subsectors.

Although this study and the FSA focus on market opening and foreign entry—as distinct from deregulation and capital account liberalization—these policies are related. Capital account liberalization involves the removal of restrictions on capital flowing in and out of an economy. De facto capital account liberalization has occurred in the past few decades because many countries have legalized foreign currency instruments in the face of increased trade flows, the internationalization of production, and improved communications.[3] Provided that there is adequate information, supervision, and risk assessment, free capital movements can facilitate efficient international allocation of savings and channel these resources to their most productive uses. This is the purpose of what we call financial reform. Domestic residents benefit from access to foreign capital markets through cheaper financing, a wider menu of options for diversifying risk and obtaining higher rates of return, and a larger pool of funds for investment.

Yet, with the explosion of cross-border capital flows, financial-sector deregulation in industrial countries frequently has been associated with excessive credit growth and a boom-bust cycle in equity and property markets. These excesses have caused serious damage to banking systems and, in many cases, have been corrected only by government bailouts and major changes in incentive systems. Emerging markets, it has been observed (White 1996), have special features that expose them to the risks of capital flow reversals, which means that as a prerequisite to fully open capital accounts, particular care should be taken to strengthen the foundations of domestic financial systems so that they can withstand shocks such as reversals of capital flows. Market opening can help to strengthen financial systems, because foreign entrants bring more advanced technologies, promote competition, and help to diversify the system. If they acquire institutional stakes, they tend to stay for the long run. Foreign entrants also require greater transparency in supervision and oversight to understand and comply with unfamiliar standards, rules, and regulations.

Deregulation, market opening, and capital account liberalization need not march in lockstep. Taiwan, for example, has not fully deregulated; it permits foreign entrants but imposes some restrictions on the capital

---

3. All OECD countries have now eliminated capital controls. By the end of 1993, a quarter of developing-country IMF members had removed restrictions on capital transactions, while 67 members maintained comprehensive controls on capital outflows and 17 on inflows (Quirk and Evans 1995).

account. The countries of Southeast Asia have not fully deregulated and still restrict foreign entry, but they have opened their capital accounts. Until its financial crisis began in late 1997, South Korea restricted foreign entry and capital flows and had many domestic reforms to make as part of its accession agreement to the OECD. In its December 1997 program with the International Monetary Fund (IMF), South Korea also agreed to remove many of these restrictions. China is the only east Asian country that still has a closed capital account (FDI inflows are encouraged, however), and foreign participation in the financial sector is still heavily restricted.

The focus of the WTO negotiations on freer cross-border trade and on foreign entry in financial services needs to be understood in two contexts. First, within the WTO, it reflects the fact that many standard policy interventions in the financial sector are untouched by GATS commitments (WTO 1997). In particular, the scope for macroeconomic policy management remains intact; prudential regulation is protected by a so-called carve-out provision in the GATS, and to the extent that other government financial policies are compatible with broad market access, national treatment, and scheduled commitments to liberalize, they can still be maintained—but in a more open context, under a multilateral agreement. Second, the FSA should be understood in terms of its contribution to financial-market development and growth. Market opening is one dimension of such development. In addition, domestic actions to strengthen financial institutions and provide public oversight are also important. They have been at the core of IMF programs aimed at stabilizing the Asian economies, for example. One implication is that WTO commitments should be part of ongoing IMF surveillance and that the WTO and the Bretton Woods institutions (the IMF and World Bank) should work closely together on oversight of national financial markets to encourage the modernization necessary to sustain long-term growth and development.

The Benefits of Financial Reform

The benefits of financial reform include faster growth. Studies of the deregulation of intrastate bank branching in the 1970s and 1980s find that annual economic growth rates increased by between 0.5 and 1.2 percentage points of gross state product for the 10 years following deregulation and by smaller, but positive, amounts in the period thereafter (Jayaratne and Strahan 1996, 651).

The benefits of better financial services are illustrated in the cost savings and quality improvements that can be realized by the households, businesses, and governments that are the main users of these services. Financial reform and internationalization in the industrialized countries have shown that as financial institutions face stiffer competition from domestic competitors and foreign entrants, they learn to exploit economies of scale and scope, reduce managerial inefficiency, and make better use of advanced technology. Savers and investors earn higher rates of return, and they have more savings instruments to choose from and more opportunities to diversify risk, as well as easier access to financial products. Those seeking funds benefit from better risk appraisal, reduced waiting times, a wider range of lending instruments, a wider range of maturities, and expanded access to funds.

In Europe, the Cecchini Commission Report (Cecchini 1988) predicted that the 1992 initiative, by opening trade in financial services, would reduce unit costs by facilitating economies of scale, increasing competition, reducing price markups, and increasing managerial efficiency. More recent studies broadly confirm these claims (WTO 1997).

Extensive empirical studies in Europe and the United States of efficiency differences among banks (with much less work available on insurance, government financial institutions, and thrifts) indicate the following: banks could reduce their costs and increase profits by between 20 and 50 percent by increasing productive efficiency; thrifts and credit unions could achieve 20 percent efficiency gains by improving managerial efficiency and by using the same sophisticated technology used by best-practice institutions; national bank regulatory agencies could make efficiency gains of a similar magnitude by achieving greater economies of scale in clearing and payments services; and insurers (where comparable data are scarce) are estimated to be between 45 and 90 percent efficient (Berger, Hunter, and Timme 1993).

Users also benefit from increased competition and access to foreign expertise in several intangible ways, such as improved quality of services and wider choice. These benefits take the form of

- access to better service channels (such as credit cards in developing countries, where they are less widely used),
- faster access to services,
- better credit assessment procedures and information-gathering techniques, and
- a wider choice of products and vendors.

Instead of lining up at the service counters of a series of strictly segregated financial institutions, for example, users can choose the most competitively priced and efficiently delivered product at a financial services "mini-mart," or they can do business by telephone or computer. Users also benefit from easier and more effective diversification of risk.

On the basis of the evidence briefly reviewed above and presented in more detail in the next chapter, we make a rough estimate, presented in

Table 1.1 Estimated benefits to users of phasing in financial services reform by 2010

Country group	Percentage of GDP		Billions of 1994 dollars		
	Welfare gain from quality improvements	Total welfare gain from reform	GNP in 2010	Total welfare gain in 2010	Present value in 1997 of cumulative welfare gains[a]
Income level					
Low	0.6	1.2	3,071	36	346
Middle	0.3	0.9	7,398	66	377
High	0.09	0.69	16,989	117	606
Region					
European Union	0.09	0.69	8,338	58	298
Latin America	0.3	0.9	2,682	24	137
East Asia	0.6	1.2	4,656	56	378
Japan	0.09	0.69	6,793	47	243
South Asia	0.6	1.2	1,158	14	94
Rest of world	ne	0.6	3,811	21	106
Total	ne	ne	27,438	219	1,256

ne = not estimated.
a. Calculated at a discount rate of 12 percent.

Source: Authors' calculations.

table 1.1, of the benefits to users of phasing in financial services reform by 2010. We assume, conservatively, that potential cost savings of 20 percent would be available from increased competition to users of financial services. We consider, based on available statistics, that a reasonable approximation of the share of financial services in total value added is 3 percent. Therefore, we estimate that cost savings would bring welfare gains of 0.6 percent of GNP (20 percent times 3 percent). We assume that quality improvements bring further welfare gains of the same magnitude to low-income countries; half that amount to middle-income countries where financial services are more developed; and 15 percent of that amount to high-income countries. Thus, total benefits from financial reform would amount to 1.2 percent of GNP in low-income countries (20 percent of financial value added for cost savings plus 20 percent for quality improvements times the share of financial value added in GNP) and 0.9 percent and 0.69 percent in middle-income and high-income countries, respectively (see the third column in table 1.1). If we assume that financial reform gradually takes place between 1997 and 2010, and if we extrapolate 1994 GNP data using World Bank (1996a) growth estimates for the next 15 years (6 percent annual growth for low-income countries, 4 percent for middle-income countries, and 2.5 percent for high-income countries), the benefit for 2010 totals $220 billion (in 1994 dollars), about half of which is realized by low- and middle-income countries, and more than half of which is realized in Asia, including Japan (see the fifth column of table 1.1). This figure actually represents a stream of annual benefits that accrue gradually throughout the reform process until 2010 and then fully thereafter. With an assumed discount rate of 12 percent, the present value of this stream is $1.3 trillion. This simple calculation shows that financial reform holds significant promise.

Objections to Deregulation and Market Opening

Those countries that have begun to reform their financial services sectors and to open their markets have begun to realize these benefits. Some countries, however, are reluctant to deregulate fully, whereas others are reluctant to open. The reasons they cite are several.

First, the experience of countries that have deregulated their financial markets, opened those markets to foreigners, and liberalized their capital accounts has been mixed. Banking and financial crises are associated with reform and internationalization or the wrong sequence of such changes. One analysis of banking crises worldwide found that, in 18 of 25 cases studied, financial liberalization had occurred some time in the previous 5 years (Kaminsky and Reinhart 1995).

Second, it is frequently argued that finance is special—some would say strategic—because of the crucially important services it provides to a growing and developing economy. These services, in this view, are best owned and controlled by domestic interests. More sophisticated foreign entrants, pursuing different objectives, could come to dominate the industry to the detriment of national objectives.

Third, reform and internationalization are often politically difficult because, although users stand to benefit, other powerful interests stand to lose. The introduction of competition threatens significant interests within the local financial industry, just as a reduction of the role of government threatens the position of certain bureaucratic interests.

Let us consider these arguments one by one, beginning with the argument that financial reform, internationalization, and financial crisis are intertwined. Reforming the domestic financial system and internationalizing it do entail risks, especially if governments continue to regulate and supervise financial systems the way they operated them before. To minimize these risks, regulatory institutions and supervisory systems must be modernized and strengthened to enable those charged with oversight to evaluate the risks inherent in a more complex, market-oriented system. Striking a balance between financial-market efficiency and economic stability is difficult, as demonstrated by the US savings and loan crisis of the 1980s and its aftermath and by Japan's ongoing struggle to work out the banking crisis that began there in the early 1990s. The Asian economic and financial crisis in 1997-98 (discussed in chapter 3) and the associated currency turmoil have stimulated renewed concern about the trade-off between economic stability and financial reform.

In evaluating this trade-off, we draw on the results of a number of careful case studies of national experiences with reform over the past two decades. These findings emphasize the importance of multiple factors in the trade-off. The general conclusion is that there is neither a universal recipe nor a standard sequence for domestic reform and internationalization. The case studies agree, however, that two major factors influence the chances of successful adjustment to these changes. The first is macroeconomic preconditions: those economies with stable and realistic prices and prudent fiscal policies do better because the creditworthiness of potential borrowers is superior. The second is that reform of the financial sector—to free up interest rates, reduce subsidization of credit, and strengthen financial institutions and their supervision—is a necessary precondition to easing restrictions on the capital account and allowing full-scale internationalization.

Both inadequate reform of the financial sector and macroeconomic preconditions played roles in the Asian crisis that began in Thailand in early 1997. Indonesia and South Korea also experienced serious stock market declines and foreign exchange depreciations and, like Thailand, they sought and received extensive international assistance organized around IMF programs. The characteristics of each country's crisis varied, but each was a combination of currency, banking, and economic problems.

Exchange rate volatility was a major macroeconomic factor. The member countries of the Association of Southeast Asian Nations (ASEAN) had fairly rigid exchange rates. The Thai baht was pegged to the US dollar, but most other ASEAN economies managed floats to the same currency. As problems in the real sector mounted, pressures on currencies were met by running down foreign exchange reserves and by raising domestic interest rates, which contributed to a rapid rise in domestic banks' nonperforming loans. Authorities faced a dilemma. Sharply devaluing the currencies or letting them float would demolish the credibility of the exchange rate pegs. But the authorities had little stomach for defending the currencies by further raising interest rates in already weakening economies burdened by banks that were accumulating nonperforming loans. As in Europe in 1992, when the United Kingdom left the European exchange rate mechanism, speculators bet, correctly, that the authorities would not be willing or able to defend their currencies at any price.

In South Korea, the won floated more freely. But a series of corporate failures in 1997, a well-known record of government-directed lending by commercial banks, political uncertainty in the lead-up to the December 1997 presidential election, and a depreciation of the Taiwan dollar in late October despite comfortable foreign reserves contributed to exchange market pressures, which the authorities countered by running down foreign exchange reserves and raising interest rates. Nonperforming loans quickly accumulated.

External factors also played a role. Large inflows of short-term capital, intermediated by inadequately supervised financial systems and weak banking institutions, led to asset inflation and boom-bust cycles in property lending. The capital was attracted by the prospects of higher rates of return than were available in the OECD countries, where interest rates had fallen to low levels as inflation fell, growth had slowed, and government borrowing had declined. Risk premiums also had declined because of increased familiarity with developing-country investments and because of an expectation after the Mexican peso crisis in 1994-95 that financial assets in developing countries would have an implicit government guarantee (i.e., that financial institutions would not be allowed to fail). Other significant external conditions had also changed: in 1996-97 the yen/US dollar exchange rate realigned as the yen weakened and the dollar rose. Growth also slowed in some key export markets such as semiconductors.

Institutional weaknesses in the financial sectors of these economies were such that banks' asset quality and their exposures to property loans and connected lending were not closely monitored. By mid-1997, many firms in Thailand and Indonesia had accumulated huge, unhedged foreign currency debts, many of which were to mature in fewer than 12 months. When the currencies were floated after strong downward market pressures, banks were faced with large nonperforming loans (because of lack of hedging and the jump in interest rates to try to halt the depreciation). In South Korea, directed lending implied public-sector guarantees for bad loans and precluded rigorous risk assessment or close inspection of asset quality.

The culprit in these crises was not internationalization per se. The culprit was not that Indonesia or Thailand had opened their capital accounts—indeed, South Korea's capital account was considerably less liberalized than either of the other two. The culprit was weaknesses in domestic financial systems that should have been corrected before or during internationalization. These weaknesses included inadequate oversight and supervision of financial institutions, inadequate risk assessment by banks, and directed lending. In addition, exchange rates were allowed to become overvalued. These shortcomings in macroeconomic policy conduct, in financial-sector infrastructure, and in market discipline[4] led borrowers and lenders in the ASEAN economies to assume,

---

4. Correcting these shortcomings was one of the intents of the Basle Committee on Banking supervision, which proposed best practices in its "Core Principles for Effective Banking Supervision" in 1997.

somewhat complacently, that interest rates and exchange rates would remain stable. Therefore, hedging of foreign debt was not a common practice. For different reasons, South Korean borrowers and lenders also felt protected against market risks. More financial reform preceding internationalization, not less, might have reduced or even eliminated the full-blown financial and economic crises that followed the currency depreciations. It is significant that Singapore and Hong Kong, both having strong financial systems, largely escaped the first phases of the crisis.

The second argument against financial reform and internationalization is that the financial system is special and, therefore, should be domestically owned and controlled. In the extreme, this argument has merit— few governments would tolerate 100 percent foreign ownership of major domestic financial institutions.[5] However, foreign participation brings substantial benefits and can be managed. Indeed, the Uruguay Round agreement explicitly allows for such management. Not only does foreign participation, judiciously supervised, provide access to foreign savings, technical transfer, and a force for modernization, but it also increases the competitiveness, efficiency, and diversity of the financial sector. The speed of innovation and the interconnectedness of markets are raising the costs of maintaining the status quo. Failure to deregulate and to open markets denies households better returns and denies businesses lower financing costs, thereby reducing growth and competitiveness. This link between real-sector activity and finance is perhaps the central issue. It is best addressed by practicing macroeconomic prudence.

With respect to the third concern, how to manage the difficult political economy of financial reform and internationalization, reluctant governments do have a point that trade negotiators should take into account. Market opening and capital account liberalization present real economic and political risks if financial supervision and financial institutions are not strengthened and if weakness in the real economy undermines borrowers' creditworthiness. But the answer is not to halt the process of reform and liberalization. Rather, it is to proceed while emphasizing the strengthening of the system's ability to evaluate risk. The implication for negotiating strategies is that diplomatic pressure should be applied to strengthen the process. This requires a delicate mixture of determined pressure for more opening and enough flexibility to ensure that the domestic political debate responds to rather than rejects that pressure, thus strengthening the hand of those who push for opening. The downside risk of complacency—of failing to insist on progress toward reform—is that nothing worthwhile gets done. However, the downside risk of too rigid a position and requirements that are too demanding is that

---

5. New Zealand is an exception; only one of its 18 banks is still domestically owned. All others are foreign owned.

antiforeign sentiment builds, eventually upsetting the domestic coalitions required to support reform.

The Organization of This Book

The next two chapters examine the pros and cons of further reform in developing economies. Chapter 2 assesses the benefits of opening the financial sector to foreign competition: macroeconomic benefits flow from the role that an improved financial sector plays in an economy's growth and development. Substantial benefits also accrue to users, as stated earlier. But these benefits are, rightly or wrongly, seen to be offset by certain risks and costs, some of which were summarized above.

Chapter 3 examines each of these risks and costs in light of available evidence and draws out their implications for the necessary ingredients of financial-sector reform and its sequencing and pacing. This chapter draws on two appendices. Appendix A examines the global financial services sector, its main players, the state of supervisory and regulatory structures, and the evolution of global capital flows. It also assesses the present state of liberalization and market opening in a number of important emerging-market economies, based on the case studies in appendix B. A particularly sobering dimension of this analysis is the extent to which financial supervisory structures remain weak and to which financial infrastructure—clearing and payments systems, modern accounting rules, and legal systems capable of enforcing property rights and accountability—remains inadequate, not only for a modern financial system, but for liberalization as well.

Chapter 4 outlines the background of the WTO financial services negotiations and places them in the context of the GATS, which is one of the two negotiating tracks in the WTO. It discusses the key negotiating positions and reviews the history of the negotiations leading up to the 13 December 1997 agreement.

Chapter 5 evaluates the significance of the 13 December 1997 agreement, including its potential contribution to financial-market development. It looks beyond the FSA to discuss the role of the multilateral negotiations in financial reform and the prospects for continuing financial services talks in the round of negotiations that will begin in 2000.

Conclusions and Recommendations

Our analysis in this book leads to four main conclusions. First, financial reform is an important contributor to growth and development strategies in developing countries. Such reform includes increasing market access to foreign institutions because they bring new skills and products, promoting competition and efficiency, and diversifying domestic financial systems.

Second, foreign entry is only part of a much broader reform process. Domestic financial institutions need to be restructured and modern financial infrastructure created to enforce market discipline. Failure to undertake these crucial changes risks depriving the users of financial services of the benefits of reform while making them more vulnerable to the costs.

Third, as the Asian financial crisis has most recently demonstrated, domestic reforms that improve risk management and strengthen supervision and oversight are essential prerequisites to full capital account liberalization. Market access and foreign entry imply that some freedom of capital movement will follow, but that freedom need not be full-blown. China, which still has an immature financial system, should seriously consider strengthening institutions that will intermediate this capital before opening the capital account. Internationalization is frequently seen to be the problem in the crisis. We see it as part of the solution because of the positive role that foreign institutions can play.

Fourth, the financial services agreement in the WTO makes a modest contribution to financial reform. It does this by providing an opportunity for most of the main players to bind the status quo in an international agreement and by providing a mechanism for settling disputes. These are not insignificant accomplishments. As finance has become truly international, international standards and multilateral rules and principles are required. Finance is too important to be left to the vagaries of political U-turns, bilateral deals, reciprocity-based measures, or unregulated markets. A multilateral commitment also provides ammunition to governments that need to undertake politically difficult reforms in the face of strong domestic interests that seek to protect privileged positions. But much reform has already been accomplished by unilateral action, regional cooperation, and, more recently, IMF conditionality.

These conclusions imply that the FSA, when it is implemented in 1999, should go beyond current commitments. It should

- secure the right of financial services firms to establish themselves and operate freely in all participating countries,

- provide national treatment for these firms once established,

- free cross-border trade in financial services and movements in personnel, and

- provide limited and transparent exemptions and MFN-compatible grandfathering of existing investments.

Industrial countries have an important responsibility in the run-up to 1999 and beyond to combine ambition with realism. They should avoid complacency and aim to keep the negotiating and liberalizing momentum, seeking guarantees of future progress by them and by developing countries.

International cooperation will be important to sustaining the momentum of market opening. Most crucial will be the implementation of international banking standards and advances in international supervision. The Asian crisis has illustrated the dangers of allowing foreign currency-denominated debt to accumulate unchecked. Cooperation is also required among the multilateral institutions involved in finance and financial services trade. In particular, IMF surveillance and IMF programs should include the financial sector, and reforms that affect market access that are based on IMF programs or prescribed in IMF Article IV consultations should also be bound in WTO commitments. Some of the reforms in the Asian economies with IMF programs, for example, have not yet been bound in the FSA. They should be.

Looking ahead to the new round in 2000, as financial innovation continues to change the financial landscape, the GATS will fall short of creating a liberalizing regime that will promote trade in financial services and services more generally. The current GATS approach accords a premium to the status quo, presenting trade liberalization as a positive, but optional, undertaking. Efforts to move the financial service negotiations forward could usefully be complemented by folding services, and financial services in particular, into a wider set of negotiations that address competition policy and foreign direct investment, which are so integral to market interdependence. This recommendation is based on the premise that market access is the central issue of the future round of trade negotiations. Because domestic policy regimes will be directly involved, governments and the WTO should seriously consider using the opportunity offered by the next round to open negotiations on the new issues of foreign direct investment and competition policy. Preparatory discussions could take place as early as 1999 to ensure that the built-in agenda of the WTO addresses these broader issues in addition to the narrower sectoral ones. While progress will be slow and difficult, these are promising issues that go to the core of globalization.

2

The Benefits of Financial Reform

The many services that financial systems provide can be grouped into five categories (Levine 1996): they mobilize an economy's resources, they facilitate the transactions necessary to carry on economic exchange and trade, they improve risk management by pooling and diversifying the risks faced by the providers and the users of funds, they collect and evaluate the information needed to make productive investment decisions, and they monitor the behavior of corporate managers, evaluating their performance and compelling them to act in the best interests of the firm. Financial institutions are considered to specialize in collecting funds from savers, evaluating potentially risky borrowers, and allocating the funds they collect to those uses that promise the highest rates of return. All these services are crucial to financing growth and promoting entrepreneurship, an objective that takes on increasing importance as a new revolution, that of information technologies, unfolds.

Many governments in industrial and emerging-market economies have introduced financial reforms. Some governments, such as those in the United Kingdom and the United States, have opted for rapid, "big bang" reform, whereas others in smaller economies, such as Canada and Malaysia, have opted for more gradual approaches. These reforms were driven by a desire not to be left behind by the dizzying pace of change in the financial services sector, and by the assessment that the benefits to users of financial services outweighed the burden that must be shouldered, sometimes unequally, by service providers.

The next two chapters examine the benefits and costs of attaining more efficient financial systems. Chapter 3 addresses the concerns that many developing-country governments have expressed about possible pitfalls of financial reforms, the links between such reforms and the FSA, and the policy and regulatory measures necessary to avoid such pitfalls. This chapter surveys the benefits that can be expected from financial reform and, more specifically, the promises of a successful WTO financial services agreement in that respect. In the context of an efficient regulatory and supervisory framework, we argue, an increase in competition, notably through granting market access and national treatment to foreign companies, will have significant implications for users of financial services in developing countries. Increased competition will result in more efficient services and improvements in their quality and range.

The next section enumerates the benefits of reform to users of financial services and develops key assumptions about possible magnitudes of cost savings, which are applied to an estimate of the benefits to users. We then briefly survey the economic literature on the relationship between financial efficiency and economic growth, we identify the major channels through which the financial system contributes to growth, and we discuss how opening to foreign competition contributes to efficiency through each of these channels.

Benefits to Users

The benefits to users of financial services take two forms: reduced costs of service to savers and borrowers with the introduction of more competition and improvements in services from more efficient, customer-friendly financial institutions. Savers receive higher rates of return, a broader choice of savings instruments, and easier access to financial products. Borrowers benefit from more accurate appraisal of risk, reduced waiting times, and expanded access to funds through more sophisticated lending instruments available in a wider range of maturities. In exploring these two sources of benefits, we draw on available theoretical studies, empirical evidence, and anecdotes.

Two past experiments in financial reform and deregulation may provide a useful benchmark: the deregulation of US intrastate bank branching in the 1980s and the financial integration undertaken by the European Union (then the European Community) as part of the 1992 single-market process. Deregulation of intrastate branching in the United States in the 1970s and 1980s boosted annual growth measured by gross state product by 0.5 to 1.19 percentage points for the 10-year period after deregulation, and by smaller, but positive, amounts thereafter—a considerable contribution. Moreover, the share of nonperforming loans in state banking systems in the 1980s dropped by between 12 and 38 percent, and connected lending (that is, lending to bank insiders) fell by between 25 and 40 percent (Jayaratne and Strahan 1996).

Before the 1992 initiative in Europe, the Cecchini Commission report (Cecchini 1988) had predicted that more open trade in financial services would reduce unit costs by facilitating economies of scale, introduce competition into oligopolistic market structures, and reduce the markup of prices over marginal costs. The commission had further predicted that financial institutions could expect to see a reduction of excess profits, as formerly protected markets were opened, and that competition would stimulate managers to control costs (that is, increase X-efficiency) as they realized economies of scale and scope (Molyneux, Altunbas, and Gardener 1996).

More recent studies tend to confirm most of these claims (see also box 3 in WTO 1997, 19). The most recent ex post evaluation undertaken for the European Commission (Economic Research Europe Ltd. et al. 1997) confirms that most of the expected consumer benefits have been achieved: a higher rate of product innovation, improved quality of service, wider consumer choice, and greater efficiency. As expected, banks have become more market oriented, and productive efficiency has risen. The study, however, finds little impact on financial services prices, except in the southern EU members. Firms have adapted to increased competition through product innovation and increased product diversity. Nonprice competition seems to have been the most frequent response to increased competitive pressures. The review relies on survey data on the magnitude of price changes related to the single-market initiative and finds that the reported change is quite small, again with the exception of southern Europe. Moreover, price divergences across countries persist, whereas the Cecchini analysis was based on the assumption that prices would converge. In some instances, prices have even risen, notably as banks strove to meet the EU Solvency Ratio and Own Funds Directives. Even when prices rose, however, consumers benefited from a less fragile financial system. The review finds little impact yet on total factor productivity. It should be emphasized, however, that financial integration in Europe is by no means complete, notably in the insurance sector, where the process has just begun and important benefits are expected.

Among the many users of financial services, small and medium-sized enterprises are likely to gain the most from more efficient and competitive financial services. Three studies of users of financial services in developing countries indicate that small firms, which might be more efficient and innovative than their larger and more established competitors, lack the relationships with banks that often predominate in noncompetitive systems. Their financing costs are higher as a result.

A study of 521 Indonesian manufacturing firms (Goeltom 1995) during 1981-88 shows that financial reform improved their performance; credit was better distributed to the small and medium-sized enterprises in the sample. Firms with personal or political relationships replaced more expensive domestic credit with cheaper foreign credit; after reform, profits and shares of total investment doubled for small firms. Less change was found for medium-sized firms.

Another study (Atiyas 1992, as reported in Caprio, Atiyas, and Hanson 1996) looked at 180 South Korean firms between 1984 and 1988. Independent variables included past investment, the degree of leverage, output, the q ratio, and a stock measure of liquidity. Results for the entire period were not significant, but when the firms in the sample were categorized by size, it was found that liquidity constraints and debt influenced the behavior of small firms. This finding implies that small firms' access to external finance is improved after reform.

In a study of 420 manufacturing firms in Ecuador during 1983-88 (Jaramillo, Schiantarelli, and Weiss 1996), results were tested for constraints that might affect the investment decisions of firms that differ on such characteristics as size and age. The main finding was that significant capital-market imperfections exist for small and young firms, but not for large and old firms. Evidence that financial reforms helped relax constraints for small firms was not found, however.

Cost Savings

Easing restrictions on financial markets and expanding competition reduce corporate and household funding costs; lower costs in turn reduce product prices and promote corporate competitiveness in international markets. These benefits are illustrated by two recent examples from the United States and South Korea.

In May 1997, US Treasury Secretary Robert E. Rubin introduced administration proposals to modernize the US financial services framework and noted the potential benefits:

> In the past, when we have permitted greater competition in the financial services industry, consumers of financial products have benefited significantly. . . . In 1995, American consumers spent nearly $300 billion on brokerage, insurance, and banking services. If increased competition from financial modernization were to reduce costs to consumers by 1 percent, that would be a savings of about $3 billion a year. Based on the efficiencies that could be realized from increased competition, it is plausible to expect ultimate savings to consumers of up to 5 percent from increased competition in the securities, banking, and insurance industries—as much as $15 billion per year. The bulk of these savings should come as financial services, driven by increased competition, adopt best practices (Rubin 1997).

Officials of a South Korean firm, in an interview with one of the authors, cited differences in trade financing costs across different Asian markets as illustrating how much lower costs are in internationally competitive markets than in the South Korean domestic market. Financing in Hong Kong is highly competitive, with a spread of approximately 20 basis points above LIBOR (the London interbank offer rate); in Shanghai, access to credit is limited and the spread over LIBOR is 80 basis points. In South Korea, the spread over LIBOR for government-approved loans is only 30 basis points, but if approval is not obtained, alternative financing must be found in the leasing market, where credit is limited and costs are high: up to 120 basis points over LIBOR.

Empirical studies estimating financial-sector efficiency in industrial countries are legion, particularly with respect to the banking industry in Europe and the United States. Some work has also been done on the efficiency of government financial institutions and thrifts and of insurance firms. These estimates tend to corroborate the more casual empiricism of the anecdotes just presented. Studies of banks focus mainly on the cost advantages resulting from increased scale and scope of production. More recently, researchers have examined other aspects of efficiency, such as technical and allocative efficiency estimated from the profit side. Because banks operate in regulated environments, researchers have developed methods to estimate the divergence of certain indicators from an efficiency frontier. Economies of scale are an important variable in this analysis. Many cost studies, based on small banks and their products, find significant economies of scale for demand deposits and mortgage loans and for certain institutions, such as unit banks (rather than branch banks), in the United States. More recently, however, one of the few studies of large banks concludes that "positive supply-side economies of scale appear to exist only in the middle range of big banks in the world, with diseconomies being the rule for the very largest banks" (Saunders and Walter 1994, 82).

Further empirical analysis has probed efficiency differences among banks; US studies indicate that managerial inefficiencies (X-inefficiencies) account for roughly 20 percent of costs, whereas inefficiencies related to scale and product mix account for less than 5 percent (Berger, Hunter, and Timme 1993). A comparison of cost studies of banks in Europe summarized the conclusions of German studies that German banks could produce the same output with roughly 76 percent of current inputs if they were operating efficiently. This is roughly the same magnitude found in the US studies (Molyneux, Altunbas, and Gardener 1996). Other national studies conclude that Italian credit cooperative banks could produce the same output with 87 percent of current inputs, UK retail banks with 94 percent of current inputs, and Turkish banks with 51 percent of current inputs (Molyneux et al. 1996). Comparable studies of the efficiency of US and Japanese commercial banks suggest an efficiency factor of around 20 percent could be realized if banks were to eliminate their technical inefficiencies and choose an appropriate scale of operation. US researchers conclude that large US banks are more efficient than small ones (Elyasiani and Mehdian 1995), and a study of Japanese banks found that they could, on average, produce the same output with 15 percent fewer resources (Fukuyama 1993).

Another set of studies, focusing on profit functions, provides insights into output inefficiencies (production of the wrong level or mix of outputs) rather than input inefficiencies. These studies find that output inefficiencies are the larger of the two; indeed, one influential survey estimates that, on average, banks appear to lose as much as half of their potential profits to inefficiency (Berger, Hunter, and Timme 1993). In another innovation, which decomposed inefficiency into allocative and X-inefficiencies, it became apparent that X-efficiency is positively related to size. In other words, as firms become larger, they realize an advantage in producing high-value outputs, and this advantage may outweigh the scale diseconomies found in other studies.

Estimates of efficiency in thrifts, government financial institutions, and insurance companies are far fewer than those for banks. The available estimates indicate that, for example, inefficient credit unions are about 20 percent less efficient than best-practice credit unions (Berger, Hunter, and Timme 1993). Other studies are of regulatory institutions, particularly the Federal Reserve Board in the United States. It was found that inefficient Federal Reserve offices were 25 to 30 percent less efficient than the most efficient offices, because of diseconomies of scale in the payments services that the Federal Reserve performs.

Studies of the insurance industry tend to use cost functions. Small and large insurers are estimated to be around 90 percent efficient, whereas medium-sized insurers are 79 percent efficient, probably because of greater dispersion in the group. X-efficiency is found to be relatively independent of organizational form or regulatory factors (Berger, Hunter, and Timme 1993). No work is yet available on insurers outside the United States.

Analysis of the efficiency of financial institutions in emerging markets is less developed than that in the industrial countries, in part because of the fragmented nature of institutional financial statistics. This dearth is attributable to the early stage of institutional analysis by official supervisory entities and market participants. Researchers must rely on basic operating statistics found in publicly available documents, such as firms' own annual reports and the reports of independent financial analysts. Operating ratios, however, must be used and interpreted with care. Interest spreads, for example, are generally wider in developing countries for several reasons: government regulations such as high reserve requirements, taxation of banks, high inflation, operating inefficiencies that contribute to excessive loan losses, and high costs due to lack of competition. Data on operating costs suffer from problems of comparability when banks offer different services or a different service mix. Furthermore, although labor costs may be lower than in industrial countries, the narrow range and low quality of services, limited use of modern technology, overstaffing, and operation of uneconomic branches also explain their relatively higher costs (Vittas 1991).

The performance indicators in table 2.1 are expense-asset and expense-

Table 2.1 Performance indicators for East Asian banks, various years (percentages)

Year	Hong Kong	South Korea	Malaysia	Singapore	Thailand
Noninterest expenses as a share of average earning assets					
1994	1.71	2.72	1.86	1.30	1.99
1995	1.60	2.73	1.60	1.23	2.01
1996	1.57	2.65	1.58	1.23	1.99
1997[a]	1.55	2.55	1.57	1.22	2.10
Noninterest expenses as a share of noninterest income					
1990	na	na	na	na	195.70
1991	na	na	na	na	189.70
1992	na	na	na	na	234.90
1993	na	na	na	na	181.70
1994	183.09	81.09	119.86	106.90	165.30
1995	165.09	66.71	125.98	131.90	178.30
1996	160.69	62.89	121.87	128.70	195.90
1997[a]	156.32	60.93	120.74	128.30	200.10
Net interest margin					
1990	na	na	na	na	3.48
1991	na	na	na	2.15	2.80
1992	na	na	na	2.10	3.90
1993	na	na	na	2.09	3.81
1994	2.91	1.94	2.90	2.19	3.96
1995	2.95	2.02	2.95	2.23	3.80
1996	3.05	2.23	3.14	2.23	3.68
1997[a]	3.08	2.33	3.12	2.25	3.63
Return on assets					
1991	na	na	na	0.93	na
1992	na	na	na	0.91	na
1993	na	na	na	1.18	2.38
1994	1.86	0.49	1.21	1.25	1.79
1995	1.78	0.32	1.23	1.25	1.76
1996	1.84	0.37	1.28	1.29	1.69
1997[a]	1.87	0.57	1.29	1.31	1.55
Return on equity					
1991	na	na	na	9.56	na
1992	na	na	na	9.10	na
1993	na	na	na	11.40	32.68
1994	22.59	8.69	21.26	11.88	23.41
1995	19.66	5.61	19.74	11.22	22.53
1996	19.89	6.48	21.18	11.30	21.15
1997[a]	20.29	10.55	21.30	11.66	19.54

na = not available.

Note: Pre- and post-1994 samples may differ in size.

a. Estimates.

Source: Salomon Brothers (1996).

income ratios for commercial banks in several East Asian economies. The relatively high noninterest expense ratios in South Korea and Thailand relative to those in Hong Kong, Malaysia, and Singapore reflect the small share of noninterest revenues, such as fees and commissions, in the product mixes of those banks. Divergence is also apparent in net interest margins; wide margins in Thailand can be attributed to oligopolistic behavior and barriers to foreign entry. Statistics on return on assets and return on equity reveal that the trend is mostly upward in return on assets; divergence among countries suggests that regulation has an impact (return is lowest in South Korea, where the government still directs lending, and highest in market-based Hong Kong and Singapore). These data imply that banks in Malaysia and Singapore are the most efficient in the group. Studies of the impact of foreign entry on domestic bank performance indicate that foreign presence has a negative relationship with cost indicators, such as net interest margins and overhead, and a positive relationship with profitability (Claessens and Glaessner 1997).

In summary, the survey by Berger, Hunter, and Timme (1993) and the overview above suggest the following conclusions regarding the benefits to users from more competitive financial services:

- Technical inefficiencies account for 20 percent of banks' costs, and scale and product mix inefficiencies account for 5 percent.

- Banks lose as much as 50 percent of their potential profits to inefficiency, as measured by profit function studies.

- Among government financial institutions, inefficient government credit unions are around 20 percent less efficient than best-practice credit unions.

- National bank regulatory agencies average around 25 to 30 percent below best-practice levels of efficiency.

- Small and large insurers are around 90 percent efficient; medium-sized ones are about 79 percent efficient.

- Not much is known about the efficiency of the financial institutions in emerging markets, but two results emerge from surveying performance data: first, the potential for improving efficiency and lowering costs through greater competition is large; and second, efficiency varies from country to country and is greater the more competitive the financial system already is.

We conclude from this survey that 20 percent, on average, is a conservative assumption of the likely cost savings that can be expected from increased competition in financial systems.

Improved Service and Quality

Users also benefit from financial services reform and internationalization in a number of qualitative ways. Increased competition brings a wider range of financial services, greater choice of institutions, new methods of service delivery, and price competition. Many products formerly available only from banks become available from competing intermediaries as well. Insurance companies have learned how to move funds from savers to borrowers more cheaply than banks and have introduced new saving instruments such as mutual funds and securitized products. Users obtain more accurate and comprehensible information—essential when choosing among, and using, innovative instruments to hedge risks. Banks have supplemented their traditional credit products with lower-risk, fee-based products such as insurance, securitized loans and guarantees, swaps, and options. Retail banking, which accounts for the largest share of earnings for many banks, is traditionally delivered in a labor-intensive fashion through branches. In industrial countries, bank branches are turning into financial services "mini-marts" offering a range of products.

Internationalization accelerates the pace at which such benefits are realized, as foreign financial institutions bring innovations in products and in service delivery. Two anecdotes illustrate this process:

- Under the terms of the North American Free Trade Agreement (NAFTA), Mexico will gradually open its insurance market by the year 2000. Insurance industry estimates suggest that by 2010, Mexico will become one of the world's top 10 insurance markets, providing potential for opportunities to serve retirement needs as Mexico privatizes its pension system; environmental regulations required by NAFTA will create demand for waste management and pollution liability insurance; and newly privatized companies in manufacturing, energy, and construction with little experience with commercial insurance and risk-management concepts will require such products (Financial Leaders Group 1997).

- Pension fund contributors will also gain. Most pension funds produce large savings pools that national governments require to be invested in low-risk domestic saving instruments. Such restrictions are understandable, but, especially in industrialized countries, funds are doomed to lower rates of return than would be possible if risk and geographic restrictions were removed. Higher returns would generate lower contribution levels, for example (Financial Leaders Group 1997).

As technological changes are introduced, users benefit from access to new distribution channels, such as automated teller machines and telephone and on-line banking. Studies of the future of retail banking in industrial countries, for example, assume that the proliferation of distribution channels associated with the entry of new service providers —supplying automated services by personal computer, telephone, and automated tellers—will reduce costs (and therefore prices) by 20 to 30 percent annually (Deloitte & Touche Consulting Group 1995). Users will also benefit from reduced waiting times for credit cards, check clearing, and loan applications. Studies of the economies of scale achievable through modern data handling in industrial countries show that such systems have already raised productivity by a factor of four (Deloitte & Touche Consulting Group 1995). These benefits are illustrated in another anecdote:

■ In Taiwan, where finance and insurance account for nearly 10 percent of GDP, deregulation and internationalization have brought substantial change: as applications for new banks have been permitted, consumers have benefited from an increased number of branches and a broader range of products; as restrictions on the money market have relaxed, banks have entered the brokerage and commercial paper business with an increase in trading volume; and relaxation of restrictions on credit cards has reduced the use of cash and improved the payments system (Financial Leaders Group 1997).

In summary, anecdotal and statistical evidence illustrate the variety of cost savings and qualitative benefits that users can realize when greater competition is introduced into the financial services sector. As we pointed out in the first chapter, simple back-of-the-envelope calculations based on the value of such benefits illustrate the substantial welfare gains of reform to users of financial services, ranging from annual gains of around two-thirds of a percent of GNP in developed countries to more than a percent of GNP in the less-developed ones.

Economywide Benefits of Financial Reform: A Review of the Literature

Benefits from financial reform will also accrue to the economy as a whole in the form of faster economic growth, as savers receive higher rates of return and entrepreneurs and innovators obtain improved access to funds. This mechanism was pointed out long ago by Schumpeter (1911), who assigned a central role to credit as an engine of innovation and entrepreneurship. The relationship between financial-sector reform and economic growth has been extensively studied in the second half of this century (Tressel 1996 provides a useful survey). Gurley and Shaw (1955) pioneered the modern empirical study of financial intermediaries' role in economic growth. They and others identified a strong positive relationship. McKinnon (1973) and Shaw (1973) argued that financial repression (associated with governments' tendency to impose ceilings on nominal interest rates) reduces the real economic growth rate and the real size of the financial system. They assumed that banks allocate credit not according to potential returns, but according to transaction costs, risks of default, and political pressures. These practices reduce capital formation, bias technical choices against labor-intensive activities, and lead to low-quality, capital-intensive investments.

The McKinnon-Shaw arguments have been remarkably durable over the years and have been buttressed by more recent studies, which model the financial intermediation process itself. Modeling the effects of financial variables, such as real interest rates, on economic growth in large samples of countries has produced mixed results:

■ Every percentage-point increase in the real deposit rate toward its market level is associated with an increase in the economic growth rate of half a percentage point (Fry 1981).

■ A rise in real interest rates by 1 percentage point will encourage more saving and translate into an increase in the economic growth rate of 0.2 to 0.3 percentage point (Gelb 1989).

■ Growth rates in countries with real interest rates below -5 percent in the 1970s averaged 1.4 percentage points below those in countries with positive real interest rates (Roubini and Sala-i-Martin 1992).

More recent empirical studies have modeled possible linkages between financial intermediation and growth and have tested such models on large samples of developing countries. King and Levine (1993a, b, and c) find positive and significant relationships between each of four financial indicators and growth.[1] Other studies have obtained similar findings (Jappelli and Pagano 1994; Roubini and Sala-i-Martin 1992; DeGregorio and Guidotti 1992). A more recent variant divides the country data into samples from prereform, reform, and postreform periods (Johnston and Pazarbasioglu 1995). Results from such studies suggest that those countries that faced financial crises had failed to adjust real interest rates, had failed to prevent inflationary credit and monetary expansion, and had allowed greater inefficiencies in their banking systems.

Pagano (1993) usefully identifies three channels of transmission through which financial development can influence long-term growth: by increasing the proportion of savings transferred to investment spending, by raising the social marginal productivity of capital, and by raising the

---

1. The four financial indicators are the ratio of M2 (a broad measure of money) to GDP; the ratio of domestic assets in banks to total domestic assets in banks and the central bank; the ratio of domestic credit to the private sector to aggregate domestic credit; and the ratio of domestic credit to the private sector to GDP.

private saving rate. The first channel has to do with the transaction costs involved in pooling available savings and allocating it to investments. The presence of these costs implies that a proportion of these savings is "lost" in the process of financial intermediation. These costs reflect the actual costs of providing financial services, but they also depend on taxes, regulations, and market structure (e.g., the presence or absence of monopoly rents). Increased competition is expected to lead to a decline in transaction costs and a larger proportion of savings being transferred to investment. An important channel through which financial development facilitates growth is the reduction of the costs of external finance (as opposed to self-financing) to firms (Gertler and Rose 1996). Typically, the development of banks and stock markets may provide substantial benefits through this first channel. Financial repression, conversely, will have negative effects on the competitiveness of the nonfinancial sectors of the economy.

The second channel concerns the efficiency of capital allocation, that is, the ability of the financial system to direct funds toward the most productive projects, where the marginal product of capital is highest. A first contribution of the financial system in that respect is the organization of the collection of information on various projects and on potential debtors. More information, of a higher quality, becomes available about investment projects. This leads to a lowering of transaction costs (the first channel) but also ensures that financial intermediation leads to a more judicious allocation of savings to better investment projects. Many economists attribute to financial intermediaries an informational superiority (for example, Levine 1996; Greenwood and Jovanovic 1990; Atje and Jovanovic 1993). But the story does not stop there: because a better-informed financial intermediary is better able to diversify its portfolio, it will presumably be ready to invest in riskier projects, proposing a higher rate of return. Financial intermediation, whether by insurance markets, banks, or securities markets, allows investors to share and diversify risk. Hence, the contribution of the financial system to long-term growth does not require an informational advantage: Saint-Paul (1992), for example, constructs an endogenous growth model in which entrepreneurs and savers share and diversify risk in a context of imperfect information, which leads to an increase of investment in riskier but more productive technologies and an increase in productivity. A third contribution to efficiency stems from a reduction of the liquidity risk faced by savers: in the absence of banks, savers will prefer more liquid assets to the neglect of more productive, but also less liquid, investment projects. Banks are able to pool the liquidity risk of depositors, reducing the need to store savings in liquid assets, and are able to invest in such projects (Bencivenga and Smith 1991).

The third channel refers to the impact of financial intermediation on the domestic saving rate. As emphasized by Pagano and as is well known empirically, the sign of the relationship here is ambiguous: financial development may actually reduce saving and (in an endogenous growth model) growth. For example, better-insured households may reduce precautionary saving. Diversification of portfolio risk through securities markets also has an ambiguous effect: risk-averse investors will save less. Moreover, financial development relaxes the liquidity constraint on households and allows for better consumption smoothing. This may lead to a decline in the saving rate unless households borrow to invest (for example, in human capital) rather than consume. (Casual discussions of the decline in the US household saving rate in the 1980s often mention this relaxation of the liquidity constraint.)

Finally, the interest rate effects also lead to ambiguous results with respect to saving. Financial repression and lack of competition imply a below-market rate of interest paid to savers. Assuming a positive dependency of saving with the rate of interest, McKinnon (1973) and Shaw (1973) argued that financial repression depresses growth by keeping saving too low. But the impact of the real interest rate on saving remains, in fact, unresolved: substitution effects imply a positive relationship, whereas income effects suggest a negative one. Pagano (1993) concludes that aggregate measures of financial development are inadequate to the extent that the growth effects of the expansion of some financial markets might be opposite to those of others. On the basis of the previous discussion, for example, greater availability of insurance and household credit might well reduce the growth rate through a negative impact on saving, whereas bank lending to businesses and stock markets would be more likely to promote growth.

Interestingly, a recent study by Holzmann (1997) on the impact of pension reform in Chile shows that the empirical evidence is consistent with most a priori claims: financial-market development, notably through pension reform, did enhance economic growth in Chile, and pension reform generated positive spillover effects on labor and financial markets, thereby accelerating growth. Contrary to expectations, the direct effect of financial-market development on the private savings rate was negative. Pension reform, however, is generally likely to contribute to an increase in public saving. In summary, this third channel seems less robust both in theory and on the basis of empirical evidence, suggesting that the contribution of financial development to growth may well hinge more on the quality of resource allocation than on the quantity of financial resources potentially available.

This theoretical framework is particularly useful in sorting out the role that foreign financial institutions can play when granted market access and national treatment and, thus, in demonstrating the interest of developing countries in reaching a successful agreement in the financial services trade negotiations. Opening to foreign competition can help to develop the financial system and contribute to growth through each of the three channels identified above. Increased competition lowers the cost of financial services and, importantly, increases the access of firms, especially small and medium-sized firms, to external finance.[2] It thus raises the competitiveness of the nonfinancial sector. For example, as Indonesia reduced restrictions on foreign banks (see appendix B) and increased competition in domestic markets, the difference in the interest rates charged by domestic and foreign banks dropped. Similarly, case studies have shown that, as restrictions eased, commission fees dropped in Turkey and interest spreads dropped in Australia (Levine 1996).

Levine (1996) argues that liberalizing foreign-bank entry bolsters financial development. Foreign banks can be expected to provide high-quality banking services at lower cost (the first two channels above); to spur quality improvement and cost-cutting in the domestic banking industry; to promote better accounting, auditing, and rating institutions; and to increase the pressure on governments to improve legal, regulatory, and supervisory systems. Much benefit can also be expected from enhanced access for foreign insurers (Skipper 1997), as it allows local markets to diversify risk more effectively and to benefit from the foreign companies' know-how and resources.

The entry of foreign financial institutions also interacts with domestic reform in several ways. First, because foreign entry is likely to make some domestic financial restrictions redundant, it may play a catalytic role in domestic reform (Edey and Hviding 1995). Such interaction can raise questions about the future conduct of regulation and competition policy. For example, free trade in the European Union led to the adoption of the "mutual recognition" principle, combining minimum harmonization with competition among national regulations. This approach has been used successfully to create a single market in banking and insurance in Europe. Second, the participation of foreign financial institutions tends to require greater transparency of domestic regulations and practices. Transparency here refers to the availability of information about laws, regulations, and administrative guidelines. Transparent regulations help market participants become fully aware of their rights and obligations arising from trade-related rules.

Finally, market opening and foreign entry also improve access to international capital markets and augment the amount of saving available for productive investment (the third channel). This benefit is especially relevant to the Asian economies in the postcrisis recovery period. The discussion above, however, suggests that most of the benefits accrue in

---

2. The Financial Leaders Group (1997, case study 6) reports how the introduction of foreign competition in consumer lending in Japan in the mid-1970s eventually brought major benefits to Japanese consumers and credit companies. It resulted in lower interest rates and a transfer of US practices with respect to credit risk assessment, loan repayment schedules, and information collection procedures. This took time, however, and many entrants failed.

the form of improvements in resource allocation rather than simply through a greater volume of available financial resources.

Anecdotal evidence confirms that foreign bank entry can contribute substantially to the development of a skilled indigenous labor force in the domestic banking system. As the president of a leading Indonesian insurance firm commented:

> It is common knowledge that the foreign banks operating in Indonesia are the source of banking expertise. They have trained a great many Indonesian men who later have become managers of national private banks. The number is so great that almost every national private bank has one of its managers originating from foreign banks. . . . It is noteworthy that the foreign banks who are operating in Indonesia have played a major role in improving the know-how and expertise of our Indonesian bankers.[3]

One example of the economywide benefits conferred by foreign financial institutions can be found in the Philippines. There, the insurance industry plays a role in mobilizing capital and channeling it to key development requirements. A US firm, which established a presence in the Philippines in 1947, developed a series of products to channel savings into investment projects. The first product was an endowment policy for farmers and small merchants, which helped them to build savings in rural areas where banks were scarce. Their savings were invested in roads and water facilities. In the 1950s a product was developed to channel funds into middle-income housing at a time of shortage. Later this firm developed the Philippines' first public mutual fund (Financial Leaders Group 1997).

Conclusion

This chapter has documented the benefits to users and to the economy at large of efficient, competition-friendly financial systems. Although the financial sectors in emerging markets are modernizing and restructuring, they are doing so at different rates (appendix A), and significant obstacles remain in all these markets, inhibiting market forces and restricting the activities of outsiders. Meanwhile, significant deficiencies exist in their capacities to ensure the safety and soundness of their financial systems. Not all governments in countries where financial services competition is lacking are convinced that reforming their financial markets is a pressing precondition for sustaining the rapid economic growth that many of them have achieved in the past decade. But the Asian financial crisis in 1997-98 points toward severe financial weak-

---

3. Munir Sjamsoeddin, president and director of TP Asuransi Bintang, at the XVth Conference of the East Asian Insurance Congress, Jakarta, 15-20 September 1990.

nesses thaᴜ demand prompt action and should have been addressed in preparation for internationalization. More, not less, competition and the active participation of foreign financial institutions would contribute greatly to improving the efficiency and resiliency of financial systems worldwide—a point explored further in the next chapter.

Governments face a choice between two alternatives. The first is to maintain existing regulations and relax them gradually and unilaterally. Indeed, they face pressures from vested interests without and from bureaucrats within to move cautiously. Although the latter may recognize that the financial system needs sustained therapy to make it more efficient, governments also have a responsibility to consider the potential side effects of the initial shock. But the consequence of failing to act would be an underdeveloped, high-cost financial sector that constantly falls behind the rapid advance of best-practice standards in terms of product diversity, product prices, and skilled personnel. Such a financial sector would follow, not lead, the economy. It would, however, be reasonably popular with established domestic financial institutions, which would welcome the prolonged protection of their favored positions.

The second alternative is to accelerate the pace of liberalization by setting targets for internationalization and binding them in a multilateral agreement and to proceed to dismantle restrictions on domestic and foreign activity in preparation for meeting those targets. The benefits, as demonstrated here, would accrue to businesses, households, and governments, which would realize lower costs and enjoy better service and wider choice. Those governments that lead the process of liberalization will see economic benefits flow to their economies from the business that will come from those of their trading partners where liberalization is proceeding at a slower pace.

The peaceful, complacent face of the domestic financial industry will undergo rapid change, however, as firms merge, foreign firms buy local ones, and local firms extend their reach by opening or acquiring foreign subsidiaries. Such restructuring, its sequence, and its pace are among the risks and costs of deregulation and market opening. These concerns are the subject of the next chapter.

3

The Pitfalls of Reform and Transitional Issues

Financial reform promises hefty benefits, but it also sets in motion a process of change that will impose some costs. The path toward greater efficiency in financial services, like the path toward freer trade, implies the closure of those firms that remain unproductive and the gradual emergence of new practices. These new practices include modern supervision and regulation and the abandonment of the special relationships and poor lending practices that bear so much responsibility for the dismal state of financial sectors in so many emerging markets. Like trade in goods, competition will bring net benefits, but those who enjoyed protection will suffer and will try to oppose change.

There are legitimate concerns about giving competitive forces free play. But the analogy with trade in goods is useful here as well: protection against foreign competition is not the best way to address these concerns. Trade in services also introduces the dimension of foreign commercial presence and national treatment, and this brings up the important issue of home-country versus host-country regulation. Important questions thus arise about the initial ingredients needed to undertake financial reform and about the best way to manage the transition, both from a purely economic standpoint and from the standpoint of political economy.

This chapter surveys these questions. First, we examine three common arguments against financial reform: that reform increases the chances of financial crisis; that finance is a "special" or "strategic" sector and therefore must remain in domestic hands and closely regulated; and that participants in the sector (and sometimes the government itself) will be hurt in bearing the burden of adjustment. Next, we examine the policy implications of these arguments and bring some evidence to bear on them, including a summary of the state of reform in leading emerging market economies, which is outlined in more detail in appendix B. Included in this examination is a review of the financial crisis that erupted in East Asia in 1997.

Three Common Concerns

How Does Financial Reform Increase the Risk of Crisis?

There is evidence that domestic deregulation and internationalization can expose or exacerbate problems in the presence of macroeconomic or regulatory weakness and may increase the risk that such weakness leads to a crisis. Such reforms, however, do not cause these difficulties, but rather bring them to light. The proper answer to legitimate concerns here is not to postpone or renounce such reforms. That would only mean forgoing the potential benefits of reform, while leaving the economy in its inefficient state, which its underlying weaknesses will only worsen. Instead, the answer is to address those weaknesses, within banking (improper risk assessment, connected lending, and insolvent banks) and in the macroeconomy, so that capital account liberalization can proceed without precipitating a major financial disruption. In many cases, a commitment to broad financial reform can help to create the incentives needed to address financial and supervisory weaknesses, as political forces may oppose such correction.

Foreign financial institutions and foreign entry are not, per se, associated with financial crises. As we argued in chapter 2, these institutions can help to strengthen and deepen the financial system, thus lessening the system's vulnerability to upheaval. We discuss these issues below, including the important distinction between opening to foreign competition and opening the capital account.

There is a popular impression that banking crises are associated with financial reform, and many governments, especially in emerging markets, consider an enhanced risk of crisis to be one of the costs. Deregulation and internationalization in Argentina, Brazil, and Chile in the 1970s ended in banking crises (a rise in the number of insolvent banks, which had to be bailed out) and broader financial crises (flight of foreign investors, capital flow reversals, and a sharp depreciation of the currency). The Mexican peso crisis in 1994-95 and its rapid spread to other economies (the so-called tequila effect) have contributed to the concerns of East Asian governments about the possible side effects of deregulation, foreign entry, and capital account liberalization.

Distinctions must be made, however, among the causal factors in such crises. One study of banking crises noted that, in 18 of 25 cases, financial reform had occurred at some time in the previous 5 years

(Kaminsky and Reinhart 1995). This and other studies have identified a number of factors behind banking crises, including macroeconomic volatility originating in the international economy—in such forms as fluctuations in the terms of trade and volatile international interest rates and real exchange rates. Other factors are volatile growth and inflation rates at home; lending booms, asset price collapses, and surges in capital inflows; asset and liability mismatches; and inadequate preparation for financial reform (Goldstein and Turner 1996). These studies underscore the fact that, although deregulation and internationalization can produce monetary shocks, the fundamental challenge for governments is to address institutional weaknesses early in the reform process. In other words, it is the quality and design of the reforms that matter for economic performance (Johnston and Pazarbasioglu 1995; Lindgren, Garcia, and Saal 1996).

In the episodes surveyed, a lending boom has generally preceded the crisis (Sachs, Tornell, and Velasco 1996; Goldstein and Turner 1996), exposing domestic banks to the risk of bank panics. Expectations of devaluation and an incipient speculative attack can cause a fall in bank deposits, which can easily lead to liquidity problems because banks lack sufficient reserves to cover their liabilities. Given the systemic implications of bank crises, the central bank can be expected to step in with an expansion of liquidity, which can in turn feed a speculative attack on its reserves. Goldstein and Turner (1996) tend to associate the cycle of excessive credit creation in part with surges in capital inflows, because those countries with the largest net capital inflows also tend to be those that experience the most rapid expansion of the banking sector. Sachs, Tornell, and Velasco (1996), however, find no obvious correlation between the size of the capital inflow and the subsequent behavior of bank credit, except in the case of Mexico.

Both studies agree on the association of credit expansion with domestic reforms. Banks react to financial reform and increased competition (both domestic and foreign) by paying higher interest rates to attract deposits and using the proceeds to expand lending and fund riskier projects. The combination of deposit insurance and inadequate supervision creates a moral hazard: banks can increase the risk and the vulnerability of their portfolios without due regard for the possible consequences, and depositors willingly cooperate. Internationalization, through short-term capital inflows, feeds the process. When these inflows reverse course, the weaknesses in the banking system are exposed.

This discussion naturally leads to the interaction between opening to foreign competition (the objective of the financial services negotiations) and opening the capital account of the balance of payments. The case for capital account liberalization rests on the argument that consumption and investment decisions within an economy can become disconnected. Consumption, and therefore saving, may be optimally distributed over time, whereas investment may be undertaken until its marginal return equals the cost of capital. Saving and investment need not balance, because any discrepancy between desired saving and desired investment is met through net capital inflows. The issues in capital account liberalization came to the fore with the costly experiences of financial reform in Chile and Argentina in the 1970s and with the Mexican peso crisis in 1994. Chile deregulated and stabilized its economy beginning in 1974, allowed foreign ownership of banks in 1976, and opened the capital account for domestic banks in 1980. When the country experienced a severe banking crisis in 1981 and renationalized its banks to prevent defaults on foreign loans, it also reintroduced capital account restrictions, some of which are still in effect (see appendix B and table 3.1). Most developing countries have become fearful of the capital flows that may follow opening, because inflows that reverse and become outflows may destabilize the domestic economic and financial situation. As a result, governments are reluctant to open fully the capital account.

Generally speaking, to the extent that a financial service transaction involves an international capital transaction, the capital account needs to be opened for the former to take place freely. But not always, and it is possible for some international trade in financial services to take place without capital flows (Price Waterhouse International Economic Consultants 1988). Capital controls (such as exchange controls), however, substantially reduce users' freedom to buy financial services directly from foreign financial institutions and may also discourage entry. Arrangements for delivering financial services across borders without affecting capital flows will also be costly. Opening the capital account, therefore, although a distinct issue from that of opening to foreign financial services competition, sooner or later becomes an issue that countries must face. As foreign financial institutions enter, and as some domestic financial institutions are strengthened through competition, pressures to grant more freedom for capital inflows and outflows will increase.

Here it is important to emphasize that the 1997 FSA negotiations left the timing and the extent of capital account opening to the discretion of each member country. Moreover, current GATS provisions allow for prudential measures to safeguard the stability of the financial system and for temporary restrictions on trade in services in the case of serious balance of payments difficulties.

Countries' experiences with capital account liberalization do not tell us as much about capital account liberalization per se as about the interaction of an open capital account with domestic macroeconomic policy choices and exchange rate policy, and with domestic banking regulatory structures. Indeed, the size and even the nature of capital inflows do not appear to be significant determinants of financial crises. Sachs, Tornell, and Velasco (1996) provide a detailed comparative study of emerging markets in the 1980s and test a number of the usual explanations of such crises. They identify three factors that determine whether

Table 3.1   Openness of financial markets, 1997

Economy	Capital account	National treatment	Foreign entry/activities	Other restrictions
Argentina	Open.	Yes.	**Current** 100 percent foreign ownership permitted in all sectors. Foreign investors permitted to control banks with less than 50 percent equity. Prior authorization required for entry. **WTO** Binds right of establishment and guarantees 100 percent foreign ownership in banking and securities.	**Current** *Insurance:* Foreign firms must establish a subsidiary to sell locally. Cross-border trading in insurance brokerage prohibited. Moratorium on new licenses for nonlife insurance.
Brazil	Still restricted.	Yes, but only if the firm is structured in accordance with Brazilian law and establishes a headquarters and administrative offices in Brazil.	**Current** Entry limited. *Banks:* Recent banking entrants limited to firms expanding minority ownership to 100 percent holdings. No new foreign subsidiaries approved since before 1988. *Insurance:* Joint ventures permitted in insurance, but establishment of new branches and subsidiaries prohibited. Foreign participation limited to 50 percent of equity and 30 percent of voting stock. 100 percent foreign ownership permitted in health sector. *Securities:* Foreign equity in investment banks limited to 49 percent of shares and 39 percent of voting shares. Foreign firms only permitted to engage in investment banking through off-shore funds or universal banks. **WTO** Guarantees right of establishment and 100 percent foreign ownership in banking and	**Current** *Banks:* Must get branch licenses to operate ATM. *Banking and Insurance:* The constitution prohibits new branches, subsidiaries, or an increase in equity in domestic firms unless it is in the national interest, based on reciprocal treatment, or reflects international treaty. *Insurance:* Government monopoly in reinsurance. *Securities:* Universal banks dominate the market; foreign bank branches are not allowed to offer universal banking services. 15 percent tax on all profit remittances. The criteria for determining whether market access will be granted is not transparent.

(Table continues on next page)

35

Table 3.1 Openness of financial markets, 1997 (continued)

Economy	Capital account	National treatment	Foreign entry/activities	Other restrictions
			securities, although new entry still subject to authorization determined on a case-by-case basis. Allows 100 percent foreign-owned insurance subsidiaries, also subject to government approval on a case-by-case basis, but no insurance branches.	
Chile	Controls on short-term capital inflows.	Yes.	**Current** 100 percent foreign ownership permitted in all financial services. *Banks:* Moratorium on new banking licenses; majority of banks are foreign controlled. *Insurance:* Over 60 percent of the market controlled by foreign companies. *Securities:* Foreign securities firms required to establish a subsidiary. Foreign firms not permitted to list on the stock market. **WTO** Guaranteed right to 100 percent foreign-owned banks, but not securities firms. Allows 100 percent foreign-owned insurance subsidiaries, but no branches. Guarantees market access in all insurance subsectors except for pensions.	**Current** *Banks:* Permitted to establish subsidiaries or branches, but subsidiaries are discouraged. Red tape burdensome. *Securities:* No investment banks exist. Investment banking takes place through commercial bank subsidiaries; therefore, a banking license is critical to offering investment banking.
China	Closed, although government committed to IMF Article VIII.	No.	**Current** Entry limited. *Banks:* Can operate only in special economic zones. Restricted branching requirements. No branching for investment banks. New products restricted. Foreign banks may enter as joint venture or wholly owned, if authorized. Must deposit 30 percent of capital requirements with the People's Bank of China.	**Current** *Banks:* Generally limited to hard currency transactions, although limited number of renminbi licenses recently issued. Limited number of foreign exchange activities. Limited to wholesale banking. Must have representative office for 3 years and 100 million renminbi to open branch. *Insurance:* Restricted repatriation of funds. Foreign firms

Country			

India — Highly restricted. — No.

...cannot compete with state-run commercial insurance and other state-run insurance companies; domestic firms can. *Securities*: Limited to B-shares transactions. Cannot introduce innovative products. Must work with domestic broker. Repatriation of profits requires government approval.

Insurance: Three-year waiting period before full business license issued. Foreign ownership limited to 49 percent of shares. Only three licenses and one joint venture approved. *Securities*: Cannot establish branches or subsidiaries. Entry through joint venture only; up to 85 percent foreign ownership permitted. No subsidiaries or branches. Representative offices cannot conduct business.

Current

Entry limited. *Banks*: Foreign banks may only enter through a branch or representative office; geographically restricted. Only eight licenses for foreign banks issued annually. Foreign banks required to lend 34 percent of net credit to priority sectors. Foreign banks limited to 15 percent of total banking assets. *Insurance*: Private ownership is prohibited. *Securities*: 100 percent ownership of nonbank financial institutions permitted. Approved on case-by-case basis.

WTO

Binds market access for foreign ownership at 49 percent for stock brokering and 51 percent for other financial services, although private ownership in insurance still prohibited.

Current

Banks: Foreign-owned banks pay higher taxes. Operating ratios based on local branch, not global, capital. Bank entry dependant on reciprocity. Foreign equity in public banks limited to 20 percent. Foreign banks cannot conduct business with public sector entities. Banks not allowed to hedge capital or unremitted profits against foreign exchange risk. *Banks and securities*: Permissible percent that can be foreign owned depends on amount invested by foreign firms (ranges from minority to 100 percent). Foreign portfolio investment limited to approved foreign institutions and nonresident Indians; discriminatory portfolio investment restrictions. Prior authorization required to remit profits or dividends.

Indonesia — Open. — Not for banks; limited to activities in insurance and securities.

Current

Entry limited. No new licenses for foreign banks, nonbanks or finance companies. *Banks*: Full ownership permitted only if branch was established before 1972. New foreign

Current

Banks: Operating ratios based on local, not global, capital. Must extend at least 50 percent of credit to export-related activities. Majority foreign-owned joint ventures cannot borrow from state-owned banks.

(Table continues on next page)

Table 3.1 Openness of financial markets, 1997 (*continued*)

Economy	Capital account	National treatment	Foreign entry/activities	Other restrictions
			financial institutions limited to 49 percent of local firms. Joint ventures limited to 85 percent of equity. Foreign banks' ATMs and commercial lending are capped. *Insurance:* Full ownership permitted only for life insurers and if branch was established before 1972. Equity participation in joint ventures limited to 80 percent; after 20 years, equity participation in joint ventures limited to 49 percent, or may be purchased by FFIs subject to government approval. Offshore companies not permitted to serve Malaysian residents. *Securities:* Entry only possible since 1989 and only as a joint venture. Foreign equity participation in joint ventures limited to 85 percent or less. **WTO** 100 percent ownership of nonbank financial institutions. Allows 100 percent ownership of insurance subsidiaries but no branches. Equity ownership in banks limited to 49 percent. **IMF** Plans to introduce legislation that would allow 100 percent foreign ownership of listed banks.	Foreign banks cannot conduct business with state-owned enterprises or the public sector. Restricted number of expatriate employees. Market access dependent upon reciprocity. *Insurance:* Higher initial equity investment required. Only joint ventures can insure Indonesian nationals and companies. Twenty percent of total capital (percentage increase annually) in form of time deposits with domestic banks. *Securities:* Foreign companies not permitted to list on domestic exchange. Portfolio investment limited to 49 percent of shares. Introduction of new financial products and services restricted. **WTO** Phases out discriminatory capital requirements in insurance. Commits to 100 percent foreign ownership of publicly listed firms. **IMF** Government lifted restrictions on branching of joint venture banks and subbranching of foreign banks.
Japan	Open.	Yes.	**Current** Requires national reciprocity. **WTO** Binds in WTO bilateral commitments made with the United States on insurance and other financial services.	**Current** *Insurance:* Protection will continue for 4 years as entry barrier to insurance sector in which foreign insurers have an advantage. *Securities:* Separate capitalization for each branch required.

Country			Current
South Korea	Restrictions being removed in IMF program.	No.	**Current** Entry limited. *Banks:* Branch operations only approved way to enter market, and foreign equity in joint ventures limited to 49 percent (to be phased out in 1998 for OECD). Discriminatory treatment in interbank market. Foreign banks limited to 15 percent of total bank assets. *Insurance:* Foreign equity participation in joint ventures in life insurance limited to 49 percent. Nonlife restricted to branches and representative offices. *Securities:* Joint ventures limited to 50 percent equity (to be phased out in 1998 for OECD). **WTO** Removes ceilings on foreign equity ownership in life insurance. Allows 100 percent foreign-owned subsidiaries and entry through branches in insurance. Removes ceilings on foreign equity ownership in securities firms. **IMF** Binds all OECD commitments on financial services in the WTO, including that allowing foreign investors to establish and have 100 percent ownership of any type of financial institution by the end of 1998. Allows foreign banks and brokerage houses to establish subsidiaries.	**Current** *Banks:* Limited access to local currency. Operating ratios based on branch, not global, capital. Must extend at least 25 percent of credit to small and medium-sized enterprises. Introduction of new products and access to credit card market restricted. *Insurance:* Premium rates regulated. Not allowed to offer all types of products. Not allowed to offer life and nonlife. *Securities:* Extremely high capital requirements. Over-the-counter market closed to foreign firms; 60 percent of bond activity on OTC. Pledge to open blue-chip bond market, but not until international/domestic interest rate differential less than 2 percent. **WTO** Allows establishment of credit card and leasing services. **IMF** Removes ceiling on aggregate foreign ownership in equities and raises individual ceiling from 7 to 50 percent.
Malaysia	Open.	In money market instruments; not in insurance.	**Current** Entry limited. No new branches or wholly owned subsidiaries. *Banks:* Foreign equity in domestic banks limited to 30 percent or less. Foreign banks have to be 100 percent locally	**Current** *Banks:* Nonfinancial joint ventures can borrow only up to 40 percent of credit from joint-venture banks. Foreign banks cannot conduct business with state-owned enterprises. Foreign banks do not have

(Table continues on next page)

Table 3.1 Openness of financial markets, 1997 (*continued*)

Economy	Capital account	National treatment	Foreign entry/activities	Other restrictions
			incorporated institutions; these may be 100 percent foreign owned. No new branches permitted; ATM's considered branches. *Insurance:* Foreign equity limited to 49 percent or less. Will not grandfather existing investment exceeding 49 percent ownership. No new branches being licensed (except reinsurance). *Securities:* Foreign equity limited to 49 percent or less. 100 percent foreign ownership permitted in fund management if company manages only foreign funds, 70 percent otherwise. **WTO** Increased permissible foreign ownership for securities brokering and foreign joint investment management firms. Binds insurance at 51 percent foreign ownership, which is less than current levels; no grandfathering of insurance investments.	access to local capital market. No sharing of credit information between domestic banks allowed. Higher capital requirements. *Insurance:* Local incorporation required by June 1998. Cannot insure ships, aircraft, property. Importers can claim 100 percent more deductions for marine cargo premiums paid to domestic insurers. *Securities:* New joint ventures subject to economic needs test. All forms of foreign equity tightly controlled. Initial public offerings generally restricted to Malaysian investors. Foreign portfolio investment restricted. **WTO** Slightly relaxes, but maintains, restrictions on number of expatriate staff.
Mexico	Open.	Yes, if same services by foreign financial institution are provided in another NAFTA country. Yes for all NAFTA countries companies.	**Current** *Banks:* Non-NAFTA banks limited to 41 percent equity. Restrictions on total foreign ownership in banking to be gradually eased out. Market access restricted to subsidiaries. *Insurance:* NAFTA country firms permitted 100 percent ownership. Non-NAFTA firms limited to 49 percent equity. *Securities:* Foreign equity limited to 49 percent. **WTO** Binds NAFTA commitments on insurance.	**Current** *Securities:* Foreign investors allowed only to acquire equity through "B" shares, American deposit receipts, or Neutral Fund. Non-NAFTA firms prohibited from pension fund management.

Country				
Philippines	Open.	Yes, in most subsectors.	**Current** *Banks*: Foreign equity in domestic bank subsidiary limited to 60 percent. Foreign banks can establish up to six wholly owned branches. Foreign equity participation in universal banks limited to 30 percent. No foreigners in investment banking or trust business. Foreign banks limited to 30 percent of total banking assets. *Insurance*: Foreign equity limited to 40 percent or less. *Securities*: Foreign equity in investment houses limited to 49 percent. Brokers are limited to representative offices and wholly owned, locally incorporated subsidiaries (no branches permitted). **WTO** Binds foreign equity participation in domestic and newly incorporated bank subsidiaries at 51 percent. Grandfathers acquired rights in banks and securities. Increases foreign equity in insurance to 51 percent, allows subsidiaries but no branches in insurance. Increases foreign equity in investment houses to 51 percent.	**Current** *Banks*: Borrowing limits based on branch, not global, capital. Not allowed to accept demand deposits. US $100 million capital infusion required, over 20 years, for new foreign banks. Larger capital requirements. No free choice on location of fourth, fifth, and sixth branches. New foreign banks must be from top 5 in home country or top 150 worldwide. *Securities*: Plans to limit number of foreign brokerages to keep domestic-to-foreign ratio at or higher than 60:40. Foreign participation in the mutual fund industry restricted. Foreign portfolio investment restricted.
Taiwan	Nearly open.	No.	**Current** *Banks*: Limited to three branches. Two-year waiting period between opening first and additional branches. Foreign exchange liability ceilings for all banks (domestic and foreign) to be replaced with reserve requirements. *Insurance*: Long approval process for new products. *Securities*: Foreign individuals banned from investing on local stock market. Foreign equity in local foreign exchange brokerages limited to	**Current** *Banks*: Limited in aggregate size of NT$ deposit. Lending limits. Restricted trade finance and guarantees for commercial paper. Cannot raise funds locally through bank debentures. *Insurance*: Foreign firms not organized as limited-liability joint stock companies unable to set up branches. *Securities*: Foreign firms restricted to investing in one local firm. Qualified foreign investors must have a minimum of

(*Table continues on next page*)

41

Table 3.1 Openness of financial markets, 1997 *(continued)*

Economy	Capital account	National treatment	Foreign entry/activities	Other restrictions
			50 percent; foreign equity in Republic of China securities firm limited to 40 percent.	US$150 million in net assets or be one of top 3,000 banks.
Thailand	Open.	Yes.	**Current** *Banks:* 100 percent foreign ownership of domestic banks and finance companies permitted until 2007, when new foreign equity limited to 49 percent.[a] Foreign banks restricted to three branches, with one outside Bangkok. ATMs regarded as branch, prohibiting foreign banks from participating in nationwide ATM network (unless approved by network members). *Insurance:* Foreign equity in domestic insurance companies limited to 25 percent. Foreign equity in services auxiliary to insurance limited to 49 percent. *Securities:* Foreign equity in domestic finance companies limited to 25 percent. Equity participation in finance company joint ventures limited to 49 percent. Foreigners prohibited from being brokers, dealers, traders, or underwriters. New entrants must be approved by minister and cabinet. **WTO** Binds status quo in banking and insurance and grandfathers any investments in the banking sector until 2007.	**Current** *Banks:* Reserve requirement of 125 million baht, invested in low-yield government bonds. Restricted number of expatriate personnel. *Insurance:* Since 1992, foreign insurance branches have been permitted but no licenses have been granted. *Securities:* No voting rights in onshore funds. Operating ratios for all financial services based on local branch, not global, capital. Foreign portfolio investment restricted to minority of shares. Foreigners not permitted to work as insurance brokers.

Notes: WTO FSA commitments, noted as WTO in the table, are scheduled to come into force in March 1999. Several countries that received IMF assistance in 1997-98 included commitments to open the financial sector in their IMF economic program. These commitments, generally scheduled to be phased in from 1998-2000, are noted in the table as "IMF."

a. Thailand's IMF economic program was in place by late summer 1997, at which time authorities agreed to raise the ceiling on foreign ownership of domestic banks from 25 percent to 49 percent and then to the current 100 percent.

a country is vulnerable: a large real appreciation of the currency, a weak banking system, and low levels of foreign exchange reserves relative to some broad measure of liquid assets such as M2 (because such assets can be converted into foreign exchange and flee the country in the event of a crisis).

In many cases, the liberalization of capital movements occurred at the same time as the choice of an exchange rate peg, to provide a nominal anchor. Such exchange rate policies may be very successful in the short to medium term, as inflation is indeed reduced dramatically. But inflation rarely drops to zero; consequently, a substantial real appreciation occurs, which helps to keep inflation low. But the appreciation also crowds out net exports, chokes off growth after an initial boom, and finally proves unsustainable, sowing the seeds of a financial crisis. The cost of real appreciation is all the more damaging when it occurs at the same time that the current account is liberalized—as McKinnon (1973) pointed out long ago. There is an inescapable dilemma between credibility (the efficacy of the peg hinges on the credible promise not to devalue) and pragmatism (the need to devalue or float the currency at the appropriate time and before a crisis develops). The lack of a pragmatic approach to exchange rate management always ends up undermining the credibility of the exchange rate commitment if nothing else happens to suggest that the real overvaluation can be tackled, for example, through productivity increases in the export sector.

Nominal exchange rate rigidity thus appears to be a major determinant of vulnerability to speculative attack and to financial crisis. Interestingly, however, capital inflows to developing countries are not always associated with real appreciation. In some cases, like Chile or Colombia in the 1980s, or like the Asian countries more recently, they are compatible with a real depreciation. Fiscal retrenchment and sterilization, together with nominal exchange rate flexibility, are conventional explanations. Sterilization, however, cannot be undertaken permanently on a very large scale, and it is costly, because it amounts to substituting high-yielding domestic assets for low-yielding foreign reserves (Fernandez-Arias and Montiel 1996).

In summary, a proper conceptual distinction among the issues at hand—opening to foreign competition, opening the capital account, addressing domestic banking-sector weaknesses, and stabilizing the macroeconomy—should help countries to realize that the challenge is not foreign competition per se. Rather, it is finding the proper mix of macroeconomic and supervisory policies that are needed to strengthen the financial system and increase the economy's growth potential. If anything, opening to foreign competition will help to find that proper mix by providing better incentives to do so. Full capital account opening, although desirable and even necessary in the longer term, is not a short-term priority. Nor is it central to the financial services negotiations.

Is Finance Special?

There is truth to the notion that finance is special, even strategic. As outlined in appendix A, the financial system is the medium through which most of the transactions of a market economy are conducted. Banks play a major role in the transmission of monetary policy to the economy; they are also expected to provide safe assets to small depositors for whom monitoring and scrutinizing financial institutions is costly, and they make loans to borrowers who are less visible in capital markets, such as small- and medium-sized enterprises that require credit to carry on their regular business. We also argued in the first chapter that the degree of development of the financial system affects the long-term growth and development of the economy.

Developing-country governments with immature financial systems often dominated by banks have tended to organize their financial systems to channel financial resources to development priorities. Both developed- and developing-country government share the concern that foreign financial institutions will have different priorities and will tend to ignore domestic objectives. There is, for example, some concern that they will leave socially important segments of the market unattended. This concern exists in the insurance industry as well. One insurance executive explained India's reluctance to open its insurance markets to foreign competition for this reason:

> I was told throughout India that one of the basic reasons why they won't allow outsiders to come back into their market is because they think outside insurers would not be concerned with underwriting the general risk and particularly those areas of risk which are socially important, like workers' compensation and agricultural risks, but rather they would be concerned only with the premium of the business, to take out profits.[1]

One of the few systematic empirical comparisons of the performance of domestic- and foreign-owned financial institutions in a host country (Australia) finds that different foreign banks pursued different strategies. Some focused on servicing corporations from the same home country, others concentrated on providing sophisticated financial products, while still others provided retail services. Domestic banks adjusted to this competition by upgrading services and providing intense competition (McFadden 1994 in Levine 1996). Casual empiricism also suggests that foreign banks' business focus is determined by market conditions and domestic regulation. Most tend to concentrate on wholesale banking (such as trade finance and selling sophisticated financial products to corporate clients)

---

1. Anthony N. Armstrong, Skandia International Insurance Company, at the XVth Conference of the East Asian Insurance Congress, Jakarta, 15-20 September 1990.

rather than on retail banking. Citibank is well known to be almost the only international bank that successfully provides retail banking services in many foreign countries. One reason for this focus is that international banks have found that they lack the assets, such as knowledge of their customers, necessary to be profitable in the retail business outside of their home countries. Domestic regulations that limit their involvement in retail banking are another reason.

These arguments that foreign financial institutions will undermine national objectives are important, but they are hardly reasons to keep foreigners out. There is very little evidence that foreign entry impairs the functioning of the domestic financial system as a whole; indeed, as the previous chapter showed, foreign financial institutions can be expected to increase the system's efficiency. Their presence helps to diversify the financial system; the diversified geographic structure of their parents also means they may escape local crises and provide badly needed stability. National objectives of providing safe assets to small depositors can be achieved by other means, such as by regulations that allow for the existence of "narrow" banks that hold government securities that match the maturity of their claims (Chant 1997). Moreover, the effectiveness of monetary policy depends more on the exchange rate regime and the degree of capital mobility than on the presence or absence of foreign banking institutions. (We return in the next section to the question of the relationship between opening to foreign competition and capital mobility through capital account convertibility.)

Another worry is that foreign investors unfamiliar with emerging and still-underdeveloped markets may exhibit a home-country bias, leading them to retreat promptly and massively at the first difficulty. This concern is related to the fear, discussed in the previous section, that an open system might be more crisis prone. Yet, evidence is scant that foreign financial institutions have undermined financial systems by, for example, retreating during recessions or by dominating the system. Like other foreign investors, their institutional presence tends to be long-term. Short-term cross-border transactions are more volatile, however. Even so, studies of the transactions of US institutional investors in emerging markets have found rather mixed evidence of such volatility. On the positive side, the Investment Company Institute found that fund managers buy when prices are falling and sell in rising markets (Rea 1995); Tesar and Werner (1995) found that the volatility of foreign equity investments declines through time as investors become more familiar with the market. Claessens, Dooley, and Warner (1995), however, show that volatility is associated more with the type of investment (portfolio, equity, or short-term) than with the duration of the investment because of interactions among the various types of investment. In banking, where more data are available, Vittas (1995) provides evidence of banks from OECD countries retreating from emerging markets in the aftermath of the 1982 debt crisis, when they were encouraged by their governments to write down or shed their nonperforming offshore loans.

Data on the distribution of financial assets provide an indication that foreign banks' share of banking assets is between 16 and 22 percent of total assets in Argentina, Chile, and Mexico, which are not financial centers like Singapore and Hong Kong. In the remaining 8 economies, foreign banks' share of total assets averages just over 5 percent (see table A.1).

Foreign banks have been active in the industrialized countries for many years. In the United States, the US banking operations of foreign banks accounted for 26.1 percent of US banking assets in 1996 (Institute of International Bankers 1997). In Latin America, Citibank's operations began 80 years ago. In the 1990s, a few large European and Canadian banks with global strategies have made numerous acquisitions of local institutions.[2] Yet, in the seven largest Latin American countries, foreign banks control on average only 15 percent of total loans and 16 percent of total deposits, with shares ranging from 10 percent in Brazil to 35 percent in Argentina and Venezuela. In most cases, foreign banks control over 50 percent of the voting stock of local institutions in which they are partners, yet their effective control of assets averages around 11 percent.

The Political Economy of Financial Reform

The third reason for governments' reluctance to undertake reform relates to a set of political economy considerations about the domestic costs of opening to foreign competition. Those considerations that traditionally apply to trade in goods also hold with respect to trade in financial services, to the entry of foreign firms, and even to the liberalization of capital flows. The benefits are widely diffused and not well understood, making coalition building difficult, whereas the costs are highly visible and concentrated among those firms that suffer from increased competition and benefit from special treatment; these firms may also provide special services to the government. This asymmetry must not be allowed to prevent reform. Binding a commitment to open the financial services sector within a multilateral framework allows governments to circumvent all the pressures that would be brought to bear on a strictly unilateral, gradual process of change. It also recognizes that all countries face the same difficulties and can address them in similar ways through multilateral negotiations.

The political economy argument against opening is linked as much to the argument that financial services are strategic and must therefore be

---

2. This section draws on Salomon Brothers (1997).

controlled by domestic interests as to concerns that crises will result. Market opening, it is held, will undermine national sovereignty and cultural integrity if it leads to domination of the sector by foreign institutions. Others point out that, at least in the past, financial repression yielded revenue to the government, because borrowing costs were lower than at market rates. To the extent that repressed financial systems were linked to lax fiscal policies, reform, by raising real interest rates, exacerbates the government debt burden. In the late 1990s, however, governments' pursuit of fiscal prudence is a necessary complement to reform, together with sound regulation and supervision of the financial system (Giovannini and De Melo 1993; Fry, Goodhart, and Almeida 1996; Fry 1997).

As Haggard and Maxfield (1993, 1996) note, a coalition of interests supporting domestic financial reform and opening may sometimes emerge. Such a coalition has been at work in many countries that have embarked on unilateral reforms. As developing countries have become more integrated into the world economy through international flows of capital, goods, and services, their governments' choices with respect to international financial policy have become more constrained—just as did those of the OECD governments during the integration of their economies. As individuals and businesses develop more foreign ties and benefit from greater openness, this increased interdependence may tilt the balance of political forces toward a more internationalist posture. For example, Japan's plans for "big bang" financial reform are in part a response to domestic investors pushing for access to foreign securities and other investment opportunities offering higher rates of return than the domestic market can provide. Foreign investors also appear on the scene and acquire more political voice, possibly supported by their home-country governments. Meanwhile, growing interdependence makes it much more difficult for governments to enforce trade and investment restrictions, not to mention capital controls. Foreign pressure is another factor; for example, in 1995-96 the United States successfully pressured Japan to increase foreigners' access to that country's insurance market.

In summary, governments' reluctance to deregulate and open financial markets responds to some very real concerns about the risk of financial crisis and about the burden of adjustment and how it will be distributed. But as this discussion has illustrated, foot dragging is not the answer. Rather than addressing these legitimate fears, it allows the weaknesses that are at the root of such fears to persist and to spread.

Policy Implications and the Management of the Transition

We have identified the essential prerequisites of domestic reform and market opening as a prudent and stable macroeconomic policy framework, adequate institutional capacity, strong prudential supervision, and adequate safety nets. We have also pointed out that it is essential that these reforms be paced and sequenced appropriately. The turmoil in East Asian financial markets in 1997 and 1998, beginning in Thailand in the middle of the year and spreading to most other countries of the region, illustrates the implications of these arguments in a timely but unfortunate way. After drawing some lessons from these events, this section turns to a discussion of the ingredients necessary for an opening to foreign competition and the issues surrounding the pacing and sequencing of domestic reform and internationalization.

Financial Turmoil in East Asia

At the beginning of 1997, few expected that Thailand would face a balance of payments crisis. Its currency was overvalued in real terms (because its current account deficit had averaged more than 6 percent of GDP from 1993 to 1997), but its budgetary position was manageable (table 3.2), and international financial markets allowed the coalition government some breathing room despite recurrent domestic concerns about the health of Thai financial institutions. Thailand's exchange rate had been pegged to the dollar for 13 years. But the appreciation of the dollar against the yen in 1996 and 1997, together with cyclical weakness in the semiconductor industry and the appearance of new competitors in labor-intensive export industries, had begun to cause competitive problems in the real sector. By 1996, the current account deficit had reached 8 percent of GDP. At the same time, high levels of domestic saving had been channeled into property-market speculation, and Thai banks and corporations had become heavily reliant on foreign capital (table 3.2). The results were currency and maturity mismatches that are typical of banking crises in other countries. By mid-1997, many Thai firms had accumulated large, short-term, unhedged debt liabilities in foreign currencies. About half of this debt, according to estimates, was held by Japanese banks, and much of it was due within 12 months.

Thailand's weak political coalition faced a dilemma: if it defended the currency by raising interest rates, it risked pushing banks and finance companies, already burdened with nonperforming loans, into insolvency. If it devalued, the credibility of its exchange rate policy would be left in shambles. Speculators bet, correctly, that the authorities would not defend the currency at any price by raising real domestic interest rates to very high levels. The Thai authorities were reluctant to ask the IMF for assistance until late in the day. On 2 July 1997, the baht was allowed to float, but when it plunged precipitously over the next month, IMF assistance was requested and a $16.7 billion rescue package was assembled by the IMF, Japan, and regional institutions and other governments,

Table 3.2 Selected economic indicators: Asian economies, 1993-97[a] (percentage of GDP unless otherwise indicated)

	Real GDP growth[b]	Inflation[b,c]	Domestic saving	Fixed capital investment	General government balance	Public-sector balance	M2 growth (end of year)[b,f]	Domestic credit growth (end of year)[b,f]	Foreign liabilities of banks[d,f]	Current account balance	External debt service
China	11	11.4	41.6	35.9	-1.7	-4	33.2	28.5	6.1	0.5	2.2
Hong Kong SAR	5.1	7.6	31.9	30.2	1.9	na	12.3	18.2	69.2	0.5[e]	na
India	6.4	8.4	23.7	24	-9.6	na	16.1	12.3	na	-1.2	3.4
Indonesia	7.2	8.8	29.1	27.4	0.7	na	23.7	22.1	10	-2.5	9
Japan	1.5	0.7	31.4	28.9	-2.9	na	2.6	0.9	10.3	2.3	na
South Korea	7.3	5	34.2	36.3	0	na	16.7	16.3	9.5	-2.2	na
Malaysia	8.5	3.6	34.6	41.3	1.9	1.3	14.8[g]	14.2[g]	8.7[g]	-6.7	6.3
Philippines	4.3	7.7	19.3	23.6	-1.2	-0.5	24.7	55.5	14.8	-4.7	7
Singapore	8.8	2.1	49	34.8	11.3	11.3	10.3	14.9	35.5	14.1	na
Taiwan	6.2	3.2	27.7	22.3	0.3	na	11.3	14.3	3.9	3.4	na
Thailand	6.6	5.2	33.8	39.5	1.6	1.9	15.2	22.2	19.9	-6.1	5.3

na = not available.
a. Averages for the 1993-1997 period. Figures for 1997 are projected.
b. Annual percentage change.
c. Consumer price index.
d. In percent of total liabilities of the banking system.
e. Includes only goods and nonfactor services.
f. Average for 1993-96, unless otherwise indicated.
g. Average for 1993-95.

Source: International Monetary Fund (1997).

subject to numerous conditions, including painful macroeconomic adjustments and structural reforms that the coalition government had been reluctant to introduce on its own.

Neighboring countries suffered contagion effects as speculative attacks spread to the Malaysian ringgit, the Philippine peso, the Indonesian rupiah, and even the Hong Kong dollar. Because the Philippines was already on an IMF program, prompt IMF assistance and quickly announced policy adjustments helped to stem the drop in the peso. Both the ringgit and the rupiah were subsequently floated. Hong Kong, with its huge reserves, repeatedly fended off speculators over the ensuing months. The Malaysian prime minister worsened the pressures on Malaysian financial markets when he publicly attacked the "capitalists" and instituted a number of interventionist measures to curb international financial transactions. Contagion effects continued to appear in regional currency and stock markets. Growth projections were downgraded further, and the downward spiral eventually precipitated a correction in US and other OECD stock markets in late October 1997.

Indonesia's crisis began, like Thailand's, with strong downward pressure on the currency, which eventually forced it to allow the currency to float. Furthermore, most short-term corporate debts to foreign institutions had not been hedged. Emergency hedging operations increased downward pressures on the currency. The South Korean won floated more freely. But a combination of domestic and external factors created severe downward pressure on the won late in the year. A series of high-profile corporate failures, which had begun earlier in the year when highly leveraged firms experienced unexpected cyclical downturns in demand for their products, together with political uncertainty in the run-up to the presidential election in December 1997 and a depreciation by its major export competitor, Taiwan (despite its large foreign exchange reserves), were contributing factors. As interest rates rose in Indonesia and South Korea, nonperforming loans accumulated at an alarming rate.

Governments in South Korea and Indonesia were forced by worsening financial and political turmoil to seek IMF-led rescue packages of $57 billion and $40 billion in late November and early December 1997, respectively. In both cases, negotiations were protracted because of uncertainties about leadership succession and political will to carry out the program conditions. These conditions included not only macroeconomic stabilization measures affecting monetary, fiscal, and exchange rate policies, but also measures to restructure the financial sectors and, in the South Korean program, measures to liberalize further the capital account (see appendix B). Measures to restructure the financial sector included restructuring the large short-term foreign debts that had been accumulated by corporations, closing insolvent banks, evaluating the balance sheets of remaining financial institutions and preparing plans to strengthen them, and identifying institutional changes to strengthen the supervisory authorities (in South Korea, for example, the Bank of Korea Act was amended in early 1998 to grant more independence).

The new political leadership in South Korea moved quickly to implement the IMF program. An important factor in restoring stability was the ability to consolidate corporate debt in the banks and to arrange with foreign institutions for credible restructuring of those debts. In Indonesia, by contrast, nonperforming loans are distributed among hundreds of banks and corporate entities, making a single restructuring package extremely difficult to implement. In early 1998, the Indonesian crisis worsened as the rupiah continued to plunge. The government imposed a debt moratorium as borrowers failed to meet their debt servicing obligations; the political leadership was reluctant to carry out the previously agreed-on terms of the IMF program with respect to fiscal policy and the exchange rate regime. (The IMF program had also been widely criticized as inappropriate for the unique Indonesian problems). Eventually, the uncertainties about the program were resolved, but it was evident that the moratorium on debt servicing would not be reversed any time soon.

The Asian financial crisis illustrates several of the implications of the analysis in this chapter. Although most of the East Asian economies had better political and economic fundamentals than Thailand, all but Hong Kong[3] protect their financial systems. The culprit in the currency crises was not the traditional combination of rising current account deficits, lax monetary and fiscal policies, and pegged exchange rates (see table 3.2). Instead, it was weak financial systems; inadequate domestic reform associated with inadequate bank supervision, especially with respect to indebtedness denominated in foreign currencies; inadequate risk assessment; a tradition of bank bailouts, which introduced moral hazard; and the interaction among these weaknesses. More extensive domestic reform before, or at the same time as, opening to foreign competition—by promoting a deeper, more resilient, and stronger financial system—would have reduced the costs of Asia's full-blown financial and economic crisis.

Extensive capital account liberalization, given the lack of domestic reforms to strengthen financial institutions, fueled the crisis. Most careful studies of financial crisis in other developing economies, particularly the southern cone countries in Latin America, have concluded that strengthening financial institutions and improving their efficiency and competitiveness are prerequisites to full capital account liberalization. In other words, the transition from a protected financial system with a closed or highly restricted capital account to an internationalized system that is open to capital flows (short-term flows in particular) should be carefully planned and managed.

---

3. Singapore introduced changes in late 1997 to match Hong Kong.

Finally, the crisis points to the urgent need to strengthen international banking supervision, as Goldstein (1997) has pointed out.[4]

Ingredients of Reform

As the discussion in this chapter has made clear, the case made in chapter 2, that development of the financial system can bolster long-term growth, does not imply that such development should be left to unregulated markets and competition. Stiglitz (1994) has analyzed the pervasive market failures that characterize financial systems; these failures primarily involve conditions of asymmetric information, in which one party to a transaction lacks important information available to the other. Mishkin (1996) describes how asymmetric information in financial systems generates problems of adverse selection and moral hazard, implying that perfect competition is not the optimal arrangement and that public intervention is required to address these market imperfections. Stiglitz and Uy (1996) build a powerful case that some financial restraint—in such forms as reducing the cost of capital to firms by, for example, holding down interest rates—can be an appropriate response to these market imperfections, improving the working of financial markets and the performance of the economy. This argument relies heavily on the examples of South Korea and Taiwan, which have spectacular growth records and governments that have intervened heavily in the financial system; indeed, financial repression in these countries has only recently been eased (see appendix B).

Yet, as others have pointed out, if market failure is possible, so is government failure (Wolf 1991; White 1995). Indeed, government failure can be at least as pervasive as market failure, and it may well be more costly. In addition, Stiglitz's arguments assume exemplary government behavior (Fry 1997), which has been rare in emerging markets. A central issue that remains is how to address market failure in financial markets by finding a proper balance between market-based regulatory systems and government intervention. The role of supervision and regulation cannot be overemphasized: looking at the factors behind 29 of the deepest bank insolvencies in the world over the last 15 years, Caprio and Klingebiel (1996) identified poor supervision and regulation in 26.

Although the financial sectors of developing countries remain segmented, countries are deregulating and restructuring them in response to internal and external pressures. Widespread deficiencies exist in regulation and supervision, large parts of the financial market remain off-limits to foreign participants, and some aspects of the capital account are still restricted in a number of countries that follow export-led growth

---

4. See Goldstein (1997) for the rationale for and details of such a proposal.

strategies. These deficiencies are illustrated in a rather striking way in tables 3.1 and 3.3 and in appendix B. Accounting practices need to be standardized; clearing and payments systems need to be modernized; supervision of banking, securities, and foreign exchange markets needs to be reinforced, through the hiring of more agents and enhancement of their skills; effective legal frameworks are required, particularly to give supervisory agencies enforcement powers; independent credit rating agencies are needed; and bureaucrats need to encourage, not resist, restructuring and market opening. Governments continue to provide safety nets in the form of financial bailouts for banks with serious loan problems. These deficiencies must be addressed if the benefits of capital account liberalization are to be realized. They are necessary ingredients of reform, no matter what sequence is adopted, but recent events in Asia suggest such reforms should be addressed before full-blown liberalization is begun.

It is significant that China largely escaped the turmoil that afflicted its neighbors in 1997 and early 1998, in part because it has not yet opened its capital account. We use China, with its immature financial system and large-scale nonperforming loans in its domestic banks, to illustrate the sequence of reforms that are needed in a developing country's financial infrastructure. Our hypothetical objective is to bring its infrastructure up to Singapore's level (see appendix B for a description of Singapore's and China's financial systems). We choose Singapore not to imply that it should be regarded as a paragon of a modern and internationalized financial system (Singapore embarked on substantial deregulation on its own in late 1997), but simply to illustrate the requirements of a transition from a still-underdeveloped system to a modern and sophisticated one. Singapore took 30 years to establish its system, so it is not unreasonable to expect that these changes will take some time in China.

What would China have to do to make the transition to Singaporean standards, practices, and institutions? Based on the analysis in appendix B, such a systematic transition would have to be undertaken in several steps. The first would be to establish a coherent legal framework, including mandates for government entities responsible for regulatory and supervisory oversight of the banking, insurance, and securities industries. This step has in part already been taken, in that the People's Bank of China is now responsible for monetary policy and banking supervision, the Financial Supervision and Regulation Department is now responsible for the insurance industry, and the China Securities Regulatory Commission has been established.

The second step would be to grant these institutions clear enforcement powers and to undertake the reforms necessary to achieve that end. The vestiges of state control are still evident in China in several ways; there remains an official fondness for top-down approvals, and

Table 3.3   Characteristics of the financial sector, 1997

Economy	Interest rate	Foreign exchange regime	Banks	Insurance	Securities	Regulatory framework
Argentina	Market determined.	Currency Board. Fixed exchange rate.	Credit market segmented. Universal banking for commercial banks. State banks control over one-third of banking assets after state bank privatization program. Large number of undercapitalized banks. Relatively high average operating costs. Industry consolidation predicted.	Large number of relatively inefficient firms. No new licenses issued, except for pension funds, life, burial services, and credit insurance. Mandatory life and disability insurance for pension funds members, driving growth of insurance industry. Private pension system. Government requires target rate of return on pension funds.	Underdeveloped. Longer-term instruments are now being supplied in government bonds. Currency-board system limits growth of credit and government securities. State privatization program dominating equity growth. Options and futures markets planned.	Prudential controls more activist. Capital requirements based on portfolio risk and market risk. Supervision, on- and off-site, frequent. Compliance also monitored through daily, monthly, and external annual reports. Deposit insurance system. Publicly listed companies require two credit ratings. Thirteen percent withholding tax for off-shore borrowing. Deposit insurance system.
Brazil	Controlled.	Unclassified.	Universal banking. State-owned commercial and mortgage banks control over one-half of banking assets. State-owned banks offer same services as private banks and	Underdeveloped insurance and pension system.	Developing. Equity market thin. State privatization program dominating equity growth. Private investment banking sector very competitive. Futures and commodities exchange very large.	Prudential supervision weak. Administrative procedures and laws not transparent. Minimum capital requirements raised. Bank for International Settlements (BIS) capital-adequacy ratios required. Disclosure

			service government finances and projects. Sector inefficient and consolidating rapidly. Banking technological infrastructure expansive.		of audited financial statements required. Auditors liable for accuracy of reports. Banks do not require external credit rating. Deposit insurance system.
Chile	Market determined.	Crawling band.	Private sector controls almost 90 percent of market. Moratorium on new bank licenses. Banking sector very competitive and efficient. Banks engage in securities activities through subsidiaries.	Private, fully funded pension system; required contribution of 10 percent of earnings. Pension can be in insurance annuity. Government requires target rate of return on pension funds. Limits on pension and insurance funds invested in each type of security.	Well-developed debt and equity markets. Short-term capital inflows subject to 30 percent reserve with central bank. Private mutual funds. Forward, options, and futures markets. Offshore market proposed.	Prudential regulations and supervision strong. Regulatory and legal system transparent. Capital requirements based on credit risk. External audit and public disclosure of statements required. Independent credit-rating agencies.
China	Adminis-tered.	Managed float. Foreign exchange rationing. Official exchange rate.	Four state-owned banks control 80 percent of market. State banks allocate credit based on central plan; ceiling on loan quotas	Small market, dominated by state-owned insurance company. Comprehensive insurance law. Premium rates set by	Underdeveloped. Bond market liquidity very thin. Nongovernment bond market insignificant; coupon rate set below government bonds. No	Regulations opaque and their application unpredictable. Regulatory agencies' roles poorly defined. Supervision aided by central bank restructure; enforcement

(Table continues on next page)

Table 3.3 Characteristics of the financial sector, 1997 *(continued)*

Economy	Interest rate	Foreign exchange regime	Banks	Insurance	Securities	Regulatory framework
		Records of FX dealings must be submitted to the government.	removed. State banks hold large proportion of deposits outside of formal channels for speculative purposes. Eleven commercial banks with no official lending requirements. SOE debt large problem.	government. Most assets required to be deposited in interest-bearing accounts; limited placement of assets in safe investments permitted.	comprehensive national securities laws. Government controls publicly listed state-owned enterprises; less than one-third of shares traded. Mutual funds prohibited.	still a problem. Lack of standard accounting practices; new loan classification guidelines by year 2000. Payments and clearing systems inadequate.
India	Controlled. Subsidies exist.	Market determined.	State-owned banks control over 80 percent of system. Required, priority loans equal to 40 percent of total loans. State-owned banks extremely inefficient. Thirteen private sector banks licensed. Minority private ownership in state-owned, publicly listed banks allowed. Nonbank financial institutions offer wide range of banking and securities products and have extensive branch network.	Government monopoly in insurance. Pension market dominated by government-owned insurance subsidiary.	Equity and bond markets developing. Equity market small but accessible to small firms. Primary dealers system. Electronic trading introduced. Listing firms required to issue share of stocks to individual investors. Mutual funds 85 percent controlled by government entity. Interest rate, currency swaps, and other derivatives approved.	Legal framework and prudential standards weak but improving. Accounting practices inconsistent and standards not enforced. BIS capital adequacy requirements for banks postponed. Regulation and supervision of nonbank financial institutions introduced. Credit-rating agencies established. Disclosure and prudential standards for publicly listed firms tightened, but no minimum capital requirements.

Indonesia	Market determined.	Managed float.	State-owned banks account for 60 percent of market. Private entry permitted since 1988. State-owned banks have much more extensive branch network than private banks. State-owned banks to be privatized. Banks can engage in securities activities through subsidiaries.	Underdeveloped. 8 percent of population covered by insurance. Numerous small firms with limited range of products. Lack of expertise in insurance. 80 percent of risk reinsured overseas. Pension funds heavily invested in government bonds.	Developing. Equity market thin and highly concentrated. Bond market small and illiquid. Secondary market inactive. Open-end mutual funds prohibited.	Prudential framework weak and laws unclear. Accounting standards poor. Risk-based supervisory practices being developed. Risk-weighted capital adequacy ratios not yet enforced. Credit analysis poor. Legal protection for minority shareholders lacking. Bankruptcy procedures ill-defined, new law planned.
Japan	Market determined.	Floating.	Segmented. City and regional banks and state-owned postal savings hold large shares of the market. Separation of banking and securities to be phased out. Banks to offer mutual funds and insurance, and underwrite securities, by 2001.	Regulations and licensing restrictions being phased out. Life and nonlife allowed in same company under separate subsidiaries. Premiums deregulated by 1998.	Developing. Corporate bond market small. Restrictions on activities of securities firms to be phased out. Securities firms to offer bank products and enter bank trust business. Brokerage commissions deregulated by 1999.	Supervision and regulation of activities, other than postal savings and life insurance, consolidated. Transparency insufficient. Disclosure inadequate. Foreign transactions taxed.

(Table continues on next page)

Table 3.3 Characteristics of the financial sector, 1997 *(continued)*

Economy	Interest rate	Foreign exchange regime	Banks	Insurance	Securities	Regulatory framework
South Korea	Controls being eased, ceiling to be phased out in 1998; subsidies low.	Floating.	Commercial banks account for one-third of market. Branch capitalization requirements onerous. Domestic banks must loan 45 percent of total to small and medium-sized enterprises; plans to abolish policy lending. Development banks important in housing and agriculture. Nonbank financial institutions deregulated before commercial banks and play significant role in sector. Banking consolidation encouraged.	Large insurance market. Life insurance market highly concentrated and difficult to penetrate. Life and nonlife not allowed in same company. Premium rates and form regulation. Insurance assets subject to investment restrictions. Reinsurance restrictions.	Range of institutions expanding. Equity market large but not a major source of funds; backlog of firms waiting to list on market. Listing requirements onerous. Mutual fund market dominated by three firms; majority of assets held in domestic bonds. Majority of bond market activity on over-the-counter market.	Prudential standards and supervision weak, but plans to strengthen. Laws and regulations not transparent. Accounting systems weak; new accounting practice and disclosure requirements to be introduced. Securities and exchange supervision weak. Difficult to introduce new products. Deposit insurance system to be established by 2000.

Malaysia	Market determined.	Floating.	Segmented and highly concentrated. Top two state-owned banks account for one-third of market. No new banking licenses since 1982. Credit allocation requirements to SMEs and indigenous Malays. Finance companies dominant in consumer, housing, and auto finance; no new licenses since 1984.	No new licenses since 1985. Auxiliary insurance services limited. Insurance companies required to place 80 percent of assets domestically and 25 percent in government bonds. Deposit insurance in the insurance sector. Mandatory contributions to pension system. Pension funds heavily invested in government bonds.	Developing. Equity market thin, despite volume. State privatization program dominating equity growth. No new seats on stock exchange. New equity price regulated. Government and corporate bond market small. Secondary bond market inactive. Government promoting bond and futures markets.	Legal and accounting framework effective. Securities and exchange supervision strong and effective. Supervision supported by audits and consolidated credit bureau reports. Moral hazard created by government record of bailouts. Open foreign exchange exposure of banks and insurance companies restricted.
Mexico	Market determined.	Unclassified.	Universal banking; commercial banks only financial institutions to offer retail banking. Most banks affiliated with financial group. State-owned, development banks account for 28 percent of the market and focus on priority sectors and export financing.	Underdeveloped. Market concentration high but market recently opened to new firms and products. Mandatory private pension scheme. Insurance and pension fund assets subject to investment restrictions.	Developing. Equity market thin and highly concentrated. Second-tier equity market growing quickly. Government debt dominates bond market. Peso and stock index futures market. Derivatives and commodities market approved.	Prudential controls strengthened. Regulations and laws transparent. Consolidated supervision of financial sector. Weak accounting framework; Generally Accepted Accounting Principles being introduced.

(*Table continues on next page*)

Table 3.3 Characteristics of the financial sector, 1997 (continued)

Economy	Interest rate	Foreign exchange regime	Banks	Insurance	Securities	Regulatory framework
Philippines	Phased liberalization began in 1980 but distorted.	Managed float.	System segmented. Universal banking encouraged in commercial banks, which control 90 percent of the sector. Commercial banking concentrated. Also, numerous small, privately owned banks. Government banks focus on wholesale market. Credit allocation requirements by sector and region.	Subsectors strictly defined. Life market highly concentrated; two firms hold 60 percent of market. Nonlife premium rates set by government. Government runs government, social, home, crop, and deposit insurance. Government insurance system required for government projects. Market highly dependent on reinsurance.	Underdeveloped. Equity and bond markets thin. State privatization program dominating equity growth. Stock exchange membership open to locally incorporated companies. Bond market dominated by government bonds. Secondary bond market inactive.	Supervisory personnel not well trained and insufficient in number. Laws and regulations not transparent. Accounting standards weak. Clearing and settlement system not efficient. Legal framework favors debtor. Capital requirements raised to encourage bank consolidation. Documentary stamp tax on collateral instruments for bonds. Transactions tax on gross sales.
Taiwan	Market determined.	Managed float.	System segmented. Three state-owned banks account for 60 percent of banking assets. Services offered by other banks restricted by loan size and geographic scope. Postal savings system mobilizes funds placed in government-owned	Diversified. Insurance companies allowed to set premium rates for group insurance policies; government sets other rates. Reserve funds used for loans, real estate, and securities investment. Insurance funds subject to investment restrictions. Pension	Developing. Corporate and government bond very thin. Secondary market inactive. Equity market thin and individual investors dominate market. Over-the-counter market for smaller firms. Securities industry very competitive.	Prudential regulations focus on assets, not liquidity. Supervision hindered by lack of skilled labor. BIS risk-weighted capital-asset ratio required. Related party transactions not prohibited. Bureaucrats resist liberalization. Financial-sector policy subordinated to industrial policy.

Country	Exchange rate	Banking	Insurance	Securities market	Supervision
	Market determined.	banks. Private banking activity increasing. Informal sector large.	funds must be in government-owned company.		
Thailand	Floating.	Segmented. Market concentration high. No new entrants since 1978. Government has control over one-third of commercial banks. 60 percent of deposits must be lent to community clients; SME and agricultural credit requirements. Banks allowed to offer some fee-based securities products. Suspended 58 of 91 finance companies.	Underdeveloped. 7.5 percent of population covered by life insurance. Life insurance market highly concentrated. Premium rates require government approval. Insurance funds subject to investment restrictions. Pension funds placed in designated finance, insurance, and securities firms.	Underdeveloped. Equity market thin and concentrated in four sectors. Government and corporate bond market thin. Government promoting the development of bond market. Secondary market inactive. Mutual funds permitted, subject to investment allocation guidelines.	Supervisory institutions lack strong exit and enforcement powers. Regulatory oversight inconsistent and weak for nonbank financial institutions in the past. Laws and regulations not transparent. New agency to restructure and supervise the financial system and guarantee deposits of suspended finance companies. Capital adequacy ratios strengthened. Moral hazard created by record of government bailouts.

Note: All references to pension funds are treated under the insurance heading, as per the WTO standard of addressing pension issues with insurance sector commitments.

Sources: Annex B; Securities Industry Association (1997); Williamson (1996); Zahid (1995).

political demands by local authorities on the local branches of banks persist.[5] The securities regulatory agency lacks a clear mandate and enforcement powers and therefore has a severe credibility problem. Enforcement will not be feasible, however, unless accounting standards are modernized and enforced so that asset quality, internal governance and controls, and strictures on insider transactions can be monitored. Nor will it be possible without major investments in training and equipping supervisory bodies with skilled staff and modern equipment. These skills and equipment are currently confined to China's major cities and special economic zones.

Finally, markets will become efficient only when the country's primitive transfer and settlement systems are modernized. These reforms are fundamental to a modern financial infrastructure capable of managing the risks of complex financial transactions. A start has been made, but until this infrastructure is better developed, China will remain a largely cash-based economy.

Taking these steps requires political will. Political will is generated when the conviction becomes widespread that the benefits of change to the users of financial services outweigh the risks and the costs of adjustment that domestic financial institutions must bear. Even if China takes such steps, however, a major underlying problem will remain in the persistence of money-losing, state-owned enterprises. The debts of these enterprises overhang the financial sector and have undermined the prospects of many of the banks to which they are indebted. Uncertainty about the future of social support for the employees of these enterprises, who traditionally have relied on their employers to provide education, health care, and retirement benefits, also prevents a clear line from being drawn between social and commercial insurance. While it grapples with these issues, China could promote technical transfer and training by permitting foreign service providers to undertake a wider range of activities. As table 3.3 illustrates, the Chinese government still heavily controls the activities of such institutions.

Sequencing and Pacing Reform

The significant problems with economic stabilization and policy reform experienced by the southern-cone countries of South America in the 1980s stimulated much study of the lessons to be learned from these experiences. Gradually, a consensus has emerged that such reforms should follow a certain sequence. Macroeconomic adjustment should come first, followed by trade liberalization; these will contribute to real depreciation of the currency where it is needed, ensuring that capital will flow

---

5. Reforms announced in early 1998 show signs of correcting this problem.

to its most productive uses (Edwards 1984; McKinnon 1991) and strengthening the competitiveness of potential borrowers. The next step is to reform and restructure financial markets; here, some argue that the banking sector should be opened first, to ensure that payments are cleared and that necessary liquidity is provided (Blommestein and Spencer 1994).

This step should precede liberalizing external financial controls. The reasons for such a sequence are as follows. First, the capital inflow will cause a real currency appreciation, lead to deterioration of competitiveness of the tradable goods sector, and raise the associated threat of a financial crisis. The Mexican peso crisis of 1994 forcefully illustrated these concerns, even though that crisis was not due to capital inflows per se. Second, capital inflows may help to sustain otherwise unsustainable budget deficits, which could also lead to a future financial crisis. Third, allowing capital inflows before liberalizing trade may cause those inflows to be channeled to the wrong industries and cause "immiserizing growth." Fourth, there is no reason to expect capital resources to be allocated to their most productive uses if the domestic financial system has not been liberalized (Williamson 1993). These concerns focus on capital inflows. With respect to capital outflows, capital flight has played a significant role in many developing countries and should be a major concern. There is an interesting interaction, which several authors have noted, between liberalizing outflows and inflows: liberalizing outflows may lead to an increase in confidence and, thus, actually stimulate inflows. If capital controls are removed when domestic real interest rates are still below market rates because of financial repression, short-term capital outflows can be expected.

The conventional approach highlights the necessary preconditions for capital account liberalization, which differ for inflows and outflows. Trade liberalization, fiscal discipline, and an efficient domestic financial system are seen as prerequisites for liberalizing inflows, whereas a stable macroeconomic policy, arrangements to limit the erosion of the tax base, and a margin of demand management through fiscal flexibility are seen as prerequisites for liberalizing outflows (Williamson 1993).

Yet, as some have documented, most Latin American countries have ignored this theoretical prescription and have undertaken stabilization at the same time as trade reform (Edwards 1984). In fact, reform is likely to be undertaken not on its theoretical merits or as part of a well-thought-out grand design, but rather under the pressure of market forces, domestic interest groups, and foreign governments and firms (Turner and van't dack 1996). In addition, a weak financial system and macroeconomic adjustment can interact in harmful ways. A strong regulatory system, adherence to clear central bank operating procedures, and overall bank portfolio quality are crucial to implementing effective adjustment policies. The conventional sequencing approach, with macroeconomic adjustment coming first, may not work (Sundarajan and Balino 1991). The higher interest rates necessary for stabilization may push poorly regulated, weakened financial institutions with doubtful loans into insolvency. There is evidence, for example, that unsatisfactory macroeconomic conditions have been a catalyst for financial reform in Egypt (Turner and van't dack 1996). In the Thai case in 1997, weak regulation and the low quality of assets of financial institutions contributed to the authorities' reluctance to raise interest rates to defend the currency and maintain macroeconomic stability.

In reality, there are a variety of possible reform sequences to choose from, depending on the country's macroeconomic, financial, legal, political, and sociological conditions (Harwood 1997). Governments interested in reform may use capital account liberalization or the expectation of a credibly scheduled opening as a spur to make domestic financial institutions more efficient and as an anchor for economic policy discipline (Turner and van't dack 1996). This opens the door to committing to a firm deadline for completion of the reform process, to generate pressure to bring about the necessary adjustments in time. Several cases illustrate the various possibilities. They include the European approach to liberalization within the 1992 single-market initiative; the Chilean case, in which liberalization was reversed and then resumed; and the Indonesian case of "reverse" sequencing, which began with opening of the capital account. It should also be recalled that in all but five of the economies reviewed in this study, capital account liberalization has already occurred (see table 3.1). The issue for these countries, therefore, is how to implement reverse sequencing. The exceptions—Brazil, China, India, South Korea, and Taiwan—are significant, however.

In the European case, the 1992 single-market project established a firm deadline, implying full capital liberalization and free trade in financial services by that date. The credibility of the deadline invited adjustment, restructuring, and changes in companies' strategies, as well as changes in governments' macroeconomic, tax, and regulatory policies.

Chile reformed its domestic financial market in 1975-77 and liberalized the capital account for domestic banks in 1980. Large capital inflows in 1980 and 1981 were intermediated by banks and nonbank financial institutions. The role of capital account liberalization in the subsequent financial crisis has been debated at length; some point emphatically to other factors, such as the lack of a prudent regulatory framework for domestic banks, overenthusiastic lending decisions by foreign banks, lack of macroeconomic prudence, and counterproductive measures taken by the central bank to stem the crisis (Caprio, Atiyas, and Hanson 1996).

Indonesia provides one of the few cases of reverse sequencing.[6] The

---

6. Japan also eased capital controls long before it deregulated and restructured the domestic financial sector (see appendix B).

capital account was initially opened in 1971, interest rate repression was abolished in 1983, trade liberalization began in 1985, and the Pakto reforms in 1988 permitted foreign ownership of financial institutions, albeit through joint ventures with domestic partners (see appendix B). The government considered that domestic banks had been given insufficient time to adjust to foreign competition, and a bad loan problem ensued, with the failure of some banks and nonbank financial institutions. The adjustment cost was high, but this reverse sequencing was made manageable by prompt fiscal adjustment, flexible interest and exchange rates, and a willingness to accept the discipline of international financial markets. Events of late 1997 and 1998 suggest, however, that such reverse sequencing is not without the risks posed by the persistence of a weak financial system.

The second challenge is that of pacing. The disadvantage of gradual broad reform, as distinct, for example, from London's "big bang" or the Europeans' 1992 deadline, is that it perpetuates the vested interests of those constituencies opposed to more domestic and international competition and leaves open the precise timing of the various steps, thus pushing the "final" step of foreign opening toward a more distant future (Bofinger 1993). Not everything needs to be done at the same time; a credible and binding commitment to pursue full reform, however, is a necessary complement to any gradual sequence, as it helps contain hostile domestic interests. Short of such a commitment, announced reforms may lack credibility.

Conclusion

Financial reform must be done out of recognition of national self-interest, not at the behest of foreigners. As the previous chapter argued, opening to foreign competition is a crucial ingredient of such reform. Left to domestic discretion, however, it may never be undertaken in any systematic way for fear of its global and parochial repercussions.

This chapter has argued that such repercussions are not consequences of opening per se, but are due to underlying weaknesses in macroeconomic policy as well as supervisory and regulatory policy, which should not be allowed to persist. Although opening exposes these weaknesses and provides incentives to address them, it does not by itself provide a solution.

The discussion in this chapter illustrates two points. The first is that certain ingredients of domestic reform are essential to successful liberalization. These include adequate prudential regulation and supervision of financial institutions, particularly commercial banks; a reasonable degree of price stability; fiscal discipline, with deficits financed through bonds sold to the private sector rather than the central bank; profit-maximizing, competitive behavior of financial institutions; and a tax system that does not impose discriminatory taxes on financial intermediation.[7]

Second, countries cannot take a cookie-cutter approach to reform. Reform requires time and the investment of political will and financial resources. The sequence of reforms, however, is for national authorities to decide in light of political realities, administrative capabilities, and economic circumstances (Williamson 1994). In particular, the conventional recommendation that opening come after the macroeconomy and the banking sector have been put on a sounder footing fails to address the political economy of reform, because it allows interest groups to build their case and to mobilize against reform and because the lack of financial reform itself contributes to maintaining and even worsening weaknesses in the macroeconomy and in the banking industry.

Political economy considerations are evident causal factors in the Asian crisis. The authorities in Thailand, Malaysia, Indonesia, and South Korea were slow to face up to the magnitude of problems in the macroeconomy —especially in the financial sector—that contributed to the crisis in part because of a reluctance to cause pain to interest groups and political allies. They were also reluctant to accept that a condition of using taxpayers' funds to rescue failing institutions must be their radical restructuring and that provisions should be made for more independent and active oversight in future.

Indeed, conclusions from the studies of financial crises in other countries cited earlier suggest a counterfactual. If financial restructuring had occurred in these economies, domestic financial institutions would have been stronger; if oversight were as active as it is, for example, in Singapore's financial system, the magnitude of the decline in asset quality in the banks and finance companies would have been known much earlier. Property lending could have been restrained (for example, Singapore took steps in 1996 to restrain speculative behavior in the property market, and the Indonesian central bank capped property lending as a share of banks' assets around the same time) and prudential controls, such as reserve requirements on foreign deposits, could have restrained the use of short-term capital inflows.

Admittedly, the challenges that policymakers face are difficult. Sound macroeconomic policy and sound banks are inextricably interlinked objectives. On the one hand, macroeconomic policy seeks to ensure a sound banking system. On the other, to conduct macroeconomic policy so as to ensure the stability of a weak banking system is to sacrifice policy flexibility (Lindgren, Garcia, and Saal 1996). It is for this reason that additional microeconomic instruments, such as reforms to strengthen the flexibility and competitiveness of the financial sector, are required.

---

7. Fry (1995) makes similar arguments with respect to banks.

This is why, again, a binding commitment to accept the discipline of foreign competition is a promising way to address the dilemma. A golden opportunity exists in those Asian countries that have IMF programs to bind their financial reforms into the WTO. South Korea, however, has agreed in its IMF program to bind only the reforms agreed with the OECD in 1996 (something it failed to do in its offer at the December 1997 FSA negotiations). The IMF program conditions should be bound in the FSA before it is implemented.

Pacing is essential. The analysis in appendix B, summarized in tables 3.1 and 3.3, suggests that countries lie on a continuum, with some further along than others toward the goal of deregulation, open markets, and a regulatory framework and financial infrastructure capable of supporting a modern financial system. These countries include Chile, Japan (obviously), Malaysia, Mexico, Singapore, and Taiwan. By and large, these countries have already set the turn of the century as the target date for achieving this goal, but they have not bound such targets into international agreements. Other countries with obstacles to safe and open markets in the form of weak regulatory systems include those involved in the 1997-98 crisis. They are developing the needed infrastructure. This list includes South Korea, Argentina, Indonesia, and Thailand, and possibly the Philippines. They will require the better part of a decade (or less, depending on political will) to reach the goal. Countries in the third category, which includes India and China (which is not yet a member of the WTO), will require the longest transition, possibly more than a decade, because of the developing state of the real economy and the rudimentary nature of the institutional structure.

There may never be a best time to liberalize and open markets. If there is, it may be at the top of the business cycle, when nonfinancial firms are in good shape. But a slow process or one plagued by reversals raises serious issues of credibility. East Asia's crisis and the questions it raises for the area's future economic prospects suggest that now is a good time to undertake the kind of reforms that would address the underlying weaknesses that the crisis has exposed. The next two chapters provide a history of the WTO negotiations in financial services and assess the 13 December 1997 agreement; its contribution to strengthening financial systems is one of the criteria used in this assessment.

Setting the Context: Toward the WTO Financial Services Agreement

Agreement was reached in the WTO financial services talks only after a protracted negotiating process that did not provide a certain outcome until the last minute. The difficulty of these negotiations and the uncertainty they involved should come as no surprise, because the negotiations addressed difficult issues that had not previously been dealt with in multilateral negotiations. However, setbacks in the course of any negotiation generally give few hints about the ultimate outcome and, thus, need not cause alarm. Not only are temporary deadlocks a constant, normal, and sometimes even tactical and strategic feature of negotiations, but they also have characterized the considerable progress achieved in multilateral liberalization of trade in goods: progress in that area has always been difficult and beset by conflict, with actual results often achieved through brinkmanship.

Important to the FSA were process and dynamics—the proper mix of foreign and domestic interests and the pressure to keep negotiations moving forward. If game theory provides a model for these negotiations, that model is the game of "chicken":[1] a cooperative outcome will prevail when, and only when, the perceived costs of defection for all

---

1. See Deutsch (1978, chapter 11) for a game-theoretic approach to international conflict. In the game of chicken, two drivers drive at high speed straight toward each other. The first to swerve is the loser, or "chicken." Failure of either to swerve results in collision, whereas both swerving simultaneously (cooperation) saves both life and honor. This is a "cooperative" game, as the drivers' perceptions of the stakes lead to mutual swerving at the last minute. Until then, however, the best strategy is to maintain uncertainty.

parties are greater than the costs of the concessions needed to make the talks a success. The Uruguay Round negotiations may have been a kind of chicken game: deadlock obtained until the last minute. The financial services negotiations were no exception to that model.

Interestingly, negotiations such as these take a life of their own. For negotiators, reaching agreement may become an objective as such, independent of considerations about the actual content of the agreement. Hence, the FSA deserves analysis on two distinct, albeit related, grounds. First, how was it achieved? Second, what does it contribute to financial reform and economic growth? These two questions are addressed in turn in the next two chapters.

This chapter focuses on the history of the financial services negotiations in the WTO, beginning with a brief account of the inclusion of services in the Uruguay Round. The next section presents the General Agreement on Trade in Services (GATS), which is the outcome of the Uruguay Round in the services industries. The third section discusses the objectives of the financial services negotiations and basic stances and strategies of the major parties to the negotiations. We conclude this chapter with a short history of these negotiations, beginning with the extension agreed on at the end of the Uruguay Round and including the interim 1995 agreement, the resumption of final talks in the spring of 1997, and the final run-up to the December FSA.

Services in the Uruguay Round

The introduction of services into the multilateral trade negotiations under the General Agreement on Tariffs and Trade (GATT) was one of the central achievements of the Uruguay Round. As far back as the 1973-79 Tokyo Round, trade and investment in services were slated for future negotiating agendas (Broadman 1994; Freeman 1997). The issue was actively debated in the United States from early 1981 on, between a number of US financial services firms led by American Express Company (under its chairman, Jim Robinson) and then-US Trade Representative Bill Brock. The US trade delegation officially raised the subject at the November 1982 GATT ministerial meeting and kept the pressure on thereafter. Eventually, the negotiating agenda was extended, despite a lack of enthusiasm and even indifference on the part of most other industrial countries and despite strong reluctance and even opposition on the part of most developing countries, led by Brazil and India.[2]

The extension of the US trade policy agenda to services is commonly attributed to three groups (McCulloch 1990). One was the US services

---

2. On the inclusion of services on the trade policy agenda see McCulloch (1987, 1990), Sapir (1985), and Sauvé (1990, 1995).

industries,[3] in particular one insurance firm, the American International Group (AIG), and American Express. These firms were interested in serving international markets both through exports and through local sales by foreign affiliates, and they insisted on market-access provisions. The second source of pressure was public officials and other business leaders, who claimed that US comparative advantage had shifted from goods to services and that, therefore, the way had to be paved to open world markets so that US firms could sell those services abroad, through both exports and direct investment. The third group consisted of trade policy experts, who saw in services a way to rejuvenate GATT and adapt it to a changing, globalizing world economy. They also saw services as a way to systematically address a range of new and important issues relating to nontariff barriers, stemming from widespread government intervention, regulation, and policies other than trade policies.

The insertion of services into a multilateral trade agreement recognized the growing importance of trade in services in the growth and development of the world economy.[4] The growing share of services in world trade suggested that most of the liberalization achieved for trade in goods should be extended to services and that the progress achieved through the GATT negotiations could usefully be extended to this area of trade. In particular, trade in financial services[5] had expanded significantly since the early 1980s as a result of the dynamic interaction between technological and financial innovation on the one hand, and financial deregulation on the other.[6]

Services were eventually included on the Uruguay Round agenda, but on a separate track that led eventually to GATS. GATS proved to be a complex arrangement, reflecting the tensions that surfaced during the negotiations. Services are a heterogeneous group of products, but with one common thread: many services are subject to widespread government intervention through regulation and other measures. Financial services are no exception: proper regulation and supervision of financial institutions are key to an efficient financial system; banks and other institutions also play a role in the transmission of monetary policy, and their behavior may conflict with the objectives of that policy should a financial crisis result and the lender-of-last-resort facilities of the central

---

3. See Freeman (1997). Interestingly, the initial push came from the financial services industry which, in the hope of getting multilateral rules on financial services, successfully endeavored to include other services in the effort.

4. In 1994, world trade amounted to $5.2 trillion, of which $1.1 trillion was in commercial services (WTO 1995).

5. For a discussion of trade in financial services, see Arndt (1984 and 1988) and McCulloch (1990).

6. On the development of finance in the 1980s, see Bryant (1987).

bank have to be used. As a result, for services in general and financial services specifically, many participants felt that the negotiating dynamics and principles inherited from GATT could not easily be extended and that a different approach was needed. Thus, separating the services talks from the other Uruguay Round negotiations served several purposes. It comforted nervous developing countries with the possibility that, in terms of commitments to market opening, the track for services might prove less demanding than that for goods. It also assuaged finance ministers in industrial countries, who, given the specificity of financial services and their own jurisdiction in that area, were opposed to treating financial services like goods and to rendering them to trade negotiators.

The final agreement of the Uruguay Round was completed in December 1993 and signed in Marrakesh on 15 April 1994 by more than 100 countries.[7] Although service negotiations remained on a separate track, and despite pressure from many countries to keep the agreement on services outside the main framework, the negotiators succeeded remarkably in making the GATS an integral part of the Uruguay Round package. No opting out of the GATS is possible for Uruguay Round signatories; all members of the WTO are bound by the agreement.

Overview of the GATS

In a globalized world in which countries are increasingly open to trade in goods and services and to capital flows, any multilateral rule should be based on the principle of nondiscrimination in the broadest sense. This means, first, nondiscrimination between trade partners—not only the granting of most favored nation (MFN) status, but also nondiscrimination between foreign and domestic firms (national treatment). For this broad concept of nondiscrimination to prevail, countries' policies and the measures they take to implement them need to be transparent. Transparency, MFN, and national treatment are therefore the three major objectives of multilateral negotiations. These principles are embodied in the GATS, albeit with various derogations that weaken the commitments and require renegotiating their application with each new set of talks.

The GATS includes two main elements:[8] a core agreement with annexes and other ancillary documents and a list of commitments by signatories (the "schedules"). The core agreement includes a preamble, 28 articles specifying the obligations of signatories, 8 annexes, 8 ministerial declarations, and an understanding on commitments in financial ser-

---

7. For an overall analysis of the results, see Hindley (1994), Messerlin (1995), and Schott and Buurman (1994).

8. For a clear and thorough description of the GATS, see Knapp (1994).

vices, also called the "memorandum of agreement" on financial services (see below). The first annex specifies the conditions under which countries may claim exemptions from the MFN obligation (see below). Other annexes list dispositions applicable to certain sectors. One of these is the Annex on Financial Services, which includes a remarkably open-ended definition of financial services,[9] thus allowing for the agreement's coverage of these services as they evolve. The ministerial declarations deal with general institutional matters such as the establishment of working groups on various issues.

Article I of GATS defines what is meant by trade in services. It follows the analysis proposed by Sampson and Snape (1985), which identifies four modes of delivery of internationally traded services: from the territory of one country into that of another; within the territory of one country to a consumer from another; by a service supplier of one country through commercial presence in the territory of another; and by a service supplier of one country through the presence of natural persons from that country in the territory of another. Although analytically useful, this distinction may have had perverse effects in the negotiations, because it allowed for selective opening along the four delivery modes, thereby introducing the possibility that countries might discriminate among them. The analysis also creates the impression that market-opening efforts along each of these modes are substitutes for each other, whereas in fact they are often complementary.[10]

Obligations accepted by GATS signatories are of two sorts: general obligations and disciplines applicable immediately to all members in all services sectors, and commitment-specific disciplines. With regard to the latter, countries are bound only in those sectors for which they have provided schedules and only to the extent of the commitments undertaken in those schedules. The main general obligations and disciplines are the MFN obligation (Article II), which rules out discrimination among trade partners; transparency (Article III); and a commitment to participate in future negotiations aimed at achieving progressively higher levels of liberalization (Articles IX to XXI). This commitment is sometimes referred to as the "built-in agenda" for future negotiations. The agreement explicitly calls for "successive rounds of negotiations beginning no later than 5 years from the date of entry into force of the Agreement Establishing the WTO and periodically thereafter" (Article XIX).

These important principles, however, suffer various weaknesses. Each country was allowed a one-time opportunity, upon signature, to notify

9. The Annex on Financial Services contains an exhaustive, but nonetheless illustrative rather than defining, list of services qualifying as financial services. It includes insurance and all insurance-related services as well as all banking and other services.

10. On the notion of market access and the various modes of supply, see the discussion in Snape and Bosworth (1996).

its own list of existing or future measures taking exception from MFN.[11] Transparency is limited to the requirement that members will publish all measures they adopt that interfere with trade in services. Members can do so locally without much publicity; in particular, there is no requirement to notify such measures to the WTO Secretariat, and therefore there will be no master list encompassing all such measures. Finally, the requirement of progressive opening usefully sets a deadline for resuming global talks and for starting a new negotiating round (no later than the year 2000), but it represents little more than a statement of principle. The agreement falls far short of demonstrating how the difficulties encountered in its negotiation should be surmounted in future talks so as to reach the "progressively higher level of liberalization" that is the avowed objective.

The commitment-specific GATS obligations are contained in the schedules of commitments notified by the members individually. These schedules include, for each member, a "positive" list of sectors in which the member is willing to make commitments and a "negative" list of derogations from the broad principles of market access and national treatment described in Articles XVI and XVII.[12] In sectors not scheduled, members make no commitment to liberalize beyond the general obligations already discussed: MFN (subject to permissible exemptions), transparency, and the commitment to engage in future negotiations. In scheduled sectors, broad obligations of market access and national treatment apply, except where members have formulated reserves individually. Moreover, members can pick and choose among the modes of delivery for which their sectoral commitments will be valid.

A number of commentators have underlined the limitation on the liberalizing dynamic implied by the positive listing of sectors. This approach establishes a bias toward the status quo, presenting further opening as a positive and optional undertaking rather than as the "default" condition, with the result that opening is likely to be undertaken only when and where it hurts least (Snape and Bosworth 1996). The approach also clearly makes transparency much more difficult to achieve,

---

11. There are other exemptions from MFN, notably those recognizing the possibility that countries might enter bilateral or regional agreements aimed at economic integration (Article V), those relating to public procurement (Article XIII), and those invoked for national security reasons (Article XIV and XIV bis). Individual exemptions taken at the time of entry into force of the WTO agreement are valid for a specified period, which "in principle" should not exceed 10 years. Those exceeding 5 years must be reviewed by the Council for Trade in Services within 5 years after entry into force, to "examine whether the conditions which created the need for the exemption still prevail." The Council for Trade in Services was created by the agreement establishing the WTO to oversee the operation of the GATS agreement.

12. On the use of positive lists versus negative lists in the GATS, see, for example, the discussion in Broadman (1994).

because the lists of sectors in which countries are willing to make commitments say nothing about the various restrictions at work in other sectors. Finally, the approach also makes countries' offers more difficult to assess.

The choice of a positive-list approach owes much to the efforts of developing countries to deflect the demands put on them and keep their options open. The United States initially advocated a more demanding negative-list approach, but the alternative emerged as the only mutually acceptable negotiating platform that parties were willing to consider. To provide for more opening in financial services, the OECD countries introduced an optional variant to scheduling: countries adopting this variant commit themselves to broad market-opening principles and list their (limited) reserves therefrom. This alternative, optional negative-list approach is embodied in the memorandum of agreement on financial services in GATS. Countries that adopt it commit themselves to extending MFN status to all other countries, whether they use the alternative, more demanding approach or the general one. Most OECD countries, but only OECD countries, have in principle chosen this variant (Woodrow 1997), with the exception of South Korea, Mexico, and Poland (Japan rallied only lately when it finally agreed to bind its bilateral agreement with the United States in the multilateral framework; see below).

Objectives, Stances, and Strategies

Financial services negotiations did not take place in a vacuum. As we noted elsewhere in this book, much had happened already, as countries, including many developing countries, deregulated and opened their financial systems. These unilateral initiatives needed to be bound into the multilateral system. Hence, a standstill commitment was one of the necessary ingredients of any financial services agreement: countries should at least bind in their schedules the level of openness achieved unilaterally so far.

As a special case of standstill, companies presently doing business in foreign countries were especially interested in a guarantee that their positions would not suffer should the host country's offer imply market-access commitments less favorable than those they already enjoy. Grandfathering these companies' existing access was necessary to ensure that these pioneers would not be penalized by a multilateral WTO agreement on financial services that is liberalizing on balance.

None of these principles is as simple to implement as it may seem. Their interaction, in particular, can be cumbersome. For example, a standstill commitment if discrimination between domestic and foreign investors persists is not easily reconcilable with MFN or national treatment, unless the country making the commitment is willing to liberalize further in subsequent talks. In the same vein, a grandfather clause also implies discrimination, but it is transparent. The implementation of such a clause should, of course, respect MFN, so that all existing foreign investors are entitled to such protection.

A further difficulty stems from the fact that freer trade in services, including financial services, implies much more than free cross-border trade; it raises the broader issues of market access and, more generally, of doing business in a foreign country, which involves investment, regulation, and public and private anticompetitive behaviors. Therefore, it implies negotiations on rules and regulations at a time when these rules and regulations are changing—as they are in developing countries that have undertaken financial reform and in the United States, where financial regulation is under close scrutiny—or have already undergone painful change—as in Europe with the creation of the single market. The European experience may provide inspiration here. Rather than fully harmonize their differing regulations, the EU countries adopted the principle of mutual recognition: a mix of minimal harmonization providing acceptable standards and competition among existing regulatory systems. This principle has been successfully implemented, for example, in the Second Banking Directive, which provides that any financial institution receiving a banking license (issued on the basis of the minimal standards agreed on among member states) in any EU member state may operate under the home-country regulatory framework in any other member state. In fact, this principle goes beyond national treatment and may differ from it; to the extent that home-country regulations are more lax than those of the host country, foreign investors may receive more favorable treatment than domestic firms. This is what leads to competition among regulatory systems.

The principle of national treatment is thus a first step into the complex issue of the compatibility, competition, or convergence of regulations. Other approaches involve mutual recognition or attempts at full harmonization. The GATS Annex on Financial Services includes provisions allowing recognition of other countries' prudential measures and specifies that "such recognition may be achieved through harmonization or otherwise" (Article 3).

Prudential measures received special treatment in the field of financial services. A special provision in the Annex on Financial Services, called the "prudential carve-out" (Article 2), specifically recognizes the right to take any measure to protect investors and depositors and to ensure the stability of the financial system. The notion of "carve-out" here means that prudential measures do not need to be scheduled and are not considered as departures from any commitment to liberalize scheduled by members. Of course, this provision applies to purely prudential measures and not to measures that would disguise limitations to market access or national treatment under prudential concerns. The prudential carve-out is therefore subject to the mechanism of dispute settlement. The Annex on Financial Services, accordingly, requires that "Panels for disputes on prudential issues and other financial matters shall have the necessary expertise relevant to the specific financial service under dispute" (Article 4).

Beyond basic standstill, a more ambitious global financial services agreement should aim at including a number of core components, going as far as possible toward meeting the following:

- MFN,

- the right of companies to establish and operate freely,

- identical treatment for foreign and domestic companies,

- free cross-border trade in services and free movement of personnel

- limited and transparent exemptions, and

- a grandfather clause protecting existing investments from any new exemptions to the principles listed above.

This is an ambitious list, whose key ingredients are market access and nondiscrimination (MFN and national treatment). However, the major actors each gave these objectives, ambitions, and priorities markedly different weights in negotiations, which explains most of the difficulties and tensions encountered all along. Before turning to the history of the negotiations and the FSA, we briefly discuss below the initial stances and strategies of developing and industrial countries and of the latter's financial institutions to shed light on the context of the negotiations.

Developing-Country Stances

Developing countries have dramatically changed their approach over the last 15 years, motivated by their increasing recognition that openness to the world economy is necessary for successful development. This recognition first led to a substantial liberalization of foreign trade, often on a unilateral basis.[13] There has been more hesitation about financial opening, and that stance seems vindicated by the rather negative experience with financial reform in the Latin American countries in the 1970s (Argentina and Chile, among others) and more recently by the 1994 Mexican peso crisis.

---

13. For an account of how this happened in Latin America, see, for example, Cardoso and Helwege (1992).

Yet, a number of developing countries have undertaken financial reform, as discussed in chapter 3. They have recognized that they cannot ignore the competition they face in attracting foreign savings to meet their huge investment needs. An increasing number of countries have awakened to the possible benefits of welcoming foreign direct investment, notably in financial services. The fear that maintaining conditions unfavorable to such investment, when other countries do not, might cost them access to foreign capital and creates an incentive to open capital markets.

Opening financial markets and liberalizing trade in financial services, however, cannot be considered separately from the broader issue of domestic financial reform. For political and economic reasons, most developing countries wish to manage deregulation and the pace that they open their financial services to foreign competition according to their own criteria and priorities. These vary across countries. They are urged to caution by the financial crises that have taken place in countries that have liberalized. That experience suggests that financial reform, although a necessary condition for lasting and stable economic growth, is not a sufficient one. Countries face pressures to accede to a "rule" on opening, yet they have to devise an indigenous phasing process that takes into account initial conditions in their financial sectors, the macroeconomic situation in the business cycle, and the need to strengthen institutions (Caprio, Atiyas, and Hanson 1996, chapter 13).

This discussion highlights one of the most important concerns of developing countries: they care about the impact of opening on domestic financial stability and domestic financial reform. Because they are not primarily interested in access to industrial countries' markets, there is a clear asymmetry of objectives between them and industrial countries' governments and firms. Few of their financial firms have reached the size and efficiency that could make them competitive in industrial countries' financial markets. Hence, they lean toward a defensive, protective posture, rather than an aggressive stance aimed at opening others' markets through a give-and-take negotiating process.

Industrial-Country Stances

Of course, the situation is different in industrial countries, where financial firms have become large and powerful. They play a crucial role in the financing of the economy and have a definite interest in market access abroad. Industrial-country governments negotiate with those of developing countries and with each other, but also with various domestic interest groups. Their exposure to domestic interests is likely to give their position a mercantilist flavor. The sequential and sectoral nature of the services negotiations makes governments even more vulnerable to such pressures. When negotiations are undertaken sector by sector, a trade-off across sectors becomes impractical, and concessions to domestic sectoral interests in one area cannot be counterbalanced by those in another. Under such conditions, a government's position is likely to reflect the position finally taken by the major domestic lobbies in the sector under consideration. This helps to explain, for example, the stance taken by the US government in the summer of 1995, when it decided that developing countries' offers were insufficient to warrant entering into a multilateral commitment with them (see below). US financial lobbies have been more vocal than others in pursuing significant market access in major developing countries.

The United States has been increasingly criticized for its tendency toward unilateralism in its trade policy strategy more generally. US officials reject this criticism (see Garten 1995). They point to the difficulty of making significant headway toward a more open world economy and to the frustration and the domestic policy costs that result. They also argue that their multifaceted policy, involving not only participation in the multilateral framework but also unilateral and bilateral initiatives, has been effective in leading some countries to open further than they might have wanted to or might have accepted in a multilateral framework. Besides, the fact that a major actor such as the United States purposely maintains pressure and uncertainty also helps to advance the negotiating process toward higher achievements.

These objections have validity. International policymaking is, of course, fraught with difficulties and in need of effective leadership. Yet, the US position also carries some risks. It imposes, rather than promotes, the spirit of openness that is so crucial to prosperous interdependence and peace. It shifts the balance along the spectrum of conflict and cooperation toward the former, making achievements fragile and further progress more uncertain. It signals a difference of approach with the EU countries and with Japan, at a time when the United States is no longer able or willing to assume full leadership of the world multilateral system, and when, therefore, joint leadership should be actively pursued. Finally, it risks mismanaging a crucial phase in the evolution of the world economy, namely, the success of some developing countries in catching up economically to the established industrial economies. As they do so, these countries have to be politically and economically integrated into the multilateral framework. Managing this process requires not only constancy and vision, but also flexibility and the talent to convince.

The Stance of Financial Institutions

Financial institutions in industrial countries have been eagerly pushing for the opening of financial markets in developing countries and for securing open access in other industrial countries' markets. In a globalized world economy, emerging markets become increasingly important locations in which to do business, and financial firms need to serve their multinational customers wherever they operate. Commercial insurers asked to cover worldwide risks are interested in providing on-site services.

Indeed, as recalled above, large US service firms have been lobbying hard to make services a more salient topic in the multilateral negotiations. Broad access to hitherto closed markets is an important objective. The financial services industries in other industrial countries share that objective, but they have tended to be less vocal than their US counterparts. Although they objected to the weakness of many developing countries' offers and insisted on their being improved, the other industrial countries seemed to be more ready to sign a multilateral agreement that would secure that objective over the longer term, at the price of less than fully satisfactory market access in the short term. Large US firms, on the contrary, have taken a more demanding stance, asking for a substantial down payment in terms of market access. They were reluctant to support a limited agreement that would bring them few benefits while granting developing countries' firms a free ride on the US market. In effect, they relied on pressure from the US government to lead to better offers and, should that fail, on denying MFN to punish developing countries and educe from them a wider degree of opening. They did not care much about having an agreement, but focused on the reality and extent of market access. Timetable mattered less than content.

The Financial Services Negotiations: A Brief History of WTO Discussions

Although the GATS covers trade in all services,[14] the negotiations could not be completed by the December 1993 deadline for the Uruguay Round in four areas: maritime services, basic telecommunications services, so-called movements of natural persons (service providers), and financial services. Rather than declare outright failure, the parties were able to secure an extension for the negotiations in these areas:[15] to 30 June 1995 (later extended to 28 July) for the talks on movements of natural per-

---

14. Article I.3.b specifies that "services" includes any service in any sector except services supplied in the exercise of governmental authority. Article I.3.c goes on: "A service supplied in the exercise of governmental authority means any service which is supplied neither on a commercial basis, nor in competition with one or more service suppliers." For financial services, that notably includes monetary and exchange rate policies and statutory social security and public retirement systems.

15. This is the function of the Second Annex on Financial Services, of the Annex on Negotiations on Basic Telecommunications, and of certain of the ministerial declarations appended to the GATS.

sons; to 1 July 1995 for those on financial services; to 30 April 1996 for basic telecommunications; and to 1 June 1996 for maritime services.

Initial progress within these extended deadlines, however, was more than sobering: the negotiations on maritime services came to a halt, with the understanding that they will resume with the next round of negotiations on services, that is, by 2000. The negotiations on basic telecommunications and on financial services could not be concluded by the new deadline; instead, interim agreements were signed to consolidate existing offers for a given period (up to 15 January 1997 for basic telecommunications and to 1 November 1997 for financial services). After that period, offers could be withdrawn, maintained, or improved during a limited period (30 and 60 days, respectively). A landmark agreement on basic telecommunications was eventually reached on 15 February 1997, following an agreement at the December 1996 Singapore ministerial on information technology. Both these agreements did much to restore hope that the negotiating process in the sectors left out of the Uruguay Round agreement was working and would eventually bear fruit. The July 1995 interim agreement on financial services (described below) set 31 December 1997 as the new deadline for a final agreement; this was advanced to 12 December when the negotiations resumed in the spring of 1997.

An obstacle to financial services negotiations was the unwillingness of many developing countries (and even Japan) to commit to a substantial and binding opening of their financial sectors. These countries were willing to make few new commitments; most of the OECD countries' financial systems were already relatively open. This discrepancy has raised the concern that some developing countries would free ride on an eventual MFN-based multilateral agreement, that is, that they would be granted wider access to the industrial countries' financial markets while keeping their own markets relatively closed. This has so far made the industrial countries reluctant or (in the case of the United States) unwilling to commit themselves to an MFN-based multilateral agreement on trade in financial services. Their unwillingness to tolerate free riding was a major determinant of the position of the industrial countries, and especially of the United States, in these negotiations.

By the time the Uruguay Round negotiations were concluded in December 1993, some 76 countries, including all the industrial-country members and 47 developing countries (out of a total of 76 developing-country signatories to the agreement), had scheduled commitments in one or more financial services industries (GATT Secretariat 1994). Unfortunately, no quantification of the value of these commitments or of their impact can be made, for lack of sufficient data on services trade broken down by mode of supply and because restrictions on services can seldom be replaced by quantitative tariff equivalents. There was nonetheless a general feeling that the major emerging markets, especially those in Southeast Asia, had offered little (Broadman 1994),[16] and that some had even committed to less than existing market access.

In the financial services negotiations that followed, significant but insufficient improvement is reckoned to have taken place. According to the WTO Secretariat, 30 countries (counting the European Union as one) have improved their offers, sometimes substantially. Japan achieved significant progress under strong pressure from a United States determined to open Japanese financial markets. A bilateral US-Japan insurance agreement was achieved on 11 October 1994, and a comprehensive bilateral financial services agreement was concluded on 13 February 1995, covering asset management, corporate securities, and cross-border financial transactions.[17] Monitoring these agreements is part of the bilateral US-Japan trade agenda. By June 1995, Japan had made a new WTO offer, but this fell short of full multilateralization of its bilateral agreement with the United States. Finally, in a letter to WTO Director General Renato Ruggiero dated 21 August 1995, Japan committed itself to full extension of the agreement with the United States to the multilateral framework. That letter, however, was a nonlegal declaration of intention, which had yet to be bound in the Japanese offer. This was one of the contentious points in the run-up toward the December 1997 agreement, with Japan agreeing to give in late in the negotiations.

In June 1995, the United States, still finding the offers of the emerging markets largely unsatisfactory, announced the withdrawal of most of its offer on financial services and the introduction of an MFN exemption on the whole sector.[18] The US position was that the degree of market access implied by existing offers was insufficient, given the initial objectives, and that the coverage of existing commitments fell short of providing the critical mass needed to reach a meaningful multilateral agreement. Private financial institutions in the United States were clearly dissatisfied with the existing offers. Trade negotiators were concerned that locking these limited offers into an agreement would be counterproductive: once committed to full MFN, the United States and other industrial countries would have no leverage left to induce developing countries to open their financial markets further. Moreover, the acceptance of offers that promised less than the status quo would raise the

---

16. Snape and Bosworth (1996, 5) note that liberalization commitments in services overall were quite modest, as they reckon that "little more than limited standstill commitments within sectors already open has been achieved even by those countries making significant commitments."

17. The agreement was called "Measures by the Government of Japan and the Government of the United States Regarding Financial Services."

18. This exemption also includes insurance services, unlike the December 1993 exemption.

possibility that some countries might reverse their previous liberalizations, leaving the industrial countries with no recourse under WTO procedures. Hence, the United States, deciding that no agreement was better than a bad agreement, withdrew MFN.[19]

The European Union's interpretation, however, was that the glass offered by the developing countries was half-full rather than half-empty,[20] that the efficacy of leverage through reciprocity was bound to be limited in any case, that the formal inclusion of financial services into a multilateral framework on the basis of a first agreement was itself worth pursuing, and that declaring failure might weaken the WTO at a time when it made sense to build up the new organization's political clout. The Europeans, therefore, moved to lock the best offers available in a provisional agreement implying standstill, and in July 1995 they were able, with the cooperation of Japan, to secure an interim Protocol on Financial Services. This protocol among 43 countries, which the United States and certain other countries joined with strong MFN exemptions,[21] meant that the best offers thus far negotiated on financial services would be implemented for an initial period, starting 30 days after acceptance by all members (scheduled to have taken place by July 1996) and continuing to 1 November 1997. Members, including the United States, would be able to modify their offers and their MFN exemptions on financial services until the 12 December deadline.

Negotiations officially resumed on 10 April 1997. By early July, only 13 countries had submitted new offers (again counting the European Union as one), none of which were from the emerging market economies whose earlier offers had been considered lacking. Convincing these countries to come up with significantly improved offers remained as difficult as ever.

Yet, the negotiators finally reached an agreement on 13 December 1997 that was hailed by most, including the United States (which withdrew its broad MFN exemption) and most developing countries, as a clear success and a milestone. Pending a detailed and documented history of the final run-up to success, three broad conjectures can be invoked as possible explanations.

First, after the 1995 interim agreement on financial services entered into force, there were signs that the United States and Europe, within the

19. Key (1997) discusses the free-rider issue and the US position.

20. On the divergences of views between the United States and Europe, see Garten (1995). For a European view on the banking discussions, see Beaurain (1996). For an assessment of insurance services commitments in the 1995 protocol, see Woodrow (1997).

21. The United States, however, supported the idea of the standstill implied by the protocol and indicated in a letter to the European Commission and to the Japanese government that their firms would continue to be granted market access and national treatment in the United States.

Quad,[22] were trying harder to cooperate to provide joint leadership in the negotiations. Unlike in other areas, including agriculture during the Uruguay Round negotiations, trade liberalization in financial services was not a transatlantic issue. US and EU negotiating efforts toward third parties were better coordinated, at both the public and the private levels. In particular, the United States and the European Union made clear that developing countries would be denied any opportunity to postpone liberalization while watching a transatlantic conflict on the issue and waiting for its resolution, unlike what happened during the Uruguay Round negotiations on agriculture. This signaled an encouraging willingness to achieve results through cooperation rather than unilateral action. The European Union's active diplomacy, seeking an agreement on the basis of substantially improved offers from different developing countries, also supported US demands and facilitated transatlantic cooperation, irrespective of the final decision that would be taken on any agreement.

Second, private firms in the United States and in the European Union set up effective cooperation through the creation, in 1996, of the Financial Leaders Group (FLG) between European and American financial service firms (see Woolcock 1997). This effort promoted a dialogue conducive to more effective and balanced lobbying and supportive of the quest for common ground on objectives and to some rapprochement of positions. It also provided a useful framework for intermediating dissensions and differences of interests among firms of different sizes and from different countries. One of the last-minute stumbling blocks in the negotiations, for example, was Malaysia's refusal to grandfather existing market access beyond the bound limit of 51 percent, thus threatening the position of the insurance leader AIG. The FLG, from its earliest pronouncements, had viewed Malaysia's position as unacceptable. Up to the end of the negotiations, the FLG and the US government supported, as a matter of principle, the importance of grandfathering all acquired rights of US financial institutions. The FLG noted that some offers still were defective or inadequate, notably those of South Korea, Thailand, Malaysia, India, and Chile,[23] but insisted that offers on the table needed to be harvested through a permanent agreement. This position helped to mollify opposition in some circles, notably the United States' Congress and Senate, to signing an agreement.

Paradoxically, the eruption of the Asian crisis, with the floating and subsequent free fall of the Thai baht from 2 July 1997 and the contagion

---

22. The Quad comprises the Canadian Minister of International Trade, the United States Trade Representative, Japan's Minister of International Trade and Industry, and the EU's Commissioner for External Relations.

23. Chile's offer for asset management was inadequate.

of the monetary and financial turmoil to other countries in Southeast Asia, provided a fresh impetus to a slow-moving negotiating process, while at the same time potentially providing these countries with further pretexts to drag their feet. The political and economic situation that unfolded in Asia may have contributed to the increased flexibility that developed on the demanders' side during the summer of 1997, when the US made clear, for example, that it was ready to consider phasing out commitments (Summers 1997). But the crisis also was widely interpreted as signaling major problems within the financial systems of emerging-market economies in Asia. The severity of the crisis and the dramatic reversal in market sentiment toward Asia prompted local governments to seek ways to restore confidence. This situation helped to make IMF demands for financial reforms acceptable, but also highlighted the benefits, in terms of credibility, of binding in a multilateral agreement some of the liberalizing measures that either had already been taken or that appeared necessary. To the extent that a multilateral agreement could help to restore credibility and contain the damage from this crisis, this may have also shifted the balance of judgments in industrial countries toward accepting an agreement that they might otherwise have been tempted to find still insufficient.

These three possible factors suggest that by the end of 1997 most parties shared the perception that failure to reach an agreement would be very costly. Thus, the chicken-game dynamic illustrated in the introduction to this chapter produced the "successful" result, after much uncertainty all along, notably with respect to the US willingness to adhere to an agreement that was still felt by some, including Chairman of the US Senate Committee on Banking, Housing, and Urban Affairs Senator Alfonse d'Amato, as being inadequate. The United States met Malaysia's refusal to grandfather existing foreign ownership that were above the bound limit of 51 percent with an option to retaliate against forced divestiture that was "carved out" from the US offer and obligations.

The FSA is to be ratified by the end of January 1999 and will enter into force by March of that year. A total of 56 new offers were eventually tabled, bringing to 102 the total number of countries that will have taken commitments in financial services under the GATTS when the FSA enters into force.

Beyond this negotiating success, however, we now turn, in the final chapter, to the content of the agreement, and we assess the FSA from the perspective, developed in chapters 2 and 3, of the relationship between financial reform and economic development. This chapter also looks ahead to ways to follow up on the FSA and to the contribution to be expected from the WTO to financial reform in developing and industrial countries.

The FSA and Beyond:
Financial Reform and the WTO

The WTO is not the only forum, nor possibly the most effective, for discussions of market opening in financial services and actions to that end. Financial reform, including opening to foreign institutions and domestic reform, has taken place through a combination of powerful market forces; diplomatic, bilateral, and multilateral pressures; and regional cooperation. The issue has been raised in bilateral talks between the United States and Japan and between the United States and China. Regional cooperation has been instrumental in promoting greater openness of financial markets to foreign competition: In Europe, the 1992 single-market program has considerably deepened financial integration among EU member states; impressive progress has also been accomplished by the United States, Canada, and Mexico within the North American Free Trade Agreement (NAFTA). The Asia Pacific Economic Cooperation (APEC) forum provides yet another setting for discussion (box 5.1). In the wake of the Asian financial crisis, IMF programs have been redirected to focus on financial reform because one of the roots of the crisis was seen to have been inefficient financial markets.

Chapters 2 and 3 describe the important role of financial reform in strategies of development. The question remains: What is the best route toward successful reform? In this chapter, we assess the FSA and conclude that it represents at best a first, insufficient yet useful, step toward more open and efficient financial systems and that the challenge remains to sustain this effort and to build a more ambitious agenda on the basis of this preliminary achievement. The second section discusses some of the limitations of the current negotiating approach and the possible contribution of GATS and WTO to promoting financial reform and

Box 5.1 Financing Growth in APEC

Since the Asia Pacific Economic Cooperation (APEC) was founded in 1989, the forum has expanded to include 18 members on both sides of the Pacific. Meetings of the leaders of the APEC members began in 1993. APEC has two objectives in addition to promoting trade liberalization. They are to promote trade facilitation and to provide economic and technical development assistance to low-income members. APEC places an emphasis on cooperation that makes it somewhat unique among trade forums. Its agenda reflects the Asian view of trade reform, which is based on the unilateral liberalization that has proved so successful in East Asia and on a preference for voluntary action based on consensus (and peer pressure) over legalistic bargaining and confrontation.

At the second meeting of APEC leaders at Bogor, Indonesia, in 1994, members agreed on the goal of achieving free trade by 2010 among the established industrial economies in the group, and by 2020 for the developing economies. At their 1995 meeting in Osaka, the leaders further defined APEC's mode of operation as one of "concerted unilateralism," in which each member proceeds toward the free trade target voluntarily, at its own speed, subject to peer pressure from other members. To make this process more transparent, members agreed to develop Individual Action Plans, in which each member would map out for itself the commitments to be made to achieve the free trade targets and ensure MFN and national treatment. These action plans are also expected to contribute to the WTO negotiations. They became the basis for the 1996 Manila Action Plan, which in turn is seen as setting the benchmark against which progress will be measured in the years ahead.

The finance ministers of the APEC members began meeting annually in 1994. Their discussions have mainly involved the exchange of information on economic trends and projections and on the impact of exchange rate changes on trade and investment. The ministers have also analyzed possible cooperative means of mobilizing cross-border capital flows within the Pacific region and increasing the funds available for social infrastructure. At their annual meeting in the Philippines in 1996, the APEC leaders called on the finance ministers to achieve financial reform and to stimulate private-sector participation in infrastructure development. This mandate is potentially far-reaching, since the growth of APEC's East Asian members is increasingly recognized as subject to infrastructure bottlenecks, whose removal must be financed by cross-border flows, using more sophisticated long-term instruments than are available locally. Reform of the financial sector through deregulation and market opening will be needed to facilitate these capital flows. Strong financial supervision and the provision of necessary financial infrastructure such as rating agencies, clearing and payments systems, sound legal frameworks, and modern accounting practices are essential prerequisites for reform. It is in this area that the intergovernmental information sharing and cooperation that are among APEC's hallmarks can be useful.

Financial services reforms were included in the Individual Action Plans of 13 of the 18 APEC members. Seven members committed themselves to reduce restrictions on market access; five made commitments to provide MFN and national treatment. Most of these commitments, however, had already been made in the context of the WTO talks.

sustaining growth. The third section sets out what could constitute an emerging agenda for financial-services liberalization and proposes some preliminary ideas about the WTO agenda for 2000. The final section presents our conclusions.

Assessing the FSA

The negotiators' perspective provides a useful way to assess the FSA. It emphasizes the progress achieved in individual offers, in terms of the number of countries willing to commit to some degree of market access and in terms of the coverage of those offers. By 12 December 1997, 56 offers (representing 70 countries, as the European Union counts as one) had been submitted with improvements, sometimes substantial, from earlier 1995 or 1993 offers. Taking into account the commitments made by other WTO members during earlier stages of the negotiations, 102 WTO members will have commitments in financial services when the FSA comes into force by 1 March 1999. Among them, five countries made offers for the first time in the run-up to the December 1997 agreement: Bolivia, Costa Rica, Mauritius, Senegal, and Sri Lanka. As for the provision and transfer of financial information, 65 countries now have commitments in these services.

Thus, more than 95 percent of world trade in banking, insurance, securities, and financial information now comes under the WTO's jurisdiction, on the basis of broad MFN and under the auspices of the dispute settlement mechanism. The essence of the agreement, however, hinges on individual countries' commitments, whose scope and ambition differ widely. Judgment of what the FSA achieves in terms of market access and national treatment is particularly difficult to make. Evaluations conducted by the Financial Leaders Group (FLG) for 20 key countries[1] suggest that significant progress was achieved in major areas of the negotiations. However, many offers were judged to be disappointing, including those of Chile (banking, asset management, and securities), Colombia (insurance), Egypt (insurance), India (all services), South Korea (all services), Malaysia (all services), Mexico (banking), Pakistan (all services), the Philippines (asset management and securities), Singapore (banking), Thailand (all services), and Venezuela (insurance).

As table 3.1 shows, the status quo already differs notably among countries, with some countries being much more open than others. The fact that the offers tabled by a number of countries have substantially improved over the course of the negotiations tells little about the degree

1. They are Argentina, Brazil, Chile, Colombia, the Czech Republic, Egypt, Hungary, India, Indonesia, South Korea, Malaysia, Mexico, Pakistan, the Philippines, Poland, Singapore, South Africa, Thailand, Turkey, and Venezuela.

of market access thus achieved; some countries may have dragged their feet in the negotiations and yet be more open than others whose offers have been substantially improved (for example, Chile versus Egypt). Unfortunately, there is no single indicator of market access that could help to rank countries on a single scale according to existing barriers so that the corresponding contribution of the FSA in removing partly or totally some of these barriers could be judged. Given the number, complexity, and lack of transparency of such barriers, we shall not attempt to provide such a ranking here.

Full details of the agreement are not available at the time of writing, but tables 5.1 and 5.2 provide a preliminary assessment. Table 5.1 compares the FSA commitment with the status quo. Table 5.2 gives our judgment on whether countries committed more or less market access than the status quo in banking, insurance, and securities markets. It is readily apparent from these tables that the FSA, save for actual advances in the field of insurance services, barely goes beyond binding the status quo. In the face of the strong reluctance by many emerging market economies, even binding the status quo was an achievement. In particular, little actual liberalization seems to have taken place in banking. Several factors seem to account for this lack of progress. Emerging market countries have underdeveloped insurance and security markets as well as embryonic asset management capacities. They may be more willing to grant wider market access there than in banking when banks dominate the domestic financial sector. They fear foreign domination and want to control the speed and the nature of the adjustments necessary to achieve greater efficiency in the sector. Insurance companies may also have been more active demanders in these negotiations because banks in OECD countries, including the United States, are preoccupied by industry consolidation at home and by changes in domestic regulations.

Remarkable though it was in terms of the negotiating challenge, especially in light of the Asian financial crisis, the FSA does not appear to provide significant new momentum on market opening. In the last few months of the FSA negotiations, the movement toward increased financial opening has come from the conditions imposed by the IMF as part of its intervention as a lender-of-last-resort (see table 3.1). As part of the Indonesian package, the IMF has secured a commitment to introduce legislation that would allow 100 percent foreign ownership of listed banks—compare that to a limit of 49 percent agreed on by Indonesia as part of the WTO negotiations. South Korea has undertaken a major financial reform as a necessary condition to OECD accession. Its WTO commitments, however, fell short of binding this reform. Here again, the IMF has secured from South Korea an agreement to bind in the WTO all OECD commitments. But other financial measures included in the IMF programs have not been bound yet.

Table 5.1 Market access in financial services: Status quo versus WTO commitments, 1997

Economy	Status quo[a]	WTO financial services agreement[b]
Argentina	Allows 100 percent ownership in all sectors.	Guarantees 100 percent ownership in banking and securities.
Brazil	Allows up to 100 percent ownership of existing banks, on case-by-case basis. Allows 49 percent ownership of investment banks. Allows 50 percent ownership in insurance, but no new branches or subsidiaries are permitted.	Guarantees 100 percent ownership in banking and securities, subject to authorization on a case-by-case basis. Commits to 100 percent-owned insurance subsidiaries, subject to authorization on a case-by-case basis, but no entry through branches.
Chile	Allows 100 percent ownership in all sectors.	Guarantees 100 percent ownership in banking. Commits to 100 percent-owned insurance subsidiaries, but no entry through branches.
India	Allows 8 licenses per year for foreign bank branches. Allows up to 100 percent ownership of nonbank financial institutions, depending on amount invested.	Commits to a limit of 12 new foreign bank branch licenses per year. Commits to 49 percent ownership for stock brokering and 51 percent ownership in other financial services.
Indonesia	Allows 85 percent ownership in banks, but new foreign equity capped at 49 percent. Allows 80 percent ownership in insurance. Allows 85 percent ownership of securities firms.	Commits to 49 percent ownership in banks.[d] Commits to 100 percent-owned insurance subsidiaries. Commits 100 percent ownership of nonbank financial institutions and securities firms.
Japan	Market access requires national reciprocity.	Binds 1996 US-Japan bilateral insurance deal in the WTO.
South Korea	49 percent ownership in banking. 49 percent ownership in life insurance. 50 percent ownership in securities.	Standstill for market access.[d]

(Table continues on next page)

Table 5.1   Market access in financial services: Status quo versus WTO commitments, 1997 (continued)

Economy	Status quo[a]	WTO financial services agreement[b]
Malaysia	Allows 30 percent ownership in domestic banks. Allows 49 percent ownership in insurance, by law, but existing practice is higher.	Commits to 51 percent equity in domestic banks. Commits to 51 percent ownership in insurance; existing investments not grandfathered.
Mexico	Allows 100 percent ownership for bank subsidiaries for NAFTA and 41 percent for non-NAFTA. Allows 100 percent ownership of insurance for NAFTA and 49 percent for non-NAFTA. Allows 49 percent ownership in securities.	Binds NAFTA commitments on insurance; commits to 100 percent ownership of insurance subsidiaries and branches.
Philippines	Allows 60 percent ownership in banks. Allows 40 percent ownership in insurance. Allows 49 percent ownership in investment houses.	Commits to 51 percent ownership in banks, and grandfathers acquired rights. Commits to 51 percent ownership in insurance. Commits to 51 percent ownership in investment houses.
Thailand	Allows 100 percent ownership of banks and finance companies until 2007, then 49 percent for new equity.[c] Allows 25 percent ownership in life and nonlife insurance. Allows 49 percent ownership in securities firms.	Commits to 100 percent ownership of banks until 2007, then 49 percent for new equity. Commits to 25 percent ownership in life and non-life insurance.

a. "Status quo" refers to market access when the WTO financial services negotiations concluded on 13 December 1997.
b. "WTO financial services agreement" column refers to commitments made in the 1997 WTO Financial Services Agreement.
c. Prior to Thailand's IMF economic program in summer 1997, foreign ownership in banking was restricted to 25 percent.
d. Indonesia and South Korea subsequently removed numerous restrictions on foreign participation in the financial services sector in the context of their IMF economic programs.

Table 5.2 World Trade Organization financial services agreement: market access in selected countries, 1997

	Banking	Insurance	Securities
Status quo plus	Malaysia Mexico	Brazil Indonesia Japan South Korea Philippines Mexico	Brazil Indonesia South Korea Malaysia Philippines
Status quo	Argentina Brazil Chile India Indonesia Japan South Korea Thailand	Chile India Thailand	Argentina Thailand
Less than status quo	Philippines	Malaysia[a]	Chile India

Notes: Based on information on offers available as of February 1998. Assessment reflects the extent to which each country's offer in the 1997 WTO FSA increases market access over what was the case prior to submission of the offer (i.e., "status quo plus"). The term "market access" refers to foreign ownership and the establishment of a commercial presence in a country. This table should not be used for cross-country comparisons. Interpretation of market access varies widely across countries. Market access, in this table, is determined relative to a country's previous level of such access; it is not determined by comparing access across countries.

a. This entry is based on a comparison of existing practice (up to 100 percent foreign ownership on a case-by-case basis) with Malaysia's commitment (up to 51 percent foreign ownership) in December 1997. This entry is not based on a comparison of existing Malaysian law, in effect when the WTO Financial Services deal concluded on 13 December 1997, which would have required foreign insurance companies to reduce their holdings to 49 percent by mid-1998.

It would be a mistake not to recognize these limitations of the FSA. The agreement simply does not address the need highlighted in chapter 2 to reform financial systems to promote growth. We have suggested in chapter 2 that foreign financial institutions can play a useful role in promoting successful reform. Their participation allows the discipline of increased competition to be forcefully combined with transfers of technology, know-how, and resources. Yet, nondiscriminatory opening to foreign entry, which should be an ingredient of developing countries' financial reform strategies, is not a major feature of the FSA. Instead, the FSA is a response to pressure from events and from foreign countries and firms. We have also argued that repressed and laggard financial markets misallocate resources and hamper growth. Even when they accept that message and look forward to gradual opening, developing countries may well misunderstand the time dimension involved. This is especially true of emerging-market economies that have engaged in a promising catch-up process with industrial countries, and that, so far, as suggested by Krugman (1994), have not focused enough on the quality of resource allocation as opposed to factor accumulation.

True, in the first three decades after World War II, the industrial countries enjoyed high growth rates despite undertaking only gradual liberalization and opening their financial markets slowly: only in the 1990s has financial integration among the industrial countries reached the degree it attained in the late nineteenth century (Obstfeld and Taylor 1997). It might thus seem to developing countries that financial reform is not as urgent as they are told and should be spread out over long periods of time. But beyond the urgency spelt by the Asian crisis, the time dimension is crucial for two interacting reasons.

First, the world economy is undergoing an information technology revolution. Whole sectors and their organization are bound to be deeply affected by the introduction of new technologies and new processes. Productivity will soar in some sectors; the pace of innovation has been steadily increasing. In such an environment, resource allocation is crucial. Even the wisest governments cannot do better than the market in anticipating where finance will be put to the most productive and promising uses. The mobility of financial resources among countries and sectors is critical to this process of discovery and innovation. Pollin and Vaubourg (1996) argue that it was the already advanced development of its financial markets that allowed the United Kingdom to become the pioneer of the Industrial Revolution. They see the same explanation behind the development of the US automobile and aeronautics industries in the twentieth century. In short, in a context of rapid industrial and economic change, the costs of resource misallocation are likely to determine which countries surf atop the wave of innovation and which are towed under.

Second, in a world of increasing capital mobility, no country can afford not to welcome foreign capital inflows, although cautious attention to and control over the nature of such inflows remains possible and sometimes desirable. Financial openness is required to augment domestic saving. Beyond the contribution of financial liberalization to increasing saving, on which theoretical and empirical evidence is arguably mixed, the fact is that capital flight is the likely outcome of excessive financial repression, as the Latin American countries found in the 1970s and early 1980s. Thus, even domestically generated savings are not likely to be invested locally if financial markets are not sufficiently free and open. The hope that restrictive measures might induce these funds to remain within the country is belied by past experience and rendered futile by the possibilities that financial technologies now offer. Moreover, the extent to which foreign investors are willing to commit resources on a lasting and stable basis depends on the degree of development of local financial markets. Investment instruments must be secure and easily tradable. In countries where financial markets are underdeveloped, foreign investment will still take place, but it will likely be volatile, ready to flee at the slightest hint of difficulties. Hence, a lack of financial modernization and openness may not prevent capital flows from coming in, but it may increase a country's vulnerability to capital flow reversals. So does also, however, liberalization conducted without due attention to the challenge of improving risk oversight and banking supervision.

The central problem of initiating a liberalizing path for financial services as part of a growth strategy, therefore, seems not to have been touched on in the WTO beyond the indisputable benefits from binding the status quo. Governments now must move the negotiations forward and prepare the talks that are scheduled for resumption in 2000 to further enhance financial reform. The objective of financial reform should be steadily pursued through a number of means, including bilateral pressures, regional negotiations, and a pursuit of the current multilateral effort at the WTO. This emerging agenda must also include the preparation of the new set of multilateral negotiations that is scheduled to start by 2000 under the WTO's so-called "Agenda 2000." Pressure exerted on developing countries must be based on persuasion rather than brinkmanship, on emphasizing that there are important benefits to expect from well-conducted reform involving wider market access, and on working jointly with them to address the costs of financial reform. Particularly, progress is needed on some of the major defects with international financial supervision and regulation as revealed by the Asian financial crisis. In the sections that follow, we discuss how the WTO can help to promote financial opening, and we venture into some of the issues relevant to Agenda 2000.

The Role of GATS and the WTO in Promoting Financial Opening

Multilateral negotiations fulfill two related functions. First, they bind opening measures, however undertaken, in a multilateral framework, creating a kind of an international constitution for trade and market access, which is based on effective dispute settlement and prevents backlashes from occurring too easily. The second function is to feed the dynamics of liberalization by pressuring each country to open its trade with foreign countries and broaden access to its markets.

The extension of the WTO jurisdiction to financial services, whatever the level of the initial commitments, is an encouraging first step. An important contribution of the multilateral framework and of the dispute-settlement mechanism that it develops is to facilitate the longer-term consistency of liberalizing efforts that are gradually undertaken. Financial reform is a process, not a one-shot policy decision, and like any gradual process it needs constant, ongoing commitment. But gradualism allows opposing interest groups to organize and oppose liberalization. Commitments to reform must be bound if they are to have lasting credibility. Binding reform is a time-proven method to prevent what is necessarily a gradual process from slipping into stagnation or reversal. The role of WTO is crucial in this respect.

More questionable, on the basis of the FSA, is the contribution of the WTO to sustaining further market opening. To improve the prospects of future multilateral negotiations in financial services, two important limitations of the current framework need to be addressed. The first lies with weaknesses in the framework of the GATS, already alluded to in chapter 4, including the positive-list approach and the difficulty of making cross-sectoral bargains. In the GATS, opening and granting market access are not the default options; for each category of financial services and each mode of delivery, they result from a deliberate decision. Positive lists identify sectors on which commitments are made rather than those on which they are not. This approach not only leaves important sectors untouched by liberalization, but also implies that as new sectors emerge they will automatically stand outside the market-opening framework until explicitly brought into it. Given the heroic effort that was needed to produce GATS during the Uruguay Round, reforming the GATS would not be an attractive task. Instead, we tentatively propose in the next section to circumvent its limitations by placing the negotiations in a broader framework.

The second limitation has to do with the traditional way that multilateral trade negotiations are conducted, namely the give-and-take process that we call the "reciprocity" approach to negotiation. Financial services are a sector in which developing countries feel that they alone make concessions. They fear the implications of financial reform and are doubtful about what they will get in return. For most of them, access to the financial markets of industrial countries is not an immediate priority. Developing countries, therefore, do not play the same negotiating game as the United States or the other industrial countries do (Ahnlid 1996). For most of the countries targeted by the United States, other industrial countries, and industrial-country firms, the threat of reduced access to the US market is of little importance. In addition, although the US market for financial services is indeed very open, it is also segmented geographically and by industry, and the policies and regulations of the 50 states may interfere with general commitments made at the federal level. This makes the US market less attractive to potential foreign entrants than its vast size and openness might suggest.

Some developing countries may over time develop comparative advantage in some financial services: according to Ryan (1990), comparative advantage can emerge in countries with a lower rate of time preference, lower interest rates, greater physical and human capital accumulation, and higher growth rates than their trading partners. Some Asian countries fit that description. Even then, however, the accumulation of necessary specialist skills takes time. And even for these potential financial services exporters, the promise of open markets in industrial countries is not immediately alluring.

Moreover, the division of the WTO negotiations along sectoral lines, separating both services from goods and individual services from each other, makes reciprocity less credible and less effective, as any reciprocal arrangements must stay within sectors. The potential for linkage and trade-offs is minimal. As Freeman (1997) has noted, the fact that the financial services talks are negotiated by finance ministers rather than trade ministers makes linkages with other trade negotiations even more difficult.[2] But even though possible linkages seldom can be identified beforehand, the potential for linkage often helps in concluding negotiations, sometimes in unexpected ways. The fact that the negotiations on telecommunications succeeded despite the same handicap provides proof that a purely sectoral approach can deliver. The results achieved by the FSA, however, cast some doubt on the potential of the current approach to produce ambitious opening in financial services.

Finally, resorting to reciprocity somewhat weakens the credibility of the case for reform that we focus on in this book: opening is in the self-interest of all countries. If that is the case, denying MFN is to shoot oneself in the foot. A message that says, "If we open our markets, it is good for us both, but if you do not open yours, I will close mine," lacks credibility. Part of the genius of GATT was its success in turning reciprocity-based mercantilism into an instrument of give-and-take multilateral liberalization (Messerlin 1995). Unfortunately, that approach, for services and especially for financial services, looks less promising. Logically, however, the negotiations should focus on taking as many countries on board as possible. Meanwhile, investors and markets will penalize those that do not participate. The notion of "critical mass" that was hailed as crucial to reaching an agreement, therefore, ignores the central reason for pursuing opening, namely, that it is in the interest of

---

2. Initially, the agenda for services negotiations had somehow created a (widely unsuccessful) linkage between financial services and movement of persons, with India claiming that movements of factors should be treated symmetrically and arguing that financial services liberalization should be matched by a liberalization of labor movements (notably in the software industry).

the opening countries to open and should not be seen as a concession to foreign service providers, even though it also serves their interests.

This discussion suggests that, unlike some earlier progress in GATT, advances in market access for financial services might not come primarily from multilateral negotiations, but might more conveniently take the form of stepwise unilateral or regional opening, eventually bound within the multilateral framework. Hence, while it is worthwhile to ask how the current WTO process could be improved, progress will have to come from the combination of several processes: unilateral opening (which may also be helped by pressures from foreign firms); regional stimulation; pressures from the IMF, the OECD, and other multilateral institutions; and the binding mechanism and dispute settlement of the WTO.

Further unilateral opening of financial markets in developing countries should not be ruled out: the revolution in information technologies and the past unhappy experience with closed economies and repressed financial sectors are likely to lead to increasing recognition of the role of finance in growth and development. Moreover, in today's globalized world, demand for private-sector capital is increasingly cross-border and competitive, as emerging-market economies tap savings worldwide. To this end, a number of developing countries have undertaken domestic financial reform and unilateral opening in the past two decades, as described in earlier chapters and in appendix B.

Domestic reform, however, is not a matter of following a standard recipe. The results so far have been mixed; much more is at stake than simply opening markets and deregulating (see Caprio, Atiyas, and Hanson 1996). Reform is everywhere an indigenous, political, unfolding process that faces many hurdles. To some extent, each country is a separate case. That is why outside pressure, if it is to be effective, must focus on the dynamics, not on the end result. With the exception of Japan[3] and those East Asian countries for which the latest round of liberalization has been IMF-imposed, the countries that have liberalized in recent years have done so unilaterally, without outside pressure or multilateral negotiations, because it served their own interests. The growing interest of the APEC economies in financial services reform as a means of achieving a larger shared objective—the financing of huge long-term infrastructure projects and the needs of aging populations—provides a case in point. Outside pressure, from the United States or the IMF, may

---

3. The US approach seems to have scored some success in Japan. The threat to deny access may have been more effective with Japanese financial firms, some of which are large and sophisticated enough to be interested in access to the US market. More likely, however, the Japanese government is finding foreign pressure helpful as it undertakes reform aimed at modernizing and opening Japan's backward, overregulated, and uncompetitive financial markets.

even be the instrument that is needed, and sometimes wanted, to carry potentially costly domestic reform.

Thus, unilateral, regional, multilateral, and interinstitutional approaches can be strongly complementary; they can jointly contribute to the formation of an effective international regime (Sauvé 1996). Regime creation under GATT was based on diffuse reciprocity and was driven by US leadership. So far, negotiations under GATS have been conducted on the basis of specific reciprocity and driven by the reluctance of the United States and other industrial countries to tolerate free riding.[4] That may well lead to more demanding negotiating stances and slower progress. Regional liberalization experiences, from that of the European Union to those of NAFTA and APEC, provide useful lessons on the considerable difficulties of liberalization and on how to achieve progress toward that goal. The ultimate test, however, is the willingness to bind progress in the WTO framework.

The Task Ahead: A Strategic Note

The FSA is open for acceptance and ratification until 29 January 1999 and will enter into force on 1 March 1999. There is still room for improvement in the existing offers before that date. The United States has indicated its willingness to negotiate further opening measures with some countries, most notably Malaysia. As we have noted, one of the objectives should also be to bind in the FSA the measures undertaken under IMF programs or as part of OECD accession. But there is a need to think to the future.

According to the so-called "built-in agenda" of the Uruguay Round, multilateral negotiations are scheduled to resume by 2000. The objectives listed in chapter 4 remain valid: the right of firms to establish themselves in host countries and to operate freely there, national treatment, free cross-border trade in financial services and free movement of personnel, limited and transparent exemptions, and an MFN-compatible grandfather clause for existing investments. These measures are compatible with prudential policies under the prudential carve out already included in the GATS Annex on Financial Services.

We conclude this chapter, however, with a discussion of some future negotiating issues that we think deserve more research and attention. GATS represented a significant breakthrough because it brought the broad range of services into the multilateral negotiations for the first time, within

---

4. Regime formation and the shift from diffuse to specific reciprocity are analyzed in Ahnlid (1996). See also the discussion by Bhagwati and Irwin (1987) on "The Return of the Reciprocitarians."

a framework of principles on which multilateral trade in goods had long been based in GATT. But some of the built-in features of GATS, as discussed in chapter 4 and recalled above, suggest that it suffers from architectural limitations that cast a doubt on its ability to create a liberalization-enhancing regime for trade in services, that is, one that exerts continuous pressure toward opening, as does GATT and as do certain regional trade agreements.[5]

A central issue in these negotiations was market access in financial services. It was addressed on a sectoral basis by working on cross-border trade and on foreign entry. Yet, market access is the key issue in the management of economic globalization well beyond financial services. Of course, it involves trade policies, but policies directed at FDI and competition policy are the crucial dimensions in a globalized economy with mobile factors of productions. These issues are central to market access for services in general and financial services in particular. FDI remains key to providing retail financial services, even though the ongoing revolution in information technology may facilitate cross-border trade. In addition, oligopolistic market structures and the potential for mergers increase the need for a multilateral approach to competition policy. This is why it might be worthwhile to extend the domain of multilateral negotiations to FDI and competition policy. Through the definition of broad principles in these areas that would apply to all goods and services, such an agenda would help to circumvent the limitations of the GATS and help the multilateral trade regime to become more liberalization enhancing. Market access in financial services could be significantly improved. As argued in this book, market access makes an important contribution to economic growth and development.

Therefore, in 1999 the Quad should consider launching a new round of negotiations to start addressing the issues of foreign direct investment and competition policy. This would be an uncertain, contentious, and probably long-term venture, as it would broach some difficult issues on which some important developing countries have already expressed reservations, even hostility. Moreover, the experience with the OECD's Multilateral Agreement on Investment (MAI) shows that it is not an easy road even for industrial countries to take. Another difficulty is that launching a new negotiating round and bringing it to a successful conclusion will require many years, especially in the face of likely negotiation fatigue compounded by poor prospects for early results.

Yet, this may be a very promising course of action that offers attractive prospects for further opening. A successful negotiation also promises major benefits: it would allow participants to capitalize on previous negotiations without jeopardizing the existing GATS and is compatible

---

5. See, for example, the discussion on the financial services chapter of NAFTA by Sauvé and Gonzalez-Hermosillo (1993).

with a pursuit of sectoral negotiating efforts as envisioned in the current plans. It would also permit the central issue of market access to be addressed in a much more coherent and cogent way by looking at what determines market access, namely, FDI and competition policy. These principles of market access deal with the whole structure of an economy, not just specific services such as financial services. Such an initiative would recognize the necessary shift of the multilateral negotiations from trade instruments and practices to the whole set of microeconomic measures and regulatory practices. It would open a major and challenging new agenda for these negotiations, thus giving them a new raison d'être. More fundamentally, it would allow the major defects of the GATS to be remedied by engaging in a parallel effort without trying to reform the agreement head-on. It would broaden the focus of the negotiations, because market-access discussions encompass all sectors, allowing cross-sectoral concessions to take place much more easily. By focusing on market access for all sectors, it should elicit strong support from various interest groups and encourage them to join forces to promote its progress. The goal is ambitious and demanding, but so is the task of managing a globalizing world economy. It gives the negotiations, which otherwise threaten to turn petty, a mobilizing political objective.

The agenda already set by the Uruguay Round agreement requires opening new negotiations on a number of issues by 2000, which, for practical purposes, amounts to a new round. Liberalization of direct investment and better coordination of competition policy would provide ambitious goals for these negotiations and would allow GATS to be improved by absorbing it into a new architectural framework that would bring more flexibility, greater consistency. It would also restore the opportunity to achieve fruitful, if unpredictable, trade-offs across sectors. While this looks like a long shot, there is little to lose in seriously tackling these new issues and considering them in a multilateral framework.

Concluding Remarks

We have argued that financial reform, involving opening markets to foreign competition and domestic reform, is a crucial ingredient of economic growth and development. We have also identified several conditions necessary for successful financial reform. The first one is that supervision of the financial sector must be substantially strengthened. This is an area in which international cooperation can bring substantial benefits, for three reasons. First, the industrial countries now have broad experience with supervisory problems and shortcomings and can contribute to establishing more efficient supervisory systems in the developing world. Second, there already exists a framework of international cooperation on these matters: under the aegis of the Bank for International

Settlements, through technical expertise available from the World Bank, from the International Association of Insurance Supervisors, from central banks and regulatory bodies in the industrial countries, and through APEC's cooperative framework. This framework continues to deepen and solidify. Third, part of the problem is international, rather than domestic, in nature. While domestic problems were largely at the root of the Asian crisis, the behavior of international investors, who miscalculated the risks, also points to severe market failures. Moreover, the "herd" behavior that characterizes international financial markets suggests that international regulation is desirable.

The second condition is that macroeconomic policy must be put on sound footing. Many developing countries made substantial progress on this front in the 1980s and early 1990s. But further financial opening, leading to a surge in capital inflows, is bound to lead time and again to the now-familiar macroeconomic dilemma of fighting inflationary pressures with an overvalued currency or resisting overvaluation by accommodating inflationary pressures. Caution and pragmatism in macroeconomic and exchange rate management are therefore necessary. At the same time, sound macroeconomic and exchange rate policy, while a prerequisite to successful financial reform, is beneficial per se, and commitment to undertake financial reform helps to create the conditions and the incentive to pursue such policies.

These two conditions, together with the misgivings in many countries about financial opening, make the whole reform process a tall order. We believe that multilateral negotiations can help, provided that the pressure is directed not toward immediate results, but toward a sustainable process of gradual opening. There may be several paths toward successful domestic reform, depending on individual countries' initial banking and financial conditions, but binding the process in a multilateral agreement is a foremost objective. Demanders from developed countries should keep in mind that rigid deadlines matter less than does the ability to sustain a dynamic process. Deadlines are, indeed, indispensable in harnessing the energy needed to bind meaningful commitments into a valuable multilateral agreement. The pressure must be kept on countries to improve their offers, before ratification and implementation of the FSA and through successive negotiations beyond 1999. But it is important not to focus on a single deadline by which any final outcome must emerge. More important is an ambitious process of opening markets that will, in a reasonable time frame, produce the desired outcome and lock in the opening dynamic that we believe most countries can be convinced to accept as part of their best negotiating strategies.

From this standpoint, the FSA, which essentially binds the status quo, should be interpreted as a first step. It provides an opportunity for a promising agenda, yet to emerge, on financial opening. 13 December 1997 did not spell the end of negotiations; instead, it gave an encouraging signal that such an agenda can realistically be pursued. However, more is needed to initiate and sustain actual financial reform as part of a growth strategy. Multilateral negotiations have a crucial role to play, not only in conveying this central message through credible pressures, as mentioned above, but also in setting up a framework conducive to further progress in the standard of openness that most countries would be willing to share.

Two recommendations emerge from this chapter. First, there is ample room for international cooperation, both on improved international financial supervision and regulation, and on the interaction between opening measures and the process of binding them in a multilateral agreement. Second, GATS not only opens a route toward market opening in financial services, but also presents limitations under which the pace of opening is likely to be slow. Negotiators and members of the WTO should investigate ways to improve the multilateral regime and make it more liberalization enhancing. An option to consider is the extension of multilateral negotiations to the two central issues of market access across sectors: FDI and competition policy.

The FSA plants the seeds of a new, multilateral constitutional framework for trade in financial services. Only through renewed efforts will the process fulfill the promises of market opening, avoid the potential costs of it, and contribute to growth. These efforts should now be undertaken.

APPENDIX A

Accelerating Change: The Global Financial Services Sector

Few industries have experienced such rapid change in the past three decades as have banking, insurance, and securities, the principal industries in the financial services sector. Rapid innovation and advances in telecommunications and computer technology have facilitated the moving of money, domestically and across borders, at ever-faster rates and in ever-greater volumes. As new financial services have proliferated, additional competitors, such as asset management companies, credit card suppliers, and securities analysts, now challenge the traditional service providers and accelerate the rate of change. Many governments have also fanned the winds of competition by removing past regulations on ownership, operations, foreign entry, and key prices such as interest rates. Many strictures remain, however, and those relating to foreign participation are the subject of the WTO talks.

Even so, regulation of financial-sector activities and institutions is still the domain of national authorities, who control the access of foreign institutions to the domestic market. The fiduciary nature of many financial activities, the sector's important role in the implementation of monetary policy, the existence of market failures due to information imperfections, and the sector's proneness to crisis all provide rationales for regulation. Marked differences in the competitiveness of financial firms and in the extent of innovation and regulation are emerging between most of the industrial countries and the principal markets in the dynamic economies of Latin America and Asia. These differences, together with the rapid rise in increasingly difficult to control cross-border transactions, are creating pressures for a more level international playing field. In the wake of the 1997-98 Asian financial crisis, pressures are also growing for greater oversight and compliance with international standards for international banking activities.

Although the boundaries between hitherto well-defined types of financial institutions are eroding, the sector is still composed of two main kinds of service providers, several distinct groups of users, and an array of government institutions that share responsibility for regulation. This appendix begins with a brief description of these players and the rationales for regulation. We then track the growth of cross-border activities and the extent of international financial integration. Next, we focus on the increasing importance of emerging markets in international financial-services trade. We then highlight how, in countries undergoing economic development, the financial system can evolve from an informal system based largely on internal generation of funds into a market-based system relying on financial intermediaries, and eventually into modern capital markets, in which providers and users of funds transact directly with each other. Finally, we assess the state of financial reform in major emerging markets and enumerate the barriers that persist in these markets.

The Players

The financial services sector is composed of users and providers of financial services and the government agencies that regulate them. These agencies enforce the rules governing what service providers can do and how they do it.

Users of financial services are households, firms, and governments. Households save, invest, and finance purchases through personal loans from banks and other providers. Corporations use the services of banks in the form of secured and unsecured loans and revolving credit facilities. They may also transact directly with savers through the sale of debt obligations, in the form of commercial paper or fixed-income securities, and equity shares. Similarly, governments borrow from financial institutions and issue securities such as bonds directly into the market. Governments and businesses may also circumvent financial intermediaries through private placements with institutional investors. All forms of debt may also be repackaged into asset-backed securities, which are sold directly to investors.

The providers of these financial services are of two types: financial intermediaries and direct finance institutions in the securities and money markets. Although the distinctions between these traditional categories are becoming increasingly blurred, it is still useful to think of financial intermediaries as including commercial banks, savings institutions, and nonbank financial intermediaries such as insurance, finance, credit, leasing, and investment companies (the last of these are better known as mutual funds or, in the United Kingdom, as unit trusts). Financial intermediaries create or acquire financial assets and obtain the funding for those assets by issuing liabilities. Their assets consist of debt and equity investments in other enterprises. The liabilities of banks and savings institutions consist mainly of deposits; those of nonbank intermediaries are more varied and include claims on insurance policies, pension obligations, and mutual fund shares. These claims, of course, represent financial assets from the claimants' perspective (White 1995).

Institutions engaging in direct finance include brokerages and securities firms.[1] Their role is to facilitate transactions undertaken directly between the providers and the users of funds, for example, by underwriting and selling bonds and equity shares. These firms may operate both in primary (original issue) and secondary (resale) markets for these securities.

Banks have traditionally dominated the financial sector for several reasons. They operate the system by which virtually all noncash payments are made, they provide liquidity to securities markets, and they have been major purchasers of government bonds (Goldstein 1997). In Japan, Germany, and most developing countries banks still hold the lion's share of the assets of financial intermediaries (see the first column of table A.1).

Banks are important in another way. Unlike all but the very largest firms in other industries, a bank that fails can have a significant impact on the rest of the economy. When depositors lose confidence in a bank, this loss of confidence can spread to other banks, leading to a run on the entire banking system. The consequences may be felt throughout the economy and spill over into the political realm. In an effort to head off such crises, governments have traditionally entered into an unspoken quid pro quo arrangement with banks. The government provides the banks with an implicit safety net, in the form of an unstated promise of a safety net by the central bank or the public treasury, or an explicit one, in the form of a public deposit insurance fund. In return, the banks submit to closer government oversight and regulation of their activities than is usual for a private-sector industry.

Deregulation and technological change have resulted in extensive innovation in the products and services provided by banks and their competitors. Banks have moved beyond traditional deposit taking and have refined their strategic goals. Market forces, allowed freer play in many countries since the late 1970s, have increased the competition that banks face from other intermediaries and from direct finance institutions. Banks have tried in various ways to adjust to this competition, sometimes with disastrous results. Since 1980, when asset growth and market share were

---

1. Rating agencies could also be included here since their role is necessary to provide information to evaluate risk.

Table A.1 Banking industry indicators in selected developing and industrial countries, 1994 (percentages)

Country	Share of banks in financial intermediation	Share of state-owned banks in total	Share of banking assets held by foreign-owned banks	Loan-loss reserves as a percentage of non-performing loans
South Asia				
India	80	98	7	na
East Asia				
Hong Kong	na	0	78	71
Singapore	71	0	80	120
South Korea	38	13	5	150
Taiwan	80	57	5	42
Southeast Asia				
Indonesia	91	48	4	23
Malaysia	64	8	16	117
Thailand	75	7	7	22
Latin America				
Argentina	98	36	22	97
Brazil	97	48	9	27
Chile	62	14	21	350
Colombia	86	23	4	76
Mexico	87	28	1	21
Industrial countries				
Germany	77	50	4	na
Japan	79	0	2	30
United States	23	0	22	169

na = not available.

Source: Goldstein and Turner (1996).

still banks' major concerns, nearly 75 percent of the member countries of the IMF have experienced significant banking problems (Lindgren, Garcia, and Saal 1996). In the 1990s, efficiency and profitability have become banks' central goals. Banks in the industrial countries have cut costs, reduced their labor forces, and augmented their credit-dispensing functions with fee-based products such as insurance, securitized loans and guarantees, derivatives, swaps, and options. Many of these new products do not appear on their balance sheets.

Nonbank financial intermediaries, similarly, have augmented their capabilities to move money from savers to borrowers more cheaply than banks and have introduced new saving instruments such as specialized mutual funds and securitized products. They have become major financial actors in industrial countries and are expanding at a fast pace, albeit from a small base, in developing countries. They play an important role in the evolution of domestic financial markets because they can compensate for banks' propensity to supply short-term debt financing. Heavy reliance on such financing often leads to maturity mismatches when borrowers need longer-term instruments. Insurance companies, in particular, are becoming more important financial intermediaries. Because they specialize in the transfer of risk, which is intrinsic to all human endeavors, they are important facilitators of economic activity. They must carry sufficient long-term assets to back large contingent liabilities that are also long-term and are therefore major sources of funds for national money and capital markets (Skipper 1996). They are the largest purchasers of government bonds. Developing countries, however, still account for a small share of insurance premiums worldwide. In 1993, insurers based in the OECD countries accounted for 92 percent of worldwide life and nonlife premiums. Premiums are typically equivalent to less than 4 percent of GDP in developing countries, compared with 6 to 12 percent or more in most OECD countries. If anything, this shows the considerable potential for the development of insurance markets in emerging-market economies.

The third set of players in the financial services sector consists of governments, which not only use financial services themselves but also determine the rules governing what service providers can do, who can do it, and how they do it. Financial services in all countries have been and will continue to be subject to government regulation. Government intervention can be inspired by political objectives or industrial policy goals. But a major rationale for regulation hinges on prudential concerns because of the special fiduciary nature of finance, maturity mismatches, and the adverse spillover effects associated with the failure of banks, mentioned above. Regulatory agencies aim, therefore, to promote the safety of depositors' assets by limiting banks' risk taking and requiring extensive and accurate disclosure of their activities.

Governments in industrial countries have developed standards for information and information processing in the form of accounting and auditing standards. National regulatory authorities also impose capital adequacy standards, liquidity requirements, and compliance reviews. To prevent the systemwide spread of problems originating in one industry, they have often enforced the segmentation of financial services by activity and in some cases (such as banking in the United States) by geography.

Financial firms in industrial countries must also provide extensive information on and analysis of lenders and borrowers. Even in these countries, however, financial systems remain far from perfect. For example, the US savings and loan debacle of the late 1980s demonstrated serious flaws in the incentive structure that the publicly funded deposit insurance system presented to service providers.

Regulatory changes can bring about large changes in industry activity and structure because they tend to impose implicit taxes on the one hand (e.g., through reserve requirements, interest ceilings, and disclosure requirements, which increase costs of intermediation) and implicit subsidies on the other (e.g., through publicly funded deposit insurance and lender-of-last-resort facilities; Walter 1993). In some cases, regulatory constraints have done more to shift activities from one location to another than to achieve their defined objectives. In 1963, the interest equalization tax introduced in the United States contributed to the creation of the eurodollar market. In the early 1980s, Japanese authorities imposed high tax rates on interest income but no taxes on capital gains. The net impact was to create demand for zero-coupon eurobonds. Germany's restrictions on derivative instruments have resulted in most futures trading in German government bonds taking place in London (Herring and Litan 1995, 20). These examples illustrate the dynamic interaction between regulation and innovation: regulation creates incentives for the regulated firms to innovate, in an effort to circumvent the regulation; as these efforts succeed, regulators are forced to counter with new regulation or, at times, deregulation.

Although parts of the financial services sector remain subject to heavy regulation, the business is increasingly competitive and internationalized. Many of the new businesses involve cross-institutional and cross-border transactions. This increasing complexity has eroded the effectiveness of regulation (which creates a moral hazard anyway by implicitly subsidizing risky activity) and increased the risk of negative spillovers—on an international scale—when things go wrong. Increasing financial integration also implies that regulatory policies become central determinants of the efficiency and competitiveness of a country's financial industry. As a result, regulatory arbitrage—that is, competition among countries' regulatory systems—has increased and become one of the central forces driving regulatory change. As Herring and Litan (1995) argue, such competition need not result in regulatory laxity. Instead, the focus can shift to the quality of regulation: its capacity to deliver results in terms of financial efficiency, stability, and security. The extent to which regulatory change should be promoted through greater harmonization of national regulatory regimes to create a level playing field or, alternatively, through competition among these regimes is the subject of intense debate (see Barfield 1996; White 1996). Nevertheless, the European Union is moving in this direction, and this is the purpose of ongoing WTO negotiations.

Cross-Border Activity and International Integration

Technological innovation in financial services has widened the choice of services, instruments, and institutions available to users and increased the ability of providers to meet their customers' financing needs. But it has also created new problems. Regulators have had to make trade-offs between achieving their domestic objectives and losing economic activity to locations with more liberal regimes, or to foreign institutions. Most

Table A.2   Net financing in international markets, 1994-96
(billions of dollars)

Component	1994	1995	1996	Stock outstanding as of end-1996
Net international bank lending	190.0	330.0	405.0	5,015.0
Net euronote placements	140.2	192.4	265.0	834.1
Net international bond financing[a]	145.2	119.2	275.1	2,391.8
Total[b]	415.0	530.0	745.0	6,390.0

Note: For bank lending and euronote placements, data in the first three columns are changes in year-end amounts outstanding, excluding exchange rate valuation effects; data for bond financing are actual flows.
a. Excludes bonds issued under EMTN programs, which are included in euronote placements.
b. Entries do not sum to totals because double counting has been excluded.
Source: Bank for International Settlements (1997, table VII.1).

countries have chosen to relax their rules and become more open and, in the process, intensify international competition and deepen international integration.

Consider some of the volumes of interinstitutional and international financial flows in 1996, reported by the Bank for International Settlements (BIS 1997) and in table A.2. Both stocks and flows are very large.

■ The stock of debt in the international interbank lending market was estimated to total $5.8 trillion.

■ Net international bank lending totaled $405 billion—an increase of 23 percent over 1995 and of 113 percent over 1994.

■ Net euronote placements totaled $265 billion—an increase of 38 percent over 1995 and of 89 percent over 1994.

■ Net international bond financing totaled $275 billion—an increase of 131 percent over 1995 and of 89 percent over 1994.

■ Daily average turnover in foreign exchange markets, much of it accounted for by banks, was estimated to total $1.6 trillion.

These data illustrate in dramatic fashion the rising volume of international financial activity, particularly in securities issues, which now exceeds international lending (although in recent years this may represent more a shift in risk management strategies than an increased financing of the real economy). The outstanding volume of exchange-traded derivatives (futures and options in interest rates, currencies, and stock market indices) reached $10 trillion at the end of 1996, twice the volume of world trade in goods and services (WTO 1997). Growth in this activity

Figure A.1 Activity in international financial markets

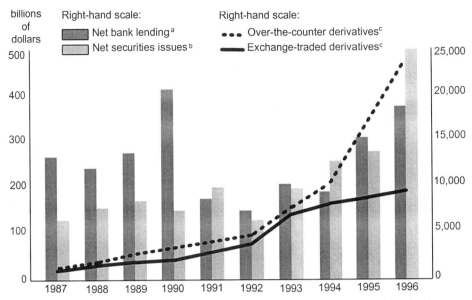

a. Changes in amount outstanding, excluding exchange rate valuation effects and interbank redepositing.
b. Net issues (excluding exchange rate valuation effects) of international bonds and euronotes.
c. Notional amounts outstanding at end-year.

Source: BIS (1997, 118).

has slowed since 1993, but meanwhile, outstanding over-the-counter derivative contracts (swaps and swap-related derivatives) have expanded rapidly. These were estimated at close to $25 trillion at the end of 1996, up from $5 trillion in 1992 and $10 trillion in 1994 (figure A.1).

Unfortunately, statistics on the size of the underlying cross-border trade in financial services are not readily available. The only source consistently offering worldwide coverage is the International Monetary Fund's *Balance of Payments Statistics.*[2] The quality and coverage of the data in this publication have improved as more countries have adopted its methodology in measuring financial services trade. These data still need to be interpreted with caution, but three presumably robust findings emerge. The first is that imports and exports of financial services are quite significant for a number of countries, including developing countries (Brazil, China, Mexico, Singapore, South Korea, Thailand, and Turkey, among

2. World Bank (1997b) includes detailed tables on exports and imports of financial services for member countries (tables 4.10 and 4.11) derived from the balance of payments data files of IMF.

others) and transition economies (such as Poland). Second, the volume of that trade and its share of worldwide trade in all services expanded dramatically between 1980 and 1995 in many countries. Third, the most dynamic trade in services is in financial, brokerage, and leasing services: this category grew at an average annual rate of 9.5 percent from 1980 to 1993, rising from 37 percent to 45 percent of commercial services trade during that period.

It should be noted, however, that cross-border trade figures provide only a partial indication of the scale of international financial activity; they omit some important dimensions of that activity covered by the WTO negotiations on financial services. The GATS distinguishes between several modes of service delivery. Cross-border trade is one of these. But an important aspect of international "trade" stems from the commercial presence of firms in countries other than their home country. The stock of foreign direct investment (FDI), which is necessary for that commercial presence, has grown dramatically, mainly among industrialized countries, but also in the emerging markets. In the 1991-94 period, total international FDI inflows grew at a 13 percent annual rate; gross product of foreign affiliates grew more than 11 percent per year, while exports of goods and services increased at only a 4 percent rate (UNCTAD 1996).

These statistical portraits suggest that financial markets have become increasingly globalized and that international financial integration is steadily increasing. It is far from complete, however, suggesting that the potential for further development of international financial activities involving trade and investment may be great. Herring and Litan (1995) carefully analyze the degree of international financial integration through the convergence of financial asset prices. They conclude that, among the leading industrial countries, short- to medium-term fixed-income assets, when insured against foreign exchange risk, are virtually perfect substitutes—that is, the condition of covered interest parity holds. This means that any country premium on such assets has disappeared. But this is certainly not the case worldwide, and even among the industrial countries, integration is far from perfect. For longer-term instruments, residual country premiums still interfere with the international substitutability of comparable assets across borders; moreover, uncertainty about future nominal and real exchange rate movements remains an irreducible obstacle to deeper integration.

The Importance of Emerging Markets

The fortunes of developing and industrial countries are increasingly linked. The former now account for 45 percent of global output on a purchasing power parity basis, 36 percent of global foreign direct investment inflows, 30 percent of global portfolio capital inflows, 11 percent of global stock market capitalization, 12 percent of global issuance of international bonds, and 11 to 13 percent of global banking assets (Goldstein 1997, 7).

Private capital flows to developing countries are growing rapidly (table A.3), with China topping the list of destinations since 1991 (World Bank 1997). In the 1990-96 period these private flows increased fivefold; they accounted for 85 percent of total flows to developing countries in 1996. Portfolio debt investment grew by 50 percent between 1995 and 1996, as an increasing volume of bonds was issued by public and private borrowers, many of them in East Asian countries. Portfolio equity investment also moved ahead strongly, as pension funds, hedge funds, and other investment vehicles invested increasing amounts in developing-country stock markets. Commercial bank loans also continued to grow, but at a more modest pace. Many of the borrowers were private-sector firms; indeed, the World Bank estimates that private-sector borrowers now account for more than two-thirds of all capital flows to developing countries (World Bank 1997).

These trends are the result of two major factors. One is that rates of return in industrial countries have declined as interest rates have dropped, inflation has declined, and public sector budget deficits are reduced. Large institutional investors have also become more familiar with developing-country financial markets and have become increasingly aggressive in seeking the higher rates of return available (despite the higher risks) in these markets.

The second factor is the change in the financial sectors of developing countries, especially in the more advanced countries of the group, which are often termed "emerging markets." Financial services in these countries are at various stages of development. A useful stylization for understanding these differences has been developed by Frankel (1995). In the first phase of development, an increasing proportion of national saving is channeled to investment, as internally generated funding and informal financing from family, friends, and business associates are gradually replaced by market transactions and institutions. Government involvement has typically been extensive at this stage, however, in an attempt to promote growth through artificially low interest rates, directed credit, and subsidies and other incentives to socially desirable activities. State-owned banks in 1994 still accounted on average for 33.5 percent of banking assets in key emerging markets (table A.1).

In the second phase, as incomes rise and development proceeds, markets are created and financial deepening (a rise in the ratio of financial to real activity) occurs. Financial intermediaries develop and improve the provision and circulation of information as well as monitoring capability. Short-term money markets begin to emerge. These institutions also raise the productivity of capital in the economy and create better incentives for saving. To allow market forces to function, governments at this stage have often removed administrative regulations, privatized state-owned assets, and allowed market forces to determine interest rates.

In the third phase, disintermediation begins as demand for longer-term assets appears and as direct finance institutions enter the market. Government bonds become the initial mainstay of the bond market; frequent and regular public-sector bond issues help to deepen and broaden these markets. Markets for corporate bonds and equities, and eventually for derivative instruments, follow.

Inherent in this process is an increasing sophistication on the part of financial institutions in mobilizing the economy's resources and securing linkages between lenders and borrowers. Savers are unlikely to lend directly to borrowers they do not know or for investment projects they do not understand without a hefty risk premium, if at all. By gathering information on the would-be users of funds and their proposed investments, financial institutions reduce this premium and stimulate economic growth (Caprio, Atiyas, and Hanson 1996).

Financial reform, through deregulation of interest rates, privatization, and relaxation of restrictions on the activities of intermediaries, is proceeding rapidly in many developing countries. But two major constraints remain. First, underdeveloped capital markets hold back the emergence of long-term private-sector finance as well as financial intermediation among developing countries. Second, strong supervisory systems are lacking. Successful development of capital markets depends, in part, on strong supervision. The huge long-term capital requirements for infrastructure financing in the East Asian economies and the rapid aging of their populations imply that those economies that have not yet done so will have little choice but to develop bond and equity markets to attract savings (both domestic, which can go out of the country, and foreign). They must also develop the financial infrastructure, including standards of disclosure and risk management, oversight and supervision, clearing and payments systems, modern accounting rules, and legal systems necessary to modern financial systems that channel savings efficiently into productive investments.

Since the mid-1980s, growth in money markets has been most rapid in Taiwan and Malaysia, followed by South Korea, Indonesia, and Thailand. In 1994, government issues dominated East Asian bond markets, followed by those of corporate and state enterprises; central banks were still lagging. By that year as well, Malaysia led the region (excluding the international financial centers of Hong Kong and Singapore) with respect to bank assets and stock market capitalization measured as shares of GDP. It was followed by Thailand and, much further back, the Philippines and South Korea. The market capitalization of the East Asian stock markets reached more than 1 trillion dollars, or 71 percent of the region's GDP (World Bank 1995a). This growth is attributed to a surge

Table A.3 Net private capital flows to developing countries, 1990-96
(billions of dollars)

	1990	1991	1992	1993	1994	1995	1996[a]
Debt	2.3	10.1	9.9	35.9	29.3	28.9	45.8
Equity	3.2	7.2	11.0	45.0	32.7	32.1	45.7
Foreign direct investment	24.2	33.8	45.9	67.7	79.4	91.8	93.2
Commercial bank debt	3.0	2.8	12.5	−0.3	11.0	26.8	34.2
Other private flows	11.3	3.3	13.5	9.2	4.6	1.7	8.3
Total	44.0	57.2	92.8	157.6	157.0	181.2	227.1

a. Preliminary estimates.

Source: World Bank (1997a).

in the supply of foreign portfolio investment, particularly from institutional investors, attracted by the regional boom.

But demand is growing. The World Bank (1995b, 4) estimates that large anticipated infrastructure financing requirements will have to be met through bond markets. The combined capitalization of East Asia's bond markets was $338 billion in 1994—a tenth the size of Japan's and a twentieth of that in the United States. Raising the necessary capital on international bond markets will be constrained by the lack of liquid swap markets in the region's currencies. Housing demand will also be met by moving beyond the current dependence on the banking industry for mortgage loans. Yet, to date only Malaysia has developed a mortgage-backed securities market. New classes of investors, including insurance companies and provident funds, emerged in the 1980s in several countries, with funds totaling more than $80 billion by 1994 (World Bank 1995a). The large contractual savings sector faced similar problems until investment policies were liberalized; these institutions are now seeking long-term fixed-income instruments to minimize mismatches.

The development of local pension funds is likely to have important implications for financial systems and regional intermediation in Asia. Currently, international capital is readily available from pension funds, hedge funds, and mutual funds in the industrial countries, as demonstrated by the large portfolio flows shown in table A.3. Pension funds alone in these countries have assets in excess of $10 trillion. Meanwhile, the US mutual fund industry is growing so rapidly that some predict that its assets may surpass those of the US banking system by 2001 (Hale 1997), although such an outcome is contingent on the continuance of current growth conditions in the US securities markets, which may be unlikely. At the same time, however, East Asian populations are aging rapidly; national pension funds are therefore likely to emerge as important new players in the industry.

Well-developed pension systems already exist in Singapore and Malaysia, and the Japanese pension fund industry is expected to expand substantially in the next 25 years. Singapore's national pension system, the Central Provident Fund (CPF), is a dominant force in financial intermediation in the city-state. Contributors to the CPF tend to be very conservative in the deployment of their savings; traditionally, the greater part of surplus CPF funds is placed in government securities through the Monetary Authority of Singapore. In 1993, the regime was liberalized to permit investment in a range of instruments, including domestic stocks, gold, government bonds, fund management accounts, and endowment-type insurance policies (Walter 1993). Japanese pension funds have poor performance records, in part because they have been managed on the basis of close relationships with the companies in which they invest, rather than strictly on a performance basis. Economic liberalization is contributing to the emergence of a shareholder lobby concerned about performance, however.

While these developments in Singapore and Japan, together with the growth of pension funds in other Asian economies (where these funds traditionally have been small), will have important implications for regional intermediation, they have a long way to go to head off some of the risks that contributed to the Asian financial crisis. Southeast Asian financial markets are not yet efficient intermediators of local or international finance. Short-term foreign capital has often been used to finance long-term domestic investment, contributing to maturity mismatches that characterized part of the crisis. Risk assessment has been inadequate, with lending decisions made on criteria other than creditworthiness of borrowers (although part of the reason for this was the practice of banks, especially those in business groups, to regard loans to connected borrowers as quasi-equity, rather than short-term debt). Better management in East Asian financial markets would help to provide high-performance vehicles for domestic and foreign savings; financial flows would be less prone to the huge swings in foreign capital experienced in the 1997-98 crisis. These shortcomings are closely related to the inadequacy of supervision and infrastructure in financial markets, the second constraint discussed below, but they also provide a strong reason for governments to undertake domestic reforms and to facilitate more entry of foreign firms.

The second constraint is inadequate supervision of financial markets and inadequate financial infrastructure. Industrial-country governments have developed strong supervisory frameworks (in part in response to past financial crises) and information disclosure requirements. Financial-market analysts also contribute much of the information required to manage risk successfully. Most developing countries still lack such systems, although the frameworks for them often exist on paper. One of the main reasons for this inadequacy is past practices of government intervention through bank ownership, artificially low interest rates, directed credit programs, and special loan approvals. These measures reduce the returns to financial institutions, limiting their incentive to invest in the information gathering necessary to manage risk; they also imply that governments will bail out failures. This underinvestment in information implies, in turn, underinvestment in human capital—in the skills required to evaluate and monitor investments and borrowers—and implies the need for large-scale change in the skills of credit analysts at banks, accountants, etc. Training such people will take time.

When financial reform occurs and governments withdraw, financial institutions may find themselves ill prepared to evaluate the creditworthiness of borrowers or the value of investment projects. Case studies also indicate that, because financial reforms often occur contemporaneously with structural adjustment of the economy, information on industries and firms rapidly becomes obsolete (Caprio, Atiyas, and Hanson 1996). In such an environment, the risk is that portfolio quality could quickly deteriorate. An essential ingredient of reform must be attention to the incentives facing financial institutions, to strengthen their systems of information collection and evaluation, which are central to successful risk management.

The State of Financial Reform in Major Emerging Markets

The evolution of financial-sector policy in developing countries over the past 20 to 25 years has been extensively surveyed (Fry, Goodhart, and Almeida 1996; Asian Development Bank 1995). Case studies of financial reform are also available (Caprio, Atiyas, and Hanson 1996; Lindgren et al. 1996). In this section we draw on this work to describe the major features of financial systems in several of the most important developing-country markets. These features are summarized in tables 3.1 and 3.3; the case studies in appendix B provide more detail. The economies examined include Argentina, Brazil, Chile, China, India, Indonesia, Malaysia, Mexico, the Philippines, South Korea, Taiwan, and Thailand. Japan, Singapore, and Hong Kong are also included. Although "big bang" reforms are slated to be enacted in Japan by 2001, the size of its market and the importance of its present domestic restrictions and barriers to entry call for that country's inclusion. Singapore and Hong Kong are included as benchmarks indicating what is possible.

In many of these countries, the status quo is anything but. Unilateral reform is occurring as governments privatize banks, free interest rates, deregulate financial services, open the domestic financial system to foreign competition and entry (albeit with reluctance, as already noted), and, to a lesser extent, free up foreign exchange transactions and the capital account. In general, governments' concerns about stability tend to outweigh the perceived benefits to users of lower-cost services and innovations spurred by greater competition and by technical transfer from foreign investors and service providers. Losers in the process, particularly those domestic service providers that have benefited from protection and lack of competition, are likely to stress concerns about institutional fragility, employment pressures, and macroeconomic stability.

Although some East Asian and Latin American economies embarked on gradual financial reform as early as the 1970s, their financial systems today are most heavily influenced by reforms undertaken since the early 1980s. As shown by Caprio, Atiyas, and Hanson (1996), the success of reform depends heavily on initial conditions. Crucial variables include the state of the banking industry, including the net worth of banks, the composition of their assets and liabilities, and their information-processing capabilities and human capital; the interest rate regime; portfolio requirements and the speed and control of portfolio diversification; the state of the supervisory system; the presence or absence of credit subsidization; the openness of the capital account; and the extent of restrictions on the entry of foreign institutions.

The characteristics of the financial sector in each of the emerging markets listed above and in Japan are summarized in table 3.3. Interest rates continue to be administered in China and India, and they were administered in Indonesia until recently. South Korea has only recently deregulated interest rates and reduced sectoral loan allocation requirements on banks; in addition, the country has committed itself to extensive reforms in connection with its accession to the OECD in 1996. In nearly all these economies, the banking, insurance, and securities industries remain segmented. Although policies toward banking have changed in the past 20 years, in most countries some form of government involvement in sectoral loan allocation persists (Asian Development Bank 1995), and the share of state-owned banks remains significant in Indonesia, Mexico, and Taiwan (table A.1). In 1994, India allowed its first privately owned bank to open, and entry restrictions on foreign banks were eased. India is encouraging the growth of markets in short-term government obligations, has established credit information bureaus, and has endorsed the standard for the adequacy of bank capital set by the Bank for International Settlements. The country's Securities and Exchange Commission has been strengthened. Indonesia has opened its banking industry to private banks through joint ventures, adopted the BIS capital standards, and imposed prudential requirements. The government has introduced more competition in the insurance sector and reformed its policies toward insurance and securities markets. Most of these economies are considering measures to develop capital markets; securities markets are already well developed in Singapore, South Korea, and Taiwan.

Indonesia and Malaysia are furthest along in developing the necessary related financial infrastructure, such as credit rating agencies.

The most sobering findings in table 3.3 are those listed in the far right-hand column, which indicate that most of these emerging-market economies, except in Malaysia, suffer from inadequate prudential supervision of banks, as shown by the recent crisis. In most, outside of Japan, the market infrastructure needed to ensure transparency between lenders and borrowers is also lacking, accounting standards are inadequate, trained supervisory manpower is inadequate, clearing and payments systems are underdeveloped, and governments are unwilling to let depositors bear the risk of bank failures. Many of these shortcomings will be addressed as part of IMF programs in Thailand, Indonesia, and South Korea. In other countries, progress will depend on whether authorities and interest groups draw the kind of lessons from the Asian financial crisis that are outlined in the first three chapters of this study.

Table 3.1 summarizes characteristics relating to economic openness. Capital account restrictions exist in Brazil, Chile, China, South Korea, and Taiwan (the last two are removing most remaining restrictions). National treatment is still not granted to foreign firms in China or Taiwan; nor is it granted to foreign insurance firms in Malaysia. Except in Argentina, Hong Kong, Japan, and South Korea, foreign entry in banking remains restricted. Foreign equity in banks is limited to 49 percent in Indonesia, 51 percent in Malaysia, 60 percent in the Philippines; new equity after 2007 is limited to 49 percent or less in Thailand. Entry in the insurance industry is also currently widely restricted, except in Argentina, Mexico (which grants liberal entry for other NAFTA countries), and Indonesia (where 49 percent holdings are permitted). Monopolies are common, and markets are crowded in life insurance, in part reflecting the absence of contractual saving, which develops as populations age and as long-term financial products emerge. In the securities industry, entry in many countries is limited to joint ventures. Foreign participation may be as much as 49 percent in Mexico. Thailand prohibits foreign participation in the industry, and Taiwan regulates tightly foreign activity and foreign ownership. As table 3.1 indicates, some progress on market-opening will be made as a result of the WTO negotiations, but it is most tangible in the insurance industry. Further progress will also occur in those countries on IMF programs; particularly in the case of Korea, reforms that go beyond what was committed in the WTO negotiations should also be bound in the WTO before the agreement is implemented in 1999.

Tables 3.1 and 3.3 show that there has been no cookie-cutter approach to financial reform in these countries. Except for the Singapore and Hong Kong international financial centers, Chile, Mexico, and Malaysia are the furthest along the road to freely functioning domestic markets. Malaysia is far less open than Mexico or Chile, but it has the best-developed supervisory system. China is the least liberalized of all and faces a major challenge to develop market-based institutions. India is also far behind, with an institutional base that is closed to entry and heavily restricted in its operations.

This analysis illustrates the variety of stages of modernization in emerging markets. As we have argued, the financial system is an important contributor to economic growth because it facilitates capital accumulation and accelerates productivity growth. One of the highest priorities of reform should be to strengthen systemic incentives for financial institutions to collect and evaluate information so that they can handle risk adequately. Yet, as we have seen, this is probably the most common barrier to safe and efficient capital markets in these emerging-market economies.

APPENDIX B

Case Studies

STEFANIE FISCHEL AND BIRGITTA WEITZ

This annex includes case studies of the financial systems in the major emerging markets, Japan, Hong Kong, and Singapore. Each study describes the regulatory framework for financial services, the institutions of financial intermediation and direct finance, conditions of foreign participation, and the remaining obstacles to the development of efficient, safe, and open financial systems in these economies. Major features of these case studies are summarized in tables 3.1 and 3.3. It is important to note that, in the wake of the Asian financial crisis in 1997-98, market forces and conditions associated with IMF rescue packages required numerous changes in regulatory frameworks and foreign entry. To the extent that these changes had occurred and were reported by February 1998, they are incorporated in these case studies.

Argentina

Introduction

Liberalization of the financial sector in Argentina has been a gradual process with many reverses. Until the 1970s the financial system was controlled and directed entirely by the public sector. In 1977-78, the government liberalized the capital account and removed many barriers to the domestic allocation of financial resources, including ceilings on interest rates.[1] Although fairly comprehensive prudential regulations were introduced, they were not adequately monitored or enforced. In 1980, as world interest rates rose, the number of nonperforming loans also rose, resulting in the failure of one major bank. The government halted and eventually reversed market opening measures in response to the loss of international reserves that precipitated the 1982 debt crisis. That year, reserve requirements of 100 percent were reintroduced and controls imposed on deposit rates. With inflation running at an average of over 250 percent annually from 1981 to 1983, the existing currency was replaced in 1985 by the austral, which was fixed at a rate of 0.8 per dollar.[2] A

1. In contrast to other countries moving from a highly controlled to an open-market economy, Argentina liberalized the capital account before opening the current account. Some steps were taken to begin opening the current account, such as the removal in 1976-78 of quantitative restrictions on goods. In 1979 a major trade liberalization program, implemented to dramatically lower tariffs over a period of five years, was initiated; however, the program was abandoned as a result of financial difficulties facing the public sector during the debt crisis. See Cavallo and Cottani (1991) for a detailed description of current and capital account liberalization in Argentina from 1977 to 1981.

2. The austral was Argentina's currency from 1985 to 1991.

dual exchange rate was also introduced. Attempts to stabilize the economy included the introduction of wage and price controls, higher tariffs, and increased foreign-sector borrowing to finance the deficit.

Confidence was not restored, however, as debt problems mounted and another major bank closed. A currency crisis ensued. Private-sector banks encountered more difficulties as deposit growth slowed in the face of low, administered interest rates. The high demand for credit by the public sector placed a further strain on the entire financial system. By mid-1988, public banks accounted for over 70 percent of outstanding loans.

During the late 1980s and early 1990s, the policy direction reversed. Privatization and deregulation measures were introduced in 1987, the exchange rate was unified in 1989, and restrictions on foreign investment were subsequently eased. High and accelerating inflation continued to be a problem, however, with the annual rate of inflation rising to 2,314 percent in 1990 (Galbis 1995, 28). In 1991, Argentina implemented the Convertibility Plan. Under the plan, Argentina adopted a currency board, eliminated all controls on foreign exchange, and required the Central Bank of the Republic of Argentina (BCRA) to back the monetary base with a combination of foreign exchange reserves, gold, and other foreign assets. Reserve requirements were reduced and financial sector supervision strengthened. Within two years after introducing the Convertibility Plan, inflation fell from 171 to 10.6 percent, interest rates dropped from 71 to 6 percent, and nonperforming loans dropped from 37 to 17 percent of all outstanding loans.

The Financial Institutions Law was adopted in 1994, significantly improving market access for foreign financial institutions. A preexisting reciprocity requirement was removed and national treatment established with the law. A moratorium on new banking licenses was also lifted, opening Argentina's financial sector to foreign competition.

Regulatory Framework

The Financial Entities Law (FEL), enacted in 1977, defines permissible activities for the following institutions: commercial banks, investment banks, mortgage banks, savings and loans associations, credit agencies, and financial companies. Commercial banks are allowed to engage in any of the services provided by any of the financial institutions subject to the FEL and thus, effectively, operate under a universal banking model. Financial service firms other than commercial banks are limited to offering those services assigned by the FEL to each specific type of institution (EIU 1996b, 12). Foreign investors can only establish commercial banks and investment banks in Argentina. Foreign commercial banks are, however, permitted to merge with or acquire 100 percent ownership of any category of financial institution. Foreign investors are also permitted to acquire 100 percent ownership of financial service firms not covered by the FEL.

All financial institutions subject to the FEL are regulated and supervised by the BCRA. Establishing a new financial entity, or acquiring or merging with existing firms covered by the FEL, is subject to authorization by the BCRA. The BCRA also has the authority to fine a firm or revoke its authorization to operate if the firm is found to be in violation of the FEL. Liquidity and capital requirements are set by the BCRA. A semiautonomous branch of the BCRA, the Superintendency of Financial and Exchange Entities, monitors and enforces compliance with the FEL and with rules promulgated by the BCRA.

Securities are regulated by the National Securities Commission (CNV). In 1990, the CNV initiated a series of reforms to deregulate the securities industry and strengthen the equity market. In 1990 and 1991, restrictions on bank ownership of brokerage firms were eliminated, as were fixed commissions and transfer taxes. The CNV has also implemented new financial and economic reporting requirements in order to increase transparency, and it is responsible for ensuring that publicly listed corporations comply with reporting requirements.

Argentine law distinguishes between a stock exchange and a securities market. Stock exchanges bring together an array of entities—private investors, traders, market makers, and firms issuing or underwriting securities—for the purpose of trading securities. Stock exchanges are self-regulating organizations that establish and enforce listing requirements and are responsible for processing and approving applications to list on the exchange. Final approval by the CNV is required in order to list on a stock exchange. The Buenos Aires Stock Exchange is the main exchange in Argentina.

Securities markets consist exclusively of businesses that trade securities. They also establish the trading requirements for their member corporations. Only five of the eleven exchanges in Argentina have securities markets, the most notable of which is the Buenos Aires Securities Market (Merval), the operating arm of the Buenos Aires Stock Exchange.

Argentina's private pension funds (AFPJs) are supervised and regulated by the Superintendency of AFPJs, which also monitors their performance. Pension funds that earn 30 percent below the average for all funds are required to inject capital into the fund so that the return to investors is no worse than 30 percent below the systemwide average return.

Financial Institutions

Finance and insurance accounted for 4.7 percent of Argentina's GDP in 1985 and 6.7 percent in 1995. The number of financial institutions in Argentina has fallen from 214 in 1991, when the Convertibility Plan was implemented, to 205 in December 1994, just before the Mexican peso crisis hit, to 146 in December 1996. Equity market capitalization as a percentage of GDP in Argentina remains low compared to other emerging markets. In 1996, market capitalization was 15.7 percent of GDP in Argentina; figures for Brazil, Mexico, and India that year are 28.6 percent, 37.1 percent, and 35.1 percent respectively (BIS 1997, 105).

Financial Intermediaries

The banking sector in Argentina is characterized by a large number of undercapitalized banks competing for a small but rapidly growing deposit base. While bank deposits in Argentina are only 19 percent of GDP (compared to 40 percent in Chile), they are projected to grow at an average annual rate of 20 percent per year.

The peso crisis and increasing competition have caused the number of financial institutions in Argentina to fall considerably over the last five years. There were 132 private banks and 35 public banks in 1991, whereas by the end of 1996 these figures had dropped to 98 and 22, respectively. The decline in the number of public banks is, in part, attributable to the privatization of provincial and municipal banks. The number of nonbank financial institutions has also dropped dramatically, however, from 47 in 1991 to 26 in 1996. Nonbank financial institutions were most affected by the peso crisis; by the end of 1996 cooperatives accounted for less than 1 percent of total loans. As a result of the decline in the number of banks in Argentina, the industry is beginning to consolidate. At the end of 1996, the top 20 banks in Argentina accounted for 75 percent of total bank deposits compared to 65 percent two years earlier.

Bank operating costs have, in the past, been extremely high in Argentina. In 1994, operating costs for private banks were 8.5 percent of total assets. By way of comparison, in the same year, bank operating costs as a percent of total assets were 3.9 percent in Mexico, 3.0 percent in Chile, and 2.3 percent in India. The industry consolidation over the past five years, however, is forcing banks to become more efficient in order to compete in the market. By the end of 1995, bank operating costs in Argentina had fallen to 5.6 percent of total assets. This figure is likely to continue to fall as a number of large banks aggressively compete for the financial services market.

Despite the fact that Argentina has privatized approximately one-third of the provincial and municipal banks, state-owned banks continue to account for a very large share of banking sector activity. In 1994, state-owned banks held 39 percent of all deposits in the banking sector, and in 1996, after the peso crisis and industry consolidation, they still accounted for 37 percent. The degree of public ownership of the financial sector has exacerbated overall financial sector difficulties because of the disproportionately high number of nonperforming loans held by publicly owned banks. At the end of 1996, nonperforming loans held by public banks represented 19 percent of total lending, compared to 8 percent in privately held banks. The recently approved privatization of the nation's largest mortgage bank will increase the role of the private sector in the banking system and is likely to promote greater attention to risk-based lending practices in a market subject to a relatively high proportion of nonperforming loans.

Argentina's credit market is relatively segmented. Subsidiaries of international firms with operations in Argentina have access to credit at low rates, as do individuals seeking financing for some consumer goods or mortgages. Foreign finance companies and banks compete aggressively in the market for large consumer goods such as automobiles and housing. Although foreign venture capital and equity funds have expanded operations in Argentina over the last five years, medium-term financing for medium-sized companies and credit for smaller companies and some consumer goods continues to be difficult to access and expensive. This situation has been made worse by the fact that the majority of banks that failed after the Mexican peso crisis were those that served the small business and individual credit market.

In 1994, Argentina created a private pension fund system that, based on the Chilean model, coexists with the public pension system. When the system was established, individuals had until July 1996 to move funds between the private and public systems. Those in the public system after that date could transfer assets to the private system at any time; however, those in the private system after that date were not allowed to return to the public pension system. More than two-thirds of the labor force belongs to a private pension fund. Individuals are permitted to move their savings from one pension fund to another (AFPJs) twice a year.

Twenty-one private pension funds have been formed by banks, insurance firms, unions, and private hospitals. Market concentration is relatively high, with six pension fund managers holding approximately 70 percent of private pension fund assets. The average rate of return for private pension funds was 20 percent in 1996, with roughly 16 percent of assets held in local equities, 49 percent in debt issued by federal and provincial governments, 14 percent in bank-issued certificates of deposit, and 3 percent in investment funds. Total assets held by private pension funds are expected to grow from $6 billion, or 2 percent of GDP, in 1997 to $118 billion, or 21 percent of GDP, in 2010 (*LatinFinance,* June 1997, 59).

Members of pension funds are required to buy disability and life insurance, thereby contributing to rapid growth in the insurance industry over the past six years. From 1991 to 1995, real premium volume in life insurance grew at an average annual rate of 32.5 percent, whereas real premium volume in nonlife insurance grew at an average annual rate of

Table B.1 Argentina: Assets of financial institutions, 1994 and 1997

	Number of institutions[a]	Percentage of assets	
		1994	1997
Public banks			
National	3	19.6	15.4
Provincial and municipal	18	22.5	19.9
Private banks			
Domestic	71	33.4	36.2
Foreign	28	15.0	19.8
Nonbank financial institutions	26	9.4	3.6
Pension fund managers[b]	21	na	5.1
Insurance companies	356	na	na

na = not available.
a. Number of institutions refers to 1997 figures.
b. The private pension fund system was created in 1994.

Sources: Republic of Argentina, Economic Report, First Quarter 1997, and authors' calculations.

6.3 percent. The insurance market, like other financial services industries in Argentina, was adversely affected by the Mexican peso crisis, with sales falling by 5.6 percent in 1995, but growth is expected to accelerate as more funds transfer from the public sector to the private pension system.

The insurance market has undergone significant changes since it was deregulated in 1992.[3] As in the banking sector, the insurance industry is characterized by a large number of inefficient firms. Increased competition following deregulation and the contraction of the industry in 1995 forced less efficient firms out of the market. From 1992 to 1997, more than 60 insurance firms were liquidated.

As of early 1997, 356 insurance companies were licensed to sell insurance in Argentina (see table B.1). Market concentration continues to be relatively low, and the industry still relatively inefficient when compared to that of other Latin American emerging markets. The top five insurance companies in Argentina control approximately 35 percent of the market; comparative estimates range from an estimated 50 percent in Brazil and Chile to 70 percent in Mexico. Acquisition fees and administrative costs are, as a percentage of total premiums, higher in Argentina than in other Latin American countries. Despite rapid premium-volume growth, the industry has sustained heavy losses since 1990 and is not likely to rebound until the market consolidates and insurance underwriting is more closely linked to the risk level of the customer base.

---

3. The following section is based on an analysis of the Latin American insurance industry reported by Sigma (1997).

Direct Finance

The Buenos Aires Stock Exchange (BASE), established in 1854, is the oldest in Latin America. In 1996, total market capitalization was $45 billion and 147 companies were listed on the BASE. The number of companies is less than it was a decade ago but market capitalization is substantially higher. Much of the growth in the equity market occurred in 1990-93, when market capitalization grew by more than 1,200 percent, from $3.3 billion to $44 billion.

A significant part of the growth in market capitalization over the past five years is due to the privatization of utility companies in Argentina. The equity market is highly concentrated; for example, three recently privatized companies—YPF, Telefonica, and Telecom—accounted for almost 50 percent of current market capitalization in 1997. The banking sector represents 8 percent of market capitalization, with roughly 90 percent of that amount accounted for by American Depository Receipts (ADRs) issued by two banks, Galicia Bank and Frances del Rio de la Plata Bank. An electronic over-the-counter market accounts for 40 percent of total private securities activity in Argentina.

Although still underdeveloped, the securities market is quickly maturing. In March 1996, the government introduced new medium- and long-term treasury bills and bonds. Loan syndications also are increasingly used as a source of medium- to long-term finance. The tradition of family-owned businesses is slowly giving way to firms willing to finance operations in the equity market. The CNV has also authorized the issuance of shares that carry voting rights. An options and futures markets is under development in Buenos Aires and was scheduled to be operational by March 1998.

Prudential Regulation

After the Mexican peso crisis, the BCRA replaced minimum reserve requirements, which applied only to demand deposits, with liquidity requirements, which apply to all financial liabilities. In contrast to reserve requirements, which were held by the BCRA in accounts earning zero interest, liquidity requirements can be held in interest-bearing "liquidity notes" or in bonds issued by an OECD country. Homogeneous liquidity requirements have been established for each type of asset held by financial institutions, and are a function of the volume of average monthly deposits or other liabilities held by a financial institution and the time until liabilities reach maturity. They range from 17 percent of demand deposits and savings accounts to 12 percent for time deposits of 90 to 179 days to zero for liabilities due to mature in over 365 days.

Capital requirements have been raised since the Mexican peso crisis and are now calculated based on the risk of assets held by a financial institution. Risk and associated capital requirements are a function of two factors: counterparty and market risk. The former is calculated according to Basle recommendations, in which assets are weighted by the type of risk associated with each. In addition to the Basle standards, firms are required to increase the weight given to assets according to the interest rate on the asset. CAMEL ratings are also considered in calculating total counterparty risk and capital-asset reserves.[4] The minimum capital-asset ratio required in Argentina, based on counterparty risk, is 11.5 percent, compared to the Basle committee recommendation of 8 percent. Banks in Argentina are required to add market risk, determined by calculating the risk of a bank's portfolio, to counterparty risk in assessing total capital-asset ratio requirements. The minimum capital required to establish a new bank is $15 million for retail banks and $10 million for wholesale banks.

Compliance with regulations is monitored through a combination of regular off-site and on-site inspections and submission of daily, monthly, and annual reports. Larger firms with higher risk are inspected at least once a year and small, less risky institutions every 18 months. Financial institutions are required to maintain detailed reports on debtors as well as on operational and administrative costs.

The Financial Entities Law requires all financial institutions to contribute to the mandatory Deposit Guarantee Fund (DGF). Contributions to the fund are equal to between 0.03 percent and 0.06 percent of the bank's monthly average deposits plus an additional assessment based on the institution's level of risk. The DGF insures deposits of under 90 days for up to $10,000, and insures deposits of over 90 days for up to $20,000 (Duggan and Fernandez 1996, 135). Deposits in both pesos and foreign currencies are covered by the fund. The DGF is managed by the Deposit Insurance Company, which is composed of representatives of both the public sector and private financial institutions.

In 1992, the CNV issued regulations requiring any company issuing public offerings to be rated by at least two local credit-rating agencies. Any corporation issuing a security is required to file an annual financial statement within 70 days after the end of the fiscal year. Securities transactions resulting in a change in ownership or acquisition of more than 5 percent of voting rights in a company must be reported to the CNV. The proportion of investments that AFPJs may allocate to different types of securities is also regulated by the CNV. Up to 50 percent of a fund may be invested in government securities, 35 percent in equity, 28 per-

---

4. CAMEL ratings evaluate an institution based on capital, assets, management, earnings, and liquidity.

cent in corporate bonds with a minimum maturity of two years, and 14 percent in mortgage-backed securities (EIU 1996b, 16).

Foreign Participation

New laws enacted during the last five years have made Argentina a much more attractive environment for most foreign investors. The Economic Emergency Law and the Foreign Investment Law guarantee foreign and local investors equal treatment. Foreign financial firms regulated by the FEL have the option of conducting business in Argentina through a local branch, subsidiary, or representative office.[5] Prior to 1993, foreign firms had to register investments in Argentina and were subject to a three-year waiting period for capital repatriation, but laws concerning foreign investment were amended in 1993 to remove restrictions on the repatriation of capital and to allow foreign firms to invest in Argentina without authorization from or registration with the government. The sole exception is in the financial services sector: firms that intend to undertake new investments or increase capitalization in the banking sector must receive authorization from the BCRA. Foreign investors are, however, allowed to have 100 percent ownership and control of commercial banks and insurance companies, subject to receipt of a license to operate from the appropriate regulatory authority. The BCRA permits residents to hold accounts in foreign and domestic currency and recently authorized financial institutions to denominate checks in either dollars or Argentine pesos.

Despite the drop over the past four years in the number of foreign-owned financial institutions in Argentina, foreign participation in the country's banking industry is substantial and growing. Following a wave of foreign investment in May 1997, only one (Banco de Galicia) of the top ten private banks remains controlled solely by Argentine interests. Foreign investors are permitted to control a financial institution with less than 50 percent ownership; Banco Santander recently took control of Banco Rio de la Plata, Argentina's fourth largest lender, with 35 percent ownership. Hongkong and Shanghai Banking Corporation (HBSC) acquired 100 percent of shares in Banco Roberts, and the Spanish-based Banco de Bilbao Vizcaya acquired 72 percent ownership of Banco de Credito during the May 1997 surge of foreign investment in the banking industry.

After the Mexican peso crisis, there was significant capital outflow as well as a flight to quality within the Argentine banking system. The flight to quality benefited large and foreign banks at the expense of deposits held by cooperatives and smaller banks. From December 1994

---

5. Although these forms of ownership are authorized under Argentine law, they are not all bound in the WTO financial services agreement.

to December 1995, the share of deposits held by foreign banks rose from 16.5 percent to 19.2 percent of total deposits in financial institutions. This percentage subsequently fell to 18.2 percent in December 1996, but the number of foreign banks also fell from 31 to 28 during those 12 months.

Deposits and lending in the hands of foreign-controlled banks are likely to continue to increase in the next five years. Banking analysts predict that Argentina's top ten banks will account for more than 80 percent of banking sector activity by the end of that time period. Given that foreign investors are heavily invested in nine of those banks, domestic market concentration is likely to benefit foreign commercial banks. In addition, a number of foreign investment banks are actively involved in mergers and acquisitions taking place in both the financial and nonfinancial sectors.

Subject to approval to operate a financial entity, foreign investors are entitled to 100 percent ownership of brokerage firms and of commercial banks engaged in securities activities. There are no restrictions on foreign ownership of stocks listed on the exchange and there are few restrictions on foreign ownership of public securities.[6] No application or authorization is required to acquire debt or equity.

In December 1996, foreign portfolio investment reached a record $16.8 billion, far exceeding the pre-peso crisis record of $13 billion in September 1994. Of the December 1996 foreign portfolio investment, 57 percent was held in government securities, 42 percent in equity, and 1 percent in corporate debt.

The Argentine insurance industry was deregulated in 1992. Foreign investors have been permitted 100 percent ownership of insurance firms since that time. Sigma (1997, 27) estimates that 40 percent of the premium volume is sold by insurance companies that are fully or partially controlled by foreign investors.

Remaining Obstacles

Argentina's financial sector is still underdeveloped. Only one in five persons has a bank account, and access to capital is difficult for small firms and consumers. Although foreign and domestic private banks are free to compete in the market, the government continues to hold a substantial market share in the financial sector. Lending limits for foreign and domestic private banks are based on local branch capital (Financial Leaders Group 1997), restricting private banks' ability to expand their market share.

---

6. Foreign firms are not yet permitted to acquire shares in mass media.

Residents are not permitted to buy insurance policies offered by firms outside Argentina. However, the high inflation of the 1970s and 1980s discouraged long-term domestic savings, so many residents illegally purchased offshore life insurance policies that are now estimated to generate returns of $200 million annually (EIU 1996b, 15). This offshore activity has also been a factor in the lack of securities market development. Numerous licensed insurance companies in Argentina are currently inactive. Although foreign and domestic firms are allowed to acquire nonlife insurance licenses from inactive firms, there is a moratorium on new licenses in the nonlife insurance industry.

Argentina made substantial commitments to the WTO financial services deal that concluded on 13 December 1997, including the right of establishment for banks and securities firms. Acquired rights have also been grandfathered and 100 percent ownership has been guaranteed for firms in these industries. However, Argentina did not commit to the establishment of insurance branches (the one area in which market access has not been guaranteed) in its offer—an omission made more obvious in an environment that generally provides an open market for foreign financial services firms.

References

Banco Central de la República Argentina. 1996. Bulletin of Monetary and Financial Affairs. Buenos Aires: Banco Central de la República Argentina (October-December).

Bank for International Settlements (BIS). 1997. *67th Annual Report*. Basle: Bank for International Settlements.

Bisat, Amer, R. Barry Johnston, and Vasudevan Sundararajan. 1992. *Issues in Managing and Sequencing Financial Sector Reforms: Lessons from Experiences in Five Developing Countries*. WP/92/82. Washington: Monetary and Exchange Affairs Department, International Monetary Fund.

Carrizosa, Mauricio, Danny M. Leipziger, and Hemant Shah. 1996. The Tequila Effect and Argentina's Banking Reform. *Finance and Development* (March).

Cavallo, Domingo, and Joaquin Cottani. 1991. Argentina. In *Liberalizing Foreign Trade: Volume 1*, ed. by D. Papageorgiou et al. Cambridge: Basil Blackwell.

Duggan, Bernardo, and Leonardo Fernandez. 1996. Banking Yearbook 1996. *International Financial Law Review*, Special Supplement (July).

Economist Intelligence Unit (EIU). 1996a. *Argentina: EIU Country Profile 1996-97*. New York: The Economist Intelligence Unit.

Economist Intelligence Unit (EIU). 1996b. *Financing Foreign Operation: Argentina*. New York: The Economist Intelligence Unit (June).

Economist Intelligence Unit (EIU). 1997. *Financing Foreign Operation: Argentina*. New York: The Economist Intelligence Unit. Flash Updater (March).

Financial Leaders Group (FLG). 1997. *Barriers to Trade in Financial Services: Case Studies*. London: Barclays Place.

Galbis, Vicente. 1995. *Financial Sector Reforms in Eight Countries: Issues and Results*. WP/95/141. Washington: Policy Development and Review Department, International Monetary Fund.

Institute of International Bankers. 1996. Global Survey. New York: Institute of International Bankers.

International Monetary Fund (IMF). 1996a. *International Capital Markets*. Washington: International Monetary Fund (September).

International Monetary Fund (IMF). 1996b. *Argentina: Selected Issues and Statistical Appendix*. Washington: International Monetary Fund (October).

Lindgren, Carl-Johan, Gillian Garcia, and Matthew Saal. 1996. *Bank Soundness and Macroeconomic Policy*. Washington: International Monetary Fund.

Ministry of Economy and Public Works and Services. 1997. *The Updated Guide to Foreign Investment in Argentina*. (http://www.mecon.ar/inver.www1.htm).

Republic of Argentina. 1996. *Economic Report*. Argentina: Ministerio de Economía y Obras y Servicios Públicos.

Rojas-Suarez, Liliana, and Steven Weisbrod. 1995. *Achieving Stability in Latin American Financial Markets in the Presence of Volatile Capital Flows*. Working Paper Series 304. Washington: Inter-American Development Bank.

Rojas-Suarez, Liliana, and Steven Wiesbrod. 1996. *Building Stability in Latin American Financial Markets*. Working Paper Series 320. Washington: Inter-American Development Bank.

Rostau, Thierry. 1996. *Banking and Finance in South America*. London: FT Financial Publishing.

Sigma. 1997. *The Insurance Industry in Latin America: A Growing Competitive Environment*. No. 2/1997. Zurich: Swiss Reinsurance Company.

World Bank. 1990. *Argentina: Reforms for Price Stability and Growth*. Washington: World Bank.

Brazil

Introduction

Brazil has a unique history of adjusting to, and continuing to grow during, periods of high inflation. From 1965 to 1979, inflation averaged 30 percent and the economy grew at an average annual rate of 5.9 percent. From 1985 to 1990, inflation averaged 856 percent (ECLAC 1995, 21) and the economy grew at an average annual rate of 4.5 percent. Despite the relatively strong growth, the high inflation had significant social costs.[1] As a result, government expenditures kept increasing, as did pressure on the government to meet foreign debt payments. In an attempt to deal with these pressures, a new Constitution was written in 1988, transferring a significant amount of financial power to the states while leaving the responsibility for social programs with the federal government. The new Constitution also barred foreign financial institutions from establishing new branches or increasing market share in Brazil, unless determined to be in the national interest, negotiated in an international agreement, or based on reciprocity.

In further attempts to stabilize the economy, five new economic plans and four new currencies were adopted between 1986 and 1991. Each was unsuccessful. Real GDP was stagnant in 1990 and fell in 1992. By June 1994, inflation had reached an annual rate of 12,000 percent and real overnight interest rates peaked at 122 percent. Later that year, Brazil adopted the Real Plan. In contrast to earlier reforms, the Real

---

1. The burden of price instability fell disproportionately on low-income earners. For example, in Rio de Janeiro between 1980 and 1990, the real minimum wage fell by 47 percent, whereas the real average wage fell by 14 percent.

Plan was based largely on market mechanisms and included provisions to reform the fiscal sector. The government passed a bill through Congress to balance the budget and successfully brought inflation under control with the introduction of another new currency, the real.

The conversion to the real was completed on 1 July 1994. Although the real was initially on par with the dollar, a band was set within which the exchange rate was allowed to fluctuate. The band has been moved a number of times during the past three years in order to allow the real to gradually depreciate against the dollar, but the government has kept interest rates fairly high to help support the real within this band. By the end of the first year of the plan the average annual inflation rate was just under 30 percent, and it fell to 4.8 percent by the end of 1997. Interest rates have been permitted to drop as inflation has fallen, but they remain relatively high. The real is currently estimated to be between 10 and 30 percent overvalued.

The banking industry in Brazil has been forced to undergo a tremendous amount of restructuring since the implementation of the Real Plan. The high inflation rates of the 1970s and 1980s had made banking extremely profitable. Banks would delay payments and clearances on accounts earning low interest and invest funds in high-yield overnight government bonds. The real gain to banks from the cash depreciation that occurred between the time a bank received and paid funds—the "inflationary float"—is estimated to have generated profits equal to 1.5 percent of client deposits per day. From 1990 to 1993, inflationary revenue averaged 4 percent of GDP, compared to 2 percent from the 1940s until 1990 (Mendonça de Barros and Fancunda de Almeida Junior 1997, 3).

The high-profit, high-inflation phase of Brazil's financial services history left an interesting legacy. In order to maximize gains in the highly inflationary environment, financial institutions implemented a vast network of bank branches and some of the world's most advanced banking technology, including computer home banking and an extensive network of ATMs. Without market discipline, however, little attention was given to accurately investing in fixed costs, pricing banking services, or developing sound risk assessment techniques.

The impact on the financial sector of the Real Plan, and the concomitant loss of the inflationary float, was instantaneous. In 1994, banks earned US$10.4 billion; within one year, their earnings fell to US$500 million. The financial sector's contribution to GDP fell from a high of 15.6 percent in 1993 to 7 percent in 1995. Rather than reorganizing operations to lower costs, many banks reacted to the change in environment by increasing lending activity:[2] in 1994-95, loans to the private sector grew by 59 percent.

---

2. The Central Bank had tried to prevent a rapid expansion in credit by raising reserve requirements on deposits from 48 to 100 percent and on savings from 10 to 30 percent.

From December 1994 to August 1995, overdue and nonperforming loans grew from 7 percent to 12.5 percent of total loans in the financial system.[3] The least efficient banks were the first affected by the combined impact of the Real Plan, poor management and unsound lending practices, and the subsequent rise in nonperforming loans. In August 1995, Banco Economico, then the eighth largest bank in Brazil, failed. By November, fear of a widespread banking crisis led the government to implement a series of measures to help strengthen the financial sector. A deposit insurance system was created that month. In an effort to encourage mergers and acquisitions, and thereby strengthen existing institutions, the government increased minimum capital requirements for new financial institutions. The Central Bank was given enhanced power to intervene in financial institutions and require recapitalization, corporate reorganization, or change in ownership as deemed necessary.

Also during this period, barriers to foreign investment in the financial sector were lowered in order to help recapitalize the banking sector. A February 1995 amendment to the Constitution created a somewhat more level playing field for foreign direct investment. Firms incorporated and maintaining national headquarters in Brazil are, under the law, considered Brazilian irrespective of the nationality of their owners. Foreign firms entering the country in this manner are legally accorded national treatment. An executive decree issued in August 1995, building on language in the 1988 Constitution, opened the door for foreign participation in financial services by resolving that it is in the national interest. Foreign investment in the financial services industry resumed in early 1996 and foreign investors are now beginning to establish a presence in the Brazilian financial services market.

Regulatory Framework

The National Monetary Council (CMN) sets monetary, foreign exchange, and credit policy and is the primary regulator of all financial services activities. Four supervisory authorities—the Central Bank, the Securities and Exchange Commission (CVM), the Private Insurance Superintendency (SUSEP), and the Complementary Pension Secretariat (SPC)—implement regulations consistent with the policy direction and decisions of the CMN. The Minister of Finance is the president of the CMN.

---

3. Statistics referring to nonperforming loans do not include the National Mortgage Bank (CEF) or state-owned banks, BANESPA and BANERJ. Since 1996, both BANESPA and BANERJ have been bailed out by the government. If these banks were included in the totals, nonperforming loans as a percentage of total loans would have been significantly higher. For example, when BANESPA's books were reviewed by the Central Bank in 1995, auditors discovered $13 billion in bad debts, compared to the $1.9 billion in nominal capital held by the bank.

According to the 1964 law that established it, the Central Bank is an autonomous institution. It authorizes the operation of every financial institution and the investment of all foreign funds in Brazil. It has the exclusive right to issue currency, and it implements monetary policy through open-market operations, changes in the reserve requirement, and financial assistance to financial services institutions that need liquidity in order to remain solvent. The Central Bank administers government programs intended to promote the stability of the financial services industry, and is authorized to intervene in, take temporary control of, or liquidate a financial institution in order to protect the solvency of the national financial system. The Central Bank also executes programs and directives necessary to meet credit policy established by the CMN. Credit policy includes measures such as fixing interest rate ceilings and requiring commercial banks to lend funds to priority sectors of the economy.

In addition, the Central Bank is responsible for managing international reserves, directing all interventions in the foreign exchange market, and overseeing the activities of dealers authorized to undertake foreign exchange transactions. All foreign exchange transactions must be authorized by the Central Bank or an authorized foreign exchange dealer. Capital controls are set by the Central Bank.

Regulation and supervision of commercial banks, savings banks, universal banks, and mortgage companies are the responsibility of the Central Bank. Regulation and supervision of investment banks, securities brokers, securities dealers, and the commodities and futures exchange are shared between the Central Bank and the CVM. The CVM has primary responsibility for funds containing assets that yield variable returns, and the Central Bank primary responsibility for those that yield fixed returns.

The CVM is authorized to regulate and supervise all activities relating to the Brazilian securities market. In order to help prevent insider trading and ensure that investors have adequate information on the market, the main focus of Brazilian securities regulations is on disclosure. All companies listed on one of the nine stock exchanges in Brazil must first be registered with the CVM. Should a market participant be found in violation of securities law, the CVM is empowered to suspend or cancel authorization for a company to list shares on the market, for a broker or dealer to trade or distribute securities, or for a stock exchange to operate.

Financial Institutions

The 1988 Constitution provided for the creation of a new type of financial institution in Brazil, the multipurpose bank. Under the multipurpose bank model, financial institutions can conduct commercial banking, investment banking, real estate finance, and consumer finance within the same firm. Thus in 1994, banks accounted for 98 percent of total assets held by financial institutions. Despite recent growth in stock market performance, the market continues to account for a relatively small part of total financing in Brazil; in 1996, market capitalization was 28.6 percent of GDP. The majority of financial-sector activity takes place in publicly or privately owned multipurpose banks, a nationally owned mortgage bank, and one of several development banks. There are 271 multipurpose, commercial, development, and investment banks in Brazil; of these, 195 are multipurpose banks.

Financial Intermediaries

The commercial banking industry in Brazil has historically been dominated by publicly owned financial institutions; in 1996, state-owned banks accounted for approximately 50 percent of total banking-sector assets (*The Economist*, 12 April 1997, 11). Publicly owned national, regional, and state banks in Brazil compete directly with private banks, frequently offering the full range of services available in a multipurpose bank. For example, state-owned banks accept deposits and offer subsidized short-, medium-, and long-term credit to priority projects. In addition, they act as the bank for the state's finances and projects while also serving local retail customers. The National Treasury has controlling ownership of the Banco do Brasil, which serves as the operating arm of government monetary policy and is the largest commercial bank, ranked by assets and deposits, in Brazil and in Latin America.

In 1996, the Banco do Brasil held 21 percent of total demand deposits and conducted approximately 16 percent of foreign exchange transactions in Brazil (EIU 1997a, 17). The largest private financial institution in Brazil, Bradesco, has total assets equal to roughly one-third of total assets held by the Banco do Brasil. Added to this is the national public mortgage bank, which in 1995 ranked higher than the Banco do Brasil in total assets, deposits, and loans. At the end of 1995, the top 25 banks in Brazil accounted for more than 81 percent of total financial assets; state-owned commercial and mortgage banks accounted for 54 percent of those assets, as well as 65 percent of the deposits held in the top 25 banks.

In addition to public participation in the mortgage, commercial, and multipurpose banking markets, development banks continue to play an active role in credit allocation throughout Brazil. The National Economic and Social Development Bank (BNDES) has a budget of just under US$12 billion for 1997 and is reported to have lent approximately US$17 billion in 1996.[4] By way of comparison, World Bank loans in 1996 totaled $13.4

---

4. Figures for 1996 may not be indicative of average annual figures. In 1996, BNDES "advanced" US$7.5 billion to the state of São Paulo against future proceeds from the privatization of state assets. As part of a US$15 billion rescue package, the advance was made to the state so that it could meet outstanding debt payments to the state-owned bank, BANESPA.

billion. The BNDES also administers the privatization of state-owned assets as directed by the National Privatization Council, has been involved in advancing resources to state-owned banks facing liquidity problems, and allocates export financing.

Since late 1995, the banking sector has undergone considerable restructuring both at the firm level and with respect to industry ownership. Given the highly inefficient nature of Brazil's financial services industry over the past two decades, many banks are closing branches and reducing staff. From December 1994 to June 1996, employment in the banking industry fell from 643,000 to 600,000, and 400 of some 17,000 bank branches were closed.

Majority ownership has been transferred in 25 financial institutions over the last two years. Although the privatization of a number of state-owned banks is planned, changes in majority ownership have largely been confined to those between private-sector market participants. By some accounts, the influence of public financial institutions has diminished. This, however, is principally due to the impact that the loss of the inflation tax has had on the services industry in general.

In 1990, participation of private and public financial institutions in GDP was 4.6 percent and 8.1 percent, respectively. By 1995, private financial institutions accounted for 3.6 percent of GDP and public financial institutions 3.2 percent. Thus, if contribution to GDP is used as a proxy for the relative impact on economic activity of private versus publicly owned financial institutions, private-sector firms are beginning to play a larger role in economic activity. This shift is largely because their contribution to GDP has fallen by less than that of public financial institutions. This is consistent with the Ministry of Finance's estimate that the public banks appropriated 63 percent of revenue made from the inflationary float (Mendonça de Barros and Fancunda de Almeida Junior 1997, 7).

The insurance industry and private pension funds are still underdeveloped in Brazil. Growth in the insurance industry was slow in the early 1990s. While real growth in premium income reached 15.7 percent in 1995, it slowed in 1996 to 4 percent. The market is expected to double, though, by 2004, and domestic and foreign firms are actively attempting to establish a market presence in Brazil. The future of the private pension system will depend on the outcome of social security reforms currently under consideration in the Brazilian Congress.

Direct Finance

There are nine regional stock exchanges in Brazil, but the exchanges in São Paulo (Bovespa) and Rio de Janeiro (IBV) account for over 95 percent of market activity. Trading value on the São Paulo Exchange is approximately five times greater than on the Rio de Janeiro Exchange. Activity on the stock market is dominated by a limited number of firms. At the end of 1996, the ten largest publicly listed firms accounted for 37 percent of total market capitalization and 62 percent of the total value traded on the market. Institutional investors account for approximately 80 percent of stock market activity and retail investors the other 20 percent.

Between 1992, when the securities market was opened to foreign investors, and 1996, total market capitalization grew from US$45 million to US$217 million. Since early 1996, the stock market has grown at an extraordinary pace. The Bovespa index rose from 100 in January 1996 to over 240 in May 1997, although shares in a single firm, Telebras, currently account for 45 percent of the weight on the Bovespa.

The São Paulo Commodities and Futures Exchange was opened in 1986, and by 1995 was the third largest futures exchange in the world. The volume of transactions on the exchange was estimated at almost $5 trillion at the end of 1996.

Prudential Regulation

In 1994, the Central Bank directed all banks to raise minimum capital to R7.9 million and to increase their capital-asset ratios to at least the 8 percent recommended by the Basle Accord. Banks were given until April 1995 to comply with these requirements. Banks are also required to place reserve requirements with the Central Bank equal to 75 percent of demand deposits and 20 percent of time deposits.

There are separate minimum capital requirements for activities other than commercial banking that occur either in the department of a multipurpose bank or in a distinct business. Investment banks and real estate departments are required to maintain minimum capital of R7 million each. Authorization to engage in foreign exchange transactions requires R3.5 million in minimum capital. Capital held for one purpose cannot be counted toward minimum capital requirements for another type of service. A multipurpose bank offering all four types of service would therefore be required to hold almost R25.5 million in minimum capital.

In late 1995, a deposit insurance system was created in which deposits of up to $20,000 are protected. Financial institutions are required to make monthly contributions to the deposit insurance fund equal to 0.025 percent of all insured deposits.

Private banks are not permitted to lend more than 30 percent of total assets to a single individual or firm or to a group of related companies. Institutional investors, including insurance companies and mutual funds, are not permitted to invest in bonds issued by foreign firms.

Banks are not required to have independent, external credit ratings. They are, however, required to publicly disclose the results of audits of their financial performance. In early 1996, auditors became liable for the quality of reports. Since that time, audits have become significantly more comprehensive and banks now disclose information on the quality of their assets and liabilities (*LatinFinance*, supplement, November 1996, 16).

Firms are required to register with the Central Bank and the CVM prior to offering shares on one of the stock exchanges. A complete economic and financial statement must be submitted to the Central Bank in order to be registered. The exchanges themselves are theoretically self-regulating and responsible for supervising adherence to market regulations, although the CVM continues to monitor activity on the exchanges. Firms wishing to engage in futures or options activities are required to hold minimum capital of US$16 million. Insider trading is prohibited by law.

Despite the fact that prudential standards have been tightened during the past three years, further attention to developing sound banking standards is required at this point in the development of Brazil's financial services industry. An assessment of the banking system in Brazil by Moody's Investor Service ranked the establishment of effective prudential supervision as one of the country's top three challenges in 1997.

Foreign Participation

From 1988 to 1995, foreign financial institutions were prohibited from establishing new branches and subsidiaries in Brazil. Existing foreign banks in Brazil were allowed to maintain operations established before 1988, but were not permitted to increase their capital stock or the number of branches. In 1993, foreign banks accounted for 16 percent of total assets in the Brazilian banking system and 13 percent of the system's net worth.

Brazil's financial services sector is in the process of transforming from one in which there was limited foreign participation and the sector was effectively nationalized, to one in which foreign participation is slowly being encouraged and the government is beginning to privatize banks. Foreign investment in the banking industry must be authorized by the Central Bank and is granted on a case-by-case basis. The Central Bank may authorize foreigners to hold 100 percent ownership of commercial banks. Most foreign investment in the financial services industry currently takes place through foreign firms' acquisition of additional shares in firms in which they already hold shares.

In April 1997, the United Kingdom's Hong Kong and Shanghai Banking Corporation (HSBC) bought 100 percent ownership of Brazil's fourth largest bank, Banco Bamerindus do Brasil. The acquisition also gave HSBC controlling interest in Bamerindus' insurance subsidiary and partial control of a pension firm that Bamerindus had previously managed jointly with another major Brazilian bank. Since 1996, Spain's Banco Santander has been authorized to expand ownership in Banco Geral de Comércio, as well as open 200 new branches of the bank throughout Brazil. France's Société Générale has, also since 1996, been approved to acquire 100 percent ownership of Banco Sogeral, in which it previously held 50 percent of equity.

In its 1997 WTO financial services offer, Brazil offered to bind the right of establishment and guarantee 100 percent ownership of foreign banks. Foreign banks will be permitted to establish new branches and subsidiaries, although authorization will continue to be granted only on a case-by-case basis.

Regulations governing permissible foreign participation in Brazilian securities have slowly changed over the last five years, opening the domestic market to foreign investors and slightly increasing opportunities for Brazilians to access foreign equity markets. In 1992, the CVM opened the domestic securities market to global fund managers, foreign insurance companies, and pension funds with assets greater than US$5 million. The minimum holding period before dividends could be repatriated was eliminated in the same year. Net foreign capital investment in the stock market grew from US$571 million (1 percent of total market capitalization) in 1991 to US$6.1 billion in 1996 (2.8 percent of total market capitalization).

Banks have been permitted to list on international markets through American Depository Receipts since December 1996. That same year, the CVM decided that, subject to prior authorization, foreign firms could list on the Brazilian exchanges through Brazilian Depository Receipts and domestic investors were allowed to acquire shares in Brazilian firms listed on foreign exchanges. Since May 1997, foreign investors have been permitted to trade derivatives on the São Paulo Futures and Commodities Exchange.

Despite these measures to gradually remove restrictions on foreign participation in the Brazilian securities market, the 1988 Constitution still prohibits foreign securities firms from establishing new operations or expanding existing operations in Brazil unless it is deemed to be in the national interest, negotiated in an international agreement, or based on reciprocity. At the end of 1997, foreign investors, limited to 30 percent of voting shares (or 49 percent of total shares), were still prohibited from majority ownership of investment banks. Brazil agreed to provide greater market access for foreign securities firms in the WTO financial services negotiations and when the agreement enters into force in early 1999, there are to be no limits on foreign participation. As is current practice in the banking sector, however, the establishment of new securities firms, as well as increases in foreign participation in these industries, will be subject to authorization on a case-by-case basis.

Under a presidential decree issued in 1996, foreign investors are permitted 100 percent ownership in health insurance firms. The director of the government agency responsible for the insurance sector noted that market access for foreigners would be extended to other areas of the insurance industry (EIU 1997a, 20). In 1996, 26 of the 130 insurance agencies in Brazil were either foreign-owned or had a foreign partner in a joint venture. Since early 1997, the US insurance groups Aetna and Cigna have announced plans to spend US$300 million and US$73 million, respectively, on separate joint ventures to offer life and health insurance in Brazil.

Brazil's WTO offer also entails some enhanced market opportunities for foreign insurance providers. New entry for foreign insurance firms will be permitted, although only subsidiaries will be authorized and foreign participation in this sector is still subject to a presidential decree authorizing such activity. The government still has a monopoly on reinsurance, but it has agreed to introduce legislation that would privatize and allow foreign participation in this sector by the year 2000.

Remaining Obstacles

Various types of capital controls have been used over the last three years to regulate the flow of foreign exchange and goods into and out of Brazil. For example, in May 1997, the government restricted financing purchases abroad with credit cards in an attempt to limit the demand for imports. To encourage a steady inflow of capital to finance the current account deficit, the 7 percent tax on foreign direct investment was recently lowered to 2 percent. In addition to the discretionary use of capital controls to limit or encourage the flow of capital, all foreign exchange transactions must be authorized by the Central Bank or an approved foreign exchange dealer. Further approval is required depending on the type of transaction. For example, foreign-owned firms operating in Brazil may borrow from abroad, but the terms of the loan must be approved by the Central Bank and there are ceilings on the amount of credit that may be acquired from foreign sources.

Although there are no limits on aggregate foreign direct or portfolio investment entering Brazil, there are restrictions on the percentage of foreign ownership permitted in some sectors. For example, foreign investors may not hold majority ownership of domestic airlines or utility companies. All foreign direct and portfolio investment must be registered with the Central Bank in order to remit profits and dividends through the commercial foreign exchange market.

Regulations concerning foreign ownership and operations in the financial services industry are not completely transparent. Despite the fact that Brazil recently authorized a number of foreign investors in financial services to expand existing multipurpose banking operations, the Constitution still prohibits such activity unless it serves national interest, is based on reciprocal treatment, or reflects agreements made in an international treaty. A 1995 presidential decree declared that foreign investment in financial services is in the national interest, but market access is not guaranteed. Thus, market access continues to depend on authorization from the Central Bank to establish operations, increase ownership, or open new branches (including ATMs). To date, no foreign investors have received authorization to establish new, wholly owned financial services subsidiaries in Brazil.

Brazil's 1997 WTO offer included provisions to guarantee foreign financial services firms 100 percent ownership in banks and securities firms. But even after this agreement takes effect in January 1999, market access will still depend upon authorization that will only be granted on a case-by-case basis. The criteria for determining whether market access will be granted to a foreign financial services firm are not transparent.

A number of joint ventures have recently been approved in the insurance industry. However, other than health insurance, the insurance industry is not yet, technically, open to foreign investors. Once the WTO financial services agreement enters into force, foreign life and nonlife insurance providers will be permitted to establish wholly owned subsidiaries in Brazil although foreign investment in the industry will, again, only be granted on a case-by-case basis.

References

Bank for International Settlements (BIS). 1996. *66th Annual Report*. Basle: Bank for International Settlements.

Bank for International Settlements (BIS). 1997. *67th Annual Report*. Basle: Bank for International Settlements.

Central Bank of Brazil. 1997. *Central Bank of Brazil—Structure and Functions*. (http://www.bcb.gov.br/ingles/fulldesc.htm).

Dornbusch, Rudiger. 1997. Brazil's Incomplete Stabilization and Reform. *Brookings Papers on Economic Activity*. Brookings Papers No. 1. Washington: Brookings Institution.

Economic Commission for Latin America and the Caribbean (ECLAC). 1990. *Economic Survey of Latin America and the Caribbean*. Santiago: Economic Commission for Latin America and the Caribbean.

Economic Commission for Latin America and the Caribbean (ECLAC). 1995. *Latin America and the Caribbean: The Economic Experience of the Last 15 Years*. Santiago: Economic Commission for Latin America and the Caribbean.

Economist Intelligence Unit (EIU). 1997a. *Financing Foreign Operation: Brazil*. New York: The Economist Intelligence Unit (April).

Economist Intelligence Unit (EIU). 1997b. *Brazil: EIU Country Profile 1996-97*. New York: The Economist Intelligence Unit.

Economist Intelligence Unit (EIU). 1997c. *Brazil: EIU Country Report 1997*. New York: The Economist Intelligence Unit (2d Quarter)

Mendonça de Barros, José Roberto, and Mansueto Fancunda de Almeida Junior. 1997. An Analysis of Financial Adjustment in Brazil. Ministry of Finance, Secretariat of Economic Policy (April). (http://www.fazenda.gov.br/ingles/infinan.html)

Moody's Investor Service. 1997. *Brazil: Banking System Outlook*. New York: Moody's Investor Service.

Rostau, Thierry. 1996. *Banking and Finance in South America*. London: FT Financial Publishing.

Sigma. 1997. *The Insurance Industry in Latin America: A Growing Competitive Environment*. No. 2/1997. Zurich: Swiss Reinsurance Company.

US Department of the Treasury. 1994. *National Treatment Study*. Washington: Government Printing Office.

Chile

Introduction

From 1974 to early 1981, a series of financial reforms gradually liberalized Chile's banking, security, and insurance markets. By 1979, quantitative controls on trade in goods were abolished and tariffs were reduced to 10 percent, and by 1982 the capital account was liberalized.[1] As a result of the 1981-83 banking crisis, the government reversed some of its earlier reforms. Chile reinstituted restrictions on the capital account and the Central Bank renationalized a number of domestic banks in order to prevent them from defaulting on foreign loans.

Having stabilized the economy and weathered the 1982-1985 recession, Chile resumed liberalizing financial services. This second phase of liberalization has been marked by a more stable macroeconomy and greater prudential controls over the financial sector. Chile has created what is now considered to be the most open and one of the safest financial markets in Latin America. That Chile was not significantly affected by the Mexican peso crisis in December 1994 is largely attributed to prudent macroeconomic management and a high domestic savings rate, coupled with the quality of the banking system and a low dependency on short-term capital inflows (IMF 1996, 111).

In 1995, financial services accounted for 12.6 percent of GDP and grew at an average annual rate of 7.2 percent. Although their growth was slightly lower than Chile's overall GDP growth rate of 8.5 percent that

---

1. Tariffs were reduced to 10 percent in all sectors except automobile imports.

year, financial services are projected to continue growing for the foreseeable future. Growth in financial services is expected, in part, because Chileans are required by law to invest 10 percent of their earnings in privately managed pension funds (AFPs). In 1996, Chile's private savings rate was 25 percent of GDP, which helped to push fixed capital investment to a record high 28 percent.

Even though Chile is open to inflows from and outflows to the rest of the world, short-term portfolio and foreign direct investment in Chile are limited by law. All foreign capital deposited or invested in the Chilean financial system is subject to a one-year, 30 percent minimum reserve (*encaje*) held with the Central Bank. Chilean authorities view the reserve requirement as a short-term measure and acknowledge that it must be removed if the country is to become a regional financial center. To pave the way for the recently negotiated bilateral free trade deal with Canada, investment classified as "productive" is now exempt from the *encaje*; investment classified as "financial" and debt on any productive investment will continue to be subject to the *encaje*. Although there exists no precise definition for productive or financial investment, most foreign direct investment is likely to fall in the former category and most foreign portfolio investment is likely to be included in the latter.

Prior to 1973, the financial sector in Chile was highly regulated. Interest rate ceilings and credit restrictions inhibited the domestic and international movement of capital. An extensive multiple exchange rate regime was used by the government to direct the flow of capital to preferred sectors of the economy. The state controlled more than 85 percent of the country's financial system. At the end of 1973 inflation was over 600 percent, GDP was 5.6 percent lower than the previous year, and Chile faced a balance of payments crisis.

In order to overcome the balance of payments crisis, control inflation, and improve allocative efficiency, the government began in 1973 a process of stabilization and liberalization. A massive devaluation was undertaken, ranging from 223 percent to over 1000 percent for items that had previously been authorized to trade at the best preferred foreign exchange rates (de la Cuadra and Hachette 1991, 223). In 1974, the multiple exchange rate regime was abolished and replaced by a crawling peg exchange regime,[2] which the government maintained from 1974 to 1979. The value of the peso and the primary goal of exchange rate policy were periodically adjusted to offset domestic and international inflation differentials and to promote the twin objectives of macroeconomic stabilization and a sustainable balance of payments.

---

2. Under a crawling peg, the nominal currency is pegged to a foreign currency and devalued at a predetermined rate against that currency. The devaluations are conducted at a rate that will offset the difference between the domestic and foreign rates of inflation and prevent a real appreciation of the domestic currency.

Elements of financial sector reform, introduced beginning in 1974, included the privatization of 19 of the country's 20 commercial banks, the removal of interest rate ceilings, and the introduction of regulations allowing 100 percent foreign ownership of domestic banks. Although the current account was liberalized and domestic regulatory financial reform introduced at the beginning of the reform process, it was not until 1977 that the government began to remove capital account controls for the financial sector.

Amendments to the Foreign Exchange Control Law allowed nonfinancial firms to borrow from foreign sources by 1974. Commercial banks were not, however, permitted to undertake independent foreign exchange transactions and were prohibited from borrowing from abroad until 1977. That year, they were authorized to borrow directly from abroad subject to quantitative restrictions on foreign capital inflow. By 1980, quantitative restrictions on foreign capital inflow by commercial banks were removed and the banks were free to borrow from abroad as well as lend funds in overseas markets.

The sequencing of financial reform in Chile from 1973 to 1980 had two specific effects on the Chilean financial sector that continue to characterize the current financial landscape. First, the one-year time lag between the removal of interest rate ceilings on short term transactions (1974) and the liberalization of commercial bank controls (1975) created a market for nonbank financial institutions (NBFIs). NBFIs are authorized to engage in consumer financing activities but are not technically considered financial intermediaries and therefore are not bound by restrictions on lending, interest rates, or other government controls over the banking sector. Lack of regulations governing the NBFIs and pent-up demand for credit resulted in rapid growth in nonbank private-sector credit from 1974-76. The NBFIs are now under greater regulatory control than in the mid-1970s, but they continue to lend more than authorities recommend and face high average risk levels and low returns on assets.

Second, in the years between 1974, when nonbank financial firms were first permitted to borrow abroad, and 1980, when banks were authorized to borrow abroad, there was "an explosion of international loans to nonfinancial firms" (Labán and Larraín 1994, 156). When the restrictions on banks' borrowing abroad were lifted in 1980, the consequent rapid increase in the demand by financial firms for funds abroad was not offset by a reduction in loans to the nonfinancial sector. As with the NBFIs, a weak supervisory framework and lack of market discipline by depositors led commercial banks to excessive risk taking and unsound lending practices. The banking system overall is now very profitable and efficient but, as discussed below, commercial banks are still clearing outstanding debt incurred during that period.

Within two years after Chile fixed its exchange rate in 1979, the peso was seriously overvalued. The real interest rate rose from 9 percent in

1980 to 29 percent in 1981 and then to 48 percent in 1982 (Bisat, Johnston, and Sundararajan 1992, 24). The combination of the overvalued peso and the sharp rise in interest rates resulted in widespread bankruptcies. By 1982, there was a run on one major bank, the stock market was 50 percent lower than in 1980, and 15.5 percent of total bank loans were judged to be nonperforming (BIS 1996, 134). Loan loss reserves in Chilean banks were not any higher in 1982 than those currently held by large banks in the United States. Many banks, therefore, were not adequately prepared for the losses that resulted from the high number of nonperforming loans and faced insolvency by the end of 1982.

The fixed exchange rate was abandoned in 1982. During the three months that the peso was allowed to float, it depreciated by 43 percent. A crawling peg regime was subsequently reinstituted. In addition to preannounced devaluations, which are typical of a crawling peg regime, the peso was allowed to float in a band around an official reference rate. Until 1992, the reference rate was the US dollar, after which the government set the reference rate based on the value of a basket of currencies.[3] The band was originally set at 2 percent around the reference rate. Since 1982, the Central Bank has revalued the peso against the reference rate when necessary and gradually widened the band to 12.5 percent around the reference rate. The combination of the fall in the value of the peso and high real interest rates, which averaged 48 percent in 1982, made it difficult to meet both domestic and external debt payments and aggravated the banking crisis.

The Central Bank attempted to deal with the crisis by making additional funds available to the banking system and to borrowers, buying nonperforming foreign currency loans, and rescheduling remaining foreign currency loans at favorable exchange rates. In 1981-83, the Central Bank intervened in 13 banks and 6 nonbank financial institutions, but this approach to dealing with the banking crisis quickly proved to be unsustainable—nonperforming loans as a percentage of total bank loans were 4 percent higher in 1983 than in 1982. Therefore, in late 1983 liberal capital account rules were abandoned. In addition to reinstituting exchange controls, the government raised the uniform tariff rate to 20 percent in an attempt to build the foreign reserves necessary to meet external debt obligations. At the same time, Chile worked with the international community to implement a bank restructuring program that would prevent Chilean banks from defaulting on foreign loans.

Under the restructuring programs, banks had the option to sell bad

---

3. The basket of currencies used as the official reference includes the dollar, deutsche mark, and yen. The weightings of the various currencies change when the Central Bank changes the reference rate. For example, in 1992 the currency was weighted 50 percent to the dollar, 30 percent to the deutsche mark, and 20 percent to the yen, whereas by early 1997 the dollar made up 80 percent of the reference exchange rate.

loan portfolios to the Central Bank with the guarantee that they would be repurchased by the bank within a scheduled time frame. Thus, the Central Bank owned 31 percent of loans by 1986. As of December 1995, five top Chilean banks still owed the Central Bank subordinated debt totaling nearly US$4.7 billion. Chilean banks are required to pay 70 percent of net income on the debt and are prohibited from paying any dividends until the debt has been repaid. Estimates of the time required to clear all subordinated debt range from 20 to 40 years (Howell 1994; SBC Warburg 1996). The final cost of restructuring the banking system is estimated to equal 19.6 percent of 1985 GDP.

Exchange controls have been gradually relaxed since Chile's recovery from the banking crisis. There are ceilings on the amount of foreign exchange that private individuals can purchase per month and requirements that any foreign exchange for interest and dividend payment be conducted through a commercial bank. The government maintains a reference exchange rate based on the value of a weighted basket of currencies and is supposed to support the peso within a band around the official reference rate. There is also a free-market exchange rate, however, which is used for the majority of foreign trade and investment. Since 1993, the government has adjusted the band around which the reference exchange rate is allowed to float in order to keep it at about the free market rate. Since 1995, the government has announced the target real interbank interest rate, which is determined by Central Bank open-market operations.

The capital account is not yet completely liberalized. As noted above, portfolio investment is still subject to the required reserve. Profits can be repatriated at any time but original foreign direct investment must remain in the country for one year.

Regulatory Framework

The banking sector in Chile is regulated by the Central Bank and the Superintendency of Banks and Financial Institutions (SBIF). The Central Bank, which has been independent since 1990, controls monetary policy and has, as its primary policy goals, responsibility for controlling inflation and maintaining the value of the peso (EIU 1995, 14). The Central Bank's normal functions include the exclusive right to issue currency, conduct rediscount and reserve operations, and control borrowing. Bank solvency appraisal, operational areas of banks and NBFIs, bank loan policies, loan diversification, and the qualification of guarantees are under the jurisdiction of the SBIF (EIU 1997, 15).

Securities companies and insurance firms are supervised by the Superintendency of Securities and Insurance (SVS). In 1995, the SVS changed regulations regarding the use of derivatives to allow limited use of futures, options, forwards, and swaps in order to hedge against interest rate and exchange rate risk. Insurance companies are regulated under Decree Law 3057 of 1979, which outlines entry-level minimums and investment restrictions. Chilean insurance companies have been permitted to create foreign affiliates since 1995.

The Chilean pension system is managed by private funds (AFPs), which are supervised by the Superintendency of Pension Fund Managers (SAFP). The SAFP sets and enforces minimum reserve requirements, recommends and interprets laws and regulations governing AFPs, and supervises legal and financial administration of AFPs. By law, AFPs must ensure a minimum rate of return on funds; those not meeting the minimum must contribute the difference. If an AFP is not able to contribute the difference, public resources will be used to make up the shortfall and the SAFP will wind up the AFP.

Rules governing foreign investment and the treatment of foreign companies are outlined in Decree Law 600, which guarantees national treatment in all sectors of the economy. Similarly, the same regulations apply to firms, both domestic and foreign owned, seeking to borrow from abroad. There are no citizenship requirements in Chile that prohibit employing foreign nationals, and no restrictions on foreign ownership or operation in the Chilean financial services industry. Decree Law 600 also guarantees foreign investors remittance of income and capital, sets forth the required reserve on short-term capital inflows, and contains provisions guaranteeing the right to remit profits from the first day of investment in Chile.

Universal banking is not permitted. As a result of a 1994 banking law amendment, however, banks are allowed to engage in securities activities (including issuing debt or equity, brokerage, investment advice, and management of investment funds) through a subsidiary, and industrial firms are allowed to invest in banks. Subsidiaries now play a significant role in the banking industry, accounting for 11 percent of total banking profit in 1995 compared to 1 percent in 1987. A new banking law would legally create a new entity known as a financial consortium, which would be able to hold majority interest in banks, pension funds, insurance companies, and securities firms, and would be allowed to offer each of these services through independent subsidiaries. Detailed regulation of financial consortiums would be carried out by the SBIF and SVS.

Financial Institutions

Chile's financial sector is considerably more diversified than those of other Latin American emerging markets. In 1994, commercial bank assets accounted for 62 percent of all financial-sector assets. By way of

Table B.2   Chile: Assets of financial institutions, 1996

	Number of institutions	Percentage of assets
Domestic private banks	13	35.1
State bank	1	6.7
Foreign banks	17	13.6
Consumer finance companies	3	1.2
Pension fund management companies	15	33.3
Insurance companies	52	10.1
Mutual funds	49	na
Foreign investment funds	18	na

na = not available.

Source: EIU 1997; Financial Times (various); authors' calculations.

comparison, bank assets accounted for an average of 94 percent of financial-sector assets in Brazil, Mexico, and Argentina. Figures for the United States and Germany for 1994 are 23 percent and 77 percent, respectively (BIS 1996, 126). Thus, financial-sector diversification in Chile is consistent with that observed in developed market economies.

Debt and equity markets are both well developed in Chile and are accessible to both the private and public sectors. Pension funds, insurance companies, and mutual funds are all privately managed and operated.

Financial Intermediaries

As of the end of 1996, there were 30 banks and 3 NBFIs in Chile (see table B.2). Since 1980, there has been a moratorium on new licenses for commercial banks and NBFIs. New market entrants must purchase an existing bank in order to operate a commercial bank.

Chile has one state-owned bank, Banco del Estado, which accounted for approximately 12 percent of banking-sector assets in 1996 (SBC Warburg 1996, 9). The Banco del Estado undertakes banking and financial operations for the government and also is authorized to compete in the market as a commercial bank.

The banking industry in Chile is extremely competitive. Prior to the 1980s firms tended to conduct business with a single bank with which they had formed a close relationship. They now tend to work with several banks at the same time, choosing banks based on costs as opposed to relationships. The competition has forced Chilean banks to lower the spread on lending and to increase the overall efficiency of their operations. Thus operating costs as a percentage of total assets in Chile were 3.0 percent in 1994, significantly lower than for the other major Latin American markets, which averaged 7.4 percent, and lower even than the US rate of 3.7 percent that year.

Intense competition in banking has kept the level of financial concentration, as measured by the percentage of financial assets held by the top five banks, low in Chile. In light of a number of major mergers and acquisitions in the banking sector during the past two years, however, financial-sector concentration is beginning to rise. In 1996, Banco Santander-Chile became Chile's largest commercial bank when it took control of Banco Orsono. It was superseded in 1997 by Banco de Santiago, which became the country's largest commercial bank when it merged with Banco O'Higgins. As a result of these mergers, financial assets held by the top five banks as a percentage of total financial-sector assets have risen from a low of 49 percent in 1994 to 62 percent in 1997. Financial-sector concentration in Chile is now on par with figures for industrialized economies such as Canada and Australia.

Chile does not have savings, mortgage, or cooperative banks. Commercial banks handle the initial transaction for most mortgages, but then sell them as securities to life insurance and pension companies. Some insurance companies participate, through subsidiaries, directly in the mortgage market.

In 1996, there were 23 companies offering general insurance and 31 involved in life insurance in Chile. As in the banking sector, there has been intense competition among insurance companies in Chile (EIU 1997, 21). Assets and reserves managed by insurance companies grew by almost 60 percent in 1994-96 alone, totaling $7.9 billion at the end of 1996. With an average of 3.1 percent of income spent on insurance in 1995, Chileans spend more per capita on insurance than residents of Mexico, Brazil, or Argentina.

The Chilean pension system is fully funded, established as a result of laws requiring individuals to contribute 10 percent of taxable earnings to privately run AFPs. Pensioners are free to move assets from one fund to another. Those not wishing to leave their money in an AFP have the option of placing their pension in an insurance annuity plan. AFPs are allowed to charge for services and compete on the basis of commission and rate of return. As of 1995, pension fund assets were 42 percent of GDP and approximately 60 percent of domestic financial savings (Budnevich and Landerretche 1997, 133).

NBFIs specialize in consumer credit and are similar to consumer finance companies. They do not offer checking accounts and are not permitted to engage in international transactions. NBFIs are permitted to handle letters of exchange and promissory notes as long as the paper is registered with the SVS. From a high of 56 in 1980, there are now only three NBFIs in Chile. In 1996, finance companies accounted for less than 2 percent of total banking assets.

Direct Finance

Chile's capital market boasts considerably more breadth than do the markets of the other major emerging markets in Latin American. In Argentina, Mexico, and Brazil, equity markets are the only major source of funds available to private firms, and any fixed-income securities issued in these markets tend to be government issued (Rojas-Suarez and Weisbrod 1996, 16). Private borrowers in Chile have the option of using fixed-income securities as well as equity markets in order to raise capital. Under Chilean law "blue chip" stock companies with a minimum risk rating of BBB+ are allowed to trade on the US stock market through American Depository Receipts (ADRs).

Chile has three stock exchanges: the Santiago Stock Exchange (SSE), the Valparaiso Stock Exchange (BCV), and the Electronic Stock Exchange (BE). The SSE is the oldest of the three exchanges and has historically accounted for the majority of turnover in the market. In 1995, intense competition between the SSE and the BE led to a "commission price war," after which the SSE held 87 percent of the fixed-income securities market and 82 percent of the equity market. In the same year, 313 companies were listed on the SSE and total market capitalization was $72.9 billion.

Insurance companies and private pension funds are significant players in the stock market. In 1993, 39 percent of the pension system's total assets of almost $165 billion was invested in shares and 10 percent of total life insurance assets of approximately $4 billion was placed in the stock market. The value of stocks held by pension and insurance companies represented approximately 15 percent of total market capitalization in the same year.

Prudential Regulation

Lack of oversight was one of the main reasons why Chile's first attempt at financial liberalization ended in a banking crisis. Since the late 1980s, Chile has implemented stringent prudential regulations governing reserve requirements, asset rating and reporting, and risk diversification. Supervision by the regulating agencies has been increased, as have public reporting requirements. The establishment of a credit bureau and public reporting requirements, coupled with use of independent credit-rating agencies, has helped enhance transparency and the overall quality of financial institutions' portfolios. For example, whereas in 1983 nonperforming loans accounted for 15.5 percent of total loans, implementation and enforcement of sound domestic banking regulations helped bring them down to 1.0 percent in 1995, lower than in any of the other Latin American economies or the United States.

Reserve requirements in Chile are calculated in terms of leverage. Liabilities must be less than 20 times a bank's capital and reserves, although in order to receive a top credit rating, it is recommended that banks keep liabilities under 17 times their total capital and reserves. Among the reforms likely to be included in the New Banking Law is the introduction of Basle guidelines on capital-asset ratios, as well as the requirement that equity be no less than 4 percent of total assets (SBC Warburg 1996, 8).

Regulations on risk diversification limit banks to lending no more than 5 percent of bank equity for unsecured loans and no more than 25 percent for secured loans. Lending to parties that hold more than 1 percent of shares in the bank must not exceed bank capital (SBC Warburg 1996, 6). Adherence to these rules is encouraged through a combination of fines for banks not in compliance with risk diversification limits and mandatory public reporting on factors such as asset quality and lending practices.

Insurance regulations are outlined in Decree Law 3057 of 1979, which sets forth minimum capital requirements and investment regulations. All financial statements concerning insurance companies must be stated in inflation-indexed units of account. Insurance companies may not invest more than 10 percent of their reserves in securities issued by a single company, and they are limited to holding 20 percent of a firm's stocks if that firm has shares in an insurance company.

Chile has stringent rules regarding which companies are allowed to trade on the stock market, as well as limitations on the amount that insurance companies and pension funds may invest in the market. Only "open corporations" may offer shares, bonds, or commercial notes. In order to be considered an open corporation, companies must meet government disclosure requirements, publish quarterly statements, and not be a closed or limited liability partnership. AFPs may invest up to 37 percent of funds in the stock market but no more than 5 percent in securities issued by a single company.

Since 1987, foreign investment funds have been permitted, subject to a minimum of $1 million in capital. Capital may not be repatriated within five years of entering Chile. Profits and dividends are subject to a 10 percent withholding tax.

Foreign Participation

Of 30 commercial banks in Chile in 1996, 17 were foreign controlled. Foreign banks represented 24 percent of total banking-sector assets in 1996, but only 14 percent of loans, 14 percent of equity, and 19 percent of net profit in the banking industry. Private domestic banks accounted for 62 percent of assets, 71 percent of loans, 67 percent of equity, and 62 percent of banking-sector profits. Other assets, loans, and profits were accounted for by the state-owned bank, Banco del Estado.

Both foreign and domestic banks must purchase an existing bank in order to enter the market. Foreign banks have the option of establishing a branch or subsidiary, although, in order to enforce bank liability on the legal parent as well as domestic lending limit laws, the Chilean government prefers that foreign banks establish branches (US Treasury 1994, 191).

At the end of 1996, over 60 percent of the insurance market was controlled by foreign companies (EIU 1997, 21). Major international companies with a presence in Chile include the European-based Allianz Versicherung-Aktien Gesellschaft and the American-based Aetna and the American International Group. Chilean insurance companies have been authorized since 1995 to establish affiliates in foreign markets.

Foreign brokerage firms are allowed to operate in Chile and, as with the banking industry, are guaranteed nondiscriminatory treatment under Decree Law 600. Securities firms establishing operations in Chile must do so through a subsidiary. In 1993, US securities firms accounted for roughly 10 percent of the Chilean stocks and bonds trading market (US Treasury 1994, 196).

Foreign firms are not allowed to list on Chile's stock market. Legislation currently under consideration would allow the creation of an offshore market on which foreign firms could list. Once such legislation is passed, foreign firms in compliance with Chilean standards would be issued a global depository receipt (GDR) and permitted to list on the offshore market.

There are no investment banks in Chile. Many of the larger domestic and foreign banks do, however, have investment banking departments. Both foreign and domestic banks have been involved in organizing share issues for Chilean companies.

AFPs, mutual funds, and insurance companies are allowed to invest in foreign securities markets, subject to limitations on the amount of funds invested abroad. AFPs and mutual funds are allowed to invest 9 percent and 30 percent, respectively, of their portfolios in overseas markets.[4] Investment in foreign securities markets is capped at 10 percent of total assets for life insurance companies and 15 percent of assets for general insurance companies.

Remaining Obstacles

Major obstacles preventing complete liberalization include the ongoing moratorium on new banking licenses and the *encaje*, a 30 percent,

---

4. In 1996, only 0.2 percent of AFP funds were invested in overseas securities markets.

one-year reserve requirement on all foreign investment classified as "financial" by authorities. The moratorium on new banking licenses may be repealed with the New Banking Law, whereas the *encaje* is not expected to change in the short run. Apart from the moratorium on new banking licenses for both domestic and foreign banks, foreigners have the right of establishment in all other financial service sectors and are allowed 100 percent ownership in these sectors. Neither foreign nor domestic firms, however, are permitted to have operations in more than one sector of the financial services market. Foreign firms wishing to establish operations in the securities or insurance markets must set up a subsidiary in Chile, and foreign firms establishing an AFP must be incorporated in Chile.

Foreign firms are guaranteed national treatment in all sectors of the economy under Decree Law 600. There is no ceiling on foreign direct or portfolio investment, although foreign investments larger than US$5 million must be approved by the Foreign Investment Committee. The country's regulatory framework is transparent, although the red tape encountered when entering the market is reported to be burdensome (US Treasury 1994, 199). Securities legislation requires firms that go public to disclose detailed information, including financial statements, which helps to increase the transparency of the market.

Chile was one of 102 countries to make commitments to the WTO financial services deal that concluded on 13 December 1997. Although Chile provides a high level of market access and national treatment for foreign financial services firms, its offer in the agreement fell short of expectations. One major area of concern for foreign financial service firms is asset management. Chile guaranteed market access for all insurance subsectors other than pension management, while commercial presence for asset management firms will only be granted on a case-by-case basis.

The New Banking Law is currently awaiting passage in the Chilean Congress. As the law has been under consideration since 1991 and has changed many times since, it is not yet clear what form the final law will take. Potential reforms include the creation of financial conglomerates, which would effectively introduce universal banking, and regulations requiring banks operating in Chile to meet requirements established by the Basle Committee on Banking Supervision. Given that Chile's largest bank, Banco de Santiago, proposed selling shares in order to meet Basle equity capital requirements in early May 1997, it appears likely that the Basle requirements will be part of the New Banking Law.

References

Bank Credit Analyst Research Group. 1996. *Emerging Markets Analyst: 1996 Annual Handbook*. Montreal: Bank Credit Analyst Publications Ltd.

Bank for International Settlements (BIS). 1996. *66th Annual Report*. Basle: Bank for International Settlements.

Bisat, Amer, R. Barry Johnston, and Vasudevan Sundararajan. 1992. *Issues in Managing and Sequencing Financial Sector Reforms: Lessons from Experiences in Five Developing Countries.* WP/92/82. Washington: Monetary and Exchange Affairs Department, International Monetary Fund.

Bosworth, Barry P., Rudiger Dornbusch, and Raúl Labán, eds. 1994. *The Chilean Economy: Policy Challenges and Lessons.* Washington: Brookings Institution.

Budnevich, Carlos L., and Oscar M. Landerretche. 1997. Macroeconomic and Financial Policy in Chile. In *The Banking and Financial Structure in the NAFTA Countries and Chile*, ed. by George M. von Furstenberg. Boston: Kluwer Academic Publishers.

de la Cuadra, Sergio, and Dominique Hachette. 1991. Chile. In *Liberalizing Foreign Trade: Volume 1*, ed. by Demetrios Papageorgiou, Armeane M. Choksi, and Michael Michaely. Cambridge: Basil Blackwell.

Economist Intelligence Unit (EIU). 1995. *Country Profile 1995-96: Chile*. New York: The Economist Intelligence Unit (April).

Economist Intelligence Unit (EIU). 1996. *Country Report: Chile*. New York: The Economist Intelligence Unit (4th Quarter).

Economist Intelligence Unit (EIU). 1997. *Financing Foreign Operation: Chile*. New York: The Economist Intelligence Unit.

Hausmann, Ricardo, and Liliana Rojas-Suarez, eds. 1996. *Banking Crisis in Latin America.* Washington: Inter-American Development Bank and Johns Hopkins University.

Howell, Mike J., ed. 1994. *Investing in Emerging Markets*. London: Euromoney Books.

International Monetary Fund (IMF). 1996. *International Capital Markets*. Washington: International Monetary Fun (September).

Labán, Raúl, and Felipe Larraín B. 1994. In *The Chilean Economy: Policy Lessons and Challenges*, ed. by Barry P. Bosworth, Rudiger Dornbusch, and Raúl Labán. Washington: Brookings Institution.

Lindgren, Carl-Johan, Gillian Garcia, and Matthew Saal. 1996. *Bank Soundness and Macroeconomic Policy.* Washington: International Monetary Fund.

Rojas-Suarez, Liliana, and Steven Weisbrod. 1995. *Achieving Stability in Latin American Financial Markets in the Presence of Volatile Capital Flows.* Working Paper Series 304. Washington: Inter-American Development Bank.

Rojas-Suarez, Liliana, and Steven Wiesbrod. 1996. *Building Stability in Latin American Financial Markets.* Working Paper Series 320. Washington: Inter-American Development Bank.

SBC Warburg. 1996. *Chilean Banks*. United Kingdom: SBC Warburg (24 September).

Sigma. 1997. *The Insurance Industry in Latin America: A Growing Competitive Environment.* No. 2/1997. Zurich: Swiss Reinsurance Company.

US Department of the Treasury. 1994. *National Treatment Study*. Washington: Government Printing Office.

Valdes-Prieto, Salvador. 1994. Financial Liberalization and the Capital Account: Chile, 1974-84. In *Financial Reform: Theory and Experience*, ed. by Gerard Caprio Jr., Izak Atiyas, and James A. Hanson. Cambridge: Cambridge University Press.

China

Introduction

China embarked on its open-door economic policy in 1979 when it established several special economic zones (SEZs) and reformed the agricultural sector. Villagers obtained control over their own farming activities, thus ending the top-down approach of central planning. In the SEZs, foreigners were allowed to invest in export-oriented sectors. Foreign-invested companies have since grown at phenomenal rates, but there has been no significant ripple effect on domestic firms, especially state-owned enterprises (SOEs). Thus, in 1996, SOEs consumed almost three-quarters of industrial investment but accounted for only a third of industrial output (Holmes 1996, 1).

Many factors, including the high export-led growth rates in the SEZs, contributed to a rising annual inflation rate that averaged over 10 percent by the late 1980s. The monetary authorities were unable to combat inflation while top-down controls were maintained in the fiscal and financial systems. The decline in fiscal revenues during the reform period prompted the Ministry of Finance (MOF) to sell bonds to the central bank in exchange for currency in order to cover its budget deficit, thus aggravating inflationary pressures. It was only in 1994 that laws were passed to create a new, more consistent, and more transparent tax system that would reverse the steady decline in fiscal revenues. The new laws also banned fiscal overdrafts on the financial system.

The open-door policy barely touched the financial system for the first five years. In that time, the central bank continued to operate as a "mono-bank," pursuing both commercial and central bank functions. Its main role was to ensure that loans were made to priority sectors, i.e., that bank branches allocated funds in accordance with the government's credit plan. It was aided in this task by three specialized banks operating in agriculture, state construction, and foreign exchange management.

The credit plan, formulated by various ministries, including the monobank and the State Planning Commission, involves a multistep, highly negotiated process in which lending quotas are allocated to the state banks (lenders) based on balancing their deposits against the funding requirements of their assigned borrowers. A relending facility allows the monobank to reallocate deposits from surplus banks, regions, or sectors to deficit ones.[1] It is funded by reserves set at 20 percent of deposits. Thus, deposit-poor lenders are assured that their allocated funding requirements will be covered by monobank loans.

Inherent in this assurance is the moral hazard problem, as banks will use the relending facility to cover lending under the credit plan and use available deposits for nonplan activities. As loans under the relending facility are generally rolled over, they represent about 30 percent of state banks' liabilities, which are estimated to equal 3 to 4 percent of GDP (Holmes 1996, 5).

The continuing allocation of investment funds to SOEs under the credit plan has allowed loss-making SOEs to remain in business. The accumulating mountain of nonperforming loans to SOEs, financed largely through increasing state bank liabilities with the central bank, suggests that any financial sector reform and resolution of the SOE debt problem are intricately linked. The continued reliance on state bank loans to subsidize SOEs has also exacerbated the MOF's fiscal weakness, as it contributes to the lack of funds for much-needed enterprise and welfare reforms.

The first signs of financial reform appeared in 1984, when the monobank discarded its commercial banking functions to become a central bank. The three specialized banks were also turned into commercial banks, passing on their policy lending to newly established policy banks. The banking system was decentralized, and interbank competition was encouraged. Urban and rural credit cooperatives were established as alternative banks. Cautiously, foreign entry was also permitted.

Interest rates, though, remained under government control. Deregulating deposit and lending rates is currently on the official agenda, although lending rates are a highly political issue because of their impact on SOE debt-servicing obligations. Preferential lending rates have been eliminated in some sectors but continue in many others.

Part of the open-door policy in 1979 was the introduction of foreign exchange certificates (FECs), or foreign money, alongside the nonconvertible

---

1. In the past, the relending facility was also extended to NBFIs.

renminbi. FECs were set at an official rate that was occasionally adjusted. In 1994, China abolished its dual exchange rate system, the official exchange rate, and strict back-up controls on foreign exchange. FECs were gradually withdrawn from circulation. The yuan, the new single rate, floats based on exchanges established at swap centers,[2] although it is not a freely convertible currency. Convertibility on the current account is under way, but on the capital account it is still only a long-term goal.

Regulatory Framework

The People's Bank of China (PBOC), China's central bank, is the financial sector's main regulatory authority. Established as a monobank, the PBOC narrowed its operations to those more consistent with a central bank when it transferred its commercial banking functions to the newly established Industrial and Commercial Bank in 1984. As the central bank, the PBOC controls the money supply, determines interest and deposit rates, and handles foreign exchange reserves through its division, the State Administration of Exchange Control. It also oversees banks' operations, using the credit plan to administratively control overall lending, and supervises the People's Insurance Company of China as well as, through its branches, trust and investment companies (TICs).

Though officially on equal footing with the MOF, in the past the PBOC frequently had to submit to MOF demands to cover the Ministry's budget deficit arising from decreasing revenues and increasing losses at SOEs. Subsidies to SOEs and other government agencies were increasingly moved off-budget, making the banking system more and more important for quasi-financing of the state sector. However, the new tax law of 1994 and the new PBOC law of 1995 put an end to this custom. The latter recast the PBOC as an apolitical central bank equipped with indirect tools for the conduct of monetary policy. It was expected to implement monetary policy under the leadership of the State Council.

Until 1993, the PBOC's discretionary authority under the credit plan was decentralized, with many decisions delegated to regional PBOC centers. This caused problems as local authorities seeking latitude for local economic activities put pressure on local PBOC branches to become profit maximizers. The profit-seeking approach led many PBOC branches to expand into commercial and financial businesses, such as TICs and securities companies. These affiliations resulted in conflicts of interest as

---

2. The introduction and concurrent depreciation of the yuan brought about an influx of foreign exchange reserves.

local PBOC officers acted as both supervisor and institutional sponsor. Absence of national legal standards in regulatory matters regarding TICs and securities companies further increased the latitude of PBOC officers, leading to inconsistent practices across regions.

In early 1998, the governor of the central bank announced reforms to centralize its economic supervision and thereby cut down on interference from local authorities who press the local affiliates to approve funding for favored projects. The proposed reorganization would include elimination of provincial level branches of the PBOC and the establishment of regional headquarters, along the lines of the US Federal Reserve System (*Los Angeles Times*, 16 January 1998). The government also removed ceilings on loan quotas for state-owned banks on 1 January 1998, in an effort to enhance the use of indirect tools for monetary policy as well as to encourage the adoption of risk-based lending practices.

Until 1995, there was no single insurance law, although a Maritime Law and a law governing foreign insurers in Shanghai did exist. In 1995, the National People's Congress passed the first comprehensive Insurance Law, which provides a legal and regulatory framework that approximates international standards. Its short-term objective is to improve both the compliance and the solvency of insurers. After the year 2000, the objective will be to establish a financially strong insurance industry with an increasing number of foreign and domestic operations nationwide.

Regulation of the insurance industry has been delegated to the Financial Supervision and Regulation Department (FSRD) under the State Council. The FSRD is responsible for formulating and regulating insurance clauses and premium rates as well as approving the establishment of domestic, foreign, or joint venture insurance operations, including the establishment of branches. It also formulated requirements regulating the establishment of new insurance companies. These requirements include: articles of association in compliance with the Insurance Law and the Company Law; minimum registered capital of RMB200 million; senior management with professional knowledge and operational expertise; a formal written application that outlines ownership, capital, and scope of business; and a feasibility study report.

National regulation for the securities market is currently being drafted. Since 1992, the Chinese Securities Regulatory Commission (CSRC), an executive agency of the State Council with offices in Beijing, Shanghai, and Shenzhen, has supervised and regulated securities markets. The CSRC is also responsible for supervising securities companies, although the PBOC continues to be the approval authority for traders and securities firms. And the State Council Securities Policy Commission (SCSPC) determines the annual number of listings and volume of issues. Other agencies also share some of the authority in regulating securities markets. However, the CSRC is the sole authority in regulating futures markets.

The China International Trust and Investment Corporation (CITIC) was established in 1979 and awarded industry-level status. As the country's major consulting firm and investment bank, it invests and lends funds raised from overseas capital markets. Its subsidiary, the China Investment Bank (CIB), invests and lends funds borrowed from international financial institutions, such as the World Bank. It is responsible for raising construction funds from abroad.

During the 1980s, many international trust and investment corporations (ITICs) were set up, offering consulting and investment banking services similar to those offered by the CITIC although not necessarily linked to the latter. While many of the ITICs were closed down during the austerity program launched in 1988, most provinces and municipalities still operate their own ITICs (Takahashi 1994, 16-17).

Financial Institutions

China is still in the early stages of financial development, as centrally allocated credit is not effective in channeling funds from savers to borrowers. The financial reforms begun in 1979 delegated some economic decisions to the microeconomic level and so necessitated the development of financial intermediaries. Positive real interest rates since 1979 have resulted in significant financial deepening. Yet developments on the stock market are still based more on speculation than on investment, indicating that securitization of financial assets still has a long way to go.

Financial Intermediaries

China has 4 state banks and 11 commercial banks. The state banks were created in 1984, when specialized banks and part of the monobank were transformed into commercial banks. The largest state bank is the Industrial and Commercial Bank of China, which extends working capital loans to SOEs for fixed-asset investment. The Agricultural Bank of China finances services in rural areas; the People's Construction Bank of China provides medium- and long-term finance for capital construction; and the Bank of China is the main international and foreign exchange bank. In fact, the last was China's only foreign exchange bank until 1986, when this function was extended to all state banks.

State banks are responsible for implementing the credit plan. They receive most of the PBOC's relending and hold the bulk of the SOEs' bad debt, and are therefore estimated to have negative net worth.

State banks have a network of branches, newly created affiliates, and special departments. This network allows them to hold the bulk of all deposits outside the credit plan; a large proportion of these deposits flows into semiformal and informal channels that are frequently of a speculative nature.

Some of the state banks' problems were addressed in the 1995 Commercial Banking Law, which adopted a "narrow banking" definition that restricts state banks to core lending businesses. The "main bank" concept was also introduced in a pilot project of 300 SOEs. It concentrates lending responsibilities to those SOEs at state bank headquarters and provincial branches. Furthermore, computer link-ups, supervised by the PBOC, are now used to conduct lender-borrower transactions.

To free the newly formed commercial state banks from policy burdens, the policy lending previously extended by the three specialized banks was transferred to three newly created, special purpose policy banks. The State Development Bank, with access to funding from postal deposits, focuses on infrastructure lending. The Agricultural Development Bank provides agricultural procurement and infrastructure funding, and the Export-Import Bank provides export-import financing for key sectors. Common problems faced by the policy banks include a lack of institutional autonomy, which makes them vulnerable to pressure in lending decisions, and a lack of secure funding despite pressures to operate profitably.

The 11 commercial banks consist of 5 national banks and 6 regional banks. Ineligible for PBOC relending, the commercial banks face no official lending requirements to SOEs and therefore hold little SOE debt. They face the same interest rate regime as do state banks, though. The regional banks, barred from national branching, are supervised by the PBOC's local branches. National banks, on the other hand, are supervised by the PBOC and owned by various state-affiliated firms and agencies. The first national bank was the Bank of Communications, a major financial institution in pre-1949 China that was permitted in 1987 to reestablish on the mainland with headquarters in Shanghai.

Urban and rural credit cooperatives were established as an alternative to banks. By 1990, they numbered more than 60,000 (EIU 1992). Urban cooperative banks, which are small and manageable, are structured in a two-tier system: in the lower tier, a number of small-scale banks handle deposits and loans; the upper tier interfaces with capital markets and acts as a supervisor for the system. The rural or agricultural cooperative banks, acting under the guidance of the Agricultural Development Bank, have little autonomy in management and lending decisions. Their clients are rural townships and enterprises. Problems arise as they divert part of the agricultural procurement moneys and use rural deposits for speculative purposes in coastal areas.

Nonbank financial institutions (NBFIs), which are more autonomous and profit driven than banks, have introduced a limited degree of competition into the financial system. In June 1993, there were 377 TICs, 66 securities companies, 22 finance companies,[3] 9 leasing companies,[4] and 3 insurance companies in China (US Treasury 1994, 249).

The state-owned People's Insurance Company of China (PICC) was a monopoly insurer until 1988. In 1993, it still handled over 95 percent of China's total insurance business. The new insurance law of 1995 limited the PICC to commercial insurance business and transferred its social insurance business to the Ministry of Labor. While the PICC and several government financial authorities own 17 regional life insurers, there are now three other regional insurers as well as two independent national insurers (Lamble and Low 1995). China's market for life insurance and household casualty insurance is still small and most casualty insurance is purchased by corporate customers. Most assets have to be deposited with domestic banks in interest-bearing accounts, and other investments are required to be spread among safe investments and are limited to short-run commitments.

TICs take and relend long-term government agency and enterprise deposits, although only a small proportion of revenues has in the past been derived from their designated core business area. As was the case with securities companies, most TIC revenues came from speculative activities until the introduction of narrow banking. Narrow banking de-linked TICs and securities companies from their sponsor shareholders, namely stock holders and government agencies, as well as from each other. These NBFIs now need to find new shareholders, but their efforts are impeded by confusion about what business activities are permitted for either of them and by entanglement in the state banks' problem of nonperforming loans.

Direct Finance

China's two stock exchanges, the Shanghai and Shenzhen Stock Exchanges, were established in 1990 and 1991, respectively. No cross-listing exists between these two exchanges. Since their founding, securities markets have grown rapidly but remain quite small in size. Securities exchange centers, which are limited to government and corporate bond trading, also exist in 18 larger cities. They were established in the mid-1980s when SOEs were allowed to sell bonds to employees, other companies, and, to some extent, to the public. The centers are linked to the stock exchanges through electronic trading networks.

---

3. Finance companies, established in 1988, are formed by industrial and commercial conglomerates to facilitate intragroup financing.

4. Leasing companies lease imported capital goods to export-oriented enterprises.

Two types of shares are offered by Chinese companies: A shares, which are exclusively sold to Chinese nationals, and B shares, denominated in renminbi but traded and purchased in foreign currency exclusively by foreigners. B shares are restricted to limited liability shareholding companies that have been profitable for at least two consecutive years; that possess sufficient foreign exchange revenues to pay dividends and cash bonuses; that provide financial statements and earning forecasts for three consecutive years; and that, at the time of listing, have a price-earning ratio of less than 15.

SOE shares[5] are compartmentalized to ensure state control while diversifying shareholding in an effort to modernize SOEs. Share capital of corporatized SOEs is segregated into several compartments, including a controlling legal person share, which is held by the government and other SOEs and which is subject to restrictions on transfer. Despite the 1994 Company Law, this compartmentalization continues, with the result that less than 33 percent of listed companies' shares are traded.[6] Confusion frequently arises as to who has authority over state shares. The absolute state shareholder also provides a buffer that protects managers from shareholder pressure.

Quotas for stock and debt listings are formulated by the state planning commission, which sets a figure for the aggregate offering price of issuances in a given year. These quotas are then allocated on a provincial level. Problems with this process include the politicized selection and approval process, the low quality of issuer, the large number of small issuers, the lack of predictability in the schedule of announcements of annual quotas, and the fact that announced quotas change yearly according to market conditions. Furthermore, the quota system pushes nonquota activity into unofficial and semiofficial channels such as the securities exchange centers.

About 80 percent of government bonds are sold to the household sector. The coupon rate, adjusted for inflation, is set well above fixed deposit rates and thus makes government bonds attractive to households. At the same time, institutional investors have been offered a lower rate not adjusted for inflation. Because households tend to hold bonds until they mature, liquidity in the market is very thin. To increase liquidity, a one-year bond was introduced in 1995, and state banks were permitted to hold treasury obligations as part of their reserves. These developments are in line with attempts to shift to institutional clientele

---

5. SOE shares can be either A shares or, provided the SOE meets the requirements, B shares.

6. The limited amount of companies' shares being traded increases trading volatility of A shares. After a year of high volatility, the share index dropped by 20 percent in 1994, leading to cancellation of A share listings in 1995.

in order to establish an open market in treasuries and to develop an efficient money market.

To date, the market for nongovernment bonds is insignificant, because coupon rates are set lower than those of treasury bills and because past payment defaults have compromised their credibility. Unlike stocks, bonds may be issued to noncorporatized SOEs. In the bond quota allocation, preference is given to infrastructure projects and to 300 priority SOEs.

The money market in China consists of an interbank market, Chibor, established in 1996 in an effort to supplant formal and informal interbank markets in bank deposits. The new system is two-tiered, consisting of a lower tier, in which trade is among bank branches and other financial institutions, and an upper tier, which links the lower-tier trading centers and the headquarters of major banks. The PBOC calculates the Chibor interbank rate based on daily trading. Eligible funds and the use of proceeds are restricted.

Also in 1996, the PBOC began open-market operations consisting of repurchase arrangements on treasury obligations with 14 major banks. Bankers' acceptances are also being developed, although this process is likely to be slow because of the near-collapse of institutional credit, which makes bankers reluctant to receive acceptances.

Until the 1994 currency unification, foreign exchange could be obtained through either foreign exchange certificates (FECs) or foreign exchange adjustment centers (FEACs).[7] By 1986, there were more than 100 FEACs, or swap centers, where foreign currency was exchanged at a floating rate that varied widely among the centers. By 1993 FEACs handled 80 percent of all foreign exchange transactions, and with the currency unification of 1994 came the gradual withdrawal of FECs altogether from foreign exchange. The swap centers determined the yuan's exchange rate. Movements toward convertibility of the current account have allowed foreign firms to make their transactions through designated foreign exchange banks and through FEACs. Chinese firms, however, must sell all foreign exchange holdings to designated banks.

Finally, China does not yet have a mutual fund market; foreign banks are prohibited from selling mutual funds to Chinese citizens or institutions; and residents may not invest overseas without government approval.

Foreign Participation

Foreign banks are generally restricted to hard currency operations, although the government, in its bid to join the World Trade Organization,

---

7. Because only authorized financial institutions and designated enterprises were permitted to deal on FEACs, a black market for other foreign exchange transactions also developed.

has announced its intention to partially open local currency business to foreign banks. Since 1985, foreign banks have been allowed to set up branches and local subsidiaries and to establish joint venture banks with Chinese partners in selected cities and SEZs. But their activities have been limited to wholesale banking and a limited number of foreign exchange transactions such as foreign exchange deposits and loans for joint ventures, foreign exchange investments and guarantees, and the settlement of import and export accounts. Extension of foreign bank branches to Shanghai was made possible in 1990 when the Pudong New Area was designated as a development zone. The PBOC approved the applications of seven foreign banks to open branches in Shanghai in 1991, and that number increased to 30 by late 1994.

To establish a branch, a bank must have total assets of over $20 million, have operated a representative office in China for at least three years, and, for branches in Shanghai, have $30 million in registered capital. In addition, $10 million in capital must be deposited in cash with the PBOC, essentially as a minimum reserve requirement (EIU 1992). In late 1994, foreign branching restrictions were somewhat eased: the minimum number of years of operation of a representative office was lowered to two, and the capital requirement is RMB100 million, of which 30 percent must be deposited with the PBOC.

As of the end of 1996, there were 538 representative offices, 131 foreign bank branches, 6 joint venture banks, and 5 wholly owned foreign banks in China. Moreover, in 1997, the PBOC issued licenses for 9 foreign banks to conduct renminbi business in Shang-hai. These banks face stringent operating requirements, including keeping two separate reserves (in local and foreign currency) equal to 18 percent of renminbi deposits and limiting local currency liabilities to less than 35 percent of their foreign exchange liabilities. Domestic banks are not subject to these requirements, and, as such, the newly licensed foreign banks are not likely to create significant competition for domestic banks yet (International Financial Law Review 1997, 21).

Foreign banks are intentionally subjected to discriminatory treatment. For example, each account held by a joint venture with a foreign bank requires official approval, which is limited to two years. In contrast, joint venture accounts with the PBOC require only one-time approval, giving the PBOC a competitive advantage over foreign banks. Foreign banks are also subject to PBOC evaluation of their "contributions to China," but the criteria for these assessments lack transparency and often are politically motivated. As is the case for all foreign companies operating in China, a bank's staff must be recruited through a Chinese government agency, which retains 55 percent of an employee's gross salary. This arrangement hinders recruitment of highly qualified personnel.

Foreign nonbank financial institutions consist of six finance companies and six fully licensed insurance companies. For foreign insurance companies to obtain a PBOC-issued insurance license generally takes about three years. Emphasis is placed on solvency and a conservative investment style, which discourages foreign companies from diversifying risk and sources of income beyond individual policies. Sixty unlicensed foreign overseas insurance companies have representative offices in China, but these are limited to operating in a few coastal areas on a trial basis. At the end of 1996, foreign insurance companies controlled less than 1 percent of the market.

Foreign securities firms may establish representative offices, but not local branches or subsidiaries. They may purchase seats on either stock exchange at the same price as that charged to domestic securities firms, but all their transactions require the partnership of a local broker. Foreign securities houses are limited to B share transactions and, subject to government approval, to underwriting. Twenty-three foreign brokers have seats on the Shanghai Stock Exchange, eight on the Shenzhen Stock Exchange. Foreign securities firms are prohibited from introducing new domestic financial products, although they may offer offshore derivatives, which have been an attractive source of business. Repatriation of profits requires government approval, while dividend payments on B shares do not.

Since 1990, foreigners have been permitted to own equity in Chinese companies through B shares.[8] The B share market developed without national guidelines, which may explain why, after an initial positive reaction to their introduction, the demand for B shares has dropped so much that they frequently trade below issuance price. Other reasons include nonstandard accounting practices, a shortage of information on listed companies, a lack of transparency and foreign direct investment strategies in China.

Offshore listings of mainland companies (the H market) are traded only outside China. They are less volatile than B shares and therefore offer better returns. In 1996, 22 mainland companies were listed on the Hong Kong Stock Exchange and 2 on the New York Stock Exchange. Future offerings in Singapore, Tokyo, London, and Sydney are under discussion.

Much of China's foreign debt consists of commercial borrowings in the form of bank loans, which accounted for 69 percent of total foreign debt in 1994. In 1995, a tighter approval regime was introduced to impose a national quota on borrowing for more than one year and to restrict all borrowing to those entities approved on a published list. Local governments are barred from this list.

---

8. As of late 1996, 78 Chinese companies were offering B shares (Holmes 1996).

Remaining Obstacles

The Chinese financial system has undergone substantial development since the mid-1980s, but it is still subject to heavy state regulation. One of the most pressing problems is the resolution of the SOE debt overhang, which undermines confidence in the system. With more than half of the country's state-owned enterprises losing money, a third of all loans are reported to be either overdue or in default. The problem of bad loans slows or even derails banking reform. To truly transform China's financial system, the SOEs, which account for 65 percent of national capital formation, must be rationalized. A new generation of bankers also needs to be recruited and trained.

The banking system needs to be moved from a credit plan to a system of prudential ratios and objective supervisory criteria. Tentative steps toward this goal have been taken with the removal of credit quota ceilings on state-owned banks in early 1998, but the development of a true commercial banking system will take years. Bankruptcy laws need to be introduced. Companies will have to provide more transparent financial information and annual reports. Skilled banking staff are still scarce, and modern equipment is largely confined to major cities or special economic zones. Supervision needs to be backed by effective powers of enforcement. Lack of a legal system, modern accounting standards, and a system for payments and clearing all contribute to problems of confidence and lack of transparency.

Some of the needed reforms are underway. In early 1998, the government outlined plans to strengthen regulation and enhance competition in the banking sector. Key reforms include plans for state-owned banks to close money-losing branches in addition to the establishment of joint-stock, local commercial banks in up to 300 cities. The plan, to be phased in within three years, will implement internationally accepted loan classification guidelines and give the central bank more autonomy.

Plans to sell many of the smaller state-owned enterprises by the end of the year 2000 were also announced in early 1998. Removing many SOE's from the banks' balance sheets will support other reforms aimed at strengthening the financial system, including plans to close many of the country's poorly regulated trust companies. To facilitate financial sector restructuring and enterprise reform, the government also intends to allocate $6 billion in 1998 and another $7 to $8.5 billion between 1999 and 2000 to cover nonperforming loans and help China's healthy banks remain solvent through the transition (*The New York Times*, 17 January 1998).

Because of current problems in the financial sector, China remains a heavily cash-based economy as other methods of payment tend to be mistrusted, so that even large deals are often still made in cash. One major reason for the persistence of this form of exchange is that the transfer and settlement system is in the early stages of development; for example, it can take up to ten days to move renminbi from one Chinese city to another through formal channels. A second reason is that local authorities have put severe political demands on local banks and branches, often treating them as little more than regional treasuries.

The Chinese government's overriding concern with limiting the number and scope of new financial institutions means that when existing institutions cannot meet the economy's financing needs, alternative means are sought through the black market.

Other obstacles include the absence of clear distinctions between social and commercial insurance; foreign exchange rationing, which presents difficulties for Chinese companies that want to borrow offshore; and the short-term mentality of the Chinese stock markets, which contributes to high volatility on the two exchanges and to speculative behavior (despite official affirmation of the role of securities markets in the ninth five-year plan). The China Securities Regulatory Commission lacks clarity as to its role and is plagued by overlapping responsibilities with competing regulatory agencies. It also operates in a legal vacuum with respect to the scope of its authority and jurisdiction.

Finally, the restricted role of foreign financial institutions reduces the forces of innovation available to the financial system. Although the government has allowed foreign banks to open a limited number of bank branches, the majority of approved foreign bank applications are for representative offices, which are still prohibited from engaging in profit-making activities. China's bid to join the World Trade Organization has increased pressure for it to expand the role of foreign institutions by providing full market access, national treatment, and a timetable for implementing specific measures to deregulate and open the financial sector.

References

Economist Intelligence Unit (EIU). 1992. *Financing Foreign Operation: China*. New York: The Economist Intelligence Unit.

Holmes, William D. 1996. China's Financial Reforms in the Global Market. Paper presented at the Conference on Regulation of Capital Markets and Financial Services in the Pacific Rim, Georgetown University Law Center, Washington (11-13 November).

International Financial Law Review. 1997. *Banking Yearbook 1997*. London: Euromoney Publications.

Lamble, Peter, and Robin Low. 1995. *The Asia Pacific Insurance Handbook*. Sydney, NWT: Coopers & Lybrand.

Takahashi, Yuichi. 1994. *Financial Sector Reform in the Asia Pacific Countries*. Photocopy.

US Department of the Treasury. 1994. *National Treatment Study* Washington: Government Printing Office.

Hong Kong

Introduction

Under British rule, Hong Kong adopted a system of common law and established a free market economy. These twin systems provided the basis for the country's transformation from a small fishing economy to one of the world's largest financial markets (Hsu 1996, 5). Before 1964, however, there were virtually no regulations governing the financial sector in Hong Kong. A banking crisis in the 1960s led authorities to enact Banking Ordinance 1964, which introduced basic standards such as minimum capital requirements and rudimentary disclosure laws. This ordinance alone was not sufficient to provide a stable and safe environment for the financial market. Bank failures, caused by poor management and excessive investment in the real estate market in the early 1980s, coupled with the stock market crash in 1987, resulted in a complete overhaul of Hong Kong financial market regulations. The country now has a transparent legal and regulatory environment that has facilitated its role as a modern regional and international financial center (US & Foreign Commercial Service 1997, 7).

Under the Sino-British Joint Declaration on the Future of Hong Kong, Chinese authorities were committed to enact the Basic Law of the Hong Kong Special Administrative Region. The Basic Law is the legal basis for the "One Country, Two System" guarantee and provides for the continuance of Hong Kong's system of common law and free market economic system after 1 July 1997.[1] The law stipulates that the Hong Kong

---

1. On 1 July 1997 China resumed sovereignty over Hong Kong.

dollar will remain freely convertible; that markets for foreign exchange, securities, futures, and other financial products will remain open; and that no controls will be placed on the flow of capital into or out of Hong Kong. The Hong Kong Special Administrative Region has the freedom to govern its own business and economic environment and maintain its own separate currency, the Hong Kong dollar. The Hong Kong dollar has been pegged to the US dollar, at HK$7.8/US$1, since 1983. Under a currency board system, the Hong Kong dollar is fully backed by US dollar reserves at the exchange rate.

Hong Kong has a competitive financial market. Laws are applied on a nondiscriminatory basis. There are no controls on the cost or flow of credit and the financial sector is completely controlled by the private sector.

Regulatory Framework

Three government agencies are responsible for regulating Hong Kong's financial market: the Hong Kong Monetary Authority (HKMA), the Securities and Futures Commission (SFC), and the Insurance Authority. In addition to being regulated and supervised by the HKMA, banks are required to become members of and adhere to the rules of the Hong Kong Association of Banks (HKAB).

The HKMA was formed in 1993 from the merger of the Office of the Exchange Fund and the Office of the Commissioner of Banking. Hong Kong has no central bank per se. The HKMA does, however, assume many of the responsibilities typically assigned to a central bank, including ensuring the safety and soundness of the banking system and the stability of the currency.

Three private banks—the Hongkong Shanghai Bank, the Bank of China, and Standard Chartered—are authorized to issue HK dollars. Under the currency board system, these banks are allowed to issue HK dollars only upon depositing US dollars in the Exchange Fund, which is regulated by the HKMA. In 1990, the HKMA began to issue Exchange Fund Bills and, in 1993, Exchange Fund Notes, which are both HK dollar debt securities. The issuance of debt securities through open-market operations provides the HKMA with a mechanism for adjusting interbank liquidity.

The Banking Ordinance is the basis of the legal framework governing the banking sector. The Bank Advisory Committee, which is composed of members of public-sector and private financial institutions, advises government authorities on issues concerning the Banking Ordinance.

The Banking Ordinance was amended in 1986 to authorize the Commissioner of Banking to regulate the banking sector, set minimum capital standards, and limit loans to customers and bank employees (US

Treasury 1994, 265). Amendments to the ordinance in 1995 gave the HKMA broader powers, including responsibility for all matters pertaining to the authorization of banks. The HKMA can suspend or revoke the license of a bank found to be in violation of regulations designed to protect the safety and soundness of the financial system. It is also authorized, after consultation with the Financial Secretary of Hong Kong, to take over a financial institution that is unable to make payments or if it is deemed in the public interest to take control of the firm (Hsu 1996, 24-25). The Banking Ordinance was further amended in 1997 to provide for the regulation of multipurpose stored value cards[2] and money brokers.

The clearing and settlements system in Hong Kong changed in April 1997. Until that time, the Hongkong Shanghai Bank managed the Clearing House of the Hong Kong Association of Banks and settled interbank payments. The Clearing House is now managed by Hong Kong Interbank Clearing Limited, which is jointly owned by HKMA and HKAB. Under the new system, interbank payments are cleared through the Exchange Fund.

The Stock Exchange of Hong Kong (SEHK) operates as a private entity. Thus when the stock market crashed in 1987, the Securities Commission had no legal authority to intervene in the affairs of the SEHK. The regulatory infrastructure for the securities industry has since been revamped and, in 1989, the Securities and Futures Commission Ordinance was enacted. This Ordinance provides the legal basis for the SFC to supervise and regulate the securities industry. The SFC now has the authority to take actions necessary to protect the safety of the securities market and to prosecute individuals who breach securities market ordinances and codes.

Financial Institutions

Services account for more than 80 percent of GDP in Hong Kong. The financial market not only contributes to a significant percentage of the service economy but also facilitates the growth of other key service sectors, such as transportation. The government's laissez-faire policies are extended to the financial sector, and the private sector owns 100 percent ownership of the country's financial services firms.

---

2. Multipurpose stored value cards (smart cards) hold a predetermined amount of money that can be used to purchase goods and services from the issuer of the card or a third party. Only those multipurpose cards used for third-party transactions are subject to regulation. Credit card issuers are not subject to HKMA regulation, but must adhere to standards of good practice set by the HKAB (Institute of International Bankers 1997, 107).

Direct Finance

There is a three-tier banking system of "authorized institutions" in Hong Kong: licensed banks, restricted-license banks, or deposit-taking companies. Only licensed banks are permitted to accept deposits of any size and maturity and to offer checking and savings accounts. They effectively function as commercial banks. Restricted-license banks are limited to accepting deposits of more than HK$500,000 and thus offer investment banking services. Deposit-taking companies are only authorized to accept deposits over HK$100,000 that have an initial maturity of at least three months.[3] As of February 1997, there were 182 licensed banks, 61 restricted-license banks, and 123 deposit-taking companies in Hong Kong (HKMA 1997a, 1).

The largest bank in Hong Kong is the Hongkong Shanghai Bank. It has majority ownership of the Hang Seng Bank, which alone has 340 branches and is estimated to hold 40 percent of Hong Kong dollar deposits (US Treasury 1994, 261). The five largest banks in Hong Kong control 40 percent of assets in the banking sector. Market concentration in Hong Kong is comparable to that of emerging markets in Asia, but is significantly higher than that in major financial centers in developed economies. Nonetheless, banks in Hong Kong are considered well placed to compete internationally; their operating costs are relatively low and, as a result of recent changes to disclosure laws, it has become apparent that their balance sheets are healthy (*The Financial Times*, 19 March 1996).

Financial Intermediaries

There were four stock exchanges in Hong Kong until 1986, when the four were merged into the Stock Exchange of Hong Kong (SEHK) in an effort to consolidate management and control of the market (Hsu 1996, 41). By the end of 1996, the SEHK was the second largest stock exchange in Asia and the seventh largest stock exchange in the world, with total market capitalization of US$446 billion. The Hong Kong Futures Exchange offers futures contracts in finance, properties, utilities, and commerce and industry (US Treasury 1994, 284).

The financial market in Hong Kong is one of the largest in the world. In April 1995, the average daily turnover of foreign exchange was US$56 billion, making Hong Kong the world's fifth largest trading center for

---

3. Until 1994, the Hong Kong Association of Banks (HKAB) set interest rates on time deposits. Deposit-taking companies were excluded from interest rate policies and developed a niche in the savings market by offering high interest rates to depositors (Takahashi 1994, 24). Since interest rates were deregulated, the number of deposit-taking companies has fallen from 143 in 1993 to 123 in 1997.

foreign exchange derivatives. Hong Kong is also the eighth largest center in the world for interest rate derivatives, with an average daily turnover of US$18 billion.

The domestic debt market is thin compared to Hong Kong's equity and foreign exchange market. In an effort to deepen the local debt market the HKMA introduced Exchange Fund Bills in 1989 and Exchange Fund Notes in 1993. At the end of 1996, outstanding Exchange Fund Bills and Notes totaled approximately US$8 billion.

Prudential Regulations

Hong Kong adheres to the Basle principles for bank supervision. The approach is one of ongoing supervision and includes on-site reviews of operations and financial records and off-site reviews of financial statements and reports. Banks are required to be incorporated and publish detailed audit reports as well as monthly returns showing assets and liabilities. In addition to information on their balance sheet and quality of assets, banks are required to disclose inner reserves, realized profits, and net assets. Authorities meet annually with internal and external auditors to review each institution's audit and determine if the institution is in compliance with prudential standards and the Banking Ordinance. The Banking Ordinance, in turn, provides a legal basis for enforcing the Basle standards. Violation of the Banking Ordinance is punishable by fines, imprisonment, or both.

The Banking Ordinance restricts the use of the word "bank" to those institutions that are either licensed or restricted-license banks. In the latter case, the word "bank" must be accompanied by either "merchant" or "investment." Only a "fit and proper person" can be issued a banking license, and there exist controls regarding the ownership and management of an authorized financial institution (Hsu 1996, 23). An authorized institution is required to inform the HKMA if it makes changes to any documents that outline the institution's procedures. Approval is also required before there can be any changes in a bank's ownership.

The Banking Ordinance also sets forth minimum capital requirements for authorized institutions. Locally incorporated banks must have paid-in capital equal to US$388 million and net assets of US$518 million dollars for authorization to operate a licensed bank. Applicants for a restricted-license bank must have paid-in capital equal to US$12.8 million (US Treasury 1994, 263).

Authorized institutions are not permitted to lend more than 25 percent of their capital base to a single customer or group of related customers, nor are they allowed to hold more than 25 percent of shares in other companies. No more than 10 percent of an authorized institution's capital base may be used for unsecured loans.

The HKMA adopted BIS capital-adequacy guidelines in 1989. The minimum standard according to BIS recommendations is a capital-adequacy ratio of 8 percent. The national requirement in Hong Kong is also 8 percent, although some banks are required to maintain 12 percent and some nonbanks at least 16 percent. The actual risk-based capital-adequacy ratio at the end of 1995 was 17.5 percent. In December 1996, the HKMA implemented reporting requirements that direct banks to address market risk in calculating their capital-adequacy ratio.

After the stock market crash of 1987, the SFC was charged with overhauling the regulations that govern securities market participants. Applicants for a license to deal in securities or operate as an investment adviser are now required to meet the "fit and proper person" criterion. Applicants seeking a dealer's license must also have minimum net capital of HK$5 million. Although there is no deposit insurance for bank customers, there is a compensating fund for individuals whose brokers default on funds owed.

In 1991 the Securities (Insider Dealing) Ordinance was amended, resulting in higher penalties for insider trading. Fraud and misrepresentation are also punishable by the SFC. Another ordinance enacted in 1991 calls on a company's directors and executives, as well as those who acquire more than 10 percent of a company's voting shares, to publicly disclose their dealings. Firms seeking to list on the SEHK must make a prospectus publicly available. The SFC has the authority to determine which clearinghouses are permitted to settle accounts and their rules of operation in order to ensure a sound clearinghouse system.

Foreign Participation

Foreign-owned commercial banks can enter the Hong Kong banking industry by establishing a branch or by acquiring ownership of a local bank. Foreign-owned firms must apply for a license to enter the financial services market. License approval is subject to four criteria: foreign-owned firms must (1) have net assets of US$16 billion, (2) be incorporated in a country that applies the Basle principles for bank supervision, (3) have approval from their home country to operate a branch in Hong Kong, and (4) come from a country that offers reciprocal access to Hong Kong banks (US Treasury 1994, 268). Of the 366 banks in Hong Kong in February 1997, 333 were owned by foreign interests. Overseas incorporated banks hold 78 percent of the country's banking assets (Goldstein and Turner 1996, 35), and bank deposits denominated in foreign currency represent 56 percent of total bank deposits.

Foreign-owned financial services firms can engage in securities market activities in Hong Kong in one of two ways. Firms that do not deal in the securities market as their primary business may engage in securities market transactions through an "exempt" license. Foreign-owned securities firms are also free to establish branches or subsidiaries in Hong Kong subject to approval from the SFC. Securities firms offer a wide range of services, from managing portfolios to selling foreign mutual funds to administering local pension plans.

Foreign firms are allowed to list on the Hong Kong stock exchange. The SEHK plays a key role in raising equity capital for firms in China. Authorities from the SEHK signed a memorandum of understanding with Chinese officials in 1993 under which Chinese state-owned enterprises are permitted to list H shares, denominated in renminbi, on the SEHK provided the firms meet Hong Kong regulatory and accounting requirements (US Treasury 1994, 280). Of the 633 companies listed on the SEHK in September 1997, 35 were incorporated in China and 21 were incorporated outside of either Hong Kong or China (SEHK 1997).

Hong Kong has a relatively well developed insurance market. Ranked by premium income, it is the 5th largest market in Asia and the 24th largest market in the world. Subject to approval from the Insurance Authority to operate in Hong Kong, foreign-owned insurance firms compete on a nondiscriminatory basis with domestic insurance firms. Of the 223 insurance firms in Hong Kong in 1996, 123 were foreign companies.

Remaining Obstacles

Hong Kong, for the most part, offers foreign financial services firms an open and transparent environment for conducting offshore and domestic business. There are no restrictions on the flow of funds into or out of the area, nor are there any restrictions on foreign firms acquiring local firms. In this laissez-faire environment, foreign and domestic financial services firms play an active role in working with the HKMA to develop laws and codes that are conducive to a safe, sound, and competitive international financial market.

Hong Kong does maintain restrictions on the number of branches that foreign banks are permitted to operate. In 1994, authorities relaxed the one-branch limit for foreign banks, allowing them to open one additional office in a separate building from the location of their main branch; however, the additional office is to be used only for "back office" functions such as processing and settling transactions conducted in the main branch office. Fully licensed banks (commercial banks) are allowed to establish operations in Hong Kong only as a bank branch. Restricted-license banks (investment banks) are permitted to open branches or subsidiaries. Licenses for deposit-taking companies are extended only to locally incorporated subsidiaries.

Hong Kong's offer in the WTO financial services agreement included measures that will remove some of the remaining barriers for foreign financial services firms when it takes effect in early 1998. First, restrictions on the number of branches foreign banks can operate will be removed for foreign fully-licensed banks that received a license before May 1978 and for foreign restricted-license banks that received a license before April 1990. Further, in contrast to current practice, locally incorporated, limited companies will no longer have to be predominantly owned by Hong Kong interests to apply for a new, full banking license. Other measures included in Hong Kong's offer—such as the guarantee that foreign insurance firms will have the right to enter Hong Kong as either a branch or subsidiary and the right to 100 percent ownership—will bind Hong Kong's current practices to the WTO framework.

References

Goldstein, Morris, and Phillip Turner. 1996. Banking Crises in Emerging Economies: Origins and Policy Options. *BIS Economic Papers*, no. 46 (October).

Hong Kong Monetary Authority (HKMA). 1997a. *Banking in Hong Kong*. (http://www.info.gov.hk/info/banking.htm).

Hong Kong Monetary Authority (HKMA). 1997b. *Linked Exchange Rate System*. (http//:www.info.gov.hk.hkma/rate.htm).

Hsu, Berry Fong-Chung. 1996. The Developing Regulatory Framework of Banking and Finance in Hong Kong. Presented at the Conference on Regulation of Capital Markets in the Pacific Rim, Georgetown University Law Center, Washington (11-13 November).

Institute of International Bankers. 1997. *Global Survey 1997*. New York: Institute of International Bankers.

The Stock Exchange of Hong Kong (SEHK). 1997. *Equity Market Statistics*. (http://www.schk.com.hk/english/markets/cash/statistics/equity.htm).

Takahashi, Yuichi. 1994. Financial Sector Reform in the Asia Pacific Countries. Photocopy.

US Department of the Treasury. 1994. *National Treatment Study*. Washington: Government Printing Office.

US & Foreign Commercial Service. 1997. Hong Kong. *International Market Insight: Market Research Report*. Stat-USA.

India

Introduction

The government of India nationalized the country's 14 largest banks in 1969, leaving 19 banks wholly owned by the government throughout the 1970s and 1980s. During the same period, the government held a monopoly on investment and production in the most important sectors of the economy.[1] Foreign investment was negligible and the domestic financial sector was dominated by the nationalized banks, which were, at the government's discretion, directed to channel investments toward priority projects and sectors. Virtually every aspect of the capital market was managed by the government, from interest rates to exchange rates to the price at which shares in publicly listed companies were allowed to trade on the stock exchange. There were few prudential standards during this period. Labor markets and international trade were both highly controlled and protected.

The impact of pervasive government control over the economy was apparent by the mid-1980s. Growth was too slow to allay rising poverty; and it was increasingly clear that inefficiencies in state-owned industries were largely responsible for the slow economic growth.[2]

---

1. The government nationalized key industries in the early 1950s.

2. For example, from 1977 to 1987, the return to public investment in manufacturing ranged from 3 to 5 percent and the return to private investment in manufacturing ranged from 17 to 23 percent.

India therefore undertook moderate attempts to liberalize the economy beginning in 1985. Although economic growth did accelerate in the late 1980s, the gains were insufficient to deal with rising internal and external imbalances. In fiscal year (FY) 1990-91 (beginning 1 April), the fiscal deficit was 8.4 percent of GDP and the current account deficit equal to 3.7 percent of GDP. The official exchange rate was fixed, and by June 1991, India's international reserves could cover only two weeks' worth of imports.

In 1991, with the goal of improving the country's fiscal position and balance of payments, India initiated a program of stabilization and structural reform. The fixed exchange rate was first devalued and then, in 1993, a market-based exchange rate was introduced. Since 1991, the trade regime has been gradually liberalized, most sectors of the economy have been opened to at least some private investment, and the market has been progressively opened to foreign direct and portfolio investment.[3]

India has succeeded in bringing about economic stability and growth in a remarkably short time. GDP growth was less than 1 percent annually in FY 1991-92. By FY 1992-93, real GDP grew 5.1 percent. Between FY 1992-93 and 1996-97, GDP growth averaged 6.0 percent annually. Within a year after the start of the stabilization plan, the fiscal deficit and current account deficit were brought down to 3.2 percent and 0.5 percent of GDP, respectively. The current account deficit subsequently began to grow again, but the concomitant floating of the currency and reduction of barriers to foreign investment have helped ease pressure on the balance of payments. Over the last five years, India's macroeconomic environment has continued to improve. Although substantial reforms have been implemented, if India is to sustain growth rates high enough to help decrease poverty levels, significant reforms still need to be made, particularly in the capital and credit markets.

Foreign exchange rules have recently been relaxed, but the capital account is not yet freely convertible. Individuals are permitted to purchase, from authorized dealers, foreign exchange of up to $3,000.[4] Authorized dealers are allowed to advance up to $15,000 dollars for advanced remittances on imports of goods and services without a bank guarantee to release the foreign exchange. Companies with a foreign exchange balance are now permitted to invest up to $15 million in projects outside

---

3. Between FY 1990-91 and FY 1994-95, the maximum import tariff fell from 300 percent to 65 percent and the average import tariff from 87 percent to 33 percent. Trade in goods and services as a percentage of GDP grew from 8 percent to 27 percent during this same period.

4. The amount of foreign exchange that an individual is permitted to purchase depends upon its intended use. Thus, individuals may acquire up to $1,000 if it is to be given as a gift or contributed to an overseas charity or cultural organization. Foreign exchange of up to $3,000 per person is authorized for basic travel.

India without approval from the central bank. Residents continue to be prohibited from holding accounts in foreign currencies, and foreign companies are not generally allowed to hold rupee accounts.[5]

After simplifying the interest rate structure during the initial phases of reform, the Reserve Bank of India (RBI) began to relax ceilings on bank deposits and floors on lending rates. In 1995, the RBI removed interest rate ceilings on term deposits over two years; controls on deposits over one year, loans larger than Rs200,000, and select export credits were removed thereafter. Interest rates on shorter-term deposits and smaller loans continue to be set by the RBI. Other significant reforms yet to be made in the financial sector include the removal of remaining barriers to foreign direct and portfolio investment and of controls that distort the domestic allocation of credit. Some controls, such as those on interest rates, have been proposed for removal while others, such as credit allocation to priority sectors, remain part of the government's economic plans.

Regulatory Framework

The Reserve Bank of India, at the direction of the government, promulgates and administers exchange regulations. Any foreign exchange transactions not specifically authorized must be approved by the RBI on a case-by-case basis. All foreign exchange transactions, whether preapproved or not, must be reported to the RBI daily.

The RBI regulates and supervises banks, nonbank financial institutions (NBFIs), and financial institutions.[6] Financial institutions under the RBI's authority include state finance and industrial development corporations. Financial services firms regulated by the RBI are required to follow its directives on lending and deposit rates and on the percent of total credit that must be lent to priority sectors of the economy. Amendments to the Banking Regulation Act in 1983 resulted in commercial banks' being allowed to establish merchant banking subsidiaries. Thus all domestic and foreign banks in India now effectively offer universal banking services.

In 1994, the RBI established the Board of Financial Supervision (BFS), which operates as a unit of the RBI. Its mandate is to strengthen supervision of the financial system by integrating oversight of the activities of financial services firms. The BFS has recently established a subcommittee to routinely examine auditing practices, quality, and coverage. The board has also recommended the establishment of a bank rating methodology based on capital adequacy, asset quality, management, earnings, and liquidity (CAMEL) criteria.

---

5. An exception is made for foreign banking, financial, shipping, and airline companies.

6. Development banks in India are considered financial institutions.

Until 1997 there was in fact very little supervision of the activities conducted by NBFIs. What regulation and supervision did exist tended to focus on protecting depositors only, and the RBI had very little recourse to require NBFIs to adhere to a wider range of prudential standards. In 1997, amendments to the Reserve Bank Act gave the RBI authority to enforce compliance with central bank regulations. Given the broad range of services provided by NBFIs (see below), new regulations were issued to focus on the management of assets as well as deposits.

In 1988, the Securities and Exchange Board of India (SEBI) was established. Four years later, it was given statutory authority, and in 1995 it was declared an autonomous government agency, free to promulgate regulations without prior approval from the Ministry of Finance. SEBI is now responsible for regulating and supervising stock exchanges, mutual funds, investment banks, and brokers. SEBI is also responsible for monitoring the activities of venture capital companies, which, starting in 1997, have been allowed to invest in unlisted companies and to provide turn-around loans and loans to start-up companies.

All firms listed on a stock exchange in India—brokers, foreign exchange dealers, and foreign financial institutions (FIIs)—must first be registered with SEBI. SEBI has the authority to impose fines or other civil penalties on those not in compliance with securities laws. These include laws against manipulating the market, making misleading statements in order to facilitate a securities market transaction, and violating listing criteria.

Foreign investors wishing to establish a commercial bank in India or to expand existing operations must first receive a license from the RBI to open a bank branch. Authorization for foreign direct investment in the securities market must be procured from SEBI. All foreign investment in financial services must also be approved by the Foreign Investment Promotion Board (FIPB). Approval is required from the RBI for offshore loans of less than $3 million and from the Ministry of Finance for loans greater than $3 million.

Financial Institutions

India's financial market is somewhat more diversified than other emerging markets and has much more depth than the markets of other countries at similar income levels. For example, in 1994 India's banks accounted for 80 percent of total assets held by both banks and nonbank financial institutions; comparable figures for Indonesia and Brazil are 91 percent and 97 percent, respectively. Bank deposits as a percentage of GDP in India have grown from 13 percent in 1969 to 41 percent in 1995. And in 1995, market capitalization as a percent of GDP was 67.2 percent in India. By way of comparison, market capitalization as a percentage of GDP was 33.2 percent in Indonesia and 21.1 percent in Brazil in the same year.

While India's financial services industry remains dominated by state-owned entities, private domestic and foreign financial services firms are slowly gaining market share in banking and securities. Prior to initiating reforms, the state controlled over 90 percent of loans and deposits, whereas by 1996, state-owned banks accounted for 80 percent of loans and 87 percent of deposits in the banking system. State-managed mutual funds still account for the majority of mutual fund investment, and the government holds a monopoly on the insurance industry.

Financial Intermediaries

In 1969, there were 89 banks and 8,262 bank branches in India. Of these, the number of public-sector banking branches grew from just over 7,000 in 1969 to more than 63,000 in 1995. As a result of policies encouraging the establishment of branches in and extension of credit to rural communities, rural branches now account for over 50 percent of all bank branches.

The private sector can enter the financial intermediary market through two main channels. First, private banks and nonbank financial intermediaries may be licensed by the RBI to open a new bank or branch. Under this option, the RBI's new guidelines on capital requirements and other standards must be met. By 1996, 10 of 13 new private banks licensed by the RBI had started operating.

In order to help banks recapitalize, the government authorized public-sector banks to raise capital on the market. Thus, the second way to participate in the provision of financial intermediary services in India is to acquire shares in state-owned banks. The maximum permissible private ownership in state-owned banks is 49 percent. As of March 1997, three state-owned banks had offered their shares in the market.

NBFIs play a fairly important role in India's financial market. The relative lack until very recently of regulations governing their activities allowed them to be more responsive to market demands than commercial and merchant banks. Thus, different NBFIs offer consumer financing, leasing and purchase financing, investment banking, underwriting, portfolio management, venture capital activities, and foreign exchange advising. The number of NBFIs has grown from just over 7,000 in 1981 to roughly 50,000 in 1997. Of these 50,000, approximately 800 have net owned funds greater than Rs5 million, the minimum amount required to get a credit rating.

The government continues to hold a monopoly on the insurance industry. There is one life insurance company, the Life Insurance Corporation of India (LIC), and one provider, the General Insurance Company (including its four subsidiaries), for all other types of insurance. India does not have any large pension fund or financial companies that provide only pension fund services. Any firm wishing to set up a pension fund for its employees can either set up its own plan or join the Group Superannuation Fund, operated by the LIC. Acquiring approval to establish a plan is difficult, and so most firms choose to work with the LIC fund.

Direct Finance

India's stock exchanges have been slow to modernize. Prior to 1992, none of the country's 21 stock exchanges were computer based. All trading was done in an open-outcry system and settlement could take weeks to process, with all trades delivered on paper and by hand, requiring dozens of signatures prior to actual delivery. In 1992, an electronic Over-the-Counter Exchange of India (OTCEI) opened in Bombay. The OTCEI was modeled after the NASDAQ in New York and designed to serve the needs of small investors and small companies. In 1994, an automated, screen-based exchange, the National Stock Exchange (NSE), began operating in Bombay, directly competing with the Bombay Stock Exchange (BSE), the nation's oldest exchange. A year after the NSE began operations, the BSE switched to electronic trading.

From 1991 to 1996, the nominal value of market capitalization in India grew by over 150 percent, reaching $122.6 million in 1996. With almost 9,000 publicly listed companies, the Indian stock exchange is less concentrated than its counterparts in many other emerging markets. In 1996, the 10 largest stocks in India represented 20 percent of total market capitalization, whereas in Argentina the 10 largest stocks accounted for 50 percent of the market; in Brazil, 38 percent; in Chile, 40 percent; and in Mexico, 33 percent.

The Unit Trust of India (UTI) enjoyed a complete monopoly in the mutual funds industry from 1963 to 1987, when public banks and insurance companies were authorized to set up mutual funds. The private sector was permitted to enter the market in 1992. Nationalized banks, government-owned insurance companies, and state development banks now control mutual funds, and compete directly with private-sector managed funds, although the UTI continues to dominate, holding, as of FY 1994-95, just over 75 percent of the market. The remainder of the mutual fund market is split evenly between private-sector and other public-sector mutual funds.

Since 1995, the RBI has undertaken an array of initiatives to widen and deepen the securities market. Prudential controls in the securities market have been tightened. In 1996, the government established a primary dealers system and authorized six agents to deal in government securities. In December 1996, an electronic securities depository began operating and, in early 1997, the government approved the use of interest-rate swaps, currency swaps, and other derivatives to hedge risk.

Prudential Regulation

A central component of the reform process has been the initiation and, in some cases, implementation of new prudential controls over banks, nonbank financial intermediaries, and firms involved in the securities market. Some of the changes, discussed above, have resulted in new regulatory bodies or increased powers for those tasked with regulating and supervising the financial services industry. The government has also undertaken measures to promote better asset management and to improve safety, soundness, and transparency in all areas of the financial services industry.

A 1985 study by the RBI concluded that there was an urgent need for financial institutions to make their financial statements more transparent. It was not until 1991, however, when the government launched economic reforms, that the recommendations of the report became a component of government policy toward financial services firms. When the Department of Supervision took over inspection of banks, NBFIs, and other financial institutions, it implemented a new reporting system for firms filing quarterly reports. The new system requires banks to determine and list the risks associated with their assets, liabilities, and off-balance sheet exposures and capital base. Credit exposure to single borrowers as well as borrowers' exposure are to be included in financial statements. Financial services firms are obligated to report information on the number of nonperforming loans, categorized by size and type of loan. Provisions made for loan losses, taxes, and other contingencies are to be included in publicly disclosed accounts. Lack of consistency in defining what constitutes a nonperforming loan and how banks account for loan losses in their financial statements has, however, precluded banks from attaining the degree of transparency intended under the regulations.

The RBI has established BIS capital adequacy requirements as the standard for public and private banks wishing to engage in operations in India. The deadline for meeting the 8 percent capital-risk weighted-asset ratio was March 1997, but it was postponed because a number of major state banks were not able to meet the deadline.

Indian regulations specify two types of reserves to be held by banks: the cash reserve ratio and the statutory lending ratio.[7] Banks are re-

7. Reserve requirements in India have historically been used, and continue to be used, as a tool of monetary and/or credit policy as opposed to being used as prudential controls. Thus, recent reductions in reserve requirements reflect the goal of lowering the cost of credit to the private sector rather than the goal of increasing the efficiency or profitability of the banking sector.

quired to maintain cash reserve ratios (CRRs) with the Reserve Bank of India. The CRR is calculated as a percentage of net demand and time liabilities. At the end of January 1997, the CRR was 10 percent.[8] The statutory liquidity ratio (SLR) establishes the investment that banks are required to make in the government and in government-approved securities; the SLR for new deposits is 25 percent and 37.5 percent for old deposits. The RBI committed to bringing the overall SLR down to 25 percent by March 1997.[9]

Prior to receiving a license to establish a new branch, banks must meet the following criteria: they must demonstrate compliance with the 8 percent capital-risk weighted asset ratio; they must have had net profits for three consecutive years; they must have minimum net owned funds of Rs100 billion; nonperforming assets must not exceed 15 percent of outstanding loans; and a plan for the new branch must be submitted to and approved by the RBI.

In January 1997, the government of India amended the Reserve Bank of India Act, resulting in changes to, among other things, the regulation and supervision of NBFIs. For the first time NBFIs, now defined to include any company whose principal business involves receiving deposits or lending funds in any manner, have to meet minimum capital criteria. In addition, RBI regulations specify that NBFIs are required to have minimum net owned funds of Rs25 million, and to keep liquid assets, which may be held in approved securities, equal to 5 percent of total deposits. NBFIs are also directed to create a reserve fund by transferring 20 percent of their net profits into the fund annually.[10]

The amendments to the act stipulate that unincorporated entities are prohibited from accepting deposits if their principal business involves accepting deposits or making loans, effectively requiring all major NBFIs to be incorporated. NBFIs are also now required to obtain a certificate of registration in order to establish or maintain operations. The RBI is authorized to extend the time frame within which banks are required to meet the prescribed minimum capital requirements and has also been given the authority to cancel the registration of NBFIs that violate the laws governing NBFI activities.

Efforts began in 1991 to increase protection of shareholders and to establish regulatory standards that will promote a stable securities market. Some improvements to date are a function of increased prudential controls established by SEBI, whereas others are a function of increased

---

8. The CRR was lowered from 14 percent in March 1996 to 10 percent in January 1997.

9. Since April 1997, scheduled commercial banks have been exempt from the SLR.

10. Reserve Bank of India, Non-Banking Financial Institutions—Summary of the Recent Amendments to the RBI Act. Press Release, 9 May 1997 (http://www.reservebank.com/pressrel/97059.html).

competition between stock exchanges. Since 1991, SEBI has banned insider trading, established rules for takeovers, and abolished controls on prices of new shares issues. Companies listing on an exchange must meet disclosure rules and register with SEBI prior to listing. In 1995, SEBI implemented regulations intended to prohibit price rigging and other unfair trading practices in securities markets.

In 1996, regulations governing requirements for companies wishing to be publicly listed were tightened. Firms issuing shares for the first time must demonstrate a track record of having paid dividends in three of the five years preceding the public offering. Those not able to meet this standard can list on the OTCEI or access the market if their project is appraised by a commercial bank and the bank supplies at least 10 percent of the equity capital in the project's total cost. An average of 5 new shareholders for new listings, and 10 for continuing listings, are required for every Rs100,000 raised on the market. SEBI also requires that at least 50 percent of a public listing be allocated to individual investors who buy less than 1,000 shares in the company. Despite repeated calls for SEBI to establish minimum capital requirements, none have been implemented to date.

Prior to the introduction of a screen-based computerized trading system on the stock exchanges, investors had no means to determine the actual price at which an exchange was conducted. Investors would place an order and the broker would execute the deal in an open-outcry system at a price that was theoretically settled on the exchange. The introduction of computer-based, instantaneous transactions has helped increase the transparency of securities trading. Similarly, the reduction of the settlement period from two weeks to one week on one exchange has not only encouraged other exchanges to follow suit and reduce settlement time but also has helped alleviate concerns that brokers were delaying fund transfers in order to retain client funds for their own use.

Foreign Participation

Foreign investors can participate in the Indian financial services market through a number of channels. Foreign direct investment in banks and nonbank financial institutions is permitted. For instance, foreign institutional investors (FIIs) are allowed to acquire equity in publicly listed firms and government securities, but only nonresident Indians and approved FIIs are allowed to invest directly in Indian securities. The percent of foreign ownership sanctioned by the government varies from one type of financial service to another. All foreign investment in financial services must be approved by the Foreign Investment Promotion Board (FIPB) and the appropriate regulatory authority.

Permission from the RBI is required in order to establish a representative office or open a new branch of a financial services firm. The share of a bank's total equity that can be held by a foreign investor depends on the amount of capital to be invested and whether the bank is a new or established entity. Foreign investors are allowed to acquire up to 20 percent of an established public-sector bank and up to 30 percent of a private domestic finance company. The FIPB guidelines delineate ownership rules for new banks. If more than $50 million is to be invested in establishing a new financial services firm, the project can be 100 percent foreign owned. For investments between $5 million and $50 million, foreign investors can own up to 75 percent of shares. Foreign investors are limited to 51 percent or less of equity in a financial services firm if the total investment is less than $5 million.

The RBI is committed to authorizing eight new foreign branch licenses, for both new and established banks, annually. Since 1993, 25 branch licenses have been approved for foreign firms. As of mid-1996, there were 38 foreign banks operating a total of 166 branches in India, and they accounted for 7.5 percent of the deposits in the system and 8.9 percent of total loans.

Operating conditions for foreign banks are fairly restrictive in India. Capital requirements are determined by the amount of capital in foreign banks' local branches. Foreign banks are subject to the same interest rate requirements as domestic banks and are required to meet RBI lending targets. Foreign banks are required to lend 34 percent of net credit to priority sectors.[11] Of this, a minimum of 10 percent must go to small-scale industries and 12 percent to export industries. Any shortfall must be deposited with the Small Industries Development Bank of India, which specializes in small-scale credit. Since foreign banks are not permitted to establish branches in rural areas, they rarely meet priority sector lending requirements. As a result, in FY 1995-65, foreign banks deposited a total of Rs1.24 billion in the Small Industries Development Bank of India. Despite these constraints on their operations in FY 1995-96, the top 23 foreign banks posted a net profit of Rs7.7 billion, approximately Rs2.5 billion more than the total profit recorded by the top 34 private domestic banks.[12] These figures represent growth in net profit of 22 percent for foreign banks and 50 percent for private domestic banks.

One hundred percent foreign ownership of nonbank financial subsidiaries engaged in securities activities is permitted, subject to authorization

---

11. Domestic banks are required to allocate 40 percent of loans to priority sectors.

12. In the same fiscal year the 19 nationalized banks had total losses of Rs2.2 billion and the State Bank of India net profit equal to Rs8.3 billion. As a result of net losses in eight state banks, state-owned banks as a group reported net losses in 1996.

from the RBI, SEBI, and the FIPB. Although investment banking continues to be dominated by publicly owned financial institutions, foreign investors have begun to develop a market presence in this area. In 1995, Goldman Sachs acquired 28 percent of the investment banking subsidiary of one of India's largest NBFIs, Kotak Magindra. The following year, Morgan Stanley was authorized to open a fully owned investment bank, and Bank of America was permitted to own 80 percent of an investment banking subsidiary. Other joint ventures have been approved in which foreign firms from France, the United States, and South Korea have acquired holdings in publicly and privately owned Indian investment banks.

In 1992, the Government of India authorized FIIs to directly invest in the country's stock markets. In the past year, permissible investments by FIIs have been considerably expanded. In 1997, gilt-edged government securities and companies not publicly listed were opened to FIIs. Individual FIIs are allowed to hold up to 10 percent of a company's equity; total FII ownership is capped at 30 percent of equity in a firm.

There are currently 427 FIIs registered in India, with the top 25 accounting for approximately 60-65 percent of debt and equity purchased by FIIs. Net investment by FIIs has risen from $4.3 million in FY 1992-93, the first year in which FII investment was permitted in India, to more than $2 billion in 1996.

Since 1992, foreign investors have been allowed to acquire equity in Indian firms through Global Depository Receipts (GDRs) listed on overseas exchanges. In 1994, annual issues of GDRs peaked at more than $3 billion. Issues of GDRs fell the next year to approximately $250 million. International equity offerings for shares in two state-owned utility companies are expected to bring $1.4 billion in foreign investment for a potential total investment of almost $2 billion for 1997.

Of the 31 mutual funds in India (excluding the Unit Trust of India) at the end of December 1996, foreign investors participated in 16 of the 21 private-sector funds and 1 of the 10 public-sector funds. Since 1995, private-sector mutual funds have been allowed to acquire government securities. Investments made by mutual funds in government securities are counted toward the government-imposed limit on external commercial borrowing (ECB) by the public and private sectors.

Government officials consider the aggregate foreign portfolio investment to be the sum of all FIIs (on domestic exchanges, through GDRs, and in any offshore funds) as well as portfolio investment from nonresident Indians and companies owned by nonresident Indians.

Foreign investment in India by nonresident Indians (NRIs) and by NRI-owned companies (called overseas corporate bodies, or OCBs) is treated differently from foreign investment by individuals not of Indian origin and the companies owned by such individuals. Nonresident Indians are defined as those who possess an Indian passport or whose parent or grandparent is or was a citizen of India.[13] OCBs are foreign firms in which NRIs own a minimum of 60 percent of shares. NRI and OCB investments are treated equally under Indian law.

NRIs are permitted to hold bank accounts in India in rupees or foreign currency and are allowed to invest in government securities and the Unit Trust of India. They are allowed to acquire shares of Indian companies and mutual funds listed on an exchange in India and to invest directly in Indian firms. NRIs may also own 100 percent of Indian firms, including those considered high priority sectors, without permission from the Reserve Bank of India.[14] Restrictions on repatriation of interest on accounts were lifted this year. Repatriation of capital and dividends depends on the percentage of NRI or OCB ownership and the sector in which the investment has been made.

NRI deposits in Indian banks represent a significant portion—14 percent in 1995—of India's external debt. Investments by NRIs count toward limits imposed on total equity in a single firm held by foreign owners as well as government-imposed limits on ECB.[15] As noted above, state-owned banks are allowed to raise capital on the market through public offers of shares, so long as the government maintains 51 percent ownership of the bank. Foreign investors are limited to acquiring 20 percent of shares in publicly listed state-owned banks, whereas NRIs are allowed to acquire up to 40 percent ownership in such banks.

Despite ceilings on permissible foreign investment, a myriad of regulations, and licenses required when investing in India, FDI and portfolio investment are substantially higher than before the economic reforms. In 1991, FDI totaled $0.2 billion and there was no portfolio investment; by 1996, FDI totaled $2.0 billion and portfolio investment $2.1 billion.

Remaining Obstacles

The reforms implemented to date have made India more open to foreign participation than it was five years ago. Once established, foreign firms in India are afforded the same treatment as domestic firms. The RBI released a report on 3 June 1997 outlining steps to complete capital account convertibility. There remain, however, numerous barriers to

---

13. This definition applies to NRI portfolio investment. The definition of an NRI for foreign direct investment is narrower: it only includes individuals who possess an Indian passport or whose father or paternal grandfather was a citizen of India.

14. NRIs and OCBs acquiring firms, directly or through portfolio investment, must obtain permission from necessary state reserve banks and other authorities as required for all foreign investors.

15. The ceiling on external commercial borrowing by a firm was $4.5 billion in 1996 and $5 billion in 1997.

investment in the financial services industry. The capital account is not yet fully convertible and regulations are not yet transparent. Market access in the banking sector is restricted by the pace at which new licenses are issued, and is limited in other financial services by ceilings on permissible foreign ownership of nonbank financial institutions; these ceilings vary according to the amount invested by a foreign firm in financial service firms. Moreover, India's commitments in the recent WTO financial services negotiations actually bind market access for foreign firms below current practice. Thus, although foreign securities firms have been authorized to hold 100 percent ownership of nonbank financial subsidiaries, India's WTO offer sets the ceiling for foreign ownership at 49 percent for stockbroker services and 51 percent for other financial services.

Prior authorization from the RBI is required, in some cases, to remit profits or dividends. Terms regarding the repatriation of capital and the remittance of interest and principal on foreign loans are determined when the investment or loan is conducted. Complete disinvestment and re-mittance of interest and principal can be written into the terms of any investment or loan agreement. Foreign firms pay corporate taxes of 48 percent versus 35 percent for domestic firms.

Foreign firms are allowed to enter the commercial banking market only by establishing a branch or representative office and they must receive a license to enter the market or open a new bank branch. Only eight new bank branch licenses are issued to foreign firms annually, and so the demand for bank branch licenses is greater than the number of licenses available (FLG 1997).[16] Foreign-owned banks are not allowed to open branches in rural areas. Foreign investors may acquire up to 20 percent of shares in state-owned banks, except for NRIs, who are permitted 40 percent ownership. Foreign banks are not permitted to hold more than 15 percent of total assets in the banking system.

Aggregate investment by foreign institutional investors, nonresident Indians, and overseas corporate investors is not allowed to exceed 30 percent of shares in single firm. No single FII is permitted to hold more than 10 percent of total issued capital in a single firm. Individual FIIs are not permitted to invest more than $100 million in corporate debt annually and may not invest in debt with maturity under one year. FII holdings of debt-based instruments, including government securities, are capped at $1.5 billion.

Private ownership in the insurance industry is prohibited and foreign

---

16. Under the terms of India's WTO financial services offer, market access will continue to be limited to eight new branch licenses for new and existing foreign banks annually. However, the offer does note that ATMs will not be considered a branch license, thereby opening the possibility for foreign banks to expand the scope of their operations in India.

participation is therefore precluded in almost every sector. Setting up a regulatory authority is considered the first step in opening the insurance industry to private-sector participation. Recent attempts to establish a regulatory authority for the insurance industry were blocked in the Indian Congress, stalling the process of liberalizing the insurance industry. Further liberalization in the financial services sector is also likely to be affected by a recent wave of strikes by employees of state-owned banks, who favor changes to their pension plan, an end to the current hiring freeze, and wage parity for employees of rural banks.

References

Center for Monitoring the Indian Economy. 1997. *Monthly Review of the Indian Economy* (April).

Economist Intelligence Unit (EIU). 1996a. *India: EIU Country Profile 1996-97.* New York: The Economist Intelligence Unit.

Economist Intelligence Unit (EIU). 1996b. *Financing Foreign Operation: India.* New York: The Economist Intelligence Unit.

Economist Intelligence Unit (EIU). 1996c. *Financing Foreign Operation: India.* New York: The Economist Intelligence Unit, Flash Updater (September).

Economist Intelligence Unit (EIU). 1997. *Financing Foreign Operation: India.* New York: The Economist Intelligence Unit, Flash Updater (March).

Financial Leaders Group (FLG). 1997. *Barriers to Trade in Financial Services: Case Studies.* London: Barclays Place.

Ministry of Finance. 1997. *Economic Survey '97.* Government of India. (http:www.nic.in/indiabudget/es97).

Reserve Bank of India. 1997. *The Annual Report on the Working of the Reserve Bank of India.* (http://www/reservebank.com/annual).

Securities Industry Association. 1997. *Asian Capital Markets.* New York: Securities Industry Association.

World Bank. 1995. *India: Country Economic Memorandum.* Report No. 14402-IN. Washington: Country Operations, Industry and Finance Division, South Asia Region, World Bank.

Indonesia

Introduction

Indonesia undertook a series of comprehensive reforms in the mid-1980s to combat sluggish growth in the early part of the decade. The terms of trade had deteriorated, reflecting the country's heavy reliance on oil revenues at a time of falling oil prices. Successive international interest rate shocks at the same time, followed by currency alignments, further widened external and internal imbalances. To revive growth rates and restore external credit worthiness, the Indonesian government switched its development strategy from the import-substitution policies of the 1960s and 1970s to an export-led growth policy that focused on promoting nonoil exports and domestic savings.

Liberalization of the real sector was achieved by changing fiscal and administrative systems, trade policy, investment licensing, and transport regulations. Fiscal policies were tightened in 1983 as large capital and import-intensive projects were rephased, public capital spending was reduced, and civil service employment and salaries were restrained. Trade liberalization focused on replacing nontariff barriers with tariffs, repeatedly reducing nominal tariff rates, and eliminating entry barriers in several previously protected sectors. The customs service was privatized in 1985. Yet, deregulation failed to affect the nearly 200 state-owned enterprises and to address the price setting of state-produced products.

In the monetary sector, the capital account was liberalized as early as 1971, when the rupiah was made freely convertible. It was pegged to a basket of currencies from 1986-97 and devalued against the US dollar in 1986 and again in 1993. Prior to reform, the main monetary instruments were credit ceilings, interest rate controls at state-owned banks,[1] and central bank refinancing of priority loans (so-called liquidity credits), the latter contributing to high inflation rates in the 1970s.

Financial liberalization, from the 1980s to the mid-1990s, occurred in two stages. The first stage, in 1983, eliminated all credit ceilings, removed interest rate controls on deposit rates at state-owned banks, and curtailed (but did not abolish) the central bank's liquidity credit programs. The second stage, begun in 1988 and known as *Pakto*, focused on promoting competition in the financial sector. It permitted entry into the banking sector (which had been closed to newcomers since 1972), allowed additional branching, eased the requirements for becoming a foreign exchange (FOREX) bank, reduced the amount that state-owned enterprises were required to deposit in state-owned banks, and lowered the reserve requirement while raising minimum paid-in capital requirements. In 1989, domestic banks obtained access to international markets, and in 1990, many of the remaining liquidity credits were phased out.

Prudential regulations were not introduced until 1991. Even then, because of an underdeveloped legal framework and accounting system, their implementation was not always very effective. Nonetheless, during the 1983-93 period, the financial sector grew at 12.1 percent annually. The reforms also mobilized savings, which, as a percentage of GDP, grew from 9.8 percent in 1970 to 20.9 percent in 1990 (Nasution 1995, 168).

Indonesia's experience with market opening and deregulation has been unconventional. Prevailing wisdom suggests that the capital account should not be liberalized before domestic financial markets are reformed; otherwise, excessive capital in- and outflows will occur as arbitragers take advantage of distorted price signals in the financial sector. In Indonesia, with a liberalized capital account prior to financial-sector reform, capital inflows and outflows caused some instability, but until the Asian currency crisis, the problem remained manageable thanks to prompt fiscal adjustment and flexibility in the interest rate. Furthermore, these capital movements speeded up the introduction of indirect monetary controls (Bisat, Johnston, and Sundararajan 1992).

According to McKinnon (1991), financial liberalization can be managed to minimize its impact on the economy as a whole by, first, closely monitoring commercial banks (possibly including temporary credit rationing) and next, recapitalizing existing banks and their customers. Finally, during the transition period, the financial sector should be temporarily closed to new entrants, who are not burdened with low-yield loans from the prereform era.

Indonesia went the opposite way. New domestic and foreign banks and branches were allowed entry with the initiation in 1988 of the *Pakto*

---

1. Interest rates charged by private banks and nonbank financial institutions were not controlled, however.

reform, and so existing banks were not given time to adjust. The pressure from increased competition led to a rapid expansion of credit without sufficient credit analysis, so that the number of bad loans increased. Furthermore, when state-owned banks badly needed financial help in the form of recapitalization, they were met with two additional problems. First, in 1987 and again in 1991, there were the Sumarlin shocks, named after the finance minister of the time who instructed state-owned enterprises to convert large amounts of their deposits, held mainly at state-owned banks, into central bank certificates (SBIs). Then Bank Indonesia in 1990 reduced the scope of refinancing, and this raised the interest costs of state-owned banks to higher levels than those of private banks.

It was only in 1992, after successive failures of banks and nonbank firms, that the government attempted to raise the capital base of state-owned banks by obtaining more than $300 million from the World Bank Financial Sector Development Project and by revaluing assets, converting Bank Indonesia's liquid credits into equity, shifting risk to other government-owned institutions, and taking over some nonperforming loans (Nasution 1995, 194).

By choosing a sequence of financial reform contrary to that suggested by conventional wisdom, Indonesia opted for a rapid pace of liberalization, but the high adjustment costs of this pace, including the failure of many banks and nonbank firms, caused economic instability. Some of the instability was increased by Bank Indonesia's inability to conduct open-market operations due to the shallowness of the money market. For example, subsidies on foreign exchange swap premiums had not been removed when commercial banks obtained access to international financial markets, resulting in massive inflows of short-term capital. Had the rupiah been allowed to appreciate, the current account would have worsened, complicating structural adjustments. Therefore, the Bank purchased foreign exchange from the public, increasing the money supply. To curtail inflationary pressures, Bank Indonesia not only tightened its credit policy and removed the subsidy on foreign exchange swap premiums, but also used discretionary policy instruments, including the Sumarlin shocks and ceilings on public-sector foreign borrowing. These measures increased interest rates and created liquidity problems for commercial banks, thereby contributing to financial-sector instability.

After the depreciation of the Thai baht on 2 July 1997, Indonesia could not longer support the rupiah at the rate at which it was pegged and on 14 August 1997 the rupiah was allowed to float. The rupiah depreciated rapidly, exposing the underlying weakness of the financial sector.[2]

---

2. The rupiah depreciated by approximately 75 percent from July 1997, when it traded at 2,400 to the US dollar, to mid-January 1998, when the rupiah traded at 10,000 to the US dollar. From late 1997 to early 1998, the value of the rupiah was extremely volatile, ranging from 5,000 to the dollar in December 1997 to a record low of 16,500 to the US dollar at the end of January 1998.

By early fall 1997, private external debt was $80 billion dollars. A significant share of this debt was unhedged and, as of 30 September 1997, an estimated $59 billion of the total private external debt was due within a year (*Financial Times* 12 January 1998), prompting Indonesia to seek assistance from the IMF. A $43 billion IMF package was announced in November 1997. The government subsequently closed 16 insolvent banks and began to implement plans to strengthen the financial sector. However, the continued depreciation of the rupiah and the flight to quality in the banking sector exacerbated the shortage of liquidity in the financial system. In an effort to reestablish confidence in the banking system, a new IMF supported economic program was announced in late January 1998 that included widespread structural reforms and a more comprehensive plan to rehabilitate the financial sector.

In the context of the IMF program, Indonesia is scheduled to undergo a new wave of financial reform. In contrast to Indonesia's earlier experience, emphasis is being placed on enhancing the safety and soundness of the domestic financial system. The government is taking steps to increase supervision over the financial sector and support for domestic financial institutions is conditional upon compliance with enhanced reporting and monitoring requirements in addition to adherence to capital adequacy rules.

Some barriers that limited the participation of foreign financial services companies in the domestic economy were removed in the context of the 1997 WTO financial services agreement. For example, Indonesia's WTO offer included the commitment to allow 100 percent ownership of nonbank financial institutions and 100 percent ownership of publicly listed companies. The IMF program includes plans that will significantly enhance market access for foreign financial institutions, beyond commitments made in the WTO agreement. For example, in an effort to help recapitalize the financial sector and attract foreign participation in the planned privatization of state-owned banks, the government intends to introduce legislation that would remove all restrictions on foreign investment in listed banks by June 1998.

Regulatory Framework

Indonesia's financial system is based on the Act on Banking Principles of 1967, which stipulates that regulation and supervision of the financial sector be divided between the Ministry of Finance (MOF) and Bank Indonesia.

The MOF is organized around six directorates: Customs and Excise, Taxation, Budgeting and Treasury, State-Owned Enterprises, Financial Institutions, and BAPEPAM, the Capital Market Supervisory Agency. The Directorate General of Budgeting and Treasury has to consult on budget allocation with the planning agency BAPENAS, which controls the allocation of the development budget. The Directorate General of State-Owned Enterprises, together with the technical ministries, controls operations of the state-owned enterprises, including banks, insurance companies, and finance companies. The Directorate General of Financial Institutions issues operating licenses for financial institutions and accountants; and also supervises nonbank financial institutions, including insurance and pension fund companies through the Insurance Law and the Pension Funds Law, both of 1992. BAPEPAM is responsible for regulating and supervising Indonesia's capital markets and securities industries, having delegated responsibility for the stock markets to private companies in 1991.

Bank Indonesia acts both as a central bank and as a regulator of financial institutions other than insurance and pension fund companies. It has the power to set the level and structure of interest rates and can control, either qualitatively or quantitatively, banks' credits. In fact, the Banking Law of 1992 explicitly permits Bank Indonesia to set maximum lending limits for banks. To support these wider activities, Bank Indonesia owns, either wholly or in part, a commercial bank in the Netherlands, two domestic commercial banks, a development finance company, a credit insurance company for small business loans, and a housing finance company.

Under the terms of Indonesia's IMF economic program, Bank Indonesia's role in the economy is rapidly changing. Bank Indonesia now provides state banks with autonomy in setting rates on credits and deposits according to market conditions. Bank Indonesia has also been given autonomy in formulating and implementing monetary policy. A new law formally establishing the central bank's independence is scheduled to be submitted to parliament by the end of 1998. Bank Indonesia's role as a supervisory agency is also changing. In early 1998, the Indonesia Bank Restructuring Agency (IBRA) was set up to supervise and rehabilitate banks. The IBRA has been given broad authority. It can now take over a troubled bank and sell off its assets, merge the bank with another institution, and/or recapitalize the bank.

Financial Institutions

The majority of financial assets in Indonesia are held by the banking sector; less than 10 percent are accounted for by nonbank financial institutions or are raised through direct finance (see table B.3). In 1991, the outstanding value of stocks and bonds issued on the Indonesian stock exchanges was only 31 percent of the banks' outstanding credit (Nasution 1995, 169). This implies that Indonesia is still in the early stages of financial

Table B.3   Indonesia: Assets of financial institutions, 1969, 1982, 1988, and 1991 (percentages)

Financial intermediaries	1969	1982	1988	1991
Bank Indonesia	57.7	42.4	36.8	23.8
State-owned banks	30.3	37.9	34.5	30.2
Private banks	3.7	5.8	13.1	25.2
Development banks	4.0	4.1	4.4	6.3
Savings banks	0.1	1.4	2.1	1.6
Foreign banks	4.3	3.6	2.8	5.2
Nonbank financial institutions	na	2.5	2.7	2.1
Insurance companies	na	1.6	1.6	3.5
Other	na	0.7	2.1	2.2

na = not available.

Source: Nasution (1995, 170).

sector development. There is some evidence of financial deepening, particularly since the beginning of financial-sector reform.

Financial Intermediaries

The traditional specialization of banks, including that of state-owned banks, was abolished with the *Pakto* reform, which recognizes only two types of banks: general banks, organized either as commercial and development banks or, less frequently, as cooperatives; and rural banks (BPRs), which are geographically bound to a specific region. Previously existing savings banks were automatically converted into commercial banks, while secondary banks were changed into BPRs. Development banks have the same status as commercial banks but focus on providing long-term credit. The banking law of 1992 provided the basis for the state-owned banks to operate more commercially by allowing them to retain profits and sell shares on the stock market.

BPRs remain relatively unimportant in the Indonesian market, and the seven state-owned banks continue to dominate the banking sector. However, the state-owned banks' monopoly power has been eroded on the liability side by increased competition from private domestic and foreign joint venture banks and on the asset side by an increasing number of nonfinancial companies selling their securities on the stock exchanges in order to avoid interest rates that have increased since the prereform era. In 1993, the seven state-owned banks held 53 percent of total outstanding credit assets, down from 71 percent in 1988. During the same period, private domestic banks increased their market share of outstanding credit assets from 23 percent to 42 percent (US Treasury 1994, 323). As of early 1998, plans are underway to merge a number of the state-owned banks and rationalize their operations with the goal of eventually privatizing them.

Except for BPRs, domestic banks with a 20-month record of having been financially sound face no quantitative or geographic limitations when extending their branch network. As a result of past discriminations, the state-owned banks have a more extensive branch network than do private banks, although the latter are catching up rapidly, accounting for 91 percent of new branches set up between 1988 and 1993 (US Treasury 1994, 318).

Indonesia's universal banking business was opened in 1985, when banks were permitted to engage in securities underwriting, brokerage, and trading. Beginning in December 1991, these activities had to be transferred to the banks' holding companies. Indonesians and foreign residents are allowed to open accounts in rupiah or in foreign currencies at specific banks. Banks wishing to deal in foreign exchange transactions require a special license, which, by 1994, had been granted to 25 private commercial banks. Newly established domestic banks must wait a minimum of two years before they may apply for a foreign exchange license.

Nonbank financial institutions operating in Indonesia consist of insurance companies, pension funds,[3] and other types of finance companies. The latter include multifinance, leasing, factoring, consumer finance, venture capital, and credit card companies. Finance companies function similarly to merchant banks in loan syndicates; they must have at least three foreign partners, each from a different country. Foreign banks may own up to 85 percent of total equity.

Insurance is the second largest financial industry in terms of assets. The market is small, however, covering only 8 percent of the population (Takahashi 1994, 31). Lack of expertise is the main obstacle to increased coverage. The industry is characterized by small-scale firms with a narrow range of products, and approximately 80 percent of risk is reinsured with foreign firms. This limits the role of insurance companies as providers of long-term investment funds for development.[4]

Most large insurance companies are either state owned or part of a business group. Their market share, though, has been eroded by the rapid growth of private domestic and joint venture insurance companies since the government discontinued setting premium levels in 1988.

---

3. The 1992 Pension Funds Law made pension funds taxable and introduced greater control for subscribers by requiring audits by public accountants.

4. The 1992 Insurance Law eliminated previous rules that attempted to reduce the amount of risk exported by requiring domestic insurance companies to retain 75 percent of the premium for business within the country. In practice, lack of domestic insurance capacity made compliance with this rule impossible.

State-owned insurance companies are the only insurers allowed to offer social insurance programs, according to the Workers Social Securities Act of 1992. In all other insurance matters, the insured is free to choose among insurers.

Direct Finance

The Jakarta Stock Exchange (JSE) opened in 1977, but was essentially inactive until the reforms of 1988-89.[5] Following deregulation, the number of companies listed increased from 24 to 207 in August 1994 (Takahashi 1994, 30), and average daily turnover of stocks grew from 27,000 to 15 million shares per day (US Treasury 1994, 325).

In 1989, the Surabaya Stock Exchange (SSE) was established in Indonesia's second largest city. The two stock exchanges operate independently of each other—trading is not integrated although both markets serve the same customers. Since 1991, both exchanges have been run by firms owned by member brokers among whom local Chinese traders are remarkably absent compared with other Southeast Asian stock exchanges.

Equities are the most common financial instrument traded on the JSE and SSE. The ratio of market capitalization to outstanding bank loans grew from 0.33 percent in 1988 to 46 percent at the end of 1993, reflecting the growth of the equity market (US Treasury 1994, 326). Nonetheless, the market constituted only 23 percent of GDP in that year. Trading is still very thin, as many companies list only a small amount of their equity, thereby avoiding the separation of ownership and management. Member firms of conglomerates tend to own a large share of each other's stock, which is not traded. Until the JSE was computerized, high transaction costs also constrained trading on this market.

Other impediments faced by the stock market are distortions introduced by the authorities, who have used the capital markets for development and redistribution purposes. Since 1989, state-owned enterprises have had to use between 1 percent and 5 percent of profits to help cooperatives and small- and medium-sized enterprises (SMEs); by 1992, Rp216.2 million had been accumulated for such purposes. To achieve equity objectives, the government stipulated in 1990 that domestic conglomerates had to redistribute a maximum of 25 percent of their shares, paid out of dividends, to cooperatives.

The bond market is still underdeveloped, despite an absence of regulatory impediments. Most bonds are bought by institutional investors, especially state-owned pension funds, who then hold on to them until maturity, resulting in an inactive secondary bond market.

---

5. The 1983-85 reform minimized a bias in the corporate income system against business financing by abolishing fiscal incentives for listing and buying securities on the JSE.

Until 1983, the money market was inactive while the dominant state-owned banks were in surplus. To compensate for low or negative interest rates at home, these banks invested much of their excess reserves in foreign assets, a policy encouraged by Bank Indonesia as a way of sterilizing the monetary impact of the oil money.

In 1984, Bank Indonesia actively began to develop the short-term money market by issuing central bank certificates (SBI), which allow the bank to conduct open-market operations. The following year saw the introduction of further money market instruments, namely SBPUs, a corporate promissory note endorsed by commercial banks, and CDs, large-denomination negotiable certificates of deposit. Bank Indonesia continued to encourage the development of the money market by establishing a credit agency in late 1994 and by developing a regulatory framework.

Mutual funds were authorized in 1991. Growth in this industry will be crucial in establishing an institutional investor base that can support a broader development of the capital markets, but so far growth has been hampered by a law preventing corporations from purchasing their own stock, thereby banning open-end funds.

Indonesian residents face no restrictions on access to foreign financial instruments as investors or to foreign markets as issuers of securities or notes. Some country funds for Indonesia are listed on the New York Stock Exchange. Since 1991, however, foreign borrowing from commercial sources except for trade financing has been restricted in an effort by the government to limit the growth of the country's foreign debt.

Prudential Regulations

The rapid pace of financial liberalization revealed several problems that financial institutions had inherited from the era of financial repression, including high debt-equity ratios of nonfinancial companies and a weak accounting system. Poor credit analysis techniques resulted in the predominance of short-term loans that were regularly rolled over and in banks demanding high-value collateral for these loans. Lack of information induced most private domestic banks to join large conglomerates (groups of firms linked by relationships). This reliance on long-term relationships contributes to the danger of subsidizing less efficient firms within the group by, for example, extending high-risk loans to them.

Nonfinancial companies' high debt-equity ratios were encouraged by low or negative real interest rates prior to financial liberalization. In times of high (positive) interest rates and slow growth, though, high debt-equity ratios strain the cash flows of a company. Hence, in 1991, when the government tightened fiscal and monetary policies in response to economic overheating, several banks were faced with bank failure as financially unsound borrowers failed to meet their obligations. Rising interest rates hit the undercapitalized state-owned banks particularly hard as they were saddled with a high proportion of nonperforming loans and illiquid (low-yield) financial instruments from the prereform era.[6] In fact, in February 1994, the Minister of Finance estimated that nonperforming loans at state-owned banks equaled 20 percent of their total loans, or three times their combined capital (US Treasury 1994, 319).

To address these problems, prudential regulations were strengthened in 1991, although compliance was not enforced until March 1997 as many banks faced severe adjustment problems. The first provision saw the rise of minimum capital requirements, which were made a function of financial institutions' assumed risks. In the banking sector, the capital-adequacy ratio linked the bank's capital base to risk-weighted assets. In the insurance industry, solvency margins, defined as the difference between a company's solid and liquid assets and its debts and required capital, were set at a minimum of 10 percent of premiums. The MOF had already set minimum capital requirements for stock exchanges and security firms in 1990.

The second provision linked new bank loans to the level of deposits. The loan-deposit ratio was set at a maximum of 110 percent. Problem loans require additional reserves.

The third provision introduced legal lending limits. The maximum amount of intragroup lending was reduced from 50 percent to 20 percent or 10 percent, depending on the amount of bank equity owned by the conglomerate. The purpose of this provision was to inhibit the concentration of financial power in order to better protect uninformed depositors by increasing overall access to banks' credits. Other new lending limits were less prudential than developmental, including the requirement that domestic banks allocate at least 20 percent of their loans to SMEs.

To reduce excessive foreign borrowing, the net open foreign exchange position of foreign exchange banks and of nonbank financial institutions was limited to 25 percent in 1989 and lowered to 20 percent in 1990.

Insurance companies are required to spread their funds among different investments. They may commit up to 5 percent of total assets in deposits with any one bank and up to 10 percent in the money market, but they are not allowed to allocate funds to high-risk investments such as derivatives, futures, and foreign exchange transactions. To avoid conflict of interest, investment in brokers and agents has been forbidden since 1993. Insurance companies are required to publish quarterly returns of financial assets to ensure transparency.

Enhanced supervision and enforcement of prudential standards is a key element of Indonesia's IMF economic program. The government is

---

6. Prior to reform, many loans extended by state-owned banks were not based on financial criteria but on development objectives.

seeking technical assistance from the IMF and World Bank to strengthen risk-based supervisory practices. Banks that are not in compliance with prudential standards, including capital-adequacy requirements, will now face severe penalties or the loss of their license. Greater transparency and disclosure will be required, including the annual publication of audited financial statements. Complementary efforts include establishing better accounting practices such as the introduction of new loan classification and provisioning guidelines. In January 1998, the government announced it would guarantee the debts and deposits of all Indonesian domestic banks for a period of at least two years. However, there is still no deposit insurance system in Indonesia.

Foreign Participation

The *Pakto* reforms of 1988 allowed not only domestic but also foreign entry into Indonesia's financial markets. Foreign financial institutions were generally required to form joint ventures with domestic partners, although those with wholly owned branches at that time were grandfathered.

In 1988, ten foreign banks were operating fully owned branches, which are permitted to provide the same range of services as domestic banks. From 1988 to 1994, 29 additional foreign banks, from countries where reciprocal access is available to Indonesian banks, penetrated the Indonesian market through joint ventures (US Treasury 1994, 321). Until 1998, foreign and joint venture banks were only permitted to establish additional subbranches in Jakarta and one branch in each of seven other cities. In a joint venture, the foreign bank's ownership was limited to 85 percent. Furthermore, the number of foreign employees has been restricted,[7] which suggests that the joint venture entry condition was not about ownership control but about transfer of business and banking know-how.

Indonesia's 1997 WTO financial services offer contains provisions—including one allowing 100 percent foreign ownership of publicly listed firms—that would have provided greater market access for foreign banks when the agreement comes into effect in early 1999. Market access in this sector was, however, subsequently significantly improved under the commitments outlined in Indonesia's January 1998 IMF economic program. The government approved a bill in January 1998 that lifts restrictions on branching of joint venture banks and sub-branching of foreign banks. The government is also scheduled to pass laws by mid-1998 that will remove restrictions on private ownership and eliminate limits on foreign ownership in banks.

---

7. This restriction applies to all foreign joint ventures and foreign firms, not only to banks.

Joint venture and foreign banks face a paid-in cash requirement twice as high as that of domestic banks, making foreign banks' capital-adequacy ratio the highest in Indonesia. The higher capital requirement acts as an effective entry barrier to protect domestic banks. In addition, these banks are required to extend 50 percent of their credits to export-related activities.[8] Joint venture companies that are majority owned by a foreign partner may not borrow from state-owned banks. The impact of the Asian currency crisis on the financial sector has made access to funds from foreign financial institutions critical for recapitalizing the banking sector and stabilizing the financial system. Therefore, some of these discriminatory barriers may be removed as the government seeks capital for the banking system from abroad.

In the insurance sector, only life insurance business was open to foreign participation before 1988; other insurers have been able to enter the market since then. Foreign firms may insure foreign nationals and foreign companies without having to form a joint venture.[9] In a joint venture, the share of equity held by the Indonesian partner must be at least 20 percent, and the agreement must stipulate a timetable for transferring up to a minimum of 51 percent of total equity to the Indonesian partner within a 20-year period (Lamble and Low 1995). This stipulation acts as a disincentive for the foreign partner to forming a joint venture; thus, by 1994 joint ventures constituted only 17 of 148 insurers (Takahashi 1994, 31).

Market access for foreign insurance providers will improve when the WTO financial services agreement comes into force in early 1999. The stipulation that foreign firms can own 100 percent of publicly listed firms will apply to the insurance sector. Furthermore, although Indonesia continues to prohibit establishing insurance branches, insurance firms will be allowed to operate 100 percent owned subsidiaries.

Foreign insurers have faced a higher initial equity investment requirement than domestic insurers, and were required to place 20 percent of their total capital in time deposits with an Indonesian commercial bank. The amount of the deposit was increased annually by a certain percentage (Lamble and Low 1995, 78). The deposit was redeemable when the foreign company ceases operation in Indonesia, but could be accessed temporarily in a liquidity crisis with MOF approval. The government agreed to phase out discriminatory capital requirements for insurance companies in its 1997 WTO financial services offer.

Foreign securities firms have been allowed to engage in securities activities since 1987, but only by establishing a joint venture with a

---

8. On the other hand, foreign and joint venture banks do not face a waiting period in order to engage in FOREX transactions.

9. They may also insure Indonesians if the domestic market offers no equivalent insurance policy provided they first obtain a special permit from the MOF.

domestic partner. Ownership by the foreign partner is limited to 80 percent. Securities firms may be 85 percent foreign owned if they are listed on the Jakarta Stock Exchange (Securities Industry Association 1997, 20). As in other sectors, publicly listed securities firms can be 100 percent foreign owned when the WTO agreement comes into force.

Until 1995, joint-venture securities firms faced minimum capital requirements twice the size of their domestic counterparts. Minimum paid-up capital requirements are now the same for joint venture and domestic securities firms, and domestic securities firms are required to have a larger net worth than joint ventures (IIB, 1997, 116).

Foreign companies may not list on the JSE and SSE, but foreign investors have been allowed entry since 1989 through joint ventures. Foreign trading, especially by large mutual funds and pension funds, dominates the JSE with more than 80 percent of all trades conducted with foreign participation. Until September 1997, this occurred despite the fact that foreigners could own only up to 49 percent of shares of any single issue.[10] Once this limit was reached,[11] foreigners could trade only among themselves, often at a significant premium that could run as high as 50 percent to 60 percent above the listed price paid by domestic investors. By listing only small issues at a time and waiting until the 49 percent limit on foreign ownership was reached before listing additional stock, domestic companies could obtain a higher price for their stock (Takahashi 1994, 30). In 1994, the government decreed that 100 percent foreign equity ownership would be permitted; however, these changes were not implemented until 1998. In contrast to the limit on foreign equity ownership, there are no limits on foreign ownership of debt instruments.

Remaining Obstacles

The biggest obstacle to financial-sector efficiency is a weak financial market infrastructure. The laws are unclear about the basis for securing contracts and credit transactions, and procedures and laws governing bankruptcy are not well defined either. Minority shareholders enjoy very little legal protection. Better supervision by the regulatory authorities has been hampered by inadequate staff training and poor accounting standards. Until 1998, there was no reporting requirement for nonpublic

---

10. Since 1992, this has included bank shares, an area previously closed to foreign investors. In September 1997, the government removed the 49 percent cap on foreign purchases of new public offerings, although aggregate foreign ownership is still capped at 49 percent.

11. By December 1992, 49 percent of stocks listed on the JSE and SSE were foreign owned.

firms. All of these factors complicated the ability of banks to properly evaluate loans. Prudential regulations began to improve in 1991, but their administration and implementation has been inconsistent, and in the financial intermediary sector they focused on credit risk while ignoring other risks, such as exchange rate risk.

Some of these factors were addressed under Indonesia's 1997 IMF program. The government announced plans to write a new bankruptcy law that will establish procedures for foreclosing on loans and attaching the assets of firms that cannot meet debt payments (*Financial Times*, 9 February 1998). It has also recognized the need for better trained supervisors and has established reporting requirements for privately held banks. Other measures to increase compliance with prudential standards are underway. The successful implementation of these measures could greatly enhance the safety and soundness of the banking sector, although other challenges to creating a stable, developed financial system remain.

The capital market remains underdeveloped. Lack of information on companies, lack of transparency in accounting procedures, inadequate protection of minority shareholders, and uneven enforcement of the legal system all contribute to a lack of confidence by the public. Capital market growth is further inhibited by government decrees regarding the distribution of conglomerate shares or the allocation of shareholder dividends in state-owned banks.

The government continues to play a very dominant role in the economy. State-owned enterprises were largely untouched by deregulation or privatization before 1998. Furthermore, although plans for privatization are underway, state-owned banks can be privatized only if sufficient capital is injected into them to solve the nonperforming loan problem.

Market access for foreign firms has generally been restricted to joint ventures. The government recently removed geographical restrictions on joint venture and foreign banks and has announced plans to remove all limits on foreign investment in listed banks. However, there are no plans for the government to issue new bank licenses; market access will be largely confined to those foreign firms that acquire rights in existing banks and that already have operations in Indonesia that can now establish more branches or sub-branches. Other barriers, such as the requirement that lending limits are based on local capital as opposed to global capital and restrictions on offering new financial products and services, continue to limit the growth of foreign banks in Indonesia. Moreover, it is not clear if, once foreign banks are afforded increased market access, they will be given national treatment allowing them to compete on an equal standing with domestic banks.

In January 1998, the government announced it would guarantee the debts and deposits of all Indonesian domestic banks for a period of at least two years. Although this commitment is likely to help restore confidence in the banking sector, the financial system as whole will need to be reformed and liberalized to help attract sufficient fund to cover the guarantee.

References

Bisat, Amer, R. Barry Johnston, and Vasudevan Sundararajan. 1992. *Issues in Managing and Sequencing Financial Sector Reforms: Lessons from Experiences in Five Developing Countries.* Washington: International Monetary Fund.

Institute of International Bankers (IIB). 1997. *Global Survey: 1997.* New York: Institute of International Bankers.

Lamble, Peter, and Robin Low. 1995. *The Asia Pacific Insurance Handbook.* Sydney, NSW: Coopers & Lybrand.

McKinnon, Ronald I. 1991. *The Order of Economic Liberalization: Financial Control in the Transition to a Market Economy.* Baltimore: Johns Hopkins University Press.

Nasution, Anwar. 1995. Financial Sector Policies in Indonesia, 1980-1993. In *Financial Sector Development in Asia: Country Studies,* ed. by Shahid N. Zahid. Hong Kong: Oxford University Press.

Securities Industry Association (SIA). 1997. *Asian Capital Markets.* New York: Securities Industry Association.

Takahashi, Yuichi. 1994. *Financial Sector Reform in the Asia Pacific Countries.* Photocopy.

US Department of the Treasury. 1994. *National Treatment Study.* Washington: Government Printing Office.

Japan

Introduction

In the first few decades after World War II, Japan transformed itself from a middle-income developing country into a highly industrialized one. Prior to the first oil shock in 1973-74, the country enjoyed years of high growth that was supported by a strictly regulated and highly repressed financial system designed to channel national savings into productive economic activity. Interest rates were set by the Ministry of Finance (MOF). The Bank of Japan (BOJ) directed banks' lending activities through window guidance;[1] and competition among financial intermediaries was limited through strict compartmentalization that forced them to operate only in designated niches. In each of these niches, competition was further restricted by prohibiting additional entry and by strictly controlling the opening of additional branches.

An additional reason for this heavy regulation was to avoid repetition of the detrimental effects of the 1920s banking crisis, which resulted in the failure of more than 75 percent of the banks in Japan from the early 1920s to 1935 (Yoshino 1996, 1). To stimulate growth after the Second World War, the Temporary Interest Rate Adjustment Law (TIRAL) of 1947 allowed the MOF to set low interest rates for different financial instruments. As price competition was thus eliminated, profit maximization required financial intermediaries, especially banks, to maximize lending.

---

1. Window guidance refers to the ceilings set on the quarterly rate of commercial bank loan increases.

To avoid excessive inflation, the BOJ adopted window guidance in 1953, limiting overall bank lending to levels it deemed consistent with its monetary policy. Banks complied with the window guidance policy for fear of potential repercussions such as exclusion from BOJ credit, with its lower interest rates than those prevalent in the call market.

Deregulation of the financial system began gradually in the mid-1970s. This was also a period of slower economic growth during which the government, pursuing countercyclical policy, started to issue a large number of bonds. To accommodate this large issue of bonds, the government bond market was deregulated; through arbitrage, the effects of deregulation spilled over into other asset markets. After the removal of foreign capital controls in 1980, firms also took advantage of another important arbitrage opportunity between the regulated domestic market and the unregulated offshore market, with the result that the Japanese corporate bond market was, effectively, moved to London. Hence, arbitrage of financial assets by the corporate sector became the driving force behind deregulation (Teranishi 1994).

The 15-year process of interest rate deregulation began in 1979 with the introduction of negotiable certificates of deposit, followed by the introduction of bankers' acceptance notes, money market certificates, and large time deposits in 1985, and treasury bills and commercial paper in 1986. It was the introduction of new financial instruments (especially deposit substitutes) and the ensuing competition among them that led to the deregulation of interest rates for individual instruments. Interest rate ceilings on time deposits were eased in a step-by-step process from 1986 to 1993, and the remaining restrictions on interest rates for nontime deposits were lifted in 1994.

Interest rate deregulation and the resulting competition for deposits forced financial institutions, especially banks, to seek optimum rather than maximum size. This development eliminated the danger of high inflation caused by excessive lending. Hence, the BOJ abolished its window guidance policy in 1993 when interest rate deregulation was almost completed.

Decompartmentalization within the banking sector started in the 1970s as different types of commercial banks expanded into each other's niches. The separation between banking and securities businesses further weakened in the 1980s. Yet universal banking was only allowed under the Financial System Reform Act (FSRA) of 1993 when, subject to cautious MOF approval, banks were permitted to own securities companies, insurance companies, and trust banks[2] as subsidiaries; securities companies could own trust bank subsidiaries; insurance companies could acquire controlling interest in banks and nonbank financial intermediaries; and the operational demarcations among different types of banks

2. Japanese trust banks are similar to North American mutual funds.

and insurance companies were largely abolished. Certain core business activities were preserved exclusively for the pre-1993 intermediaries, thus remaining closed to the new subsidiaries. Furthermore, to limit the expansion of bank power, restrictions were imposed on these new subsidiaries: for example, they had to be separately capitalized, and the amount of business between parent company and subsidiary was limited.

Although the yen has been fully convertible for several decades, the MOF has continued to restrict foreign exchange transactions by setting limits on banks' net foreign currency positions and on margins between buying and selling positions for spot and forward commitments. Fixed or set interest rates made many domestic financial instruments unattractive as market participants' wealth grew in the late 1980s and the excess liquidity flowed into the real estate and stock markets, driving up prices and creating asset inflation. When the BOJ ended its easy monetary policy in the early 1990s, the asset bubble created in the late 1980s collapsed, causing a major financial crisis. By some estimates, falling asset prices and land values since 1992 have destroyed a decade's worth of wealth creation (*The Economist*, 28 June 1997).

The first impact of the insolvency crisis occurred in housing loan companies, which were exposed to real estate lending when land prices collapsed. They received a highly controversial public rescue. As widespread insolvency problems began to appear in the banking system, domestic and foreign pressure grew for workouts and rationalization of the sector. At the same time, it was becoming evident that Japan's position as an international financial center was slipping because of the high-cost business environment, continued heavy regulation, and restrictions on foreign transactions and foreign entry.

Japan has been slow to get its financial house in order in the 1990s. Far-reaching reform of the financial sector is required, but it has taken some time to form the necessary consensus to proceed. In late 1996, the Japanese government unveiled plans for a "big bang"-style deregulation and market opening by 2001.

First, the Bank of Japan Law was revised in April 1997 to increase the BOJ's independence from the MOF. Second, the Foreign Exchange Control Act was redrafted to remove banks' traditional monopoly in, and reduce reporting requirements on, foreign exchange transactions. Effective April 1998, licenses and prior notification for cross-border capital transactions and settlement of debts will no longer be required, and the authorized foreign exchange bank and money-exchanger systems will be abolished (Institute of International Bankers 1997, 127). Third, the government will implement the following measures to phase out restrictions on the types of financial products traded and offered in Japan:

- fixed brokerage commissions will be deregulated by 1999;
- banks will be allowed to underwrite securities and to trade stocks;

- banks will be allowed to sell mutual fund-type products and insurance policies by 2001;

- securities firms will be allowed to offer bank-type accounts as of 1997 and to enter trust banking as of 1998;

- a ban on financial holding companies will be lifted in 1998; and

- a new financial services law governing the banking, securities, and insurance sectors will be enacted.

These changes do not include explicit measures to allow foreign firms more access, although many assume that greater competition will allow this implicitly.

The "big bang" reforms will help to address the problem of declining international competitiveness of the banking system, but little progress has been made on strengthening the domestic banking sector throughout the early 1990s. The protracted downturn in Japan's macroeconomy, combined with events in Asia, eroded banks' capital bases and, by late 1997, resulted in a decline in consumer confidence in the banking sector. For the first time since 1945, the government allowed a bank and a security house to collapse. By January 1998 corporate failures were at a record high, and there was concern that the stock index would slip below 15,000—prompting a wave of bank failures (*The Economist*, 21 February 1998). Aiming to restore consumer confidence in the financial system and prevent a major economic crisis, the Ministry of Finance introduced "Emergency Measures to Stabilize the Financial System" in early 1998 (MOF 1998, 1). Key components of this plan include expanding the authority of the Deposit Insurance Corporation (DIC) to facilitate its ability to restructure the financial system, as well as the commitment of 30 trillion yen to strengthen the financial base of the DIC.

Regulatory Framework

The most prominent regulatory agency of Japan's financial institutions is the MOF and its various bureaus and departments. The Insurance Department of the Banking Bureau supervises and regulates insurance companies according to the insurance law last amended in 1995. The Banking Inspection Department of the Banking Bureau is responsible for supervising and regulating commercial and trust banks as well as for issuing new licenses.[3] Its activities are based on the Banking Law of 1928, which was enacted as a reaction to the banking crisis of the time with the aim to reduce the number of banks, avoid excess competition,

---

3. The MOF also regulates consumer finance companies (US Treasury 1994).

and strengthen healthy management of banks (Yoshino 1996). Other laws governing the activities of the Banking Inspection Department are the Long-Term Credit Banking Law of 1952, which separates commercial and long-term banking businesses, and the Temporary Interest Rate Adjustment Law (TIRAL), which, from 1947 to 1992, ensured a low interest rate policy. By June 1998, the MOF bureau and departments responsible for supervising banks, securities, and insurance firms are to be transferred to an independent Financial Services Agency. The MOF will retain authority for promulgating rules governing the financial sector.

The MOF's Securities Bureau, together with the Securities and Exchange Surveillance Commission (SESC),[4] regulates and supervises securities firms according to the Securities and Exchange Act (SEA) of 1948. The SEA, modeled after the US Glass-Steagall Act, strictly separates banking and securities business into separate institutions. Initially, it was intended to protect securities firms from the consolidated power of the prewar *zaibatsu* banks. The SEA also provides for the establishment of subsidiaries of foreign securities firms, while the Foreign Securities Firm Law regulates branches of those firms.

The International Finance Bureau regulates all cross-border banking activities such as foreign exchange transactions under the Foreign Exchange and Trade Control Law.

The MOF also oversees the activities of self-regulatory bodies such as the Tokyo International Financial Futures Exchange (TIFFE) and the Japan Securities Dealers Association (JSDA), which administers over-the-counter (OTC) equities markets.

The other main regulatory body of the Japanese financial system is the BOJ, which also supervises individual banks based on contractual agreements. Operating under the Bank of Japan Law of 1942, it has been under strict government control, although moves began in 1997 to give it more independence. The MOF can overrule BOJ policy, and the cabinet can dismiss the Bank governor, who is selected alternately from the MOF and the BOJ. Nonetheless the BOJ has acted independently in controlling the money supply and, in doing so, the exchange rate. This became very apparent in 1990 when it drastically increased the discount rate, thus causing the speculative bubble of the late 1980s to burst (*The Economist*, 25 January 1992).[5]

---

4. The SESC was established in 1992 after a series of securities market scandals in 1991 shed doubts on MOF's dual role as industry regulator and industry advocate. The SESC has limited powers—it can investigate problems but not impose penalties (US Treasury 1994, 351).

5. The bursting of the speculative bubble prompted the BOJ to argue for rapid financial deregulation as market-determined interest rates would be economically more efficient to expand liquidity in the money market. The MOF, on the other hand, favored a slower pace of deregulation to avoid the disruption of many financial institutions (Takahashi 1994).

Legislation enacted in June 1997 and effective April 1998 supports the Bank of Japan's independence from the government in setting monetary policy. Together with the Deposit Insurance Corporation, the BOJ has ensured that no depositor has lost money when ailing banks were merged with larger ones or when banks were allowed to fail starting in 1995. The DIC was established in 1971 to cover individual accounts, and its capital is contributed by the MOF, the BOJ, and banks in equal amounts. Though the DIC was asked to extend loans in connection with two rescues in 1992, it was not asked to pay depositors in the first 25 years of its history due to the MOF's no fail policy until 1995 and insufficient funds to fulfill its purpose.

As outlined in the 1998 "Emergency Measures to Stabilize the Financial System," the DIC's operations will be enlarged to cover all financial institutions and the DIC's ability to collect nonperforming loans will be strengthened by giving it the authority, for the first time, to impose penalties. To support these enhanced responsibilities the government has agreed to set aside 17 trillion yen to protect depositors and a further 13 trillion yen to help recapitalize Japanese banks. A separate account at the DIC will be established for operations that increase the capital base of banks, and decisions to use the fund will be made by an examination board that includes the governor of the DIC, the minister of finance, the commissioner of the new Financial Supervisory Agency, the governor of the Bank of Japan, and three private sector representatives.

Neither the MOF nor the BOJ has jurisdiction over the huge postal savings accounts and life insurance systems managed by post offices, both of which are regulated by the Ministry of Post and Telecommunications (MPT). The MPT has full autonomy in setting interest rates on postal savings accounts, which compete with bank deposits. The funds collected are invested in money market instruments and public securities or are allocated to the Fiscal Investment and Loan Program (FILP). The FILP, which is also referred to as the government's second budget, constitutes between 60 percent and 70 percent of MOF funds (Takahashi 1994). It makes long-term loans available to strategically and socially important sectors. Given the immense size of the postal savings system, the fact that the interest rate on postal savings accounts is not market determined is the last major obstacle to full financial deregulation.

Financial Institutions

Despite Japan's developed-country status in the real sector, its financial sector is still developing, as data on financial depth indicate. For example, banks still dominate the system. In 1995, total bank loans accounted for 105 percent of GDP in Japan, compared to 37 percent in the United States (*The Economist*, 9 March 1996). The lack of financial deepening is further

Table B.4 Japan: Assets of financial institutions, 1970, 1980, 1989, and 1993 (percentages)

Institution	1970	1980	1989	1993
City banks	27.5	21.0	22.3	35
Regional banks	12.8	11.8	11.2	28
Sogo banks (2nd-tier regional)	8.6	5.6	4.3	–
Foreign banks	–	1.3	1.0	2.5
Long-term credit banks	4.8	4.6	4.7	8
Trust banks	7.6	7.6	11.6	–
Other	6.6	8.1	5.4	na
Insurance companies	5.4	5.7	9.5	na
Securities and securities finance companies[a]	0.6	0.6	1.1	na
Intermediaries for small and medium firms				
Shinkin banks (credit assoc.)	7.0	7.0	5.9	na
Credit cooperatives	1.6	1.6	1.4	na
Shoko-chukin Bank	1.0	1.0	0.8	na
Government institutions				
Postal saving system[b]	10.9	17.1	15.5	na
Other	5.6	7.3	5.2	na

na = Not applicable.
– = Not available.

Notes:
a. Securities held for own account plus loans to clients.
b. Assets of the Trust Fund Bureau of the Ministry of Finance.

Sources: Bank of Japan, *Economic Statistics Annual*, various issues (for example, the 1991 edition, tables 16-50, 41-104, gives a variety of annual data series for most of these institutions); Teranishi (1994) and US Treasury (1994) for 1989 and 1993 data.

evidenced by the distribution of assets held by various financial institutions through the 1980s (see table B.4). From 1980 to 1989, the share of financial assets held by commercial banks, including foreign banks and long-term credit banks, remained almost constant at around 44 percent of the total. The share held by trust banks, insurance companies, and securities companies—namely, by financial institutions that facilitate direct finance rather than intermediation—increased from 13.9 percent to 22.2 percent during the same period, although some of this increase can be attributed to the asset price bubble of the late 1980s rather than to financial deepening. Overall, the distribution of financial assets is fairly diffuse, with only city banks and the postal savings system accounting for significant shares.

Financial Intermediaries

Traditionally, the Japanese financial sector has been characterized by strict compartmentalization, along both regional and business lines. Over the past 20 years, the individual niches have been slowly eroded, first, in the 1970s, by allowing different kinds of banks to offer a wider, overlapping variety of interest-bearing instruments, then, since the 1980s, by permitting bank and nonbank financial intermediaries to partly enter each other's businesses. Since 1992, financial institutions have been allowed to own subsidiaries in a different niche.

For decades, the number of banks did not change much as it was the declared policy of the MOF not to allow banks to fail. In contrast, with the exception of insurance companies, the number of specialized intermediaries has declined drastically since 1960. Many of these small, highly specialized nonbank financial intermediaries lost their niches as a result of deregulation and had to be taken over by larger banks to avoid failure. Other financial intermediaries chose to merge to exploit either economies of scale by combining operations in different regions or economies of scope by expanding business activities into separate niches (Kitagawa and Kurosawa 1994, 114-17).

Commercial banks are divided into city banks, regional banks, and second-tier regional banks. These banks have traditionally specialized in short-term loans, their funds coming from time deposits with maturities of less than three years. In the 1980s, city banks began using instruments such as interest rate swaps, dollar-denominated five-year certificates of deposit (CDs), floating rate loans, European transactions, and the sale of loans to circumvent the three-year limit on time deposits, thus adjusting their term structure.

City banks have a nationwide branch network. Six of them are the main banks of major business groups known as horizontal *keiretsu*. The main bank not only provides loans to group members but also guarantees group members' loans from other (nonmember) financial institutions. This assumption increased the *keiretsu* members' overall credit standing.

As interest rate deregulation proceeded, companies became more cost-sensitive. In particular, large companies with access to capital markets became less dependent on bank financing. Slower economic growth further decreased the demand for loans. City banks thus expanded their clientele and offered more long-term loans, e.g., residential loans.[6] This development led to a mismatch of maturities between assets (increasingly long-term) and liabilities (mainly short-term), which exposed the banks to interest rate and liquidity risk.

---

6. Maturities on deposits, not loans, were regulated by the MOF. Yet prudent banking practices will result in short-term loans when deposits are short-term.

Whereas city banks, especially those that are members of a *keiretsu*, focus their business on large-scale clients, regional banks deal with small and medium-sized enterprises (SMEs) in one or two prefectures, although some of the regional banks are quite large by asset size. Second-tier regional banks are smaller in size. In fact, they have been in existence only since 1989, when *sogo* banks, or mutual savings and loan associations, were allowed to convert into second-tier regional banks. *Sogo* banks had been losing their business niche as city banks expanded their clientele among SMEs. The last *sogo* bank merged out of existence in 1992.

In the 1980s, regulations were changed to allow commercial banks to sell government bonds (1983) and deal in government bonds and commercial paper (both in 1987). This weakened the separation of the banking and securities business. In 1993, the FSRA permitted banks to own securities subsidiaries. Similarly, since 1986, city banks have been allowed both to link medical insurance with time deposits and to have subsidiaries in the insurance business, two practices that have weakened the separation between banking and nonlife insurance.

The long-term credit banks provide long-term loans to private industry. Their source of funds is limited to medium-term bank debentures with maturities in excess of five years. These banks, which invest in the bond market and issue corporate debt instruments, have only a small branch network, although since 1993 they have been permitted to convert into commercial banks or to merge with them. The FSRA of 1993 also allowed them—like city banks—to have securities firm subsidiaries, which are barred from engaging in brokerage activities and from underwriting equities. Staggered entry enabled long-term credit banks to set up such subsidiaries before city banks did.

Until recently, trust banks, which are similar to mutual funds, had (along with life insurers) the exclusive right to manage pension funds.[7] In other, noncore trust business activities, the seven original trust banks (as well as one city bank that had been grandfathered to engage in trust banking) have faced increasing competition since 1993, when regulations on entry were relaxed and several banks and securities companies were licensed to operate trust bank subsidiaries. Even before 1993, though, the increasing maturity pattern of city bank loans was a source of competition for trust banks.

The majority of bank loans are collateralized, a practice that was standardized in 1962. In the 1970s, 60 percent to 70 percent of bank loans were collateralized through third-party guarantees. The 1980s saw a shift toward real estate collateralization—especially in the case of city banks, in which the growth in lending secured by real estate exceeded overall

---

7. Trust banks and life insurers lost their monopoly in pension fund management as part of the "big bang" financial reforms.

lending growth. As the real estate asset bubble collapsed and many companies were faced with bankruptcy, the banks were burdened with an increasing amount of nonperforming loans or bad debt.

To help banks reduce their bad loan exposure and to bolster confidence in the Japanese financial system, in 1993 the government established the Cooperative Credit Purchasing Corporation,[8] a lifeboat institution to which banks can sell nonperforming loans. The following year, the government created Special Purpose Companies, to which banks can transfer their restructured loans off their balance sheets. Banks have responded by aggressively writing off their problem loans: in 1993, write-offs increased by more than 100 percent over the previous year and, in 1994, there were five times as many write-offs as in 1992. Nonetheless, these write-offs constituted only 20 percent of total disclosed bad loans.

When the real estate bubble collapsed, the housing loan companies (*jusen*) were left with 60 percent nonperforming assets. Unfortunately, the *jusen* fiasco was just the tip of the iceberg. The liberal definition of problem loans prevents anyone from knowing the exact extent of Japan's bad loan problem.[9] However, by early 1998 nonperforming loans were estimated to total $600 billion dollars, or roughly 25 percent of 1996 GDP (*The Economist*, 23 February 1998). In order to address the mounting crisis in 1998, the government made 13 trillion yen available to the Deposit Insurance Corporation to purchase preferred stock and subordinated debt of financial institutions to increase their capital base; another 17 trillion yen was available to protect deposits and allow the Resolution and Collection Bank to secure any failed financial institution. It is not yet clear, however, how the nonperforming loan problem will be addressed under Japan's 1998 emergency measures to stabilize the financial system.

Japan's nonbank financial intermediaries in 1994 included 428 credit associations or credit unions, 381 credit cooperatives, and more than 2,000 agricultural cooperatives, which specialize in taking deposits from and making loans to farmers. Together with the forestry and fishery cooperatives, the agricultural cooperatives own the Norin-chukin Bank, which acts as their central bank and, since 1959, has been entirely privately owned. This contrasts with the Shoko-chukin Bank, the central cooperative bank that provides finance to small business cooperatives and is almost 73 percent government owned. Both banks may issue bank debentures.

---

8. Similar institutions include the Housing Loan Administration Corporation, which was established in response to the *jusen* failures, and the Resolution and Collection Bank, which targets failed credit associations and credit cooperatives.

9. Bad loans, according to this definition, are equal to loans of bankrupt borrowers plus those on which interest in arrears totals at least six months, but this definition excludes restructured loans and bad loans if an additional loan was made to cover the interest arrears.

Until 1996, the insurance market was strictly separated into life and nonlife insurance sectors, with 27 domestic life insurers and 24 domestic nonlife insurers in 1994 (Lamble and Low 1995, 87). Since the new Insurance Law came into effect in April 1996, both sectors have been allowed to enter each other's area of specialization through subsidiaries.[10] They are also allowed to own controlling interest in other financial institutions.

The insurance industry was, in the past, heavily regulated through administrative guidance by the MOF, which set uniform premium rates and prohibited insurance companies from advertising their products based on comparisons of dividend yields. According to the new Insurance Law, beginning in 1998, premiums will no longer be set by the MOF; companies will only have to notify the MOF of rate changes. The law also introduces solvency standards, enhanced monitoring, and improved disclosure (Lamble and Low 1995, 89). In addition, the law promotes the establishment of a mutually funded assistance company, resembling the deposit insurance corporation, to help insurance companies in financial difficulty meet their obligations to policyholders.

Although a brokerage system is supposedly planned, the insurance industry relies on an agent network. Life insurance agents may work only for a single life insurance company, which effectively makes them company employees. In contrast, many nonlife insurance agents are multiagents and sell on behalf of several insurance companies.

An obstacle to competition in the insurance industry is the *keiretsu* membership of the larger insurance companies. For example, in 1987, 75 percent of the largest Japanese companies cited group affiliation as the reason for selecting their fire and marine insurer.

The slow pace of interest rate deregulation in the 1980s allowed life insurance companies to accumulate a larger share of additional savings. Their investment in stocks is limited to 30 percent of assets; in real estate, to 20 percent. After limits of 10 percent of assets on their overseas investments were raised to 30 percent in 1986, insurers became major investors in foreign securities.

Securities companies perform the multiple tasks of broker, dealer, underwriter, and distributor, with each task requiring a separate license from the MOF. Since the enactment in 1993 of the FSRA law, they are also

---

10. Under a 1996 bilateral insurance deal with the United States, the MOF has to ensure that nonlife insurers who enter the personal accident insurance market do not do so at the expense of foreign life insurers. Entry into a third sector, the medical and cancer insurance market, in which foreign insurers enjoy competitive advantage, will not be allowed until 2001 (*Nikkei Weekly*, 23 December 1996). Japan agreed to bind the commitments made in the 1996 US-Japan bilateral insurance deal in the 1997 WTO financial services agreement. When this agreement comes into effect in early 1999, the provisions of the US-Japan insurance deal will therefore be subject to the WTO dispute settlement mechanism.

allowed to own subsidiaries in the banking sector. By size, securities companies have historically been divided into three groups: the "big four," ten smaller securities companies, and an agglomeration of the rest. The big four are members of a *keiretsu* and many of the other securities companies are affiliated with them. They dominate both the issue market, with 70 percent of new issues, and the secondary market, although their market share declined from 40-50 percent in the early 1980s to 30 percent 10 years later. Shares in Yamaichi, Japan's fourth largest securities company, fell sharply in early November 1997 and within two weeks it closed. Given increased competition from domestic and foreign securities firms, the dominant market position of the now "big three" is likely to continue its decline.

Brokers are now less dependent on bank borrowing and credit from securities firms than they used to be. Their funds stem from retained earnings and better access to the money market, which improves their capacity for risk taking. This interval financing ability is a result of an oligopolistic market structure with fixed commissions and restricted entry. In 1994, the stock brokerage fee was liberalized, resulting in several foreign securities firms charging no fee at all. Small and medium-sized securities firms are expected to follow suit, unlike the big four. Besides the commission, there is a 0.3 percent securities transaction tax.

Japan's privately owned financial institutions have to compete against government-owned ones. Among these, the postal savings system is the most prevalent. With roughly 19,000 of its more than 24,000 post offices offering banking services, the postal savings system has the most extensive branch network of all the financial institutions. In addition, it offers higher interest rates than do commercial banks. One type of deposit account that is particularly attractive to savers offers fixed interest rates for ten years, and customers are further protected from falling interest rates by being allowed to withdraw their savings without notice after six months.

The postal savings system lost its tax-free status in 1988. As compensation, the MPT was awarded in-house management of postal savings funds. Furthermore, post offices were permitted over-the-counter (OTC) sales of up to ¥1 trillion worth of government bonds, and the ceiling on deposits was raised in two stages to ¥10 million. Post offices are also allowed to exchange foreign currencies and to sell traveler's checks.

Like the postal savings system, the postal insurance system is also operated nationwide by post offices. Created at the end of the last century to provide small-sum-insured life policies to low-income households, it is still limited to small insurance policies. Nonetheless, the postal insurance system is the biggest life insurer in the world. The demands of the MPT to be permitted to expand into bigger insurance policies are strongly opposed by private life insurers.

Other government-owned financial institutions include the Japan Development Bank, the Export-Import Bank, and specialized financial co-operatives such as the Housing Loan Corporation, which provides 80 percent of Japanese mortgages.

Direct Finance

Japan has eight licensed stock exchanges, the largest of which is the Tokyo Stock Exchange (TSE).[11] With the exception of the TSE, where banks may become special members to participate in government bond dealing, membership is restricted to licensed securities firms. Companies wishing to list on the exchanges require MOF approval. In 1996, stock market access was made easier.

The market value of equity listed on the TSE peaked with the asset bubble in late 1989. In the following four years, the market value fell by almost 50 percent and trading volume declined by 60 percent (US Treasury 1994, 347). Equity trading was suspended in April 1990 because of the sharp downturn in the stock market. This development is opposite to that in the registered OTC market, where the annual turnover has doubled since 1989.

Government bonds have dominated the bond market since 1975, when massive offerings of government bond issues began. Since October 1990, the BOJ has auctioned off 60 percent of government bond issues; the remaining 40 percent are underwritten by the straight syndicate method with the issuing price set at the average auction price. This practice ensures that small underwriters, who might otherwise not compete successfully, participate in the market.

The corporate bond market has been growing lately, though it is still small at only 1.2 percent of GDP. Part of the problem has been Japan's restrictive primary market, which, in the past, limited the amount of issuance allowed and charged high fees by international standards. In fact, in 1991, Japanese companies issued more than 60 percent of their securities outside of Japan (Takahashi 1994, 41).

Since 1988, companies no longer require permission to issue bonds, and in 1993 the limit on the maximum number of new issues was lifted. Restrictions on European bonds were also abolished.[12] Other measures that explain the recent surge in the corporate bond market include a fee reduction of approximately 50 percent and a lowering of the minimum credit rating for bond-issuing companies to triple-B. Yet, the MOF continues to be hesitant about permitting innovative instruments tailored to

---

11. Prior to the asset bubble crash of 1990, the TSE had become the world's largest stock exchange.

12. European bonds had been introduced for nonresident private issuers in 1984 and for resident private issuers in 1985.

the issuers' needs. An outdated bond registration law and the lack of an efficient clearing system explain why the sec-ondary bond market is almost nonexistent despite the growing primary market.

Growth of the money market was triggered in 1969 by the introduction of repurchase agreements. The following two decades saw the introduction of various other money market instruments. Recent instruments include the introduction of a bid-offer system in the collateralized call money market (1990), and postdated transactions in both the unsecured call money market (1991) and the bill discount market (1992).

In the CP market, which was launched in 1987, no direct issue by borrowers is permitted. Securities houses may act as arrangers, but domestic banks dominate the CP market with 77 percent of the total. Recent liberalization of CP market regulations includes lowering the required minimum rating threshold and permitting nonbanks to issue CP on a limited basis provided the proceeds are not to be used for loans (1993). In 1994, the latter deregulation was extended to insurance companies. That year, the MOF also permitted the issue of overseas asset-backed Euro-yen bonds.

Financial futures are traded in the Tokyo International Financial Futures Exchange (TIFFE), which was established in 1989 and specializes in bank-related financial futures and options. Initially limited to three-month Euro-yen and Euro-dollar interest rates and the yen/dollar exchange rate, permissible transactions on the TIFFE were extended in 1994 to include forward rate agreements (FRAs) and forward exchange rate agreements (FXAs). As managers became more familiar with such instruments, demand grew and trading in the TIFFE took off in 1993, with annual turnover increasing by 60 percent. Basic capital requirements are high, which might explain a membership decline of 20 percent from 1989 to 1994. Membership among foreign securities firms has increased slightly, though, despite the abrogation of lower capital requirements for them.

Since 1989, the markets for securities derivative products have stagnated, although a slight improvement was recorded in 1993. The sharp decline in cash stock prices led the government to tighten controls on stock index derivative trading starting in 1990.

Investment trusts, aimed at retail investors, are the Japanese version of mutual funds. Money management funds are similar to investment funds, but specialize in investing in short-term instruments, which makes them very liquid. The market for both funds has been lackluster since the collapse of the speculative bubble.

Investment trusts are managed by investment trust management companies (ITMCs), most of which are affiliated with one of the *keiretsu*. Since 1983 ITMCs have been permitted to sell investment trusts established overseas. Derivative trading is discouraged, and investment in gold, real estate, and many other nonfinancial assets prohibited. Investment advisory services are licensed to engage in discretionary fund management. Since 1993, they have also been permitted to manage pension funds, although they cannot enter the investment trust business except through subsidiaries. Investment advisory firms and ITMCs have been regulated as separate entities. Under the terms of Japan's 1997 WTO financial services offer—which comes into effect in early 1999—investment trust management services and discretionary investment management services will be permitted to be supplied by one entity, subject to adherence to prudential standards.

Pension funds are either public or private. Everyone is required to enroll in the public pension fund system, which invests most of its funds in low-interest public loans through the MOF's Trust Fund Bureau.

The most important private pension funds are the Tax-Qualified Group Pension Plan (TQPP) and the Employer Pension Fund (EPF). The TQPP is regulated by the MOF and is targeted at companies of 15 or more employees. The government recently removed restrictions stipulating that only trust banks and life insurance companies could manage TQPP funds. The EPF, regulated by the Ministry of Health and Welfare, is for companies with at least 500 employees. EPFs must make a minimum return of 5.5 percent; any shortfalls must be made up by the participating companies.

Traditionally, trust banks and pension funds have managed EPFs, but since 1990 investment advisory firms have been permitted to manage new contributions to the funds. In 1994, the regulation was extended to allow investment advisory firms to manage up to 33 percent of all EPF assets; the share was increased in 1997 to 50 percent and, as of 1999, all limits will be removed. In 1993, 62 percent of EPF assets were managed by trust banks, 36 percent by life insurance companies, and 2 percent by investment advisory firms.

Besides allowing entry of investment advisory firms, the Ministry of Health and Welfare has also gradually relaxed its 5-3-3-2 rule in order to promote higher pension fund returns. According to the 5-3-3-2 rule, at least 50 percent of a pension fund had to be invested in assets with a guaranteed return on principal; no more than 30 percent could be invested in domestic equities; no more than 30 percent in foreign securities, and no more than 20 percent in real estate. Furthermore, no single investment was to exceed 10 percent of the fund. Such deregulation measures caused money to move from trust banks and life insurance companies to investment advisory firms (*The Economist*, 28 June 1997). Japan's WTO financial services offer contains provisions that will remove asset allocation guidelines for EPF and Pension Welfare Public Service Corporation funds managed by—as well as ceilings on the amount that can be invested by—discretionary investment management services by March 1999 (*Inside U.S. Trade*, 15 December 1997). Finally, the big bang plan forces all fund managers to disclose the market value, rather than the book value, of their investments. This will facilitate comparisons with Western competitors.

Foreign exchange (FOREX) transactions have been limited to designated FOREX banks, which include all city, regional, long-term, and foreign banks, most second-tier banks, and all trust banks. Amendments to the Foreign Exchange Law, passed as part of the big bang plan of financial reform, state that these banks will lose their monopoly power over FOREX transactions by April 1998. The 1980 New Foreign Exchange Control Law permitted all capital transactions that were not explicitly prohibited. Exchange controls are, under the law, to be introduced in emergencies only. Nonetheless, the MOF controls the overall currency position of FOREX banks, special settlement methods, and resident deposits in overseas accounts. The MOF also must be notified of direct investments in Japan (FAIR 1996, 6).Under the 1997 amendments to the Foreign Exchange Law, the government will retain power over capital transactions in emergencies and will continue to require prior notification for foreign direct investment in Japan.

Prudential Regulations

Prudential regulations were introduced in Japan's financial system shortly after World War II. However, these prudential regulations were not comprehensive; they allowed for various loopholes, and the regulatory authorities did not always ensure compliance with them.

The Antitrust Law of 1947 limits to 5 percent the amount of assets a bank can hold in another company.[13] This limit was raised to 10 percent in 1953, only to be lowered back to 5 percent in 1977, when banks were given a ten-year grace period to comply with the lower limit.

Regulations to diversify risk by restricting individual loan sizes were introduced in 1974, first through administrative guidance, then, in 1981, by law. A commercial bank's loan to any one company is limited to 20 percent of the bank's equity, and the limit for long-term banks is 30 percent. These restrictions, though, do not include other types of credits or the value of equity holdings involving the client. Furthermore, loan restrictions do not apply to subsidiaries. Thus it is possible to exceed loan limits.

Liquidity regulations, imposed in 1959, stipulate that current assets exceed 30 percent of deposits and CDs. Prior to 1980, city banks generally

---

13. The Antitrust Law forbids any Japanese company to hold stock in a competitor company. Hence, city banks cannot own each other's shares but may hold shares of a financial institution operating in a separate niche. The decrees of the Antitrust Law that govern acquisitions, takeovers, mergers, and joint ventures can be overruled by the Japan Fair Trade Commission.

did not meet this requirement. In fact, they only met the regulation after taking time deposits in the Euro-market, which are not subject to liquidity requirements, and making call loans, which are included in current assets.

In 1954, the MOF stipulated that equity constitute at least 10 percent of total assets. In general, though, city banks have not complied with this regulation. Their low equity ratio has been the result of high lending growth rates and the MOF's strict control of their dividend policy. In 1986, the MOF lowered the required 10 percent minimum equity ratio to 6 percent for banks with foreign branches and 4 percent for those without foreign branches.

In 1988, the Bank for International Settlements (BIS) guidelines for risk weighting of assets were introduced. This capital-risk asset ratio includes all on and off balance sheet risk-related items on the asset side and 45 percent of unrealized capital gains in securities on the equity side. The MOF stipulated that Japanese banks had to meet a risk-weighted capital-adequacy ratio of 7.25 percent by 1991 and the BIS recommended ratio of 8 percent by 1993. Risk-weighted capital adequacy for securities firms was introduced in 1990. And in 1992, the MOF repealed the 10 to 1 ratio of liabilities to capital.

To meet the BIS capital requirements, banks issued a large amount of equity and convertible bonds between 1985 and 1989, in an amount that equaled over half of new issues on the TSE in those years. Banks also enjoyed unrealized capital gains on long-standing securities in other firms. These returns compensated them for the lower profits associated with lending activities.

As long as stock prices were rising, compliance with BIS capital adequacy rules seemed easy. But the stock market declines of the early 1990s wiped out much of the banks' hidden reserves. It was estimated that each 100-point drop in the Nikkei index lowered the overall bank equity ratio by 0.2 percent.

In the last few years, Japanese banks have continuously improved their risk-weighted capital-adequacy ratios, and they are scheduled to meet new, more stringent capital adequacy ratios by the end of the 1997 fiscal year (March 1998). But stock market losses, beginning in late 1997, combined with slow economic growth once again wiped out banks' hidden reserves, eroding the value of their capital base. Regulators implemented a number of emergency measures in early 1998 that will enable banks to meet required capital-adequacy reserve ratios. Of the 30 trillion yen emergency stabilization package announced in late January 1998, 13 trillion is earmarked for improving banks' balance sheets. The MOF has offered a one-year grace period for small banks to meet these requirements; it also plans to allow banks to count property assets as reserves to help them meet capital requires in the current fiscal year (*The Wall Street Journal* 27 January 1998).

Foreign Participation

Foreign commercial banks enjoy national treatment or better. They benefited from many of the deregulation measures introduced for domestic banks in 1993, and so have since lost some of their better-than-national treatment. They were, however, grandfathered to engage in certain activities not yet open to domestic commercial banks.

Nonetheless, the 145 branches of 90 foreign banks in Japan (US Treasury 1994, 343) have only a small market share. Rather than take deposits, foreign banks rely on the money market for funding. Part of the reason for their limited success is the difficulty in penetrating the *keiretsu* system. Cross-shareholding, which ensures that only a limited number of shares are traded, also makes it difficult to acquire existing Japanese banks. The MOF has stated that such acquisitions are possible and will be approved should a foreign bank make such a request, but this has not happened because of the current dismal financial state of domestic banks.

In 1985, trust banking opened to foreign participation. Nine foreign trust bank subsidiaries are permitted to engage in a full range of trust banking, including pension fund management. Foreign banks have had some success in the discretionary fund trust market, capturing a market share of 12.5 percent by the early 1990s. They have not, however, been able to gain ground in pension fund management, as management mandates of private pension funds are awarded to *keiretsu* members based on corporate relationship rather than economic performance. Since the size of Japanese corporate pension funds makes them attractive, foreign trust banks have pushed for a more rapid elimination of asset allocation guidelines (e.g., the 5-3-3-2 rule). They have welcomed the big bang plan and its proposal to introduce standardized evaluation methods by valuing pension funds at current market value.

In 1994, there were 3 foreign life insurers and 30 foreign nonlife insurers, all of which are allowed to join the mutually funded assistance corporation. Foreign insurers' market share is small, as the *keiretsu* system and the insurer agent system (rather than a broker system) make it difficult to penetrate the market. Hence, by 1994, foreign insurance companies had captured only 3.2 percent of the casualty insurance market and 2.5 percent of the life insurance market (Lamble and Low 1995). A third sector, the medical and cancer insurance market, makes up about 3 percent of the total insurance market but accounts for approximately 50 percent of total foreign insurance company income (*Nikkei Weekly*, 23 December 1996). In this sector, foreign insurance companies have a 35 percent market share (*The Economist*, 15 June 1996). The current liberalization process, which eliminates barriers between the insurance sectors, calls for continued protection of this third sector until 2001. Thus, while foreign insurers will be allowed to expand into other insurance sectors, they will remain protected for four more years from the competition of the very large, *keiretsu*-affiliated Japanese insurance companies in the medical and cancer insurance market. Authorities agreed to prevent life and casualty insurance companies from entering the third sector, until other deregulation measures had been implemented under the terms of the 1996 US-Japan insurance pact. This bilateral pact was subsequently incorporated into Japan's 1997 WTO financial services offer. Key reforms outlined in the 1997 offer include allowing life and nonlife insurance subsidiaries to offer a wide range of services, introducing new payment options for automobile insurance customers, and offering increased flexibility to set automobile insurance rates based on risk (*Inside US Trade*, 15 December 1997).

There were 97 foreign securities companies in Japan in 1994, down from a peak of 127 in 1991, a downsizing due in large part to high and rising overhead costs. Twenty-four of these companies had a seat on the TSE, up from six when foreign securities companies were first permitted to join in 1986. In contrast to the banking sector, establishing a securities company does not require reciprocity. The primary business of foreign securities companies is intermediation of international securities transactions, although they have enjoyed an expanding business role since 1985. In 1993, foreign securities houses accounted for 17.8 percent of securities market turnover in equities and 12 percent in government bonds. The latter represents an increase of 100 percent over the previous year (US Treasury 1994).

Foreign bank subsidiaries operating in Japan may open securities branches with less than 50 percent of operating capital, which until recently was better-than-national treatment. Each securities branch requires a separate MOF license and must be separately capitalized, which discourages multiple branches. The latter rule does not apply to domestic securities houses and therefore places foreign securities houses at a disadvantage vis-à-vis their domestic counterparts. Subsidiaries of foreign securities houses have to apply according to the provision of the SEA, whereas representative offices are required only to notify the MOF.

Foreign investment trust management companies (ITMCs) have been allowed to enter the market since 1990. In mid-1997, five foreign ITMCs, specializing in the sale of investment trusts established overseas, were operating in Japan. To manage both investment trust and pension funds, foreign companies have to establish separate branches—one ITMC and one investment advisory firm—which increases overhead. These high entry costs deter foreign participation. Furthermore, as investment trusts can be marketed only by securities companies and foreign securities companies do not have extensive branch networks, foreign ITMCs generally have to market their products through Japanese securities houses. Yet, many Japanese securities houses are already affiliated with ITMCs through their *keiretsu* network. Hence, penetrating the trust and pension fund market is difficult for foreign firms.

Remaining Obstacles

Some, but not all, of the obstacles to an open, safe and efficient financial system in Japan will be removed as the big bang proceeds to its scheduled completion by 2001. Explicit barriers to foreign entry are few, but implicit obstacles presented by existing business and business-government relationships persist. Market forces are only beginning to be a factor. Important supervisory and prudential changes are still required to increase efficiency. The bad loan problems of the 1990s have revealed low audit standards, insufficient disclosure in accounting practices, and low standards of regulation and enforcement, in part because of insufficient numbers of regulatory staff.

Major questions also remain about the future MOF and the BOJ: Can the MOF establish a truly independent Financial Services Agency (as it is scheduled to do by June 1998) to deliver impartial advisory oversight of financial institutions? How much independence will the BOJ actually have? Will its independence and credibility continue to rely on the personality of the BOJ governor? Other questions remain: How quickly and far-reaching will the big bang reform process actually be? And will the limited access for foreign financial institutions continue to be blocked by the dominance of cross-shareholding and *keiretsu* relationships? Finally, the future of the postal savings system appears to be untouched by the big bang. As interest rates are deregulated in the rest of the economy, and as a new range of innovative financial products become available to consumers, will the postal savings system be rationalized into a market-driven institution?

References

Foundation for Advanced Information and Research (FAIR). 1996. *Capital Flow Liberalization and Financial Market Opening in the APEC Economies: An East Asian Perspective.* Tokyo: Foundation for Advanced Information and Research.

Frankel, Jeffrey A. 1995. Recent Changes in the Financial Systems of Asian and Pacific Countries. In *Financial Stability in a Changing Environment,* ed. by Kuniho Sawamoto, Zenta Nakajima, and Hiroo Taguchi. New York: MacMillan Press.

Institute of International Bankers. 1997. *Global Survey 1997.* New York: Institute of International Bankers.

Kitagawa, Hiroshi, and Yoshitaka Kurosawa. 1994. Japan: Development and Structural Change of the Banking System. In *The Financial Development of Japan, Korea, and Taiwan,* ed. by Hugh T. Patrick and Yung Chul Park. New York: Oxford University Press.

Lamble, Peter, and Robin Low. 1995. *The Asia Pacific Insurance Handbook.* Sydney, NWT: Coopers & Lybrand.

Ministry of Finance (MOF). 1998. Outline of the Emergency Measures to Stabilize the Financial System. (http://www.mof.go.jp/english/emergency/e1sfs1.htm).

Patrick, Hugh T., and Yung Chul Park, eds. 1994. *The Financial Development of Japan, Korea, and Taiwan.* New York: Oxford University Press.

Takahashi, Yuichi. 1994. Financial Sector Reform in the Asia Pacific Countries. Photocopy.

Teranishi, Juro. 1994. Japan: Development and Structural Change of the Financial System. In *The Financial Development of Japan, Korea, and Taiwan*, ed. by Hugh T. Patrick and Yung Chul Park. New York: Oxford University Press.

US Department of the Treasury. 1994. *National Treatment Study*. Washington: Government Printing Office.

Yoshino, Naoyuki. 1996. The Role of Government Banks in Japanese Development and Its Lessons. Paper presented at the Conference on Regulation of Capital Markets and Financial Services in the Pacific Rim, Georgetown University Law Center, Washington (11-13 November).

South Korea

Introduction

During the immediate postwar reconstruction period, the South Korean government pursued an inward-looking, import-substitution economic development strategy. In 1961, development policy was reoriented and an outward-looking strategy, based on export expansion and heavy government involvement in economic activity, was implemented. At the same time, the government nationalized the banking sector. Throughout the 1960s and 1970s, the financial system was used as a key instrument to promote national development objectives. Extensive capital and interest rate controls, in addition to a variety of subsidies and export credits, were used to ensure the flow of credit to export-oriented industries. In 1973, government intervention increased with the implementation of the Heavy Chemical and Industrial Drive (HCI), in which key industries received the majority of credit at below-market interest rates.[1] By the end of the 1970s, approximately 80 percent of fixed investment in the manufacturing sector was in HCI industries.

Between 1962 and 1982, annual growth averaged 8.4 percent, although by the end of the 1970s production efficiency in priority sectors was falling. As a result of the myriad of government incentives and controls, there was excessive investment in the HCI industries and little allocative efficiency in the capital market. The financial sector was highly repressed,

---

1. The HCI industries are steel, petrochemicals, metals, shipbuilding, electronics, and machinery.

with the government controlling virtually every aspect of the domestic financial market and with high barriers to entry for foreign financial services firms.

In 1982, the South Korean government undertook efforts to liberalize the financial sector. It began to privatize commercial banking, abolished preferential rates for policy loans by commercial banks, introduced commercial paper at unregulated rates, and allowed corporate bond yields to fluctuate around the basic bank loan rate by plus or minus 1 percent.

Despite these initial measures, the financial sector and capital market remained highly controlled throughout most of the 1980s. For example, interest rates remained, for the most part, under the control of the government. And in order to compensate for the lack of financing for firms other than the large HCI industries, the government directed commercial banks to allocate at least 35 percent of loans to small and medium-sized enterprises. In addition, all foreign exchange transactions were required to take place through an official, state-designated, foreign exchange bank.[2]

From 1980 to 1984, South Korea ran a chronic current account deficit and therefore maintained strict controls on capital outflows while allowing limited capital inflows, most notably through public financial institutions and public borrowing. Foreign banks were allowed to enter the market in order to help attract foreign capital. From 1985 to 1989, the situation was reversed, and South Korea ran a considerable current account surplus. During this period, the government began to liberalize capital outflows but tightened regulations concerning capital inflows. Throughout the 1980s, the exchange rate was determined by a Multiple Currency Basket Peg System (MCBS).

Beginning in 1988, South Korea began to relax restrictions on foreign exchange transactions. That year, South Korea agreed to accept the obligations of IMF Article VIII on foreign exchange controls.[3] A foreign currency call market subsequently opened and, in 1990, the MCBS was replaced by a market average rate (MAR) system. Under the MAR, a daily exchange rate for the won/US dollar rate is calculated based on the previous day's won/dollar transactions. The won/dollar rate was permitted to fluctuate by a maximum of 0.4 percent per day.

Foreign exchange controls are regulated by the Ministry of Finance as outlined in the Foreign Exchange Control Act (FECA). The FECA was amended in 1991, replacing a positive system of foreign exchange controls with a negative system. That is, rather than allowing only those foreign exchange transactions specifically permitted by the government,

---

2. Although foreign exchange controls have been relaxed since the 1980s, all foreign exchange transactions must still be conducted through an official foreign exchange bank.

3. IMF's Article VIII prohibits the imposition of restrictions on payments and transfers for current account transactions.

all such transactions are allowed unless specifically prohibited by the government. There remains a wide range of controls on foreign exchange, although the government has committed to phasing out foreign exchange controls in conjunction with other financial sector reforms.

In 1988, the government attempted to liberalize interest rates, but within a few months the rates skyrocketed and the government reversed the majority of reforms. Another schedule for interest rate liberalization was put forth three years later. By 1993, controls had been removed on all lending rates except for policy loans, on deposit rates longer than two years, and on all bond rates.

In its 1993 Blueprint for Financial Reform, the government outlined a five-year program of gradual financial sector deregulation. Under the plan, all interest rate controls, except those on demand deposits, were scheduled to be removed by 1997.[4] Other principal measures of the blueprint include reducing controls on short- and long-term capital flows, giving banks greater autonomy in managing their business, and reducing policy loans from the central bank. Immediate reforms included widening the margin of fluctuation for the exchange rate to plus or minus 1 percent[5] and raising the ceiling on long-term foreign portfolio inflows.

The timetable for liberalizing capital movements was subsequently expedited with the 1995 Revision to the Foreign Exchange Program. Foreign portfolio outflows for purchases of securities and overseas deposits are scheduled to be completely liberalized by the end of 1998. By the end of 1999, there are to be no restrictions on the amount of domestic securities that may be issued overseas. Foreign loans used by South Korean firms to finance capital goods will be liberalized by 1999. Controls on the flow of short-term capital are scheduled to be gradually loosened until 1999.

South Korea's 1996 accession to the OECD was contingent upon its acceptance of the obligations of the OECD Codes of Liberalization of Capital Movements and Current Invisibles Operations. The codes are binding on OECD member countries and require them to remove specific restrictions on the movement of capital and invisible operations. Foreign direct investment in financial services and foreign portfolio investment

---

4. As of February 1996, interest rates were estimated to be deregulated on 83 percent of deposits and 96 percent of all lending. Under South Korea's 1981 General Banking Act, however, interest rates remained capped at 25 percent until December 1997, when the ceiling was raised to 40 percent. In keeping with Korea's IMF program, the ceiling on interest rates is scheduled to be eliminated in 1998.

5. The MAR was allowed to fluctuate plus or minus 2.25 percent per day until November 1997, when the won trading band was expanded to 10 percent around the daily mid rate. By late December 1997, to help the financial system stabilize during the Asian currency crisis, the government abolished the daily fluctuation band and allowed the won to float.

are addressed in the capital movements code, and cross-border trade in financial services is covered in the code on invisible operations. All countries seeking membership in the OECD must also endorse national treatment principles, as outlined in the 1976 OECD Declaration on International Investment and Multinational Enterprises.

Reservations to both codes and exceptions to the national treatment principles are permitted, and South Korea has availed itself of the opportunity to exercise this option, particularly with respect to the financial services sector. The average acceptance rate among the OECD member countries of the codes on financial liberalization is 89 percent; South Korea accepted only 65 percent of the codes, although many of its reservations and exceptions are to be phased out by 2000.

In keeping with its obligations as a member of the OECD, the South Korean government announced in September 1996 specific reforms that gradually remove barriers to the flow of foreign portfolio investment and foreign direct investment in financial services from OECD countries. Under South Korea's 1996 OECD commitments, the following reforms were scheduled to be phased in: foreign banks and securities firms from OECD countries would be permitted to establish subsidiaries in South Korea by 1998; aggregate foreign investment ceilings for investors from OECD countries were scheduled to be phased out by 2000; foreign investors from OECD countries would be allowed to establish and hold 100 percent ownership of any type of financial institution by December 1998; and, by 1999, foreign investment consulting firms from OECD countries would be able to offer their services without establishing a commercial presence in South Korea.

Despite these changes, the South Korean financial system has been under increasing strain since early 1997, when a chain of corporate defaults exposed a shortage of liquidity in the market. Cash-flow problems facing several large corporations have resulted in an increase in the proportion of nonperforming loans held by commercial banks. The government accelerated plans to deregulate the financial sector, encouraging consolidation in order to help ease liquidity constraints and increasing the government's capacity to effectively supervise the industry. In early 1997, it appointed a presidential commission to recommend corrective action. Far-reaching proposals emerged by mid-year and were initially rejected at the political levels. As the crisis deepened, however, many of these proposals have been adopted.

By late August 1997, the government planned to help finance any troubled financial institution that submitted a self-rescue plan. At that time total aid was estimated at $3.9 billion; bad loans held by the financial sector had reached $29 billion. Through the fall of 1997, the situation worsened and by early December South Korea and the IMF agreed to a $55 billion loan package, the IMF's largest rescue package ever.

The WTO financial services negotiations were underway at the same time that South Korea was seeking assistance from the IMF in the wake of the Asian currency crisis. Within the context of the WTO agreement, South Korea was pressed to bind its OECD commitments to open its banking, securities, and insurance industry to foreign competition. Such an offer was not forthcoming. As the WTO financial services negotiations drew to a close on 13 December 1997, there also remained many barriers to foreign entry in the South Korean financial services market. By the end of December, many of these remaining barriers were addressed in South Korea's letter of intent to the IMF, including the commitment to bind its OECD commitments in banking, securities, and insurance in the WTO financial services agreement. Since the end of December 1997, South Korea has implemented plans to open the financial services sector to foreign competition at a pace that is, in some cases, even quicker than the schedule outlined in South Korea's OECD commitment. New bills regarding supervision and regulation of the financial service sector were subsequently passed, as were bills regarding permissible domestic and foreign ownership of Korean firms. As of early 1998, the Korean financial system is beginning a long process of restructuring and reorganization.

Regulatory Framework

The Ministry of Finance and Economy (MOFE) directly or indirectly controls monetary and credit policy, as well as policies governing the entire financial sector in South Korea. The MOFE and the Bank of Korea (BOK) are the primary regulators of financial institutions. The BOK comprises three main offices: the executive office, the Office of Bank Supervision (OBS), and the Monetary Board. The latter is composed of banking industry and government representatives and is chaired by the Minister of Finance, who is authorized to request a review of any resolution adopted by the Board (Nam 1995, 27). The Board's responsibilities include formulation of credit and monetary policy, supervision of the BOK, and regulation of commercial banks.

Commercial banks are directly supervised by the OBS, whose responsibilities include the establishment of capital and liquidity requirements, reporting requirements, and the proportion of loans targeted to small and medium-sized enterprises. The OBS also conducts bank inspections, reviews applications to establish new banks, and makes recommendations to the Monetary Board about whether to grant a license to open a new bank or revoke an existing license. Approval to operate a bank or nonbank financial intermediary must be granted by the Monetary Board for each type of service an applicant wishes to offer.

The Securities and Exchange Act (SEA), which is the major law governing securities market activities, mandates the separation of securities and banking activities. It requires all financial institutions to obtain permission from the MOFE prior to engaging in securities activities and prohibits securities firms from engaging in business other than securities activities without authorization from the MOFE. The SEA further requires securities companies and securities investment trust companies to receive a license in order to establish a business; and under a 1987 amendment to the SEA, investment advisory businesses must register with the MOFE. The Securities and Exchange Commission (SEC) was created under the SEA.

The SEC and the Securities Supervisory Board (SSB), the executive body of the SEC, regulate primary and secondary market activities. The SEC is responsible for supervising and monitoring securities firms and exchanges and for establishing fair trading practices. It is structured as an independent organization, but the MOFE has the authority to repeal the SEC's decisions, has final rule on any policy relating to the securities market, and is responsible for approving any application to establish a securities firm. The SSB supervises securities companies and transactions, both in and out of the securities market, and monitors compliance with disclosure requirements.

The Korean Stock Exchange (KSE) and Korean Securities Dealers Association (KSDA) both function as self-regulatory agencies. Only licensed securities companies are permitted to be members of the KSE. As mandated by the SEA, the KSE monitors member firms and price movements, establishes listing requirements, discloses information about publicly listed firms, and investigates any potential violation of trading practices. KSDA membership comprises securities firms, securities investment trust companies, banks, and the KSE. The KSDA supervises an over-the-counter market, functions as an information clearinghouse and coordinates activities among members, and manages the Securities Investment Protection Center.

While the Insurance Supervisory Board supervises the insurance industry, the MOFE approves applications for foreign insurance firms to open branch offices or for domestic firms to enter the market, and also establishes premiums, interest rates, and asset management in the insurance industry. The 1962 Insurance Business Act mandates the separation of life and nonlife insurance business.

In December 1997, the Korean National Assembly passed 13 financial reform bills, including a bill to consolidate supervision of the financial services sector in an independent agency reporting to the prime minister's office. A new Financial Supervisory Commission is to be established by 1 April 1998. The activities of the Office of Bank Supervision, the Securities Supervisory Board, and the Insurance Supervisory Board are scheduled to be taken over by the Financial Supervisory Commission in 1999. The MOFE will retain the authority to establish financial policies, revise and amend financial laws, issue financial services licenses, and set foreign exchange policies.

The financial reform bills also include provisions to give the central bank greater autonomy in the conduct of monetary policy. The Monetary Board of the central bank will assume responsibility for setting monetary and credit policy. The Bank of Korea has the mandate to implement monetary and credit policy and has primary responsibility for maintaining price stability. Under the December 1997 financial reforms, the Monetary Board is to be headed by the Governor of the Bank of Korea instead of the Minister of Finance, as has been the traditional practice. Three of the Monetary Board's other six members will be recommended by the Minister of Finance, Governor of the Bank of Korea, and Chairman of the Financial Supervisory Board, and the other three members will be recommended by representatives from the financial services business community.

Financial Institutions

The share of assets held by commercial banks in South Korea has fallen dramatically during the last 25 years, from over 70 percent in 1970 to 35.5 percent in 1995 (see table B.5). Nonbank financial institutions (NBFIs), particularly savings institutions, gained a significant market share during this period. As discussed below, this financial deeping is a result of policies designed to encourage the use of NBFIs instead of the informal credit market. These policies served to tilt the playing field in favor of NBFIs at the expense of commercial banks, which have remained subject to much greater government control than NBFIs over the last 15 years.

The South Korean equity market has expanded rapidly since the mid-1980s. The stock market index rose from 272 in 1986 to 525 in 1987, and peaked in 1989 at 1,007. Although liberalization contributed to the growth of the equity market, the rapid growth of the stock market in the late 1980s was due to the large current account surplus and excess liquidity in the market between 1986 and 1989. In 1989 the stock market bubble burst, and by the end of 1990 the market index stood at 696. The market has since been relatively volatile. Since 1986, the government has made greater use of government bonds (as opposed to credit policy) to manage the money supply and, since 1989, the corporate debt market has become a significant source of capital for South Korean firms. In 1995, the value of traded bonds was roughly 50 percent greater than the value of traded stocks.

Financial Intermediaries

There are two categories of deposit-taking financial intermediaries in South Korea. The first, deposit money banks, is com"posed of commercial

Table B.5 South Korea: Assets of financial institutions, 1970, 1980, and 1995

	Date of formation[a]	No. of institutions[b]	1970 Won[c]	1970 Percentage share	1980 Won[c]	1980 Percentage share	1995 Won[c]	1995 Percentage share
Banks	1945, 1967	101	1.99	72.1	38.3	67.2	290.2	35.5
Nonbank financial institutions								
Development		3	0.63	22.8	9.43	16.6	32.3[f]	7.97
Investment	1970, 1976	46[d]	0		2.43	4.3	54.1[f]	13.3
Savings[e]		6,646	0.103	3.7	4.34	7.6	96.9[f]	23.9
Insurance	1922, 1946	49	0.034	1.2	1.43	2.5	30.5[f]	7.51
Domestic securities companies	1949	25	0.003	0.1	1.04	1.8	18.7[f]	4.62
Foreign securities companies	1980	22	na					
Leasing companies	1972	20	na					
Venture capital companies	1974	51	na					
Credit card companies	1983	6	na					

na = not available.

Notes:
a. Date of formation of the first institution.
b. Number in 1995, unless otherwise specified.
c. In trillions.
d. Includes six merchant banking companies established from 1969 to 1979.
e. Includes trust accounts at banks, established in 1910; credit unions, established in 1960; mutual funds, established in 1969; and mutual savings and finance companies, established in 1972.
f. Figures are for 1990.

Source: Republic of Korea (1996).

banks and specialized banks; the second, nonbank financial institutions, includes development banks, investment banks, and savings institutions.

After privatizing four national banks in the early 1980s,[6] the government authorized the establishment of new national commercial banks in 1982 and 1989-92. From 1967 to 1971, ten privately owned local commercial banks were established to ensure that each region in the country had access to credit. There are currently 15 national commercial banks and 10 local commercial banks in South Korea, accounting for approximately 30 percent of total assets held by financial institutions.

Specialized banks, created in the 1960s to direct resources to specific sectors, have since expanded into commercial banking. Four specialized banks—the Industrial Bank of Korea, the Citizens National Bank, the Korean Housing Bank, and the National Agricultural Cooperative—account for more than a quarter of total assets held by deposit money banks and 12 percent of assets held by all financial institutions. The Citizens National Bank was privatized at the end of 1994; the other specialized banks continue to be controlled by the government and thus complement government-directed lending done through official development banks.

Gradual deregulation of the financial services sector has changed the shape of the industry over the last 15 years. On the one hand, the government not only opened the commercial banking market to new participants but also allowed commercial banks to conduct a wider range of new services, albeit on a very incremental basis. Regional banks and national commercial banks were allowed to enter the trust business in 1983 and 1984, respectively. By 1985, all deposit money banks were authorized to offer negotiable certificates of deposit. On the other hand, throughout this period the government maintained strict controls over the lending activities and management of banks while lowering barriers to entry for investment, savings, and finance companies.[7]

The result of this uneven pace of deregulation was an explosive growth in the number of savings institutions and a dramatic loss in the total market share held by commercial banks.[8] The growth in both the number of savings institutions and the shares of assets held by them reflects

---

6. One of the five nationalized commercial banks, the Commercial Bank of Korea, had been privatized in 1972.

7. Investment and finance companies and mutual savings and finance companies were established in conjunction with the 1972 Presidential Emergency Decree. Nam (1995) also attributes rapid growth of NBFIs to the fact that they were able to offer new financial instruments and that interest rate controls for NBFIs were periodically relaxed throughout the 1980s.

8. Savings institutions include bank trust accounts, credit unions, postal savings and mutual savings, and finance companies.

a deliberate strategy on the part of the government to institutionalize the financial sector. In the early 1980s, the informal credit, or curb-loan, market accounted for approximately 40 percent of the financial system. The deregulation of financial institutions, other than commercial banks, helped reduce the size of the curb market by creating a medium through which individuals and small businesses could access formal credit, with the result that the curb-loan market is now estimated to represent less than 10 percent of total credit (Noland 1996, 8).

With a total of $41 billion in premiums written in fiscal year 1995-96, the South Korean life insurance market is the sixth largest in the world. Following the 1987 deregulation of the industry, 27 new life insurance companies entered the insurance market. The top six companies currently control a combined 73 percent of the total life insurance market, leaving little room for smaller firms seeking to establish a presence in the market. The difficulty for smaller firms seeking to establish a company of a size that will enable them to compete with larger firms is exacerbated by the mandated separation of life and nonlife insurance operations, which prevents them from achieving economies of scope.

Of the 28 life insurance companies in South Korea, 17 are considered effectively insolvent. In March 1997, the government announced plans to revoke a longstanding prohibition on the five largest *chaebols* (conglomerates) entering the life insurance business,[9] on the condition that they each take over at least one insolvent life insurance business in order to enter the market.

Nonlife insurance premiums written in South Korea totaled $13 billion in fiscal year 1995-96, making South Korea the eleventh largest nonlife insurance market in the world. There are currently 14 nonlife insurance firms in South Korea.

The government has, over the past decade, removed some restrictions on large domestic firms seeking to establish financing and investment trust companies. As a result, *chaebol* have become increasingly involved in the financial services sector. In 1996, the 30 largest *chaebol* owned 85 financial subsidiaries, representing 13 percent of the 669 companies affiliated with these conglomerates. Since the Asian currency crisis, South Korea has instituted measures to facilitate mergers and acquisitions between, as well as ease the exit of, firms in the financial services industry. The new regulations are intended to help to recapitalize the financial system and increase the competitiveness of financial institutions. The new mergers and acquisitions laws do not allow a firm

---

9. Samsung had been exempted from this ban because it had established the Samsung Life Insurance Company before the prohibition went into effect. Thus, despite the apparent prohibition on the involvement of *chaebols* in the insurance industry, the early entry of Samsung accounts for 36.5 percent of the life insurance business controlled by the largest five business groups.

to change its underlying business orientation. The laws do, however, permit firms to expand the range of services offered within the company by, for example, allowing mergers between commercial banks and securities firms. The government is presently considering moving to a universal banking system.

Direct Finance

The Korea Stock Exchange (KSE) is the country's only stock exchange. In 1994, market capitalization was $192 billion (50 percent of GDP) and 721 firms were listed on the KSE; the top ten of these firms account for 38 percent of total market value. There are also two over-the-counter markets in South Korea. The first is operated by the Korean Securities Dealers Association and is open to firms not able to meet the KSE's listing requirements; it is not open to foreign investors. In 1994, 340 firms were listed on this exchange and the volume of transactions was 0.25 percent of the volume of transactions on the KSE. The second OTC market is open to foreign investment. Little information is available regarding activity on this exchange.

The South Korean stock market is now the sixth largest market in the world. Nonetheless, the equity market in South Korea is not yet a major source of funds for many South Korean firms. In 1990, the government established a quota system that limits the number of new issues each quarter. As of June 1996, there were 360 firms waiting to list on the KSE (*The Economist*, 3 July 1996). Other barriers to entry are also extremely high. Among other requirements, firms must be at least five years old, have paid-in capital of 3 billion won and total equity of 5 billion won, and have average sales of at least 15 billion won to list on the KSE. Despite these onerous listing requirements, the securities market has grown significantly over the last decade as the government has slowly liberalized it.

In 1981, the South Korean government announced plans to gradually open the securities industry to foreign competition and liberalize the industry in order to help deepen the domestic capital market. During the first phase of the reforms, from 1981 to 1984, international investment funds were established, allowing foreigners to indirectly invest in South Korea, and domestic securities firms were permitted to underwrite and sell foreign securities. As part of the second phase, in 1985 the government allowed domestic companies to issue convertible bonds on overseas markets. By 1991, the government had authorized South Korean securities companies to expand abroad, allowing them to establish overseas branches and subsidiaries and to form joint ventures with foreign securities firms.

When the South Korean market was opened to foreign securities firms in 1991, the government revised the SEA to implement new requirements for all securities firms. In addition to a license from the MOFE, securities companies must have paid-in capital greater than 50 billion won in order to establish operations in South Korea. In 1996, there were 33 domestic firms and 19 foreign branches offering securities services. The main business of these firms is securities underwriting, dealing, and brokerage; ancillary businesses include extending credit for securities transactions and securities savings.

Securities investment trust companies have operated in South Korea since 1970. In recent years they have helped contribute to the development of capital markets and supported corporate financing by issuing securities savings plans to the public and investing the savings in stocks and bonds. Three national and five regional investment trust companies currently dominate the South Korean mutual fund market; the three national firms account for more than 70 percent of the market. Domestic bond funds account for an estimated 85 percent of all assets held in South Korean mutual funds.

There are three types of bonds in South Korea: government, public, and corporate. Corporate bonds accounted for 60 percent of all bonds issued in 1995. Approximately one-quarter of all government and public bonds are monetary stabilization bonds, issued by the central bank to conduct open market operations. In contrast to the equity market, the majority of bond market activity (60 percent) takes place on the over-the-counter exchange.

Prudential Regulations

The government's inordinate control over the financial sector did little to promote transparency and accountability. Further, because interest rates were highly controlled and the majority of lending was directed by the government, domestic financial institutions had little incentive to develop risk-based lending practices or mechanisms to evaluate the risk of their portfolios. The government has, however, gradually strengthened prudential standards, particularly in the last five years.

In a 1982 amendment to the Bank Act, the government placed an 8 percent ceiling on the amount of equity any one individual company could hold in a national commercial bank. This limit was subsequently lowered to 4 percent. Such limits are intended to help to prevent any one company from acquiring control over a bank and directing its resources to potentially risky or inefficient uses.[10] The government has

---

10. Included in the late 1997 financial reform bills is a provision to allow domestic and foreign investors to acquire more than 4 percent of a commercial bank. Foreign investors will be required to receive approval for holdings that exceed 4 percent of equity. Each domestic industrial conglomerate will be allowed to acquire more than 4 percent of total equity in only one bank.

also attempted to increase the autonomy, and thus the accountability, of bank management. For example, in 1993 South Korea replaced a system in which the government nominated bank presidents with one in which a committee nominates bank presidents.

Commercial banks were directed in 1992 to meet minimum BIS capital adequacy ratios by 1995. Liquid assets must be greater than 30 percent of total liabilities. Reporting standards for banks are based on the CAMEL criteria (capital adequacy, asset quality, management ability, earnings quality, and liquidity level).

Credit is classified according to a system that ranks loans from "normal," for which payment is expected, to "substandard," for which a debtor has an unfavorable payment history, to "doubtful" and "estimated loss," for which payment is not expected. Nonperforming assets in the doubtful and estimated loss categories and 20 percent of those in the substandard category must be kept at less than 2 percent of a bank's outstanding loans.

The safety and soundness of the South Korean financial system has, in the past, also been jeopardized by the association of fictitious names with financial transactions. Without proper identification on financial transactions, it is difficult to monitor fraudulent activities, such as insider trading, and it is not possible to enforce laws regarding the collection of outstanding credit. In 1993, the government introduced the Real Name System for Financial Transactions in order to help increase transparency and accountability in the financial sector. The law mandates the use of real names for all types of financial transactions.

Despite these efforts, the presidential review commission found that, when US accounting standards were used, nonperforming loans in South Korea's top six national banks totaled 14.3 percent of all outstanding loans, or more than twice the government's official estimate for nonperforming loans in all commercial banks. By the fall of 1997, when the currency crisis hit South East Asia, it became apparent that existing prudential controls were not sufficient to reverse unsound banking practices arising from well-entrenched business standards.

In keeping with Korea's IMF economic reform program, since late December 1997 the government has announced a number of measures to enhance the safety and soundness of, as well as help to recapitalize, the financial system. The Real Name System law has been revised to allow the state to issue unregistered bonds and thereby encourage more capital to flow into the financial system. Prudential standards are to be upgraded to reflect the Basle Core Principles for Banking Supervision. These reforms include the introduction of internationally accepted loan classification guidelines and classification criteria for nonperforming loans. Financial institutions will be required to have statements audited by independent, internationally recognized firms, and all firms will be required to submit consolidated financial statements.

In April 1997, the SEC was designated as a deposit insurance body for the stock market. At that time, there was no deposit insurance system in South Korea for the banking industry. Since the currency crisis, the government has established a consolidated deposit insurance corporation to protect deposits not honored by any ailing financial institution. The deposit insurance system is intended, in conjunction with new mergers and acquisitions laws, to facilitate the restructuring of the financial system. The government has committed to guaranteeing payments from the new deposit insurance system while the financial industry in undergoing necessary restructuring. After 30 December 2000, however, the consolidated deposit insurance system is to be funded by contributions from the financial sector and is only intended to protect small deposits.

Foreign Participation

The treatment and role of foreign banks in the South Korean markets have varied considerably over the last 15 years, usually changing in response to shifts in the government's macroeconomic policy. Thus, when the country was running a chronic current account deficit in the early 1980s, foreign banks were encouraged to establish bank branches in South Korea in order to help supply foreign exchange to the market. Authorities announced in 1984 that foreign banks would receive national treatment in South Korea. The next year foreign banks were given access to the Bank of Korea's rediscount facility for export financing and were authorized to become members of the Korean Bank Association and the Korean Clearing House.

When the current account deficit turned to a surplus in 1986, South Korea's policies toward foreign banks also changed, eliminating any advantages that foreign bank branches had enjoyed in the South Korean market. In 1986, foreign banks were allowed to access the rediscount window for loans only if at least 35 percent of them were extended to small and medium-sized firms. By 1987, the South Korean government had begun to reduce ceilings on swap limits, thereby reducing banks' capacity for local currency lending. The percentage of foreign banks in total local currency loans and discounts fell from 5.8 percent in 1987 to 2.5 percent in 1993 (US Treasury 1994, 366).

The treatment of foreign banks has, for the most part, gradually improved since 1991. Following the Financial Policy Talks that year between the United States and South Korea, South Korea agreed to stop reducing the ceiling on swaps and to remove the ceiling on foreign bank capital. Foreign banks are now allowed to fully engage in the trust business, open multiple branches in South Korea, and, since 1992, aggregate total capital held in all branches in determining lending limits.[11]

---

11. Before that, capital requirements were calculated on a branch-by-branch basis.

Other barriers to entry, such as economic means tests and the requirement to establish a representative office prior to opening a bank branch, have recently been removed. Foreign banks are scheduled to be allowed to establish wholly owned subsidiaries in South Korea by 31 March 1998.[12]

There are 52 foreign banks operating 72 bank branches in South Korea; Citibank, the largest of the foreign banks, operates 11 branches in the country. With 3.5 percent of the assets held by all financial institutions, foreign banks continue to account for a relatively small part of the South Korean financial market.[13] Foreign banks tend to focus on corporate financing, as opposed to retail banking, in part because they continue to have limited access to local currency. The introduction of new products also has been tightly controlled, making it expensive for foreign banks to exploit their comparative advantage in South Korea.

The securities market has, since 1981, gradually been opened to foreign participation. During the initial stages of liberalization, South Korea permitted foreign indirect portfolio investment through overseas unit trust companies and allowed foreign securities companies to establish representative offices in South Korea. In 1984, the Korea Fund was authorized to list on the New York Stock Exchange in order to access deeper financial markets, and in 1990 Samsung Co. became the first company permitted to offer depository receipts on overseas markets.

Following these tentative initial steps toward liberalizing the domestic securities industry, the pace of liberalization accelerated. In 1991, foreign securities firms were legally permitted to establish branches in South Korea and enter into joint ventures with domestic firms. Also in 1991, membership in the Korea Stock Exchange was opened to foreign market participants. The following year, foreign securities firms held a 1.1 percent share of the domestic securities brokerage market. By May 1996, there were 19 branches of foreign securities firms and 2 additional local securities firms with minority foreign ownership in South Korea. Under South Korea's OECD commitments, foreign securities firms from OECD economies were to be allowed to establish subsidiaries in South Korea and hold majority ownership in a joint venture as of 1 December 1998. The timetable for foreign participation in the South Korean securities industry was subsequently expedited and expanded to include all foreign firms. Under the WTO Financial Service agreement, South Korea offered to remove restrictions on foreign equity participation in existing security firms, investment trusts, and investment advisory services. For-

---

12. Under Korea's 1996 OECD commitments, foreign banks from OECD countries were scheduled to be allowed to establish subsidiaries in Korea by December 1998. According to Korea's December 1997 letter of intent to the IMF, foreign banks and brokerage houses are now to be allowed to establish subsidiaries in Korea by 31 March 1998.

13. Data refer to 1993 figures (OECD 1996, 42).

eign securities firms are now scheduled to be permitted to establish subsidiaries in South Korea by mid-1998.

In 1992, South Korean authorities opened the domestic market to foreign portfolio investment, subject to limitations on total portfolio investment by foreigners. Initial ceilings on foreign portfolio investment were, for individual investors, 3 percent of outstanding shares in a company and, for aggregate foreign investment, 10 percent of total portfolio investment. Total foreign portfolio investment accounted for 3 percent of outstanding shares by the end of the first quarter of 1992, and aggregate foreign portfolio investment had reached the 10 percent ceiling by the end of 1994. Authorities have since raised the limit on permissible foreign portfolio investment numerous times. As of November 1997, aggregate foreign portfolio investment was capped at 26 percent of total portfolio investment, aggregate investment in public companies limited to 18 percent of total shares, and individual foreign investment in private companies restricted to 7 percent of outstanding shares for the company. In 1995, net foreign investment in the domestic securities market reached a record high $12 billion.

The ceiling on aggregate foreign portfolio investment was scheduled, in South Korea's OECD accession commitments, to rise to 26 percent in 1998 and be phased out by the end of 2000. As with other specific market opening measures in South Korea's OECD commitment, it did not match the offer in the WTO financial services deal concluded on 13 December 1997—South Korea subsequently offered more market access in its IMF letter of intent. By the end of December 1997, the ceiling on aggregate foreign equity ownership in South Korea had been raised to 55 percent. It is scheduled to be eliminated by the end of 1998. The cap on individual equity ownership was also raised in December 1997, from 7 percent to 50 percent. And, in early 1998, South Korea passed legislation that permits foreign investors to take over up to a third of a company's outstanding shares either with or without the approval of the board of directors.

Since 1994, foreign investors have been permitted to acquire convertible bonds issued by small and medium-sized firms, subject to a 50 percent ceiling on aggregate foreign ownership and a 10 percent ceiling on individual foreign ownership. The individual investment ceiling on corporate bonds was lifted in December 1997. In addition, foreigners may subscribe to public bonds, as long as these are offered on the primary markets and bought at interest rates comparable to international rates. The government announced plans in November 1997 to open the market for guaranteed corporate bonds with maturities over three years to foreign investors. As part of South Korea's IMF program, South Korea opened the short-term corporate bond market to foreign investors.

Foreign participation in the insurance market was not permitted until 1987, when foreign branches were first allowed to establish operations in South Korea. Two years later the government authorized foreign investors to establish insurance subsidiaries and joint ventures in South Korea. Between 1989 and 1997, five foreign firms (three subsidiaries and two branches) and seven joint ventures received licenses to participate in South Korea's life insurance market. In fiscal year 1996, the twelve life insurance companies with foreign ownership or foreign equity had a combined loss of more than $350 million.

The only foreign nonlife insurance market participants are three US firms with branch offices in South Korea. Total premiums written by these three companies account for less than 0.5 percent of the South Korean nonlife insurance market.

A perception that the insurance market was overcrowded led the government to refrain from issuing licenses for foreign or domestic firms to establish new life insurance operations from 1994 to early 1997; on 1 March 1997, South Korea resumed issuing new licenses to establish insurance firms. Foreign life and nonlife insurance companies are required to meet the same minimum capital requirements ($30 billion) as domestic firms and are also required to produce a statement from their home country's regulator confirming the company's sound financial status.

In the WTO financial services agreement, South Korea offered to bind its current practice of allowing foreign insurance firms to establish subsidiaries or branches. Although the ceiling on equity ownership was maintained at the time of the WTO deal, South Korea has since lifted permissible foreign equity ownership in South Korea and if further reforms go through as scheduled, foreign insurance firms will be allowed to hold 100 percent ownership of domestic firms by the end of 1998.

Under the 1996 Foreign Direct Investment Liberalization Plan, other specific sectors of the financial services industry are scheduled to be opened to foreign participation, in part or in full, by 2000. As outlined in the plan, market-opening measures for mutual credit companies and some auxiliary financial services were to be implemented beginning on 1 January 1997. Liberalization of insurance appraisal and brokerage services and of auxiliary insurance and pension fund services is scheduled to start in April 1998. Beginning 1 December 1998 foreigners will be permitted to serve as CEOs of joint venture banks and securities firms, and as board representatives as long as no more than one-third of the board members are foreign nationals.

Remaining Obstacles

Although Korea's WTO commitments and IMF program will remove many obstacles discussed below, the list of obstacles is long and complex, and it will take time for planned reforms to translate into a more competitive environment for financial services. Following decades of government control, the banking sector remains highly bureaucratic and inefficient; many domestic banks in 1998 are in considerable difficulty, despite a major rescheduling effort to reorganize their foreign debts. Banks still tend to administer interest rates and to make loans to favored sectors of the economy. Despite the ongoing deregulation of the financial system and removal of barriers for foreign market participants, foreign firms have not significantly increased their presence in the market. This is due in part to the fact that foreign banks have a difficult time accessing foreign exchange at competitive rates and therefore have limited lending capacity. High minimum capital requirements and the fact that foreign banks, in contrast to domestic banks, are not permitted to count retained earnings toward their total available branch capital further restrict foreign banks' ability to expand in the domestic market. Foreign banks controlled an estimated 5 percent of total banking assets in 1996, compared to 9 percent in 1985. Foreign financial institutions are not allowed to control more than 15 percent of the financial services sector. It is not clear if, in the wake of the currency crisis, restrictions on total foreign control of the financial services sector will be removed to help to recapitalize the banking industry.

Despite recent liberalization measures, the government continues to be heavily involved in certain aspects of the banking sector, maintaining restrictions on overseas investment, equity finance, and overseas finance. Participation in the financial system depends on an existing list of products: services cannot be offered unless they are expressly permitted by the government.

Although foreign banks were not legally prohibited from establishing subsidiaries in South Korea, prior to the new market opening commitments no licenses for foreign bank subsidiaries were actually issued. Paradoxically, the 52 foreign banks operating branches in South Korea are treated like subsidiaries, in that capital requirements are based on total branch level holdings as opposed to global capital endowments. Domestic bank branches are not subject to individual branch capital requirements, placing foreign branches at a disadvantage vis-à-vis their domestic competitors. Banks are required to lend at least 25 percent of their total loan portfolio to small and medium-sized enterprises (SMEs). Although less than the 45 percent of domestic banks are required to lend to SMEs, foreign banks have difficulty meeting these requirements, because they tend to serve the wholesale market.[14]

The minimum capital requirement for establishing a foreign bank or securities branch remains very high. For example, a foreign securities branch that plans to offer underwriting, dealing, and brokerage services must have a minimum capital of 15 billion won.

---

14. Since the Asian currency crisis, the government has indicated that it intends to abolish policy lending requirements for domestic and foreign banks.

Access to the securities market remains difficult. Foreign investors are required to get a special identification card before they can purchase equity. Foreign investors are not permitted to trade on the main OTC market, an exclusion that creates a significant barrier to entry since 60 percent of all bonds are traded on the OTC market.

It is difficult for foreign investment funds to register in South Korea. Once registered, foreign firms offering mutual funds in South Korea are required to use one distributor of funds, whereas domestic investment trust and brokerage firms are permitted to use an unlimited number of distributors and market funds from foreign companies. Complications associated with setting up the required foreign currency account create an extra obstacle that keeps many foreign investment trust and brokerage firms out of the South Korean market. The most onerous requirement, however, is that foreign investment management firms have assets under management equal to $18 billion in order to establish operations in South Korea.

Finally, lack of transparency continues to create obstacles for foreign firms trying to enter the South Korean market. English translations of laws and regulations have to be provided by local lawyers, and foreign firms have restricted access to regulators or authorities, thus limiting their ability to clarify inconsistencies between de jure and de facto practices.

References

Ministry of Finance and Economy. 1996. *Financial System of Korea: Overview and Prospects.* Republic of Korea. February.

Ministry of Finance and Economy. 1997. Foreign Direct Investment Liberalization Plan. (http://www.mofe.go.kr/PR/press14.html).

Nam, Sang Woo. 1995. Korea's Financial Markets and Policies, in *Financial Sector Development in Asia: Country Studies,* ed. by Shahid N. Zahid. Hong Kong: Oxford University Press.

Noland, Marcus. 1996. *Restructuring Korea's Financial Sector for Greater Competitiveness.* Working Paper Series on Asia Pacific Economic Cooperation 96-14. Washington: Institute for International Economics.

Organization for Economic Cooperation and Development (OECD). 1996. *OECD Economic Surveys: Korea 1996.* Paris: Organization for Economic Cooperation and Development.

Organization for Economic Cooperation and Development (OECD). 1997. Korea: Reservations and Exceptions. (http://www.oecd.org/daf/cmis/country/korea.htm#nti).

Park, Daekun. 1995. Financial Opening and Capital Inflow: The Korean Experience and Policy Issues. In *Financial Opening: Policy Lessons for Korea,* ed. by Rudiger Dornbusch and Yung Chul Park. Seoul: Korea Institute of Finance.

Park, Joon. 1996. Regulation of Capital Market and Financial Services in Korea. Paper presented at the Conference on Regulation of Capital Markets and Financial Services in the Pacific Rim, Georgetown University Law Center, Washington (11-13 November).

Presidential Commission for Financial Reform. 1997. *Financial Reform in Korea: The*

Second Report. Seoul, Korea: Presidential Commission for Financial Reform (3 June).

Republic of Korea. 1996. Financial System of Korea. Seoul: Ministry of Finance and Economy.

Takahashi, Yuichi. 1994. Financial Sector Reform in the Asia Pacific Countries. Photocopy.

US Department of the Treasury. 1994. *National Treatment Study.* Washington: Government Printing Office.

Malaysia

Introduction

Financial sector reform in Malaysia followed a severe financial sector crisis in the early 1980s. For decades, Malaysia had followed prudent macroeconomic policies, focusing on low inflation, strong external reserves, and current account surpluses. In the 1970s, an income redistribution program aimed at alleviating economic distinctions along racial lines was introduced. In 1979-80, however, Malaysia experienced its sharpest deflation since the Korean War. Deteriorating terms of trade (TOT) had a devastating effect on the small, open, resource-based economy. Implementation of countercyclical policies led to a deterioration of the federal fiscal deficit. A stringent structural adjustment program and fiscal restraint in 1983, complemented by temporary TOT improvement, brought some relief. But falling resource prices led to a renewed TOT deterioration in the mid-1980s, precipitating a crisis in the real and financial sectors.

In the late 1970s and early 1980s investment flowed into the nontradable sector, resulting in a real estate boom. A subsequent economic slowdown in 1985 led to a contraction in the cash flow of many companies, which fell behind in debt repayments and frequently resorted to distress borrowing at exceptionally high interest rates to meet temporary liquidity shortages. Rapidly falling share and property prices led to declining asset values and, hence, collateral, so that an increasing number of nonperforming loans hit financial institutions in 1985-86.[1] Commercial banks experienced sporadic runs. Subsequently, cumulative losses of financial institutions were estimated to equal 4.7 percent of GDP (Sheng 1995, 109).

To rebuild confidence in the financial sector, the central bank intervened in the operations of many banks and finance companies. It replaced the management of ailing financial institutions and required that shareholders inject as much new capital as possible; it then supplied the remaining necessary capital, which it held in trust with buy-back options for shareholders.

To promote greater efficiency in dealing with the financial sector crisis, the central bank made the ringgit freely convertible in 1986 as a means to adjust the balance of payments.[2] The bank also reformed its export credit refinance scheme, reduced liquidity and reserve requirement ratios of commercial banks to lower their costs of funds, created investment funds to shift bank lending out of real estate, introduced more flexible interest rates, abolished deposit rate controls, and encouraged the establishment of a secondary mortgage market. In 1991, the basic lending rate (BLR), akin to the US prime rate, was freed from direct administrative control by the central bank; it is currently computed on a monthly basis using a four-element formula.

The central bank's crisis intervention, though, excluded financial institutions beyond its jurisdiction, such as deposit-taking cooperatives, which were particularly hard hit, and informal deposit-taking institutions, such as pawnbrokers and credit and leasing companies. To address this problem, prudential regulations were tightened and the legal framework was radically changed. As a result, central bank supervision has broadened since 1989 to include all deposit-taking financial institutions, and legislative changes have given the central bank wide powers to pursue illegal deposit-taking institutions and to act quickly in emergency situations.

These measures helped the country to overcome the financial-sector crisis in the 1980s. Confidence in the economy was further enhanced by the government's financial restraint during the 1984-85 recession. In the late 1980s, large foreign direct investment inflows occurred.[3] A large scale government program to privatize infrastructure and growing private-sector financial needs led to a boom in Malaysian capital markets in the early 1990s.

---

1. Other reasons for the financial sector crisis included mismanagement, fraud, and poor internal controls. For example, four relatively new banks aggressively attempted to increase their market share of total loans in the late 1970s, frequently without adequate attention to loan quality.

2. Between September 1985 and the end of 1986, the ringgit depreciated by 16.7 percent in national terms.

3. From 1991 to 1994, foreign direct investment averaged 7.9 percent of GDP (Sachs, Tornell, and Velasco 1996, 29).

Regulatory Framework

Malaysia's main laws governing financial institutions are administered by the central bank, the Bank Negara Malaysia, established in 1959. Bank Negara supervises the nation's banking system, which includes commercial banks, finance companies, merchant banks, and discount houses. Until 1989, banking institutions were governed by the Finance Companies Act of 1969, the Banking Act of 1973, the Essential (Protection of Depositors) Regulation of 1986, and the Finance (Banking and Financial Institutions) Act of 1986.[4] The Banking and Financial Institutions Act, adopted in October 1989, includes the main features of all of these laws. Tighter banking supervision was also introduced when the central bank expanded the roles of some of these institutions to facilitate market development. Finance companies were permitted to participate in the interbank market, and merchant banks were permitted to issue certificates of deposit. Three commercial banks were also issued stock brokering licenses. In 1988, Bank Negara took over supervision of the insurance industry as part of the government's policy to streamline financial supervision and to encourage a more prominent role for insurance companies in capital markets.[5] Finally, Bank Negara controls the availability and allocation of credit and deposits by setting the borrowing rates for commercial banks.

Other regulatory agencies include the Registrar of Companies and the Malaysian Securities Commission (SC). The former supervises private debt securities and shares responsibility for regulating stock exchanges; the SC has assumed, since 1993, the main regulatory responsibility for the securities industries and also supervises the Kuala Lumpur Futures Market (KLFM) and the Kuala Lumpur Options and Financial Futures Exchange (KLOFFE). Previously, regulation was done by a number of government bodies, which resulted in inconsistent rulings.

Finally, Malaysia has set up an offshore financial center, regulated by the Labuan Offshore Financial Services Authority. Banks, life insurance companies, and trust companies have established facilities in Labuan.

Financial Institutions

In 1987, at the end of the financial sector crisis, just over 70 percent of financial sector assets were raised by the banking system, which includes the central bank and nonmonetary institutions such as finance compa-

---

4. The Exchange Control Act of 1953 is also administered by Bank Negara.

5. Offshore insurance business is separately regulated following a 1990 amendment to the insurance law.

Table B.6 Malaysia: Assets of financial institutions, 1987 and 1993 (percentages)

	Share	
Financial intermediary	1987	1993
Commercial banks[a]	42.3	39.4
Central bank	11.9	17.6
Finance companies	10.5	11.1
Merchant banks	3.1	3.3
Discount houses	1.5	1.2
Employment Provident Fund	15.9	12.7
Other NBFIs	4.7	4.6
Development finance institutions[b]	2.3	1.6
Savings institutions[c]	3.6	2.4
Other	4.2	6.1

a. Includes the Islamic bank.
b. Includes all development banks.
c. Includes the national savings bank and deposit-taking cooperatives.

Source: Sheng (1995, 118); Bank Negara Malaysia.

nies, merchant banks, and discount houses (see table B.6). Commercial banks accounted for just over 40 percent of financial sector assets.

The type of securities raised in capital markets has changed significantly over time. Of the capital raised between 1976 and 1980, 94 percent was in the form of government securities and 6 percent was in the form of equities. In 1995, 59 percent and 41 percent of capital raised was in the form of equities and corporate bonds, respectively.

Financial Intermediaries

The banking sector is characterized by high market concentration, which has been exacerbated by the fact that no new banking licenses have been issued since 1982. In 1996, there were 38 commercial banks, 24 of which were domestic banks and most of which had some foreign participation. A handful of these banks, which are either partially or totally government-owned, dominate the industry. In 1992, the top five banks held 52 percent of banking sector assets; the two largest government-controlled banks accounted for almost a third of banking sector assets.

An Islamic bank was established in 1993. Based on Islamic law, the bank and its depositors are prohibited from taking interest. Instead, the bank provides its depositors with a share of its profits and receives in turn a percentage of its borrowers' profits. The rapidly increasing popularity of the bank led the government in 1993 to encourage other financial institutions to offer such services. By year-end, 20 commercial banks, including one foreign one, had followed suit. A year later, the government instituted the Islamic interbank market for trading financial instruments and investments and for clearing checks.

The financial reforms of 1989 allowed commercial banks to diversify into stock brokering. Commercial banks may also hold equity in other stock brokering firms, as well as in insurance companies, although they require a license from the Ministry of Finance (MOF) when diversifying into nontraditional areas.

Since 1986, deposit rates have been market determined and lending rates have been more flexible. Despite the improving general liquidity, gross interest margins increased from 4.2 percent in 1985 to 5.2 percent in 1988 because banks did not lower lending rates in line with falling deposit rates. Banks did not lower these rates because they were not collecting interest on nonperforming loans and were attempting to recover lost profits. Thus, depositors and good borrowers effectively subsidized banks' losses. The long-term effect of low deposit rates and high lending rates was to discourage intermediation and deter the new investments needed for economic recovery. It took persuasion for Bank Negara to reduce lending rates in the late 1980s. Currently, the maximum interest rate that banks may charge is 4 percentage points above the basic lending rate.

Bank Negara requests commercial banks to target their loans toward certain groups and sectors. In line with the income redistribution efforts along racial lines of the 1970s, 20 percent of outstanding credit must be allocated to the Bumiputra (indigenous Malays). At least 150 million ringgit must be allotted to small enterprises, and half of those funds must be granted to Bumiputra enterprises. Commercial banks must meet these guidelines as a group (US Treasury 1994, 390).

Commercial banks are permitted to engage in foreign exchange transactions, both lending in foreign currency and accepting foreign currency accounts from nonresidents. The banks may not borrow ringgit from nonresidents without approval from the central bank. Central bank permission is also required for nonresidents to borrow locally in excess of 10 million ringgit and for residents to borrow overseas in excess of 5 million ringgit.

To facilitate offshore transactions and complement onshore ones, the Labuan International Offshore Financial Center (IOFC) was established in 1990. The MOF has awarded licenses to 31 banks and 3 insurance companies and has approved 11 trust companies to conduct business in the IOFC.

There are 40 finance companies in Malaysia, 36 of which are domestic firms. Seven of these have some foreign participation. Finance companies specialize in small loans for consumer and housing finance and have a significant market presence in the auto finance sector. Since the

1987 financial sector reforms, finance companies have been permitted to diversify into the interbank market.

Given their close links to the real estate sector, finance companies were particularly hard hit by the 1985-86 financial sector crisis. The crisis resulted in the merger of seven ailing finance companies with stronger ones, and this, in turn, further increased market concentration in a sector where entry has been barred since 1984. The three largest firms now hold 47 percent of the total assets of Malaysia's finance industry. In an effort to strengthen finance companies by promoting further consolidation in the industry, after January 1999 only finance companies with shareholder's funds in excess of US$178 million will be allowed to access the interbank market for funds (*The Financial Times*, 8 October 1997).

There are 12 merchant banks (9 of them domestic) and 7 discount houses in Malaysia. Merchant banks must obtain at least 30 percent of their income from fee-based activities. The 1989 reforms allowed merchant banks to issue CDs and to take equity in stock brokering firms. Since 1991, they may also hold shares in companies listed on the Malaysian stock exchange. Besides underwriting private debt securities, they may also underwrite foreign debt securities with permission from Bank Negara.

Important nonbank financial institutions (NBFIs) include insurance companies, deposit-taking cooperatives,[6] development banks, and the Employee Provident Fund (EPF). Development banks, together with commercial banks, provide the bulk of credit to the industrial sector. They have benefited from concessional lending from Japan and the ASEAN-Japan development fund.

In 1994, there were 60 insurance companies in Malaysia, of which 51 were domestic companies. There was also one Islamic insurance company and a number of insurance brokers and loss adjusters. Domestic insurers are required to divest a minimum of 30 percent of ownership, control, and management of the industry to the Bumiputra. Bank Negara encourages insurance companies to play a more prominent role in the capital market and to set up operations in the Labuan IOFC.

During the financial crisis of 1985-86, 30 percent of insurance companies could not meet the minimum solvency requirement of 20 percent of net premium income. As a result industry consolidation has been promoted; to advance this goal Bank Negara encourages mergers and has not issued new licenses since the crisis. The Insurance Guarantee

---

6. As deposit-taking cooperatives were not under Bank Negara's supervision until 1989, they were not required to observe the reserve requirement and the 25 percent liquidity requirement; as a result, they were particularly imprudent in their lending habits. To avoid social unrest, Bank Negara eventually rescued these cooperatives. The rescue plan reimbursed depositors (but without interest), though in more financially troubled cooperatives, 50 percent of deposits were turned into equity. Since cooperatives have been under central bank supervision, they may take deposits only for housing and educational purposes.

Scheme Fund (IGSF) was established to meet liabilities of insolvent insurers to private policy holders for certain mandatory policies. The IGSF is financed through fees levied on all general insurers, who pay up to 1 percent of the value of the premiums written during the previous year.

The EPF, a pension scheme for the labor force, is a significant feature of Malaysia's financial system. Employees and employers make monthly contributions that are invested, according to statutory requirements, mainly in government bonds.

Direct Finance

The Kuala Lumpur Stock Exchange (KLSE) was founded in 1973 after it separated from the Singapore Stock Exchange. In October 1989, when the MOF prohibited firms incorporated in Malaysia from cross-listing in Singapore, trading volume on the KLSE started to increase rapidly. The introduction of a computerized trading system in 1992 helped the KLSE cope with the increased volume, much of which was due to the government's massive privatization programs.

In contrast to the stock market, the bond market is small. Trading is particularly sluggish in the secondary market. Malaysian Government Securities (MGS) constitute the bulk of the bond market even though fiscal surpluses in recent years have prevented the government from issuing more bonds. As most bonds are held to fulfill reserve requirements, the secondary market for MGS is essentially captive.

The corporate bond market is very small, although the government is actively promoting its development and, in this context, established the Rating Agency of Malaysia (RAM) in 1990. Issuance of corporate debt papers involves the approval of four regulatory authorities, a process that usually takes six to nine months. In the money market, short-term treasury bills dominate. Similar to MGS, fiscal surpluses in recent years have prevented additional issues. Of late, short-term Bank Negara bills have been used by the central bank as a means of exerting monetary control.

The EPF, to which both employers and employees contribute, accounted for 13 percent of financial sector assets in 1993. More than 70 percent of the EPF must be invested in government bonds; in 1992, these bonds exceeded 90 percent of total EPF assets.

In the foreign exchange market, the development of currency swap transactions has been restricted since 1989 by daily limits on nontrade-related swaps. The market has a forward exchange market (the Malaysia Monetary Exchange [MME]) to hedge risk.

Other forward contracts and futures are traded on the KLOFFE, which started operating in December 1995 after a long gestation period. The Malaysian Derivatives Clearing House (MDCH), in which the MME and KLOFFE each hold 50 percent equity, was established at the same time.

Commodity futures are traded on the Kuala Lumpur Commodity Exchange (KLCE), which was established in 1980. So far, though, palm oil contracts are the only actively traded contracts.

Prudential Regulation

Prudential regulations address issues of shareholder diversification, risk diversification, reserve requirements, and foreign exchange exposure. Shareholder diversification requires that an individual's equity share be limited to 10 percent, and a company's equity share to 20 percent, of a financial institution's assets.

Regulations on risk diversification limit banks from lending more than 30 percent of capital to any single customer. Extending loans to bank directors or staff is prohibited. Banks cannot acquire shares without Bank Negara approval. They are not allowed to make property investments (except for operating needs), and investments in manufacturing companies are limited to 25 percent of the bank's capital. Investments by insurance companies in unsecured debt are limited to 10 percent, and those in secured debts to 20 percent, of the insurer's assets.

The reserve requirement for insurance companies is a solvency margin of 20 percent of net premium income. A minimum of 80 percent of insurance funds must be invested in authorized Malaysian assets, of which 25 percent must be placed with Malaysian government securities.

Foreign exchange exposure by commercial banks is limited to an open position of 80 million ringgit unless the bank holds an equivalent amount in foreign currency. Similarly, insurance companies are prohibited from investing in foreign securities unless such investments are offset by an equivalent amount of liability overseas.

In support of these prudential regulations, the central bank has introduced standardized accounting treatment of income from bad or questionable debts. It has also established audit and examination committees and a consolidated credit bureau to monitor and improve consolidated credit information on bank and finance company customers. Capital adequacy ratios are currently estimated at 10 percent, 2 percent higher than the minimum recommended by the Bank for International Settlements.

Foreign Participation

Foreign participation in domestic banks is limited to 30 percent ownership.[7] The restrictions regarding the maximum amount of a foreign

---

7. The definitions and restrictions are different in other businesses. Companies with more than 50 percent foreign ownership are classified as nonresident-controlled companies

individual's or company's equity are the same as those for domestic residents and companies. To encourage greater expertise in the securities market, 49 percent foreign participation in stock brokering firms is permitted.

In 1982, when the banking sector was closed to additional entry, there were 16 foreign bank branches in Malaysia.[8] A 1989 law required that these branches be converted into locally incorporated institutions by October 1994. The resulting new subsidiaries were allowed to remain 100 percent foreign owned.[9] Further, while foreign bank branches had been excluded from a law that precludes banks from sharing credit information with foreign parents, the law has since been extended to them.

Foreign banks cannot establish additional branches in Malaysia. This restriction applies to nonresident controlled companies (NRCCs) and, therefore, includes 100 percent foreign-owned subsidiaries. As an additional barrier, automatic teller machines (ATMs) are considered branches, so foreign bank subsidiaries cannot join the ATM pool. This limits their attraction to depositors and has contributed to foreign banks' declining market share. Foreign bank subsidiaries also cannot extend more than 40 percent toward NRCCs' domestic borrowing, which accounts for approximately 10 percent of the domestic banking credit market.[10] As lending to NRCCs is an area of competitive advantage to foreign bank subsidiaries, this lending limit further impedes potential expansion of their market share.[11]

Foreign bank subsidiaries are given the opportunity to comment on proposed regulatory changes and are accorded national treatment in money market instruments, access to Bank Negara discount windows, and use of swaps to bring offshore capital into Malaysia. While each

---

(NRCCs). Until 1986, all newly established companies had to be resident owned if they either depended primarily on the domestic market or used nonrenewable domestic resources. These limitations were relaxed in 1986 as the government sought to attract more foreign investment. Since then, 100 percent of foreign equity has been permitted for projects exceeding 50 million ringgit if (1) no local partner can be found, (2) at least 50 percent of output is exported, and (3) that output contains at least 50 percent local value added. If the last two restrictions are not met, foreign equity is limited to 79 percent.

8. The number of foreign bank branches has since dropped to 14 due to sales to domestic shareholders. These 14 banks earned 45 percent of all pretax bank profits and held 50.9 percent of the sector's net working funds to be paid in capital in 1993 (US Treasury 1994, 388).

9. Nonetheless, local incorporation represented a less efficient form of organization as none of the foreign banks, when they still had the choice, had opted to locally incorporate their branches.

10. The ceiling on the amount of credit that foreign-owned firms can borrow from foreign-owned banks is scheduled to rise to 50 percent by the year 2000.

11. It constitutes yet another method by Bank Negara to strengthen domestic banks.

subsidiary is limited to hiring two expatriate personnel,[12] this restriction is less stringent than that imposed on domestic banks. Furthermore, the restriction has been somewhat relaxed lately to allow for intracorporate exchanges and short-term assignments. Yet, the capital requirement—10 percent of risk-weighted assets—is higher for foreign bank subsidiaries than for domestic banks. The foreign subsidiaries are also limited to 20 percent of assets when using the interbank market to fund their capital requirements.

Under current regulations, foreign fund managers are not permitted to own more than 30 percent of a trust fund, and foreign asset managers are not permitted to hold more than 49 percent of a foreign joint venture asset management company. The latter restrictions were eased under the terms of Malaysia's 1997 WTO financial services offer. When the agreement enters into force in early 1999, foreign firms will be allowed to have majority ownership of asset management companies, subject to prior authorization from the government. Malaysia has, however, noted that it intends to issue only 10 licenses for the establishment of foreign asset management subsidiaries and will require such firms to manage assets of at least $100 million outside of the country in order to be eligible.

Foreign equity in domestic insurance companies has been limited to 49 percent, although some exceptions have been granted. Under the 1996 Insurance Law, companies whose existing investments in the insurance sector exceed 49 percent ownership would have been required to divest their holdings to the 49 percent ceiling by June 1998.

In its 1997 WTO offer, Malaysia agreed to allow foreign firms to hold up to 51 percent of equity in insurance companies that are locally incorporated by 30 June 1998. Although an improvement to the earlier law—because it will allow foreign insurance providers to maintain majority control over Malaysian operations—the offer is contentious since it requires a few large international insurance firms to divest their holdings in Malaysia, (a five-year deferral was granted in May 1998). While the offer allows majority foreign ownership for insurance companies that are locally incorporated prior to 30 June 1998, new firms cannot have more than 30 percent foreign ownership.

Foreign insurers may not open additional branches or insure ships, aircraft, and property.[13] They are also disadvantaged vis-à-vis domestic insurers as importers may claim double deduction for marine cargo premiums paid to domestic insurers. On the other hand, they face no Bumiputra participation requirement.

---

12. Within the commitments outlined in Malaysia's 1997 WTO financial services offer, each subsidiary will be allowed to hire five expatriate personnel when the agreement comes into effect in early 1999.

13. As of early 1998, direct insurance companies with less than 50 percent foreign ownership will be permitted to establish new branches.

Remaining Obstacles

Obstacles to efficiency and openness in the Malaysian financial services sector include its history of the use of government bailouts as a form of safety net in the event of a crisis. Although tighter prudential supervision in the 1990s should reduce this problem, some concerns about moral hazard remain.

Capital markets are underdeveloped, except for the equity market, which remains thin; despite an impressive volume, the equity market is dominated by shares of privatized government companies, in many of which the government maintains significant ownership interest. There is recent evidence, however, that significant steps will be taken to stimulate development of capital markets.

Another obstacle to efficiency and openness is the lack of competition. The financial services sector continues to be segmented as internal liberalization is incomplete and both domestic and foreign entry is restricted. No new bank branches or wholly owned subsidiaries are permitted; entry into most financial services (except, for example, credit card firms) is limited to acquiring shares of existing firms or establishing joint ventures (FLG 1997, 16). Foreign firms are prohibited from opening subbranches or operating ATMs. Foreign banks are not allowed to offer certain services (such as underwriting equity issues) and are restricted in the number of expatriate staff they may employ, further limiting both competition and technology transfer in the banking sector. There exist similar barriers to entry in the insurance and securities sectors. For example, foreign insurance brokers are confined to the reinsurance business, and foreign insurance companies are permitted to own shares in only one type of insurance business (FLG 1997).

Foreign participation in domestic banks is limited to 30 percent and, in most other financial services firms, 49 percent ownership. Malaysia will allow foreign asset managers to have majority control and to allow foreign insurers 51 percent ownership in its 1997 WTO financial services agreement. This ceiling for foreign insurers is, however, below current practice. Further, the concessions that Malaysia made in the agreement to permit direct insurance companies to establish new branches will only apply to those companies with minority foreign ownership.

References

Financial Leaders Group (FLG). 1997. *Barriers to Trade in Financial Services: Case Studies.* London: Barclays Place.

Frankel, Jeffrey A. 1995. Recent Changes in the Financial Systems of Asian and Pacific Countries. In *Financial Stability in a Changing Environment*, ed. by Kuniho Sawamoto, Zenta Nakajima, and Hiroo Taguchi. New York: MacMillan Press.

Lamble, Peter, and Robin Low. 1995. *The Asia Pacific Insurance Handbook*. Sydney, NWT: Coopers & Lybrand.

Mahmood, Nik Ramlah. 1996. Malaysia: Issues in Capital Market Regulation & Development. Paper presented at the Conference on Regulation of Capital Markets and Financial Services in the Pacific Rim, Georgetown University Law Center, Washington (11-3 November).

Sachs, Jeffrey, Aaron Tornell, and Andrés Velasco. 1996. *Financial Crisis in Emerging Markets: The Lessons from 1995*. National Bureau of Economic Research Working Paper No. 5576. National Bureau of Economic Research. Cambridge, MA: National Bureau of Economic Research.

Sheng, Andrew. 1995. Malaysia's Bank Restructuring, 1985-88. In *Bank Restructuring: Lessons from the 1980s*, ed. by Andrew Sheng. Washington: World Bank.

Takahashi, Yuichi. 1994. *Financial Sector Reform in the Asia Pacific Countries*. Photocopy.

US Department of the Treasury. 1994. *National Treatment Study*. Washington: Government Printing Office.

Mexico

Introduction

In the early 1970s, policies that supported economic growth led by the private sector gave way to policies based on active government participation in the economy. For the next decade, this policy direction was supported by foreign loans and revenue from oil exports. But with rising inflation, repressed domestic interest rates, and falling oil prices, Mexico was unable to meet its huge accumulated external debt obligations, and in 1982 this resulted in a major financial crisis. In response, the government nationalized 58 of 60 private banks and, in the first months of the debt crisis, imposed controls on trade and foreign exchange. Thus from 1982 to 1988, the financial sector was highly repressed. Regulated interest rates, high reserve requirements, and required public lending distorted credit allocation and crowded out private-sector lending (IMF 1992, 38). The government also consolidated the banking system; of the 58 banks nationalized in 1982, 18 remained in operation a decade later.

Mexico's agreement to join the General Agreement on Tariffs and Trade (GATT) in 1986 prompted the government to initiate efforts to remove trade and investment barriers, and led to the liberalization of the financial sector beginning in the late 1980s. First, interest rate and quantitative credit controls[1] were phased out and then, in 1991-92, the

---

1. In 1988, only 25 percent of lending was unrestricted; by 1991, 100 percent of commercial bank lending was unrestricted.

government privatized the banking industry. Foreigners were excluded from buying or having voting rights in the newly privatized banking sector. Intense competition among domestic investors resulted in the banks being sold at an average price over three times their book value. Although the government netted $12.4 billion, the high price-to-value ratio left new owners with liabilities far in excess of earnings at the time of the buyout.

When the banking sector was privatized, authorities did not significantly strengthen prudential controls or increase bank supervision, nor did they establish criteria for lending or for evaluating portfolio risk. The combination of pent-up demand for consumer credit and pressure on newly privatized banks to recover the cost of acquiring the banks resulted in an explosion of lending. From year-end 1991 to 1994, loans grew at an average annual rate of 23.7 percent, more than eight times the average annual rate of growth of real GDP (Karaoglan and Lubrano 1995, 2).

From 1982 to 1991, the government maintained a dual exchange rate. The rates were unified in 1991, and a band was established within which the peso was allowed to fluctuate. For the next three years the peso was kept within this band. During this same period, Mexico ran a growing trade and current account deficit and kept real interest rates high in order to meet external liabilities. By the end of 1994, international reserves had fallen to $12.5 billion. With $30 billion in short-term dollar-linked bonds due to mature in early 1995, the government was no longer able to support the peso. The peso/dollar exchange rate band was widened on 20 December 1994, resulting in an effective devaluation of 15 percent in one day. The next day, Mexico abandoned the exchange rate band altogether. The peso fell sharply against the US dollar, depreciating by 54 percent over the following twelve months.

With international support, Mexico was successfully able to begin to meet external debt obligations and convert outstanding loans into long-term, more manageable debt. The government's economic plan for dealing with external debt obligations included allowing real interest rates to rise significantly in order to prevent the depreciation of the peso from accelerating. By March 1995, the interest rate on government securities exceeded 80 percent and commercial interest rates topped 100 percent. The impact of post-privatization lending patterns on domestic commercial banks quickly became apparent as nonperforming loans jumped from 2.3 percent of total outstanding loans in 1990 to 10.5 percent in 1994 and 19.1 percent in 1995.[2]

In order to protect the solvency of the banking industry and help stabilize the economy, the government implemented a number of do-

---

2. These estimates are based on Mexican accounting standards. Using internationally accepted accounting principles, the actual figure may be as much as 10 percent higher than the cited estimates (GAO 1996, 22).

mestic programs for banks holding a large number of nonperforming loans.[3] Emphasis in these programs was placed on enforcing a higher level of discipline on the financial sector. In addition to these measures, the government began redesigning regulation and supervision of financial services activities. The changes center on increasing prudential controls while reducing constraints on the provision of financial services by both domestic and foreign financial service firms. Notably, since the peso crisis, the Mexican government has not taken any measures to reverse the process of financial market liberalization. In 1995, the central bank intervened in the exchange market on 24 occasions but exchange controls were not implemented. Although various post-crisis programs have in effect subsidized loans to certain sectors of the economy, banks remain free to make credit and interest decisions based on market criteria.

Regulatory Framework

Financial services regulation and supervision in Mexico are conducted at the federal level. The Ministry of Finance and Public Credit (SCHP) is the primary regulator of financial services and has a wide array of responsibilities, including the establishment of credit limits and capital reserve requirements, assessment of national and international banking transactions in order to monitor systemic risk, issuance of permits to domestic and foreign financial firms, interpretation of financial laws, and supervision of bank holding companies (Demetrio Guerra-Sanchez 1996, 1).

Universal banking was permitted in Mexico from 1974 until 1982, when the banking system was nationalized and banks were required to sever affiliations with nonfinancial institutions, securities firms, and insurance companies. With the liberalization of Mexico's financial services industry, the Law on Credit Institutions has been amended and, since 1991, universal banking has once again been permitted in Mexico.

In 1995, the National Banking Commission and National Securities Commission merged to form the National Banking and Securities Commission (CNBV), which is responsible for supervising and regulating all firms engaged in banking and securities activity. The CNBV also, in conjunction with the SCHP, authorizes commercial bank and securities firm activities. The merger consolidated oversight of the financial industry and is intended to ensure uniform, effective supervision and regulatory standards for services offered by different types of financial groups.

Financial groups are governed under the rules set forth in the Law of Financial Groups, enacted in 1990. Three different types of structure are

---

3. See Karaoglan and Lubrano (1995) for a description of government programs implemented in the wake of the peso crisis that assisted with both temporary and long-term recapitalization and that helped banks restructure debt.

permitted for financial groups. The first two types must be headed by either a bank or a brokerage firm and must offer leasing, factoring, foreign exchange, and mutual fund management services. In the third and most common type, each firm is headed by a holding company and may include one bank, one brokerage house, and one leasing company. More than one mutual fund and insurance company are allowed to operate in each holding company, subject to the requirement that they serve different markets. Regardless of the model chosen, financial conglomerates must receive authorization first from the SCHP in order to establish a financial group, and then from the appropriate regulator in order to operate each company within the group.

Since mid-1997, Mexico's pension system has been administered by private pension fund managers (AFOREs). The National Commission for the Retirement Savings System (CONSAR) now has regulatory and supervisory authority for the AFOREs and for the pension funds (SIEFOREs) they manage. Insurance companies are regulated and supervised by the National Insurance and Bonding Commission.

The Bank of Mexico, which has been independent since 1994, is directed by Mexico's constitution to make price stability the top priority in monetary policy. It has sole authority for issuing currency and is responsible for holding the reserves of and acting as a clearinghouse for financial institutions. The Bank of Mexico is also responsible for assessing and enforcing civil monetary penalties on financial institutions engaged in activities that place the safety and soundness of the market at risk.

Financial Institutions

The financial market in Mexico is not very deep. In 1994, bank assets accounted for 87 percent of all financial sector assets, and state-owned banks represented 23 percent of total bank assets (BIS 1996, 126). The bond market is overwhelmingly dominated by government debt, and equity markets are dominated by a few large firms. Since the 1990 amendments to the Law on Credit Institutions, most banks have become affiliated with a financial group.

Financial Intermediaries

When the banking sector was privatized in 1991-92, there were 19 domestic banks and 1 foreign bank operating in Mexico.[4] Although the

---

4. Citibank had been restricted to a single branch when the banking sector was nationalized, and therefore virtually the entire commercial banking sector was, until recently, controlled by domestic interests.

number of authorized banks has increased rapidly since the banking sector was privatized, with 56 commercial banks currently licensed to operate in Mexico, the commercial banking industry remains highly concentrated. For example, in 1995, the top three banks accounted for 58.3 percent of all outstanding loans (EIU 1996a, 21). Mexican commercial banks provide the services of savings banks, mortgage banks, and deposit-taking institutions; apart from development banks, which were, in the past, authorized to accept deposits, no other type of financial firm offers these retail services.

Development banks, though few in number (six), play a large role in the Mexican economy. The largest development banks are Nacional Financiera (Nafin) and Banco Nacional de Comercio Exterior (Bancomext). Prior to 1989, Nafin was permitted to accept deposits and directly offer financing to businesses with majority Mexican ownership. Nafin now operates as a development bank: it manages its own fund, underwrites and purchases Mexican bonds and equity, channels funds to priority sectors of the economy, and allocates resources from foreign funds. Bancomext offers export financing and credit for developing companies that intend to produce goods for export. Although Nafin and Bancomext extended credit at preferential rates in the past, they now offer financing at market rates. As of 1994, state-owned development banks accounted for 28 percent of total assets in the Mexican banking industry.

Direct Finance

The Mexican Stock Exchange was established in 1894 and has had a turbulent history. It was virtually ignored until the mid-1970s. Market capitalization has since then risen and plummeted in response to the debt crisis in 1982, the stock market crash in 1987, and the peso crisis in 1995. Stock market capitalization averaged 25 percent of GDP from 1983 to 1985, 12 percent from 1986 to 1990, and 30 percent from 1991 to 1994. In 1993, market capitalization stood at $200.7 billion; by 1995 this figure had fallen to $90.7 billion (BCA 1996, 46). The market has since started to slowly climb back to pre-peso crisis levels, with market capitalization totaling $106 billion at the end of 1996.

The equity market, like the banking industry, is highly concentrated, with a few firms accounting for the majority of shares. For example, in 1995, one company accounted for almost one-quarter of capital on the stock market and between 20 percent and 40 percent of daily trading (EIU 1996b, 36). High market concentration is due, in part, to the fact that few public firms are considered highly marketable: only 20 of 198 stocks measured for marketability in September 1996 were ranked as highly marketable (US Embassy 1997, 72). One of these firms, Telmex, accounted for almost half of total foreign equity investment.

In 1993, a second-tier market, the Market for Medium-Size Companies (MMex), opened on the stock exchange in order to provide a means for small and medium-sized enterprises to obtain equity financing. In contrast to the dramatic drop in investment on the main exchange, investment in the intermediate market grew by 31 percent in 1995 and 15 percent in 1996.

Despite the instability that followed the peso crisis, the government has continued to take steps toward liberalizing financial services in the securities industry and to remove restrictions on derivatives. For example, the Bank of Mexico has authorized trading in Mexican peso futures and stock index futures on the Chicago Mercantile Exchange. In addition, there are plans to open a domestic derivatives trading exchange for products currently offered on the Chicago Mercantile Exchange and to create a Mexican commodities market.

Although financial instruments available in Mexico are becoming increasingly sophisticated, the market continues to be dominated by government securities. In 1992, for example, the turnover in government securities was estimated at $3.4 trillion, compared to an aggregate turnover of $29 billion in corporate debt for the same year (Johnson 1995, 141). Similarly, compared to other Latin American emerging markets, new equity issues represent a relatively small part of total private-sector credit. In 1993-94, the ratio of new equity issues to growth in private bank credit was 12.0 percent in Mexico, 27.0 percent in Chile, and 46.2 percent in Argentina. By this measure, Brazil was the only major Latin American economy to perform worse than Mexico, with new equity less than 1 percent of growth in private domestic credit (Rojas-Suarez and Weisbrod 1996, 17).

The new mandatory private pension scheme should help deepen the Mexican securities market. As of mid-1997, contributions of at least 8.5 percent of salaries must be placed in a privately managed pension fund. Each pension fund management company (AFORE) will invest in one or more funds (SIEFOREs) managed by the company. Eighteen financial groups and firms are currently authorized to operate as AFOREs. Individuals are free to place pension contributions in the AFORE and SIEFORE of their choice but are not allowed to change AFOREs more than once a year in order to keep administration costs down (OECD 1996, 149). The government projects that the new private pension system will help increase the private domestic savings rate from 16.1 percent of GDP in 1996 to 17.7 percent in 2000, three years after the new system is scheduled to begin operating.

Mexico's securities market should also benefit from projected growth in the insurance industry. At present, the Mexican insurance market is underdeveloped and highly concentrated. Insurance premiums as a percentage of GDP are lower in Mexico than in the other major Latin American emerging economies, ranging from a low of 1.5 percent of

GDP in Mexico to a high of 3.1 percent of GDP in Chile in 1995 (Sigma 1997, 14).[5] In the same year, the five largest insurance companies accounted for more than 70 percent of Mexican insurance premiums. This situation is likely to change as the market responds to recent measures to liberalize foreign participation in insurance by increasing the number of products offered on the insurance market and lowering the cost of providing insurance in the Mexican market.

Prudential Regulation

Prior to the peso crisis, the Bank of Mexico directed commercial banks to increase their capital-to-risk weighted asset ratio to 8 percent by 1993 (Karaoglan and Lubrano 1995, 4). Despite this attempt to prevent inadequate reserves from causing instability in the banking sector, poor risk management and the consequent increase in nonperforming loans were major causes of the peso crisis. The programs implemented by the Mexican government to assist banks in the wake of the peso crisis have forced a higher level of discipline on banks and, in essence, changed the standards under which they operate.

The creation of an improved financial regulatory framework was one of the central components of the financial support package developed by the Mexican government in response to the peso crisis. With the merger of the banking and securities supervisory authorities in the CNBV, stricter rules were enacted to protect against losses from nonperforming loans. Since February 1995, financial institutions have been required to maintain reserves equal to the larger of either 60 percent of nonperforming loans or 4 percent of their entire portfolio (Banco de Mexico 1996, 164).

A number of other recent legislative changes have closed loopholes that had been left open under the 1991 privatization legislation and have more narrowly defined permissible lending activities. For example, as of April 1996, financial conglomerates may no longer use their stock as collateral for loans or engage in financing arrangements to purchase shares in their own conglomerate (US Embassy 1997, 79); and no individual or firm may hold more than 5 percent of total shares in any commercial bank.

Mexico has also announced that it intends to apply stricter accounting standards according to the internationally recognized generally accepted accounting principles (GAAP). Differences in the definition of nonperforming loans in the current accounting framework and in the

---

5. All of Latin America is considered underinsured: its countries accounted for 6 percent of global GDP but only 1.5 percent of world insurance premiums in 1995.

GAAP will raise the number of loans classified as nonperforming, but over time, use of the GAAP should help promote financial stability by increasing transparency in the Mexican banking industry.

As in the banking sector, brokerage houses are required to maintain reserves equal to 8 percent of risk-weighted capital requirements. The CNBV requires publicly listed firms to disclose financial statements and prohibits insider trading. Debt and equity traded on the stock exchange must be authorized by the CNBV, and financial statements must be submitted and approved before securities are made available to the public.

In contrast to other areas of the financial services industry, the securities industry is largely self-regulated. Amendments to the 1993 Securities Market Law enhanced the opportunity for self-regulation by the stock exchange, which, along with the Mexican Association of Trading Intermediaries, operates as a self-regulating organization (US Treasury 1994, 149). Although government directives concerning disclosure requirements are not considered to be as well enforced as those in the United States, the recent authorization and establishment of ratings agencies has increased transparency in the securities market.

CONSAR has established minimum capital requirements for both the AFOREs and the SIEFOREs managed by the AFOREs. Each AFORE must keep an initial minimum capital requirement of $3.2 million in reserve in order to operate. SIEFOREs are required to have up-front capital of $500,000. In order to prevent any pension fund manager from gaining control of the market, no AFORE will be permitted to hold assets accounting for more than 17 percent of the market in the first four years after the public pension system begins. Thereafter, an AFORE's market share will be limited to 20 percent (Banco de Mexico 1997, 2). SIEFOREs will be allowed to invest only in government securities and specific gilt-edged stocks, known as List No. 40, reported in the National Registry of Securities and Intermediaries. Insurance companies may invest only in the same securities as those that are permissible for SIEFORE investment.

Foreign Participation

Regulations governing foreign participation in financial services were first amended in 1993, to allow banks and other financial institutions market access to compete in the newly privatized banking sector. They were changed again in 1995 to attract foreign funds to help recapitalize commercial banks after the peso crisis seriously weakened their balance sheets. Market access and national treatment differ, on paper, for NAFTA and non-NAFTA countries. Financial firms from NAFTA countries are permitted higher levels of foreign ownership than are firms from non-NAFTA countries. NAFTA also guarantees that firms from NAFTA countries will receive national treatment. Under NAFTA, however, any non-NAFTA firm that provides financial services in one NAFTA country must receive the same treatment as do firms headquartered in a NAFTA country. Thus, non-NAFTA firms that engage in financial services activities in the United States must receive the same treatment and market access in Mexico as do US firms.

The 1993 Foreign Investment Law removed barriers to foreign direct investment in roughly three-quarters of Mexico's industrial sectors. Limits on foreign ownership were reduced in banking, brokerage, and insurance, but prohibitions remained on majority foreign ownership in financial services. Firms from non-NAFTA countries were permitted 30 percent ownership of financial groups and 49 percent ownership of banks, brokerages, and insurance companies.

When NAFTA took effect in 1994, Mexico committed to national treatment in financial services for US and Canadian firms. US and Canadian firms are entitled to 100 percent ownership of Mexican bank subsidiaries, subject to restrictions limiting the rate of expansion in the Mexican market and the amount of total market capital that a single foreign institution may hold. The original NAFTA implementation schedule stipulated that US and Canadian investors could invest in the Mexican banking industry as long as foreign ownership did not exceed 8 percent of total capital in the first year after NAFTA was signed. This limit was to be raised by 1 percent annually until it reached 15 percent, at which point there were to be no remaining restrictions on total foreign ownership as a percentage of total banking capital. The implementing legislation also stated that no bank was permitted to control more than 4 percent of total capital in the banking industry, which effectively prohibited US and Canadian firms from acquiring any of the six largest Mexican banks (US Treasury 1994, 144-45).[6] US and Canadian firms seeking to control a commercial bank in Mexico were required under the original terms of agreement to secure 100 percent ownership of the bank.

These terms and conditions changed when the Law on Credit Institutions was amended in 1995, following the peso crisis. The amendments increased permissible foreign ownership for both NAFTA and non-NAFTA firms entering the financial services sector. The limit on foreign ownership of financial groups by firms from non-NAFTA countries was raised to 49 percent. US and Canadian firms may now hold, in total, up to 25 percent of total capital in the banking industry. A single firm from Canada or the United States may acquire banks that control up to 6 percent of the capital of the banking industry. The new rules also lowered limits on the percentage of shares required for control of Mexican banks. Firms from the United States and Canada are now permitted to own 51 percent

6. Under NAFTA, no single financial institution from the United States or Canada could control more than 1.5 percent of the total net capital of all domestic and foreign banks until 2000, when the 4 percent figure was to be applicable.

of a bank's shares and, therefore, may participate with domestic share-holders in joint ventures.

NAFTA contains other provisions to promote market access. The participating governments must be more transparent, publish their regulations, and establish offices to address foreigners' regulatory questions. Completed applications for foreign firms seeking to invest in the financial services sector must be answered within 120 days. Other measures designed to facilitate the cross-border provision and establishment of financial services stipulate that countries may not prohibit citizens from buying the services of firms in other NAFTA countries, nor dictate the citizenship of a firm's senior management.

In 1994, the Mexican government authorized 18 foreign commercial banking licenses. By the end of 1995, two-thirds of the new banking licenses had resulted in new bank subsidiaries. Even so, assets of the top ten commercial banks totaled less than 4 percent of all banking sector assets at the end of 1995. A year later, only four of Mexico's 18 privatized commercial banks were still wholly Mexican-owned and almost 20 percent of the banking system assets were under the direct control of foreign institutions (Institute of International Bankers 1997, 140).[7] The extent of foreign involvement in the Mexican commercial banking industry is difficult to gauge, however, because foreign banks are heavily involved in recapitalizing the banks and indirectly control a significant share of the financial sector.

The stock market was opened to foreign participation earlier than other financial service sectors. Following the 1987 stock market crash, the Mexican government amended the securities laws to permit foreigners to invest in Mexican equities through a "neutral" fund, which gives foreigners pecuniary rights over shares but no voting rights. Commercial debt is currently categorized as either A shares, which can be purchased only by Mexicans; B shares, which can be purchased only by foreigners; American Depository Receipts (ADRs), which are shares in Mexican firms that are listed on overseas markets; and the Neutral Fund, a trust managed by Nafin that represents companies not listed on the stock market. Foreign investors are permitted to participate in the Mexican securities market by investing in the Neutral Fund, acquiring B shares, or purchasing ADRs.

Foreigners have been permitted since 1990 to hold shares in brokerage houses and other stock market intermediaries. Under NAFTA, individual firms from the United States and Canada may not hold more than 4 percent of the entire capital of the securities market until January 2000, after which there will be no limits for NAFTA firms. Permissible foreign ownership of total ordinary capital stock in brokerage houses

---

7. The 18 commercial banks were denationalized from 1991 to 1992.

was raised in 1995 from 30 percent to 49 percent, of which an individual firm may hold up to 20 percent. There are currently no restrictions on foreign ownership of government debt securities. No foreign firms are listed on the stock exchange, although they are allowed to trade.

Foreign investment in Mexico has been extremely volatile over the last five years. Foreign investment in Mexican equity peaked in January 1994 at $60.9 billion, accounting for 30 percent of market capitalization. By February 1995, it had fallen to 24 percent of market capitalization, totaling $18.9 billion. Foreign portfolio investment began to return to Mexico in the first half of 1996, with most concentrated in ADRs, although diversification is slowly growing.[8] Only six of the twelve foreign brokerages licensed to establish subsidiaries in Mexico had taken seats on the stock exchange as of 1996. As the market expands and moves away from a reliance on overseas placements of Mexican securities, more foreign brokerages are likely to set up operations in Mexico.

The Mexican insurance market has recently become significantly more open for foreign firms. Before NAFTA was signed, residents and businesses were prohibited from buying insurance from non-Mexican insurance firms, and foreign investors were not permitted to hold the majority of shares in domestic insurance firms. With NAFTA, the insurance industry was allowed the same level and type of foreign investment as permitted for foreign pension fund managers—that is, 100 percent ownership for firms from NAFTA countries and 49 percent ownership for firms from non-NAFTA countries. Mexico bound NAFTA commitments on insurance in the 1997 WTO financial services agreement. Thus, when it comes into effect in early 1998, foreign insurance firms from non-NAFTA countries will be afforded the same market access as insurance firms from NAFTA countries. Market share restrictions will be phased out by 2000, after which it is likely that foreign-owned companies will account for a much larger share of the market. One US-headquartered insurance company expects to see annual growth of 20 percent in Mexico over the next four years and projects that the Mexican insurance market will, by 2010, represent one of the top ten insurance markets in the world, with an estimated premium volume of $50 billion. By 1995, 25 of 54 insurance companies were foreign-owned or had a foreign joint venture partner, and foreigners controlled 23 percent of the insurance market (Sigma 1997).

Under the government's new privately managed pension system, firms from NAFTA countries will be permitted 100 percent ownership, and from non-NAFTA countries 49 percent ownership, of AFOREs (EIU 1996b, 13). Eighteen requests to operate AFOREs were approved by the Mexican

---

8. As of May 1997, 51 percent of foreign investment in stocks was held in ADR shares, 34 percent in B shares, and the remainder in Mexican investment funds.

government for 1 July 1997, the day the new pension plan was scheduled to start; Of those approved, ten have foreign partners or affiliates (EIU 1997b, 3).

Remaining Obstacles

In less than a decade, Mexico's financial services sector has been transformed from one in which foreign participation was effectively prohibited to one in which the market is relatively accessible to foreign firms. Although there continue to be limits on market access, many of these will be phased out by the year 2000 for firms from or with operations in other NAFTA countries. Under NAFTA, there are to be no restrictions on the total share of the banking sector that may be controlled by foreign interests after 2000. Individual foreign firms will be limited to controlling a market share no larger than 15 percent of the total market. Foreign banks wishing to enter Mexico under NAFTA must establish a subsidiary in the country.

Firms from non-NAFTA countries will continue to face higher barriers to market access in financial services than do firms from NAFTA countries, although some of the differences in treatment were removed with Mexico's 1997 WTO financial services agreement. For example, when it comes into force there will be no difference in the treatment of foreign insurance providers: non-NAFTA firms will continue to be restricted to holding a minority position in banking, but will now be permitted to acquire 30 percent voting rights in addition to 40 percent equity in that sector; firms from both NAFTA and non-NAFTA countries will continue to be subject to a 49 percent ceiling on the ownership of a financial group.

Given the pace at which the government has been issuing new licenses to foreign firms in all financial sectors over the past two years, there do not appear to be bureaucratic barriers to market access. New procedures to help make regulations more transparent should further facilitate the expansion of foreign firms throughout Mexico. Some securities products have not been authorized as quickly as planned. It is likely, however, that domestic and foreign firms with operations in Mexico will have a much wider range of derivatives available in the near future.

For the most part, Mexico is very open to and nondiscriminatory toward foreign investment. In 1994, the withholding tax on interest payments to nonresidents was lowered from 15 percent to 4.9 percent, and this rate applies to financial services firms from both NAFTA and non-NAFTA countries. Foreign firms operating in Mexico have access to peso credit and often are given better terms than domestic companies seeking financing (EIU 1996a, 9). But insurance companies and pension fund managers are prohibited from placing funds in foreign securities, a restriction that stands out as one of the more significant remaining barriers to financial market liberalization.

References

Banco de Mexico. 1996. *The Mexican Economy 1996*. Mexico City: Banco de Mexico.

Banco de Mexico. 1997. *The Mexican Economy 1997*. Mexico City: Banco de Mexico.

Bank for International Settlements (BIS). 1996. *66th Annual Report*. Basle: Bank for International Settlements.

Bank for International Settlements (BIS). 1997. *67th Annual Report*. Basle: Bank for International Settlements.

Bank Credit Analyst Research Group (BCA). 1996. *Emerging Markets Analyst—1996 Annual Handbook*. Montreal: BCA Publications Ltd.

Demetrio Guerra-Sanchez, Jose. 1996. *Overview of the Regulation of Banks in Mexico*. National Law Center for Inter-American Free Trade. (http://www.natlaw.com/pubs/spmxbk2.htm).

Economist Intelligence Unit (EIU). 1996a. *Financing Foreign Operation: Mexico*. New York: The Economist Intelligence Unit (April).

Economist Intelligence Unit (EIU). 1996b. *Financing Foreign Operation: Mexico*. New York: The Economist Intelligence Unit, Semi-Annual Updater (October).

Economist Intelligence Unit (EIU). 1997a. *Country Report: Mexico*. New York: The Economist Intelligence Unit (1st Quarter).

Economist Intelligence Unit (EIU). 1997b. *Financing Foreign Operation: Mexico*. New York: The Economist Intelligence Unit, Flash Updater (January).

General Accounting Office (GAO). 1996. *Mexico's Financial Crisis*. Washington: Government Printing Office, GCD-96-56.

Hausmann, Ricardo, and Liliana Rojas-Suarez, eds. 1996. *Banking Crisis in Latin America*. Washington: Inter-American Development Bank and Johns Hopkins University.

Hufbauer, Gary Clyde, and Jeffrey Schott. 1993. *NAFTA: An Assessment*. Washington: Institute for International Economics.

Institute of International Bankers. 1997. *Global Survey 1997*. New York: Institute of International Bankers.

International Monetary Fund (IMF). 1992. *Mexico: The Strategy to Achieve Sustained Economic Growth*. Washington: International Monetary Fund.

Johnson, Hazel. 1995. *Banking Without Borders*. Chicago: Probus Publishing.

Karaoglan, Roy, and Mike Lubrano. 1995. Mexico's Banks After the December 1994 Devaluation. *Northwestern Journal of Law & Business* 16, no. 1.

Libby, Barbara. 1994. The Impact of the North American Free Trade Agreement on Commercial Banking. *Journal of Economic Issues* 28, no. 2.

Lindgren, Carl-Johan, Gillian Garcia, and Matthew Saal. *Bank Soundness and Macroeconomic Policy*. Washington: International Monetary Fund.

North American Free Trade Agreement (NAFTA). 1992. *Chapter Fourteen: Financial Services*. Washington: Government Printing Office.

Organization for Economic Cooperation and Development (OECD). 1996. *OECD Economic Surveys: Mexico 1997*. Paris: Organization for Economic Cooperation and Development.

Organization for Economic Cooperation and Development (OECD). 1997. *OECD Economic Outlook*. No. 61. Paris: Organization for Economic Cooperation and Development.

Rojas-Suarez, Liliana, and Steven Weisbrod. 1995. *Achieving Stability in Latin American Financial Markets in the Presence of Volatile Capital Flows*. Working Paper Series No. 304. Washington: Inter-American Development Bank.

Rojas-Suarez, Liliana, and Steven Weisbrod. 1996. *Building Stability in Latin American Financial Markets*. Working Paper Series No. 320. Washington: Inter-American Development Bank.

Schwartz, Moises J. 1997. Recovering Stability and Growth in Mexico's Economy and Financial System. In *The Banking and Financial Structure in the NAFTA Countries and Chile*, ed. by George Furstenberg. Boston: Kluwer Academic Publishers.

Sigma. 1997. *The Insurance Industry in Latin America: A Growing Competitive Environment*. No. 2/1997. Zurich: Swiss Reinsurance Company.

US Department of the Treasury. 1994. *National Treatment Study*. Washington: Government Printing Office.

US Embassy. 1997. *Mexico: Economic and Financial Report*. Mexico City: US Embassy.

Philippines

Introduction

Compared to those of other member countries of the Association of Southeast Asian Nations (ASEAN), the Philippine financial system is underdeveloped. Although most financial institutions are private, the sector has a legacy of government control and limited foreign entry. There is a moderately wide range of services and institutions, but credit is directed and interest rates continue to be subsidized.

The financial sector experienced repeated crises in the 1980s because of poor supervision, concentrated lending to single borrowers, politically motivated loans, and restrictive regulation. When several banks collapsed in the early 1980s, the government responded by infusing fresh capital. Comprehensive financial reforms were introduced from 1981 to 1984: restrictions on financial intermediation were lifted, market-oriented credit and monetary policies were implemented, all interest rates were gradually liberalized, and agricultural credit programs were eliminated, as was forced specialization in the banking sector. Universal banking was introduced, and banks were encouraged to mobilize savings from the private sector. But the objective of these reforms—to encourage commercial banks to engage in long-term lending—was not achieved. The immediate effect of the reform process was a surge in credit to the private sector that far outstripped deposit growth. Weak credit analysis resulted in many financial institutions being burdened with nonperforming loans (Bisat, Johnston, and Sundararajan 1992, 66). Political crises during the 1986-89 period added to the atmosphere of uncertainty, and after several runs on financial institutions and large capital outflows, a balance of payments crisis occurred that required an IMF adjustment program and extensive domestic reform.

In 1997, the Philippines was affected by speculative attacks following those on the troubled Thai baht. The presence of the IMF, plus additional adjustments, helped to minimize the fallout. With the domestic economy growing at a fast rate and real estate speculation a concern, the central bank has moved proactively to limit US dollar lending and to cap loan exposures. It imposed a 20 percent ceiling on real estate exposure of banks, reduced the lendable value of real estate to 60 percent, and required borrowers to supply more equity (*Asian Business*, July 1997, 14-21). Nevertheless, after unsuccessfully defending the currency with high interest rates and expenditure of foreign reserves, in July 1997 the central bank allowed the peso to float.

Regulatory Framework

The Philippine Central Bank (BSP) controls and supervises the monetary system and, in 1993, spearheaded the country's financial restructuring. Primary objectives of the BSP are to ensure internal and external monetary stability, and to sustain the peso's value and preserve its convertibility. In addition, the BSP monitors foreign exchange transactions and regulates exports, imports, and invisibles. Under the General Banking Act, the BSP is responsible for regulating commercial banks, savings and mortgage banks, building and loan associations, trust companies, finance and leasing companies, investment houses, and pawnshops. It also issues loans to state-owned enterprises (SOEs).

The Monetary Board is the other primary institution responsible for controlling and supervising the monetary system. It directs the management, operations, and administration of the BSP and consists of the BSP governor, government officials, and two private-sector representatives.

The Securities and Exchange Commission (SEC) was established in 1936 to supervise stock exchanges and the activities of stock brokers and security dealers. Since 1975, it has also been responsible for the registration and regulation of commercial paper.

Finance companies, which carry on quasi-banking functions and issue commercial paper, are regulated by both the BSP and the SEC. Credit unions are not supervised by any government agency, although cooperative credit unions fall under the supervision of the Cooperatives Development Authority.

The Insurance Commission regulates insurance companies, registers new providers, and administers a security fund, which is used to pay outstanding claims against insolvent insurance companies.

The Bureau of Internal Revenue is responsible for administering a transaction tax of 0.25 percent levied on gross financial sales. The Philippines has no capital gains tax on transactions involving listed securities.

Financial Institutions

The banking system dominates the financial sector, accounting for more than 80 percent of total financial assets. Although the equity market continues to be thin, market capitalization grew from US$10 billion in 1991 to US$80 billion in 1996.

Financial Intermediaries

Commercial banks account for 90 percent of banking-sector assets; thrift banks, specialized government banks, and rural banks make up the remainder. The banking sector is highly concentrated, with the top five commercial banks holding half of total assets. The Central Bank lowered barriers to entry into banking as part of its 1993 financial reform initiative and the number of commercial banks has grown from 24 in 1991 to 44 in 1997 (*Far Eastern Economic Review*, 25 September 1997, 104).

Commercial banks, which account for the largest segment of the banking sector, are encouraged to provide universal banking services. For example, they may perform investment activities such as securities underwriting, and they may invest in direct equity in allied commercial undertakings. By 1994, 15 commercial banks operated in this fashion.

Private banks constitute a second segment of the banking sector. Half of these are still relatively small in asset size, and more than half are banks that are controlled by one or two families. The third segment comprises government banks, which concentrate on wholesale lending. Since 1989 these banks have been gradually privatized, with the exception of banks that have been assigned special development roles in the agricultural and industrial sectors. Government agencies and government-owned corporations are required to bank with government financial institutions, and this has slowed privatization. By 1994, the government retained controlling interest in two commercial banks, including the country's largest commercial bank, Philippines National Bank (PNB) (US Treasury 1994, 422).

Prior to the financial reforms of the 1980s only commercial banks were allowed to accept demand deposits, and they were prohibited from giving interest on these deposits because of antiusury laws, which were repealed in 1980. Thrift banks and rural banks continue to function as savings and mortgage banks or savings and loan associations. Thrift banks focus on medium- and long-term loans and on home mortgages; rural banks are largely privately owned and extend loans to medium-sized farms and rural nonfarm enterprises. Both types of institution are encouraged to promote private-sector investments and, until the 1980s, the government participated as a silent partner on loans to the private sector, matching them peso for peso. This kind of subsidized borrowing compensated rural banks for the lack of demand deposits.

Domestic entry into the banking sector was relaxed in the late 1980s when the BSP approved the conversion of two thrift banks into commercial banks. But capital requirements, which had been imposed to strengthen the domestic banking sector by giving incentives to merge and consolidate, rose steadily until 1993 and thus deterred additional entry. The barriers to entry resulted in oligopoly profits from the increasing interest rate spreads that followed interest rate liberalization.

Philippine banks face restrictive loan portfolio regulation that is intended to aid the economy in its development objectives. A deposit retention scheme requires that at least 75 percent of a bank's total deposits in a geographic region must be invested in that region, although this regulation was eased in 1990 to apply to 3, instead of 13, regions. A second restriction is that 25 percent of net incremental lendable funds must be used for agricultural lending, 40 percent of which must be earmarked for agrarian reform and the remainder for general agricultural purposes. Finally, a requirement of mandatory credit to small-scale enterprises stipulates that at least 10 percent of loans must be allocated to small enterprises with total assets of less than 5 million pesos (Lamberte and Llanto 1995).

Innovation in banking channels has been introduced since 1990, when the government abolished the requirement that off-site automatic teller machines could open only in areas in which a bank operated a branch. By 1993 commercial and thrift banks faced no geographic restrictions when extending their branch network.

The main nonbank financial institutions are finance companies, investment and securities institutions, insurance companies, and a number of less formal institutions. Finance companies are heavily involved in consumer credit; more recently they have been allowed to engage in securities trading and residential mortgage finance. They may also engage in quasi-banking functions but require a special license to do so. Investment houses underwrite securities, administer various private and government-run trust funds, and provide medium- and long-term investment funds. Like finance companies, they may engage in quasi-banking practices subject to obtaining a special license. Recent liberalization of the banking sector has weakened these institutions and created incentives for mergers or transfers to commercial bank ownership. Since 1990, they have been subjected to a minimum fee-based income requirement to encourage them to diversify into fee-based activities other than securities underwriting.

The insurance sector includes two government-owned social insurance institutions, the Government Service Insurance System (GSIS) and the Social Securities System (SSS), which provide coverage for hospitalization, disability, and death, as well as some nonlife insurance. Three other government insurance agencies provide crop insurance, home insurance, and deposit insurance (Takahashi 1994, 80). Private insurance companies are highly concentrated. For example, the two largest life insurers account for 60 percent of assets in their market, although new entry into this sector has been permitted since March 1992. The insurance market is highly dependent on reinsurance. More than 56 percent of insurance companies' assets are invested in stocks, government securities, and bonds. The life insurance sector is well capitalized, with 60 percent of liabilities covered by reserves and unassigned surpluses. The nonlife sector is not as well capitalized, with only 32 percent of liabilities covered by reserves and surpluses (Lamble and Low 1995). Nonlife premiums are set by the Philippine insurance rating association, a statutory body with compulsory membership. Since June 1991 banks have been permitted to own up to 35 percent of an insurance company.

Direct Finance

There are two stock exchanges in the Philippines: the Manila Stock Exchange, established in 1927, and the Makati Stock Exchange, established in 1963. Brokers could have a seat on only one exchange until 1994, when the Philippine Stock Exchange was established by linking both exchanges through automated trading arrangements. A book entry system and greater automation are proposed for the future.

The Philippines equity market is thin, highly concentrated in the stocks of five companies that, in 1992, accounted for about 55 percent of market capitalization. Since the early 1990s, equity financing has surged because of privatization, new offerings of high-grade stocks by well-known corporations, and an influx of foreign investment. High economic growth rates since the mid-1990s have continued this deepening of the equity market. Two types of shares are available: A shares, which may be purchased by Philippine nationals only, and B shares, which may be purchased by anyone and which trade at a premium. Since 1994, though, this distinction is no longer required under SEC regulation (US Treasury 1994, 434).

The bond market, dominated by government bonds, also is thin. Apart from a three-year, floating-rate treasury note, there are virtually no issues of longer-term public debt instruments. Most outstanding bonds are held to fulfill reserve requirements, so the secondary market is still relatively inactive. The private bond market is underdeveloped, dominated by a few prominent companies. As in other countries, the lack of development is linked to a strong preference for short-term instruments due to the history of high and volatile interest rates, the absence of a secondary market, and the lack of transparent and critical information on the credit worthiness of corporate bond issuers.

A credit rating system, the Credit Information Bureau, Inc., was established in 1982. Its coverage is limited, however, because of the small number of public listings and the cost involved in obtaining and updating information.

Money markets include the interbank call loan market, a deposit substitute market, a commercial paper market, and a government securities market. The interbank call loan market accounted for 43 percent of money market transactions in 1992. Commercial banks are the main participants, using the call loan market to adjust liquidity positions and to finance regular lending operations. Compared to deposit substitutes, this instrument is relatively cheap because the reserve requirement is only 1 percent. The commercial paper market is dominated by the nonfinancial corporate sector and is strictly regulated. Borrowers must maintain a debt-equity ratio of 2.5:1 for new issues, and the SEC may require that a commercial bank secure as much as 20 percent of a company's aggregate commercial paper issue. Government securities account for 49 percent of the money market and are used mainly to finance the government deficit.

Other recent innovations include the introduction of mutual funds in 1989, although brokers and dealers are prohibited from managing such funds. Investment houses are permitted to do so subject to central bank approval and acceptance of a higher capital requirement. The futures market is geared mainly toward agricultural commodities, although treasury bill futures are quoted. Futures trading is limited. The foreign exchange market was reformed in 1991 to liberalize trade- and nontrade-related foreign exchange transactions. Overseas borrowing by private and public sectors continues to be restricted, though, especially for loans guaranteed by the national government or by government financial institutions. All foreign-currency borrowings and transfers of pesos outside the country that exceed P10,000 must be approved by the Central Bank (SIA 1997, 34). The Philippine Dealing System, created in 1992, provides quick and adequate information about the foreign exchange market to participants at low transaction costs.

Prudential Regulations

Prudential regulation has been successfully tightened and improved since 1980. The BSP has raised the minimum capital requirements for banks three times since 1980. In December 1996, the minimum capital requirement was raised from P1.5 billion to P2 billion for regular banks, from P2.5 billion to P4.5 billion for universal banks, and from P150 million to

P250 million for thrifts. Limits on credit to a single borrower[1] are set at 25 percent of unimpaired capital. Since several banks failed in the 1980s, contingent liabilities must be included within the 25 percent ratio. In addition, loans to insiders are subject to regulations that limit all insider loans to less than 15 percent of the bank's loan portfolio or less than 100 percent of its capital, whichever amount is lower. Finally, banks are subjected to a reserve requirement that was set at 17 percent in 1994 (Sachs, Tornell, and Velasco 1996, 33).

Depositor protection requires compulsory membership by banks in the government-owned Philippine Deposit Insurance Corporation (PDIC). The PDIC is the official receiver of troubled banks. In view of past problems, maximum coverage per depositor was raised in 1992. Even so, the PDIC has had difficulty meeting claims promptly.

Insurance companies are required to have a minimum of five shareholders. New insurance companies must meet minimum capital requirements of 100 million pesos, 75 percent of which must be in paid-up share capital. They must also maintain a solvency margin of 500,000 pesos or 10 percent of the previous year's net premiums, whichever is higher.

Foreign Participation

No new foreign bank licenses were granted in the Philippines until 1994. At that time, only four foreign banks operated as commercial banks; they were not allowed to accept demand deposits, but they could establish additional branches with central bank approval. Since 1994, 12 additional foreign banks have entered the market (*The Economist*, 12 April 1997), some of them taking advantage of a five-year window, established in 1994, during which up to 10 foreign banks may establish full-service branches (US Treasury 1994). These entrants are each required to provide $100 million in capital infusions, staggered over 20 years. At the same time, prohibitions on the expansion of the branch network were partially removed, so foreign banks operating on a full-service basis may add up to six new branches. They are also allowed to become universal banks and engage in securities underwriting for the local market. They may not, however, operate as investment banks or engage in the trust business.

Foreign equity participation, limited to 40 percent of stock with 30 percent voting rights and 10 percent nonvoting rights, has been allowed in domestic banks since 1972. Since 1986, in order to help alleviate the

---

1. This regulation applies to banks and finance companies, but not to investment houses with quasi-banking functions.

country's foreign debt problem, foreign banks have been permitted to buy additional shares in domestic banks through a debt-equity conversion scheme.

In 1994, limits on foreign ownership in new subsidiaries incorporated in the Philippines and in existing domestic banks was raised to 60 percent, although foreign participation in Philippine-owned universal banks remains limited to 30 percent and in life insurance companies to 40 percent. New banks are permitted to enter the Philippine market as either a branch or a subsidiary if they are among the top five banks (measured by assets) in their home countries or among the top 150 worldwide.[2]

In 1976, Offshore Banking Units (OBU) were established, and the number of participants rose annually until the recession of 1983. Since then, tighter regulations have prohibited OBUs from renewing medium-term loans and restrained them from permitting letters of credit. OBUs are limited to foreign currency transactions, and concentrate on trade finance, correspondent banking, foreign currency lending, and foreign currency deposit-taking. They are not allowed to establish branches, although foreign banks that do not operate branches in the Philippines may join. Finally, foreigners are permitted to repatriate cash dividends without BSP approval.

Foreign insurance providers are just beginning to establish a presence in the insurance market. There is presently a 40 percent limit on foreign ownership in this sector, but this figure is scheduled to rise to 51 percent when the WTO financial services agreement comes into force in January 1999. The local insurance market, in which only 11 percent of the population holds an insurance policy, is considered to be a high growth market, and foreign insurance providers are now positioning themselves to take advantage of enhanced market access and greater competition in this sector (*Journal of Commerce*, 8 January 1998).

Remaining Obstacles

The obstacles to an efficient and open financial system in the Philippines are numerous. Capitalization requirements for banks and other financial institutions lack uniformity. Continuing segmentation of the country's credit markets makes mobilization of funds for the larger capital needs of small and medium-sized enterprises virtually impossible. Supervisory agencies lack skilled personnel. Many small and medium-sized enterprises do not abide by standard accounting practices, and this makes credit analysis by banks difficult. The legal framework is not conducive to lending; indeed, it is biased in favor of borrowers.

---

2. New banks will not be permitted to enter the market as a branch after early 1999.

The Philippines lacks an efficient clearing and settlement system. It continues to impose a documentary stamp tax on collateral instruments for bonds. The secondary bond market is nonexistent. Despite complete interest rate liberalization, the Philippines still has a distorted interest rate structure because government entities continue to subsidize interest rates in special government credit programs.

Foreign banks are not permitted to control more than 30 percent of total banking assets. There are restrictions on the number of branches a foreign bank is permitted to operate. Lending limits are set based on branch, as opposed to global, capital (FLG 1997), further restricting foreign banks' ability to compete in the domestic economy.

Further, the commitments outlined in the Philippines' offer in the 1997 WTO financial services agreement will result in market access bound below current practice in the banking sector when it comes into effect in early 1999. Current ownership is capped at 60 percent, and foreign ownership in the banking industry will be limited to 51 percent.

References

Bisat, Amer, R. Barry Johnston, and Vasudevan Sundararajan. 1992. *Issues in Managing and Sequencing Financial Sector Reforms: Lessons from Experiences in Five Developing Countries*. Washington: International Monetary Fund.

Economist Intelligence Unit (EIU). 1992. *Financing Foreign Operation: Philippines*. New York: The Economist Intelligence Unit.

Financial Leaders Group (FLG). 1997. *Barriers to Trade in Financial Services: Case Studies*. London: Barclays Place.

Lamberte, Mario B., and Gilberto M. Llanto. 1995. A Study of Financial Sector Policies: The Philippines Case. In *Financial Sector Development in Asia: Country Studies*, ed. by Shahid N. Zahid. Hong Kong: Oxford University Press for Asian Development Bank.

Lamble, Peter, and Robin Low. 1995. *The Asia Pacific Insurance Handbook*. Sydney, NWT: Coopers & Lybrand.

Sachs, Jeffrey, Aaron Tornell, and Andrés Velasco. 1996. *Financial Crisis in Emerging Markets: The Lessons from 1995*. National Bureau of Economic Research Working Paper 5576. Cambridge, MA: National Bureau of Economic Research.

Securities Industry Association (SIA). 1997. *Asian Capital Markets*. New York: Securities Industry Association.

Takahashi, Yuichi. 1994. Financial Sector Reform in the Asia Pacific Countries. Photocopy.

US Department of the Treasury. 1994. *National Treatment Study*. Washington: Government Printing Office.

Singapore

Introduction

Since Singapore separated from Malaysia in 1965, the country's government has followed a sophisticated strategy to develop a diversified economy based on manufacturing and regional services, including finance. Singapore has fine telecommunications facilities, easy accessibility, political stability, and a well-educated workforce. It has become a highly sophisticated regional financial center that draws on and contributes to dynamic growth in nearby economies.

Since 1980, financial and business services have been the second largest sector in the economy; they currently account for 28 percent of GDP (*Far Eastern Economic Review*, 25 September 1997). Singapore has developed a particular competitive advantage in supplying financial services to nonresidents by focusing on creating good conditions for domestic and foreign financial institutions. The international banking facility was created in 1968, followed in 1973 by the establishment of fully competitive foreign exchange and gold markets. A futures market for gold was introduced in 1978 and the Singapore International Monetary Exchange (SIMEX) in 1984.

Offshore income from banking, securities, and insurance business receives favorable treatment, with a 10 percent concessionary rate phased in for various types of lending, securities trading, and fund management activities over a 20-year period. International syndicated lending, nonresidents' securities transactions, and nonresident mutual fund income are tax exempt. Tax concessions are also available for financial institutions that establish regional headquarters in Singapore. Overall, the government's policies provide a moderate regulatory environment.

An increasingly prominent feature of Singapore's financial system is the Central Provident Fund (CPF), the country's compulsory pension scheme. Employees under the age of 55 are required to save 40 percent of their wages, and employers contribute a further 40 percent. This high rate of compulsory savings has helped Singapore sustain a high level of public investment. The entire fund was invested in government bonds until 1993, when changes were initiated to facilitate diversification of investment into blue chip stocks and real estate. As of March 1996, S$45 billion of the CPF's outstanding balance due to members of S$69 billion was, however, in government securities. In early 1998, the government removed restrictions on the investment of CPF funds, allowing it to be placed in foreign denominated securities and corporate bonds as long as such investments are made by approved professional fund managers.

The Post Office Savings Bank, established in 1877 as part of the postal service department, was incorporated as an independent statutory entity in 1972.

Regulatory Framework

Singapore does not have a central bank, but the Monetary Authority of Singapore (MAS) acts as a quasi-central bank, performing all functions except issuing currency. The MAS is the supervisory body for the financial system, as well as the government's banker and financial agent. Its functions include issuing securities on the government's behalf, raising loans in overseas capital markets for the government, and, along with the Singapore Investment Corporation, jointly managing of the country's official exchange reserves.

The local currency, the Singapore dollar, is issued by the Board of Commissioners of Currency. Singapore's Finance Minister chairs both the MAS and the Currency Board. The MAS governs the financial services industry by enforcing five pieces of legislation: the Banking Act, the Finance Companies Act, the Securities Industry Act, the Futures Trading Act, and the Insurance Companies Act. The MAS also administers other statutes, including the Local Treasury Bills Act and the Development Loan Act.

In the conduct of monetary policy, the MAS focuses on exchange rate stability rather than on money supply or interest rates. The exchange rate regime is a managed float in which the currency is allowed to fluctuate within a band based on a trade-weighted basket of currencies dominated by the US dollar.

Financial Institutions

Singapore has a well developed, privately owned financial sector. Commercial banks are the most important financial institutions in Singapore, accounting for two-thirds of financial assets in 1994. The equity market is deep; market capitalization grew from 91.6 percent of GDP in 1990 to 169 percent of GDP in 1996 (BIS 1997, 105).

Financial Intermediaries

Commercial banks in Singapore are of three kinds: fully licensed, restricted license, and offshore. Fully licensed banks are permitted to carry out a full range of banking services approved under the Banking Act. Locally incorporated banks as well as foreign banks established before 1971 have full licenses. Restricted-license banks do not have free access to the local market and differ from fully licensed banks in the size of the deposits they are permitted to collect.[1] Offshore banks are limited to wholesale banking services sold to nonresidents. They are restricted to one branch and are not allowed to accept interest-bearing Singapore-dollar deposits from residents.

Singapore has 132 commercial banks: 119 of these are foreign owned (see table B.7). Four commercial banks—the Development Bank of Singapore, the United Overseas Bank, the Overseas Chinese Bank, and the Overseas Union Bank—rank among the world's top 500 banks. The remaining 128 commercial banks are divided between those that are fully licensed (35), restricted licensed (14), and engaged in offshore business (82). Other significant financial institutions include merchant banks, finance companies, and insurance firms.

Merchant banks, 76 of which operate in Singapore, are permitted to offer corporate finance, investment management, equipment financing, and gold and foreign exchange trading. They are prohibited, with some exceptions, from raising funds from the public; issuing promissory notes, commercial paper, or certificates of deposit; establishing branches; or operating an Asian currency unit. MAS regulations prohibit merchant banks from granting any person or company credit facilities in excess of 30 percent of their capital (unless specific MAS approval is given).

Singapore's 27 finance companies are active in car and home finance. They have also diversified into leasing and factoring, dealing mainly with small firms and individuals. Finance companies are subject to a well-developed legal framework and relatively strict regulation. Through

---

1. The restricted-license banks are allowed to open only one branch each and are not permitted to operate Singapore-dollar savings accounts or to accept Singapore-dollar fixed deposits smaller than S$250,000.

**Table B.7 Singapore: Assets of financial institutions,
1987 and 1993** (percentages)

	Number of institutions, 1994	Assets (percentage shares)	
		1987	1993
Commercial banks	132	60.2	66.7
Local	13		
Foreign	119		
Full banks	22		
Restricted banks	14		
Offshore banks	83		
Finance companies	27	5.3	6.2
Post office savings banks	140	7.7	6.7
Merchant banks	76	23.1	14.8
Insurance companies	142	3.7	5.6

Source: Monetary Authority of Singapore, Annual Report 1996.

interbank deposits, they play an important role as suppliers of funds to merchant banks, which lack fund-raising capabilities of their own.

As of March 1996, there were 146 registered insurance companies in Singapore. Of these, 59 were general business and life insurers, 38 professional reinsurers, and 49 captive insurers. Although there are many insurers serving the economy, the market is highly concentrated. For example, two companies control two-thirds of the life-insurance market (Dow Jones International News, 16 December 1997).

Two areas targeted for growth in the future are offshore reinsurance and captive insurance.

Direct Finance

Singapore's treasury bond market is modeled on the US treasury bond market and involves primary dealers and market makers, which tend to be commercial banks. Since the government does not engage in deficit finance, few government bonds are floated and the market is not particularly liquid.

Singapore does not have a significant domestic market for corporate bonds, either, since companies are able to secure funds in the form of equities and commercial loans with ease.

Securities are traded on the Stock Exchange of Singapore (SES), which was deregulated in 1987 to allow full access to local and foreign securities firms and banks. The SES is owned by its members; nonmembers are required to trade shares through member firms.

To obtain a listing on the main board, a company must have a minimum paid-in capital of S$20 million, 25 percent of which must be owned by at least 500 shareholders. The company must also have a minimum track record of five years and must have been profitable for the three most recent years. Alternatively, it must have adequate working capital and continuity in management. A minimum of 20 percent of issued and paid-in capital must be in the hands of shareholders. If the nominal value of issued and paid-in capital is less than S$50 million, shareholders may hold no more than 10,000 shares and no fewer than 500 shares.

The Securities Industries Act, introduced in 1986, allows the SES to be self-regulating, buttressed by the MAS as the final regulator. There are four elected stockbroker members on the SES board; they are joined by five non-stockbroker members appointed with the approval of the MAS.

Under other reforms, also introduced in 1986, the securities industry was opened to financial institutions, including foreign ones. Singapore-incorporated commercial banks have been allowed to set up wholly owned stockbroking subsidiaries. Other brokerages have attracted foreign financial institutions, which are allowed to acquire up to 49 percent of the voting capital of member firms.

In the effort to develop Singapore's financial system as a major world financial center, the Stock Exchange of Singapore Dealing and Automated Quotation system (SESDAQ) was launched in 1987 to enable small- and medium-sized domestic companies with good growth prospects to raise funds for expansion. The listing requirements for SESDAQ are less stringent than those for the main exchange. There are no specific criteria for size, but potential candidates must have at least a three-year trading record; and at least 500,000 shares or 15 percent of the issued and paid-in capital (whichever is greater) must be in public hands when dealing starts.

In March 1988, the SES established a link with the US NASDAQ to promote international securities trading in Singapore. The link enables the exchange of price and trading information on a selected list of NASDAQ stocks, allowing Asian investors to deal in selected US and European stocks. The SES also has a custodial agreement with the Japan Securities Clearing Corporation that allows investors to settle transactions in Japanese securities through the Central Depository (CDP) book-entry system. Japanese stocks account for two-thirds of the total amount of foreign securities traded in Singapore.

In 1990, the SES and the Kuala Lumpur Stock Exchange separated, and Malaysian-incorporated stocks were removed from SES listing and vice versa. Singapore subsequently set up an over-the-counter market for foreign shares, known as the Central Limit Order Book (CLOB) International, which has been very successful.

Also in 1990, the SES created an international membership category, which includes international members that are wholly owned by major foreign securities houses. They are allowed to deal with, for, or on behalf of nonresidents and their related companies in transactions of any size on the SES main board, on the SESDAQ, and on the CLOB International.

The Singapore International Monetary Exchange (SIMEX), launched in 1984, conducts transactions in three-month Euro-dollar interest rate futures, three-month Euro-yen interest rates, and the Nikkei 225 stock average index. The growth of SIMEX as an international exchange is partly due to the successful implementation of a mutual-offset system with the Chicago Mercantile Exchange.

A tax-exemption package in effect since the mid-1980s applies to the income of nonresidents that is derived from investment funds handled by approved fund managers. Fee income of these managers is taxed at a concessionary rate of 10 percent. To further promote fee-based off-shore fund-management activities, the exemption has been extended to include investments in the local stock market.

Prudential Regulation

A distinguishing characteristic of prudential regulation is the activist stance taken by MAS regulators in promoting the objective of a safe and sound financial system. Foreign institutions seeking entry are carefully reviewed. Regular onsite inspections emphasize sound internal controls, asset quality, and management practices and regularly examined internal controls. BIS standards are enforced among banks. External auditors are held to high standards of accuracy and transparency. MAS eschews deposit insurance, arguing that its existence would erode self-discipline expected of banks.

The MAS limits credit to any single customer or group of customers to 25 percent of a bank's capital (Goldstein and Turner 1996), and loans in excess of 15 percent of a bank's capital must not exceed 50 percent of its total credit portfolio.[2] Banks are also prohibited from acquiring interests in financial, commercial, industrial, or other undertakings that exceed 40 percent of its capital. The 40 percent ceiling does not apply to MAS-approved investments in other banks or in bank subsidiaries formed to carry out functions relevant to banking.

Well-defined rules guide mergers and acquisitions; any shareholder who possesses 25 percent control of a company must inform the stock exchange and make a general offer for the remaining shares. The Securities Industry Council, which has supervisory responsibility, conducts investigations in this area. No takeover or acquisition of more than 20 percent of the voting rights of a merchant bank is permitted without

---

2. These restrictions apply to finance companies as well as commercial banks.

MAS approval. Similarly, merchant banks are not allowed to buy more than 20 percent of a company's shares without MAS approval.

The insurance industry is regulated by the Insurance Act, which was amended in 1987 to provide for a Policyowners' Protection Fund, established by the MAS. This fund covers policyholders whose insurance com-panies have become bankrupt. A fee, not to exceed 1 percent of the annual premium income of an insurer, may be imposed by the MAS on registered insurers to maintain the fund, which will meet the full amount of claims payable for compulsory insurance policies and 90 percent of total claims payable for life policies. Insurers are also required to maintain a solvency margin on their entire business. Insurance regulations were again amended in November 1997, raising the minimum paid-up share capital requirements for direct insurers and reinsurers from S$5 million and S$10 million, respectively, to S$25 million for both types of insurers. Finally, Singapore has an Insurance Ombudsman Committee to handle complaints or disputes of individual policy holders.

Foreign Participation

Foreign financial institutions are subject to some restrictions. Foreign banks and finance and insurance companies seeking to set up offices or branches require MAS approval. Although 22 foreign banks have full banking licenses, they are not permitted to operate ATMs beyond their banking premises or open additional branches. Being barred from the ATM network hinders foreign banks' ability to compete in the equity market, since 95 percent of applications for Initial Public Offerings are made at an ATM.

Among the fully licensed foreign banks, only Citibank, Hongkong Bank, Malaysian Bank, and Standard Chartered Bank are active in retail banking. These four and Chase Manhattan Bank are the only foreign banks operating in the highly competitive credit card business.

The MAS controls the level of foreign ownership of local banks through a number of legislative restrictions. For example, it controls the takeover of a local bank in which an individual acquires 20 percent of the bank's shares, as well as any arrangement that enables foreigners to determine a domestic bank's policy.

Foreign companies are allowed to publicly list in Singapore, but those applying for listing on the SES must comply with different requirements. They must already be listed on their home exchange; they must have net tangible assets of at least S$50 million; they must enjoy a cumulative pretax income of at least S$50 million for the preceding three years or a minimum of S$20 million for any one of those three years; and they must have a minimum of 2,000 shareholders.

Portfolio investment by foreigners is strongly encouraged by the government; nonresidents are not restricted in the purchase or sale of stocks, bonds, or other capital or money market instruments.

Remaining Obstacles

Singapore's dual financial system includes world-class competitive institutions for offshore transactions, while the domestic business is fairly heavily regulated. Offshore banks are not permitted to offer key services in Singapore dollars, access to electronic banking services is restricted (FLG 1997), and new onshore foreign bank licenses are not permitted. Foreign entry into the insurance sector is difficult, although the government agreed to allow foreign companies to have management control—with 49 percent ownership—of domestic insurance firms in the 1997 WTO financial services agreement.

While Singapore excels as a base for international financial activity, domestic financial intermediation continues to be costly, and the positioning of Singapore banks in the broader international competitive environment is uncertain (Walter 1993). Recognizing these challenges, the government commissioned a study on the competitiveness of the financial services sector that was submitted to parliament in late February 1998. The government accepted nearly all of the study's recommendations covering fund management, equities markets, and insurance. Key reforms include: removing fixed rate brokerage commissions within three years; streamlining approval procedures for IPOs; initiatives to promote the growth of the captive insurance market; and plans to list more regional equity and interest rate products and derivatives on the SIMEX to strengthen Singapore's position as an international financial center (MAS 1998a). Domestic banking reform and liberalization were absent from both the study and ensuing financial reforms. This was recognized by parliament as an area for further review, given the trend toward greater international competition in banking (MAS 1998b).

References

Bank for International Settlements (BIS). 1997. *67th Annual Report*. Basle: Bank for International Settlements.

Financial Leaders Group (FLG). 1997. *Barriers to Trade in Financial Services: Case Studies*. London: Barclays Place.

Goldstein, Morris, and Philip Turner. 1996. *Banking Crises in Emerging Economies: Origins and Policy Options*. BIS Economic Papers No. 46. Basle: Monetary and Economic Department, Bank for International Settlements (October).

Monetary Authority of Singapore (MAS). 1998a. Government's Response to Recommendation by CSC Finance and Banking Sub-Committee. (http://www.mas.gov.sg/cyber/release2-c.html).

Monetary Authority of Singapore (MAS). 1998b. Answer to Parliamentary Question on: Policy towards the Domestic Banking Sector. (http://www.mas.gov.sg/cyber/parliament7-c.html).

Walter, Ingo. 1993. *High Performance Financial Systems: Blueprint for Development.* Singapore: Institute of Southeast Asian Studies.

Taiwan

Introduction

The regulation and structure of the financial sector in Taiwan reflects the evolution of the country's overall economic development policy. Prior to the mid-1980s, the Taiwanese government's goal was to industrialize and transform the basis of the economic structure from subsistence agriculture to industry. Mercantilist use of import substitution to build up heavy industries supported industrial development. Monetary and fiscal policy were also oriented to these goals, and, as a result of these policies, the financial system was highly repressed. Foreign direct investment was subjected to close scrutiny and strictly controlled. The government kept interest rates artificially low, implemented strict foreign exchange controls, maintained a fixed exchange rate, and directed credit with the goal of promoting the rapid growth of the domestic economy. By the mid-1980s, Taiwan had become a successful exporter and had built up a substantial current account surplus and foreign exchange reserves. But the high degree of government intervention had distorted the economy and, in particular, the financial sector.

Financial repression led to a significant share of financial sector activity in the informal market and, as a result, the formal intermediated market and securities market were both underdeveloped. The regulatory system was not sufficiently developed to provide a basis from which authorities could adequately monitor or enforce laws against illicit financial sector activity. This was the context for major policy changes in the mid-1980s.

Martial law was lifted in 1987. In response to foreign pressure, capital controls were lifted that year, the undervalued exchange rate was freed up, and direct foreign investment reviews were eased. Trade policy was liberalized and tariff and nontariff barriers were reduced.[1] The 1989 New Banking Law reforms were aimed at strengthening regulatory controls over potentially destabilizing, unmonitored financial sector activity and helping banks become more competitive vis-à-vis the informal financial sector. Major reforms included steps toward privatizing commercial banks, removing controls on interest rates, and developing laws to punish those engaged in illegal financial activities (Yang 1994, 293).

In 1995, with a new emphasis on improving Taiwan's overall international competitiveness, the government launched the Asia Pacific Regional Operations Center (APROC) Plan. This plan was designed to liberalize the flow of goods, services, people, capital, and information in order to promote Taiwan as a hub in the global trading system. One of APROC's goals is to make Taiwan a regional financial center.

Despite these efforts to begin liberalizing the financial sector, many limitations in the regulatory environment of financial institutions can still be explained by Taiwan's growth and stability promotion objectives. Indeed, stability is so important to government policy that considerable efficiency has been traded off to achieve it. Monetary policy has traditionally been conducted with considerable prudence. Interest rate policy has been seen as an effective instrument for fighting inflation. However, interest rates have also been strictly controlled by the Central Bank of China (CBC), often below market-clearing rates, in order to stimulate investment (Shea 1994, 255).

Foreign exchange policy has also been one of strict control. At various times, dual and multiple exchange rate systems have been adopted, the rationale being to alleviate a severe shortage of foreign exchange. In 1978, a floating exchange rate system was adopted in order to make the economy less vulnerable to external disturbances, particularly those resulting from huge trade surpluses. The related accumulation of net foreign assets contributed to rapid growth of the money supply in the 1980s as the authorities chose to control exchange rate movements, in order to promote exports, rather than inflationary pressure. These very tight restrictions on exchange rate fluctuations were eliminated in 1989; all trade-related transactions involving foreign exchange are now unrestricted. Nontrade-related transactions are, however, subject to restrictions on inward remittances by individuals, outward remittances by companies and individuals, and prior approval from the CBC for large remittances. Although access to foreign exchange has been significantly relaxed since

---

1. Subsequently, the New Taiwan Dollar (NTD) appreciated substantially, exposing distortions in the real sector. Small businesses adjusted to the related loss of competitiveness by investing and relocating abroad.

1989, the exchange rate remains virtually fixed through central bank intervention.

Regulatory Framework

The two main regulatory agencies are the Ministry of Finance (MOF), which carries out administrative regulation of banking institutions, and the CBC. Insurance companies are regulated by the Insurance Department and securities firms by the Securities and Exchange Commission (SEC), both of which are divisions of the MOF. The MOF also governs the Central Deposit Insurance Corporation (CDIC), which administers deposit insurance.

The CBC carries out both regulatory and central banking functions. As a regulator, its main task is to regulate foreign exchange under the Statute for Administration of Foreign Exchange (SAFE). It also regulates and audits banks and financial institutions. The CBC's responsibilities to manage the money supply and the allocation of credit include such tasks as issuing currency, being a fiscal agent, and controlling the money supply in two ways: by acting through government-owned banks and by manipulating deposits in the postal savings system. The CBC, for example, redeposits funds accumulated in the postal savings system into the CBC or into four specialized funds.

The laws that aid the MOF and CBC in their regulatory function include the Securities and Exchange Law, enacted in 1988 (to update regulations established in 1968); the 1989 reform of the Banking Law, including reform of the Bureau of Monetary Affairs in the MOF; the 1992 reform of the Insurance Law, by which the Insurance Department in the MOF allowed private groups to set up insurance companies; the Foreign Futures Trading Law, enacted in 1992; the Futures Reform of 1993; and the Fair Trade Law, enacted in 1991 and made effective in 1992.

Financial Institutions

Over the past two decades, a large majority of financial assets in Taiwan has been lodged in banks (see table B.8), although this dominance began to decline in 1995 as the share of assets held by investment and trust companies and by insurance companies increased. These rising shares represent successful competition from nonbank financial institutions, and the government encourages the development of such institutions in order to reduce the oligopolistic behavior of banks. Direct finance continues to represent a negligible share of total financial assets.

**Table B.8 Taiwan: Assets of financial institutions: 1970,
1980, and 1990** (percentages)

Institution	1970	1980	1990
Full-service banks	80.2	64.5	53.3
Foreign banks	0.9	5.5	2.9
Small business banks	3.1	3.7	7.3
Credit cooperatives	7.8	6.8	9.2
Credit departments	5.2	5.0	6.8
Investment and trust companies	1.3	4.3	4.3
Postal savings	0.8	8.3	11.7
Insurance	0.9	1.8	4.4

Source: Shea 1994, 285.

Financial Intermediaries

The majority of financial assets in Taiwan continue to be held by government-controlled banks, which dominate the financial system; three
state-owned banks represent 60 percent of Taiwan's total banking business (Liu 1996, 12a). These banks have been constrained by a variety of
portfolio restrictions and regulations. For example, loan officers have
been held responsible for bad loans; not surprisingly, bank behavior has
therefore tended to be bureaucratic rather than entrepreneurial. But despite criticisms of excessive bureaucracy, the banking system has done
little damage to the economy, thanks to the dedication of public-sector
institutions and the implementation of macroeconomic policy to promote rapid economic growth. The number of privately owned banks is
increasing, partly because of privatization policies and partly because of
approvals for the establishment of new banks since 1991. Credit policies,
nevertheless, are extremely conservative, and some banks, such as the
medium-business banks, are limited in both their geographic scope and
the scope of services they are permitted to provide.

A significant component of the Taiwanese financial system is its large
informal sector, where transactions include deposits with firms, loans
against post-dated checks, installment credit, leasing, mutual savings and
loans, mutual credit, and secured and unsecured borrowing and lending
(Shea 1994, 234). Between 1964 and 1990, the informal system accounted
for 24 percent of domestic financing in the business sector, roughly half
the amount of financing done by formal financial institutions (Shea 1994,
235). Analysis of the curb market share of private enterprise financing
shows a close relationship to developments in the formal financial system. The curb market share declined from 1964 to 1973 as the formal

financial system was being developed; however, interest rate controls during a period of high inflation resulted in an increase in the share of financial transactions conducted through the curb market from 1975 to 1980. When interest rates were decontrolled in 1980, the curb market share dropped again, only to resurge during the 1985-86 recession and the continued financial market intervention by the authorities.

In the formal sector, full-service domestic banks account for the greatest, although declining, share of financial assets. Full-service domestic banks include commercial banks and specialized banks; there are no savings banks, nor are there investment banks per se in Taiwan. Investment banking functions are performed by commercial and specialized banks, as well as by investment and trust companies.[2] With full-service banks engaging in a variety of financial services, ranging from operating savings departments to making longer-term credit available,[3] universal banking is common (Shea 1995, 110-11). Other domestic banks focus on areas such as short-term credit supply and export financing. Most lending is collateral based, suggesting that credit analysis techniques are still underdeveloped.

Prior to 1991, there were six specialized banks and ten commercial banks in Taiwan, with six of the commercial banks owned by the government. The number of bank licenses had been frozen at that level since the late 1970s and the number of branch licenses strictly controlled by the government. From 1991 to 1993, 17 additional bank licenses were issued. Restrictions on branching were also reduced and the number of branches grew by over 25 percent during this same time period. At the end of 1993, however, government-owned banks still represented more than 25 percent of all bank branches and 80 percent of full-service bank assets.

Taiwan also has a number of medium- and small-business banks that developed from privately owned mutual savings and loan companies in the late 1970s. These banks are required by the Banking Law of 1975 to specialize in extending medium- and long-term credit to small- and medium-sized enterprises. The banks are restricted in geographic scope and do not compete with one another.

Cooperatives accept deposits from and grant loans to members. They are separately examined and supervised by the Cooperative Bank, a government-owned institution that also acts as the central bank for cooperatives. At the end of 1993, cooperatives accounted for one-third of all bank branches but held only 16 percent of total bank assets. A ban

---

2. Investment and trust companies deal only in securitized financial products and are addressed under "Direct Finance."

3. Specialized banks are the predominant source of domestic long-term credit. While they are similar to development banks in that they channel funds to priority sectors of the economy, they have both private- and public-sector ownership.

on setting up new credit cooperatives was lifted that year, but the growth of cooperatives has generally been constrained by strict regulations limiting their lending activities to individual members, as opposed to local small-scale enterprises, and prohibiting them from engaging in foreign exchange and trust activities.

Other financial institutions include the postal savings system and insurance companies. The postal savings system was set up by the Japanese; it accepts savings deposits and conducts life insurance business through the post office network. Although these units do not make loans, they have been effective in mobilizing savings. Most deposits are redeposited in four government-owned specialized banks. This redeposit ratio has, since 1984, been an instrument used by the CBC to control the money supply and to ration credit.

Insurance companies have traditionally played a limited role in Taiwan's financial system, as cultural barriers and government provision of some forms of insurance limited the growth of the insurance market. Since the mid-1980s, however, such institutions have played an increasingly prominent role. In the late 1980s, the government began to issue new licenses in the nonlife insurance market, and in 1993 the first domestic life insurance license in 31 years was issued (Takahashi 1994, 95). Reserve funds are used for loans, real estate, and securities investments, although the government controls the proportion of funds that may be placed in any type of investment. Pension funds must be placed with a government-owned trust company.

Direct Finance

The Taiwan Stock Exchange (TSE) began operating in 1961. A short-term bills market was established in 1976, primarily to assist smaller firms, which found accessing loans from banks difficult, in raising funds (Shih 1996, 128). Other available money market instruments include treasury bills, bankers' acceptances, commercial paper, and negotiable CDs. Despite the availability of money market instruments, they have not become a significant source of debt. Moreover, strict controls on domestic stock market activity and the exclusion of foreign investment in the market resulted in negligible trading on the TSE during its first 20 years of operation.

In 1981, the Securities and Exchange Commission (SEC), which regulates all aspects of issuing and trading securities, was transferred from the Ministry of Economic Affairs to the Ministry of Finance. Reform of the capital market began in 1982 with a three-stage plan to internationalize Taiwan's securities market. The first step involved setting up mutual fund management companies to manage foreign-invested Taiwanese mutual funds. The second phase, implemented in 1991, allowed qualified foreign institutional investors to invest in publicly listed stocks; foreigners are limited to a certain quota. The third phase, implemented in early 1996, allows general foreign investors (GFI) to invest, again up to a certain limit. The degree of internationalization of Taiwan's capital market is limited by the continued existence of foreign exchange controls.

As authorities began to open the market to foreign capital, they also began to remove impediments to stock market activity for domestic capital and firms. Until 1980, there were only eight investment and trust companies in Taiwan and no other firms specializing in securities trans-actions.[4] A securities finance company was set up that year to help increase market liquidity by providing loans for securities transactions (Shea 1994, 230). In the mid-1980s, the stock exchange was computerized and the permitted daily fluctuation of stock prices was increased to 7 percent of the share price.[5] Tax incentives were used to encourage companies to raise funds on the equity market. In 1988, the Securities Exchange Law (SEL) was amended, removing restrictions on the total number of securities firm licenses and creating the Integrated Securities Firm company structure, under which licensed firms are permitted to underwrite, deal, and broker securities. New bills finance companies and securities finance companies were not permitted to enter the market until 1994.

With the exchange rate still effectively controlled until 1989 and Taiwan running a large trade surplus, the country attracted large capital inflows, which resulted in a boom in equities investment in the mid- to late 1980s. The TSE index did not break 1,000 until 1986, but by 1990 it had peaked at 12,495. When the bubble burst, the stock index fell by 80 percent, to 2,560, in less than a year (Shea 1994, 232). The stock market had, however, considerably developed during the late 1980s and continued to grow after stock prices fell back to more sustainable levels.

As of May 1996, with 362 companies listed on the main exchange and an over-the-counter market for smaller firms, total market capitalization was US$210 billion and 226 securities brokers and 54 securities dealers were in operation.[6] Morgan Stanley recently included Taiwan's share prices in its Emerging Market Free Index. Although the equity market has become significantly deeper over the last 15 years, stifled competition in the securities industry has left a legacy on investment patterns. More than 90 percent of all share transactions are still conducted by individual

---

4. The China Development Corporation, a government-owned investment and trust company, was Taiwan's first institution of this kind. Market opening occurred in 1971-72 to increase long term loans, and seven new institutions were permitted at that time.

5. Stock prices are still limited to fluctuating by no more than 7 percent per day.

6. Thus, despite the fact that the number of firms listed on the TSE grew by over one-third from 1992 to 1996, the ratio of listed companies to securities firms is still less than 1.5:1.

investors, leading to high turnover rates and speculative behavior in the market (Shih 1996, 131).

The bond market had historically been far less developed than the equity market, in large measure because of the low level of government bond issues and strict regulation on the bond issue of private companies. The number of government bond issues is small, and the combination of the transactions tax on corporate bonds and the lack of credit rating agencies to help accurately price corporate debt have contributed to the underdevelopment of the corporate bond markets. Thus in 1995, corporate and government bonds together accounted for only 9 percent of the capital market. As banks are allowed to use government bonds and bonds issued by government enterprises to satisfy their reserve requirements, most of these instruments (some estimate as much as 90 percent of the market) are held by banks and are not traded. As a result, the secondary market is seriously underdeveloped.

As part of Taiwan's plan to become a regional financial center, it has recently introduced new money market instruments that are likely to help deepen the bond market. Taiwan introduced Asian Development Bank bonds, denominated in US dollars, yen, and NTD. By the end of 1996, the total value of trading in these bonds, in addition to Taiwanese government and corporate debt, was more than twice the value of trading in the equity market. Authorities are now planning to set up Taiwan's first futures exchange.

Prudential Regulation

Poor management, concentration of credit, and lack of transparency in investments have been responsible for problems in Taiwan's financial sector from the 1960s to the present (Shea 1995, 104). Since the mid-1980s, the government has gradually improved prudential controls in an attempt to try to prevent the types of financial crises that have affected the country's financial system in the past.

In 1985, the government created the Central Deposit Insurance Corporation (CDIC). Membership in the CDIC is voluntary and so far only 35 percent of financial institutions have opted to use the deposit insurance system. Government-owned banks, in particular, tend not to contribute to the CDIC; the government considers contribution to the fund a waste of money since the government is responsible for the liabilities of government-owned banks. Concerns about moral hazard continue to be an issue in the financial sector.

Other problems, such as those associated with illegal transactions and concentration of credit, were addressed when the New Banking Law was implemented in 1989. This law requires banks to meet the BIS' recommended 8 percent risk-weighted capital-asset ratio and limits individual and group ownership of banks to 5 percent and 15 percent, respectively. Minimum capital requirements for new bank branches were subsequently set at NT$10 billion. The New Banking Law was also intended to help establish rules that would allow the government to prosecute those conducting illegal financial activities, but lack of qualified personnel to evaluate and monitor banking activity continues to hinder the effective enforcement of financial sector laws.

In early September 1997, the first credit agency started operating. Laws governing the accuracy of financial statements were also recently strengthened to allow the government to prosecute accountants issuing false reports. Both actions are likely to increase transparency and discipline in the banking and securities markets.

Foreign Participation

Foreign commercial banks play a small role in Taiwan's financial markets, controlling an estimated 3 percent of total assets in the banking system. Although foreign banks were allowed to enter the market as early as 1964, they were subject to strict numerical and geographical limits until the mid-1980s. Operational restrictions on foreign banks have been eased in the last ten years; foreign bank branches can now locate outside of Taipei and handle foreign exchange transactions, extend loans to firms and individuals, and engage in the trust business (Shea 1994, 227). By 1996, 62 branches of 39 foreign banks had been established in Taiwan.

Remaining restrictions on the activities of foreign banks hinder the banks' ability to expand into some areas of the market. For example, foreign banks are still limited to three branches. Until 1985, they were not permitted to accept local currency savings deposits, and the aggregate size of NT dollar deposits continues to be limited. Trade finance is also restricted, as are guarantees of commercial paper. Lending limits, including those for total foreign currency credit extended to a single customer, still exist. Hence, foreign bank participation in the Taiwanese economy tends to be limited to corporate lending, private banking, and advisory work.

Although Taiwan began to open its capital market to foreign investors in the early 1980s, the degree of internationalization continues to be constrained by foreign exchange controls and restrictions on portfolio investment. It is planned that foreign exchange controls will be lifted by the end of 2000, subject to emergency powers held by the Central Bank of China. Qualified foreign institutional investors (QFIIs) and individual investors are limited to US$600 million and $5 million in investment, respectively. Individual foreign investors are not allowed to acquire more than 10 percent of shares in a company and total foreign investment may not exceed 25 percent of shares.

The securities market has become considerably more accessible to foreign securities firms in the last two years. In 1995, foreign securities firms were allowed to set up branches to engage in local business, and by the end of that year, seven firms had branch offices in Taiwan (Liu 1996, 9A). A year later, authorities abolished foreign ownership limits on investing in domestic securities investment and trust companies. Although foreign securities firms have only recently been allowed to enter the market, they did have some limited opportunities before then to develop a presence in the market. Many had already established relations with publicly listed companies through the GDR and convertible bond projects, prior to entering the market through a branch office (Liu 1996, 9A). Foreign firms have also had a notable impact on the secondary market because they effectively control QFII-GFI trading, which has become one of the benchmarks for market movement.

In January 1993, domestic investors were permitted to purchase futures traded on international exchanges. The purpose of this step was to develop a domestic futures trading capability. Foreign companies listed on the New York, Tokyo, and London Stock Exchanges are also permitted to issue shares in the form of depository receipts.

Remaining Obstacles

The remaining obstacles to deregulation and market opening in Taiwan include uncertainty as to whether there will, in fact, be complete liberalization of foreign exchange controls and the financial system by 2000, as outlined in the APROC plan. To pave the way for WTO accession, Taiwan concluded a bilateral market opening agreement with the United States in early 1998 that addressed market access in the financial sector. In the agreement, Taiwan agreed to provide "substantially full market access and national treatment, in the full range of financial services" (US Trade Representative, The United States and Taiwan Conclude Comprehensive Market Access Agreement, Press Release, 20 February 1998, 3). It is not yet clear, however, how much foreign participation would be permitted under a WTO financial services offer from Taiwan. Regardless, other barriers to an efficient and sound financial sector continue to exist in Taiwan. The financial system continues to be heavily regulated and staunchly defended by the Central Bank of China. Financial sector policies remain subordinated to industrial policy goals, despite Taiwan's ambitions to become a regional hub. Regulatory emphasis tends to focus on assets, with insufficient emphasis on market liquidity considerations. There is also a persistent tendency to engage in related-party transactions, which implies that the prudential supervisory infrastructure needs to be developed and given credible enforcement powers. The legal system lacks personnel with deep knowledge of financial law and of how to administer insolvency legislation. Finally, regulators must be consulted before judicial review (Liu 1996).

References

Liu, Lawrence S. 1996. The Law and Political Economy of Regulating Capital Markets and Financial Services in the Republic of China on Taiwan. Paper presented at the Conference on Regulation of Capital Markets and Financial Services in the Pacific Rim, Georgetown University Law Center, Washington (11-13 November).

Shea, Jia-dong. 1994. Taiwan: Development and Structural Change of the Financial System. In *The Financial Development of Japan, Korea, and Taiwan*, ed. by Hugh T. Patrick and Yung Chul Park. New York: Oxford University Press.

Shea, Jia-dong. 1995. Financial Sector Development and Policies in Taipei, China. In *Financial Sector Development in Asia: Country Studies*, ed. by Shahid N. Zahid. Hong Kong: Oxford University Press for Asian Development Bank.

Shih, Yen Chrystal. 1996. The Changing Financial System in Taiwan. In *Changing Financial Systems in Small Open Economies*. Policy Papers No. 1. Basle: Bank for International Settlements, Monetary and Economic Department.

Takahashi, Yuichi. 1994. *Financial Sector Reform in the Asia Pacific Countries*. Photocopy.

Yang, Ya-Hwei. 1994. Taiwan: Development and Structural Change of the Banking System. In *The Financial Development of Japan, Korea, and Taiwan*, ed. by Hugh T. Patrick and Yung Chul Park. New York: Oxford University Press.

Thailand

Introduction

Thailand began to liberalize its financial markets in the early 1990s to support the market-oriented, export-led development policy that it had initiated ten years earlier. Previous development policies, such as infrastructure development and agricultural production diversification in the 1960s and import substitution in the 1970s, had required little change in the financial sector for their support.

With the shift to a more outward-oriented economic policy, the fixed exchange rate system vis-à-vis the US dollar was replaced in 1978 by a fixed rate, announced daily, based on a basket of currencies of major trading partners.[1] Nonetheless, apparent attempts to stabilize the baht-US dollar exchange rate in the early 1980s led to overvaluation of the baht. Speculation against the baht and an appreciating US dollar resulted in major devaluations of the baht against the US dollar, by 8.7 percent in 1981 and by 15 percent in 1984, when fluctuations of major currencies became the reference point in the daily fixing scheme.

Despite attempts to link the baht to a currency basket, close links to the US dollar were maintained. This caused an export boom in the 1980s and early 1990s, when the baht was undervalued because of the weak US dollar. The recent surge of the US dollar and the consequent overvaluation of the baht caused another speculative attack on the baht in

---

1. These include the US dollar, the deutsche mark, the pound sterling, the Japanese yen, the Malaysian ringgit, and the Singapore and Hong Kong dollars.

early 1997. It was finally devalued on 2 June 1997, and subsequently allowed to float but the prolonged defense of the baht had caused foreign exchange reserves to drop. The eventual depreciation resulted in huge exchange rate losses for domestic financial and nonfinancial companies. Nonperforming loans as a percentage of total loans were already high, averaging 7.6 percent in 1994-95 and reaching over 12 percent in 1996. With external debt at over 40 percent of GDP, the depreciation of the baht culminated in a banking crisis. On 5 August 1997 Thailand agreed to an IMF rescue package of US$17.2 billion.

The government also made some early attempts to reform interest rates. After the second oil price shock, the ceiling on lending rates for different financial institutions was raised from 15 percent to a level deemed appropriate by the Ministry of Finance. The resulting increased volatility in interest rates, coupled with increased exchange rate volatility and the concurrent world recession, severely affected many Thai financial institutions. Excessive exchange rate speculation, mismanagement, fraud, and bad loans brought many of them to the brink of ruin. The government intervened with the "Lifeboat Scheme" to restore public confidence. Under this scheme, the government bailed out or nationalized several financial institutions facing fiscal ruin, forced others to merge, or withdrew their licenses. It also founded the Financial Institutions Development Fund to reconstruct and develop the financial institutions system.[2] Hence, in the mid-1980s, priority was given to economic and financial stability rather than to financial reform.

Once the financial system was stabilized, the government embarked on its first three-year plan of financial liberalization (1990-92). The objective was to mobilize savings for future economic development, to increase the competitiveness of financial institutions, to encourage the development of new financial instruments and services, and to become a regional financial center. Achieving these objectives would in turn reduce the need for intervention by the monetary authorities.

Specifically, the reform package consisted of four components. The first emphasized the market mechanism: interest rates were deregulated (1989, 1990, 1992); controls on foreign exchange (FOREX) transactions were relaxed (1990, 1991, 1992); and financial liberalization was encouraged by widening the scope of business opportunities for financial institutions (1991, 1992). The second component focused on prudential regulation, including measures such as the development of a supervisory system, monitoring procedures, and an information system; provision of training for bank examiners; and adjustment of certain requirements like the risk-weighted capital asset ratio in line with the Bank for International Settle-

---

2. To fund the Financial Institutions Development Fund, each financial institution must contribute to the Fund up to 0.5 percent of deposits, borrowings, or funds received from the public. The Bank of Thailand may allocate some of its reserves as well.

ment (BIS) guidelines. The third component of the reforms dealt with financial innovation in the primary and secondary capital markets and included the establishment of a credit rating agency. The fourth component aimed at reforming the interbank clearing system and establishing second-note printing works.

The second three-year plan (1993-95) largely supported and built on the reforms of the first plan: deregulation and financial development continued, supervision improved, and the payment system further developed. The government also pursued its efforts to develop into a regional financial center by establishing the Bangkok International Banking Facility (BIBF) in 1993 by which banks were issued licenses to attract foreign funds subject to preferred rates of taxation.

Reforms planned for Thailand's 1997 IMF economic program further advance the goal of financial reform and liberalization. Elements of the program include: the adoption of international loan classification and provisioning standards, the introduction of a deposit insurance system, the implementation of new bankruptcy laws, and the commitment to remove restrictions on foreign equity ownership in banks and finance companies for the next 10 years. The latter reforms were subsequently bound in the WTO financial services agreement. Thailand's WTO offer and IMF economic program include the provision that, although foreign equity ownership will be capped at 49 percent after 10 years, investments in the banking and financial services sector will be permanently grandfathered.

Regulatory Framework

The Bank of Thailand (BOT) and the Ministry of Finance (MOF) are responsible for conducting monetary policy in Thailand. The MOF is responsible for monetary affairs, while monetary management is delegated to the BOT. The BOT, which enjoys a high degree of autonomy from other government agencies, formulates and conducts monetary policy with the objective of ensuring the stability of the economic and financial system. The Bank also acts as a fiscal agent in providing development finance.

As the sole agent in charge of exchange rate policy, the BOT is responsible for administering Exchange Equalization Funds. The BOT also administers the Commercial Banking Act, which was passed in 1962 and revised in 1979, 1985, and 1992. Under this act, the BOT supervises commercial banks and is authorized to deal with troubled financial institutions. The third element in the BOT's legislative framework is the Act on the Undertaking of Finance Business, Securities Business, and Credit Foncier Business, which was passed in 1979 and amended in 1983, 1985, and 1992. Under this act, the BOT regulates and supervises finance companies, securities institutions (until 1992), and credit foncier companies.

Table B.9   Thailand: Assets of financial institutions
(percentages)

Financial Institution	1983	1989	1992
Commercial banks	69.6	69.55	68.02
Finance companies	13.9	13.93	18.05
Life insurance	1.6	1.86	1.80
Agricultural cooperatives	1.3	0.88	0.48
Savings cooperatives	1.0	1.93	2.02
Pawn shops	0.5	0.36	0.25
Credit foncier companies	0.7	0.20	0.17
Government Savings Bank	5.9	6.22	4.06
Government Housing Bank	1.4	1.37	1.53
Other	3.9	3.70	3.62

Sources: Vichyanond 1995, 307, and author's calculations.

In conjunction with the 1997 IMF rescue package, Thailand agreed to establish a separate regulatory and supervisory agency, the Financial Restructuring Agency (FRA), to manage the liquidation of the 58 suspended finance companies. The FRA was also charged with guaranteeing the interest and principal of the finance company's depositors and creditors. The Asset Management Company (AMC) was created by the government to assist in the process and is charged with appropriating, managing, and selling bad debt held by the finance companies.

The Securities and Exchange Commission (SEC), established in 1992, supervises securities companies. It is an independent regulatory body made up of both independent members and members drawn from the MOF and the BOT.

The MOF is responsible for the Government Housing Bank, the Government Savings Bank, the Industrial Finance Corporation of Thailand (IFCT), and the Bank for Agriculture and Agricultural Cooperatives (BAAC). The MOF owns all or part of these four institutions.

The regulatory framework is further dispersed. The Ministry of Commerce regulates life insurance companies under the Life Insurance Act of 1967, the Ministry of Agriculture and Cooperatives regulates and supervises agricultural cooperatives and savings cooperatives under the Cooperative Act of 1968, and the Ministry of Industry is responsible for industrial promotion and state industrial finance.

Financial Institutions

Over the past two decades, commercial banks have consistently held just under 70 percent of financial assets in Thailand (see table B.9). The share of other banking institutions has almost halved in that time. Finance companies, the most dominant of the nonbank financial institutions, significantly expanded their market share of financial assets over this time period. The capital market remains underdeveloped; in 1992, the outstanding value of stocks and bonds was only 10 percent of financial intermediaries' outstanding credit (Vichyanond 1995, 309). In other words, companies in Thailand rely more on intermediation than on securitization to raise capital.

Financial Intermediaries

Until late 1997, at least 75 percent of shareholders and directors had to be Thai nationals for a bank to qualify as domestic. Fifteen of the 29 commercial banks[3] were domestic banks, and the government retained ownership interest in 10 of them. Following the Asian currency crisis, Thailand agreed to relax restrictions regarding the nationality of bank directors as well as ceilings on foreign equity ownership in domestic banks. At the time of this writing, a number of international mergers and acquisitions with Thai banks are pending.

Market concentration in the banking sector is very high. In 1993, the three largest domestic banks accounted for 50 percent of all banking system assets, while the five smallest domestic banks held only 6 percent, a share similar to that of foreign banks (Vichyanond 1995, 304).

Thai banks no longer face any legal restrictions in extending their branch networks. Prior to 1993, though, they had to place a minimum of 16 percent of outstanding deposits in government bonds in order to be eligible for a branch network. This was intended to help the government finance its budget deficit. After 1992, however, there was no issue of government bonds since the budget was in surplus, and so the 16 percent requirement was gradually lowered until it was abolished in 1993.

For a bank to open a branch in a suburban district, it had to commit at least 60 percent of the branch's deposits in credits to community clients. In 1991, this requirement was changed so that all the bank's branches in the region collectively (rather than each branch individually) extend at least 60 percent of their deposits to community clients. In rural districts, one-third of community credits must be agriculture-related. If these community targets cannot be met, the branch must deposit the residual with the Bank of Thailand.

There are no other explicit compulsory credit requirements, although the BOT has formally requested collaborative efforts in helping to develop certain sectors of the economy. Beginning in 1975, banks were asked to allocate at least 5 percent of their deposits as credits to the

---

3. A commercial bank must be a limited company licensed by the MOF.

agricultural sector. This level was subsequently increased until, by 1987, a minimum of 14 percent of deposits was to be extended to agriculture and 6 percent to small and medium enterprises (SMEs). The more credits a bank extended to these priority sectors the more privileges, such as access to rediscount windows, it could obtain from the BOT.

No new banks entered the banking sector from 1978-98.[4] Under the Lifeboat Scheme, the government either nationalized or injected capital into ailing banks so that the total number of banks has remained constant. This allowed banks to reap oligopoly profits when interest rates and foreign exchange transactions were decontrolled.

In 1989, the Bank of Thailand lifted the ceiling on term deposits with maturities greater than 12 months; the following year, it removed ceilings on all term deposits; and in 1992, controls on lending rates were abolished. The ceiling on mortgage rates, though, was fixed at commercial banks' minimum lending rate for low-income individuals holding a mortgage prior to June 1992. Given the oligopolistic structure of the industry, formalized in the Thai Bankers' Association, these interest rate reforms allowed the interest rate spread of commercial banks to increase from 3 percent in 1988 to 4 percent in 1992 (Vichyanond 1995, 369). In effect, the Thai Bankers' Association now sets commercial bank interest rates.

All commercial banks are allowed to engage in foreign exchange transactions. The requirement of BOT approval to purchase foreign exchange was dropped in 1990, and in 1991 all foreign exchange transactions for current account purposes were decontrolled. Since 1992, Thai nationals and companies have been allowed to hold foreign currency accounts, and nonresidents have been permitted to open baht accounts.

To facilitate and reduce the cost of foreign borrowing, the monetary authorities created the Bangkok International Banking Facility (BIBF). All domestic commercial banks and most foreign banks were granted licenses to operate offshore banking units under the BIBF. These licenses permit the acceptance of deposits in foreign currencies, lending in foreign currencies to residents and nonresidents, and foreign exchange transactions across foreign currencies. BIBF's aim was to encourage the inflow of foreign funds in order to finance the current account deficit and to create a link to other financial systems in the region. It was also intended to help promote Thailand as a regional financial center. The BIBF's major competitors are the offshore markets in Singapore and Hong Kong.

---

4. In January 1998 the Ministry of Finance (MOF) approved one new commercial bank license. The MOF will be the major shareholder in the new bank, which will play a central role in bidding for assets put to auction from the 58 finance companies that were closed in the wake of the Asian currency crisis. The new bank, capitalized by loans from the World Bank and Asian Development Bank, will be listed on the Stock Exchange and subject to the rules and regulations governing publicly listed companies.

In 1992, internal liberalization allowed commercial banks to conduct more business related to financial instruments, such as financial consulting; debt instrument and securities issuing, underwriting, and trading; managing personal funds; and acting as trustees for mutual funds.[5] These fee-based activities compensate commercial banks for the loss in business they face as the economy moves from intermediation to securitization.

In addition to the commercial banks, there are three government banking institutions. The purpose of the Government Savings Bank, with its many branches, is to mobilize small savings. Until 1989, a large portion of its funds were held in government securities. Since then the bank has diversified its credit to state-owned and private enterprises. Because it operates subject to the restrictions of the (outdated) Government Savings Bank Act of 1946, the bank has been able to capture only a declining portion of deposits.

The Bank for Agriculture and Agricultural Cooperatives (BAAC), founded in 1966 and majority-owned (99 percent) by the MOF, provides credits for farmers and agricultural cooperatives at low interest rates. It obtains its resources from commercial banks that lend to the BAAC in order to fulfill their compulsory rural lending requirement. At times, the Bank of Thailand provides additional credit facilities. Besides problems similar to those of the Government Savings Bank, the BAAC's main constraint is a continuously inadequate inflow of funds.

The Government Housing Bank, entirely government-owned and supervised by the MOF, was established in 1953 to assist people of moderate income in purchasing their own houses. Deposits constitute most of its funds, which tend to be insufficient because the bank does not have many branches. Regulations regarding the use of the bank's funds introduce rigidities into its fund management, further restricting its competitive edge. Of late, it has faced increasing competition from commercial banks that are diversifying into the housing credit business.

The nonbank financial institutions comprise finance companies, credit foncier companies,[6] insurance companies, pawn shops,[7] the IFCT, and the Small Industry Finance Corporation of Thailand (SIFCT).[8] There are no investment companies.

---

5. Commercial banks are permitted to hold up to 25 percent of new mutual funds that were established in 1992.

6. Credit foncier companies are similar to finance companies, except that they specialize in immobile properties and issue medium-term notes. At the end of 1993, there were 16 credit foncier companies in Thailand (US Treasury 1994, 478)

7. Pawn shops are not regulated; their diminishing importance (table B.9) shows that financial intermediation is replacing the last elements of internal finance.

8. The SIFCT is the IFCT counterpart for small-scale businesses. It is regulated by the Department of Industrial Promotion in the Ministry of Industry and is allowed to mobilize funds from the public.

A finance company must be a limited company, licensed by the MOF. In many ways, it acts similarly to an investment company, issuing promissory notes and borrowing from banks. The market concentration of finance companies is typically less than that of commercial banks: in 1990, the assets of the five largest constituted 28.9 percent of all finance companies' assets (Vichyanond 1995, 332). As with commercial banks, prior to the recent financial crisis, 75 percent of a domestic finance company's shares were required to be held by Thai nationals. Finance companies may set up additional branches subject to MOF approval, although the MOF may attach any kind of conditions it deems necessary to the license. Finance companies can also apply for an additional MOF license to conduct securities business. Generally, a finance company may not hold shares in another finance company, accept deposits, or engage in foreign exchange transactions.

Many finance and credit foncier companies were particularly hard hit by the financial crisis of the early 1980s. Speculation, fraud, mismanagement, and poor credit analysis caused liquidity shortages among major finance companies. The MOF revoked the licenses of 22 finance and 8 credit foncier companies, forcing them to merge with other, more financially sound companies. Under the Lifeboat Scheme, the Bank of Thailand rehabilitated another 25 finance (and securities) companies as well as 6 credit foncier companies by extending soft loans, injecting new equity, and replacing the management team. The program was successful: by 1991, only ten of the Lifeboat Scheme finance companies and six other finance companies were unable to meet their reserve requirement.

Financial reform in the early 1990s has largely benefited finance companies and hampered credit foncier companies. Interest rate deregulation eliminated ceilings on the interest rates that finance companies could charge,[9] and internal liberalization allowed them to conduct leasing business (1991), to act as selling agents of government bonds (1992), and to provide information and advisory services to companies wishing to go public. Credit foncier companies, on the other hand, have been negatively affected by internal liberalization: they now face increasing competition from commercial banks and finance companies expanding into the mortgage business, but they are not allowed to diversify into short-term funds or issue mortgage-based securities.

Despite the competitive advantage afforded finance companies in Thailand's financial sector, finance companies were again hit particularly hard by the banking crisis in 1997. In June 1997, the government suspended

---

9. As in the banking sector, the exception was that the ceiling on mortgage rates for mortgages signed prior to June 1992 with low-income individuals was fixed at 1.5 percent lower than the minimum lending rate.

58 of the 91 finance companies. Viable assets held by these institutions are to be sold to the remaining 33 finance companies and 15 domestic banks.

Insurance companies experienced rapid growth, almost doubling in size, from 1990 to 1993. Nonetheless, their share in total financial assets remains small because most Thais do not yet have the resources to acquire a significant amount of insurance. In 1994, for example, only 7.5 percent of the population held a life insurance policy (Lamble and Low 1995, 204). Another impediment to growth is the lack of personnel trained in actuarial science.

Most insurance companies are local. In 1994, there were 11 local and 1 foreign life insurers, and 77 local and 5 foreign nonlife insurers in Thailand (Lamble and Low 1995, 201). The life insurance market is thus highly concentrated, the nonlife insurance market less so.

In 1992, the Insurance Act was revised to introduce better supervisory measures and to establish an insurance arbiter. Most regulations remain stringent and outdated, though. For example, a change in premiums requires approval from the Ministry of Commerce. The ministry also requires that most funds be invested within Thailand in investments sanctioned by the ministry. Reinsurance abroad has to be approved by the registrar.

Agricultural cooperatives are organized by farmers to make low-interest credits for agricultural activities available to members. The cooperatives are small and there is little cooperation among them. Because their members' incomes and savings are too small to serve as a reliable source of funds, the cooperatives are highly dependent on the BAAC and its policies. Another impediment is the lack of trained staff able to analyze creditworthiness.

Savings cooperatives are formed on the basis of occupation, so most of their members are salary earners. These cooperatives grew rapidly in the early 1990s, but do not seem to be able to effectively mobilize their funds. In addition to the lack of capable managers, the Ministry of Agriculture and Cooperatives, the regulatory agency responsible for these institutions, is itself a major impediment to their growth as it focuses on agricultural issues.

The Industrial Finance Corporation of Thailand (IFCT), established in 1959, is owned partly by the MOF and partly by private entities, especially commercial banks. Its aim is the development of industries and the capital market, and it operates similarly to a private development bank or a development finance company. It finances fixed assets through medium- and long-term loans but is not allowed to extend credit to companies that are more than 33 percent government-owned. Because the IFCT was prohibited from tapping funds directly from savers, foreign debt was its most important source of funds until 1985, when exchange rate devaluations caused it to incur major foreign exchange losses. Since then, the IFCT has turned to issuing bonds and debentures in the domestic market.

Direct Finance

The Stock Exchange of Thailand (SET) was established in 1975 under the Securities Exchange of Thailand Act as the center for trading of listed companies. Initially trading was slow and early developments in the market were reversed by the second oil price shock in 1979. To revitalize the market, the government established in 1979 the Capital Market Development Fund, which was operated by the IFCT and funded with contributions from the Bank of Thailand, the Government Savings Bank, and the Thai Bankers' Association. The fund was intended to intervene in the SET when share prices dropped drastically. Nonetheless, with the financial sector crisis of 1981-83, share prices continued to plummet, reaching an all-time low in 1983. It was not until the boom years, starting in 1986, that trading on the SET accelerated.

These developments, which were outside the SET's control, were aggravated by the number of laws and supervisory agencies that controlled activities on the SET. The Securities Exchange of Thailand Act stipulated that SET supervise activities on the exchange. The Act on the Undertaking of Finance Business, Securities Business, and Credit Foncier Business governed the business of securities companies under the auspices of the BOT. The Public Company Act, under MOF direction, governed the public offering of shares and debentures. The Ministry of Commerce, through the Civil and Commercial Codes, was responsible for general provisions regarding civil and commercial practices. Obviously, the greater the number of laws and supervisory agencies governing the stock exchange, its participants, and their activities, the greater the possibility of inconsistent rulings. In fact, the listing and trading rules were so restrictive that by 1983 only ten companies had become public.

To address these problems, the Securities Exchange Act (SEA) of 1992 established the Securities and Exchange Commission (SEC) and reorganized the SET as a nonprofit, self-regulatory organization that served as the secondary market for securities. The aim of the SEA is to set up a framework to develop financial instruments, provide greater investor protection through information disclosure by the issuer, make the supervisory system more transparent, and facilitate the development of securities businesses and the SET.

Since 1992, the SEC has replaced the Bank of Thailand as an independent regulator of securities companies, which specialize in the issuance and trading of securities.[10] Securities companies must register with and

---

10. When the securities business was first developed, finance companies were encouraged to diversify into the securities business to ensure adequate financial backing. In

obtain primary issue listing approval from the SEC. In the 1992 reforms, the SEC permitted securities companies to diversify into providing information and advisory services and to act as sales agents for government bonds and securities.

These regulatory and financial liberalization measures of the early 1990s continued the momentum for the SET growth that had begun in 1986. By August 1996, 364 companies were listed on the SET. Equity market capitalization grew from US$35 billion in 1991 to US$131 billion in 1996. Computerized trading, developed with the help of the Midwest Stock Exchange, was introduced in 1991 to increase the transparency of trading, to provide efficiency and fairness for investors, and to promote confidence in the SET.

The great majority of securities traded on the SET are common stocks. In fact, over 60 percent of market capital originates in equities from only four sectors: banking, building and furnishing materials, finance and securities, and property development.

In contrast to the equity market, the bond market is only emerging. Traditionally, companies have relied more on loans from financial institutions and on the equity market to mobilize funds. Legal constraints have served to prohibit companies from issuing bonds. Furthermore, the government bond market is captive; government bonds are used to fulfill capital adequacy and branching requirements, preventing the development of a secondary market. Because of fiscal surpluses from 1988 to 1992, the government did not issue additional bonds, and so the market steadily diminished. Only when the branch opening requirements of commercial banks were abolished in 1993 were a large number of government bonds released to the secondary market.

The BOT first issued bonds in 1987 to absorb excess liquidity from the financial system. Commercial banks used these bonds to fulfill branch opening requirements, and foreign banks used them to meet capital adequacy rules. Hence this is also a captive market. Limited supply due to infrequent issuance and the short-dated nature of these bonds has further hindered the development of a secondary market.

Despite these impediments, the government is actively promoting the development of a bond market. The SEC has encouraged securities companies to form a network of bond dealers that will devise a trading and quotation system to help develop the bond market. The system is to be

---

some firms, the intermingling of finance and securities affairs caused problems such as excessive margin lending. The attempt by the authorities to separate finance and securities dealings, as was done with the Glass-Steagall Act in the United States, was shelved at first as it was feared that the close link between both activities in some companies might lead to unrest in the money market. Many companies, though, have opted to divide their finance and securities activities on their own. The idea of compulsory separation for the remaining companies has resurfaced.

market-driven and self-regulated. The SEC also plans regulations that will protect clients, impose capital adequacy requirements for brokers and dealers, promote the development of derivative products to hedge risk, and eliminate tax discrimination against bond holders.

With the cooperation of Standard and Poor's, the government encouraged the development of an independent rating system in 1993; this led immediately to a dramatic increase in the number of private bonds issued that year. At the same time, the BOT began using its bonds and those of state-owned enterprises to conduct open-market policies.

The money market consists of the interbank market, the government bond repurchase market, and the treasury bill market.[11] The well-developed interbank market deals in unsecured transactions. Interbank rates have been volatile because of seasonal patterns in agriculture, the thinness and shallowness of the market, and limited day-to-day management by the BOT. The low efficiency of the market is due to the small number of participants and the oligopolistic practices of the lenders, who consist of the large Thai banks that use their power to set multiple interest rates.

The government bond repurchase market was established in 1979, partly to reduce the oligopolistic edge of lenders in the interbank market. It is an anonymous money market in which transactions are secured against government bonds. Its objective is to increase the liquidity of government bonds held by commercial banks and to provide a new channel through which the BOT can conduct monetary policy. The treasury bill market is very restricted; in weekly auctions, its bills are purchased by the BOT and by financial institutions that use them to satisfy capital and liquidity requirements.

Until 1992, only one mutual fund was authorized by the BOT to mobilize domestic funds. Since then, financial institutions have been permitted to jointly establish mutual fund companies. To diversify shareholding, the maximum amount of equity holding in these companies is 25 percent for commercial banks, 50 percent for finance and securities firms combined, and 25 percent for foreign companies. By 1993, eight mutual fund companies had been established, all of which were closed-end funds, i.e., the investor bears the long-term risk that the capital markets may experience a long recession.

Offshore funds were first created in 1986. The Bangkok Fund and the Thailand Fund were both set up in New York and London to attract foreign investors. In the following years, several more offshore funds were established to guarantee SET stability. Thai investors wishing to invest in foreign mutual funds must obtain approval from the BOT.

---

11. Bank of Thailand bonds, which remain short-dated, have been considered part of the money market.

Pension funds have been regulated since 1984 by the MOF. Funds must be placed with designated depositors, including certain finance, securities, and insurance companies.

Commercial banks and the BOT's Exchange Equalization Fund are permitted to conduct foreign exchange transactions on the foreign exchange market. Since exchange control deregulation took effect, commercial banks have relied much more on foreign borrowing and have, therefore, become a major supplier of foreign exchange. While the baht-US dollar exchange rate was stable, the forward exchange rate market was inactive.

Futures and options trading are still undeveloped in Thailand, and the speed of introduction has been affected by the 1997 financial crisis.

Prudential Regulations

Prudential regulations are centered on shareholder diversification, risk diversification, liquidity reserve ratios, and foreign exchange exposure. Regulations regarding shareholder diversification stipulate that a commercial bank and a finance company must have a minimum of 250 and 100 shareholders, respectively, who together must hold at least 50 percent of shares issued. No shareholder may hold more than 0.5 percent of a bank's shares or 0.6 percent of a finance company's shares. Other holding limits restrict a "person," defined as a family or partner in a limited company, to owning no more than 5 percent of a bank's or insurance company's shares. This restriction does not apply to government ownership or to families that privately own a bank.

The government has sought to ensure risk diversification by setting conditions on the customer profile and lending targets. For commercial banks, credits to any individual client are limited to 25 percent of capital funds, and off-balance sheet obligations to any customer are restricted to 50 percent of capital funds. The banks are not allowed to invest more than 20 percent of capital funds in shares or debentures of another incorporated company, and may not commit more than 10 percent of capital funds to holding another company's equity. They also may not extend credit to bank executives or their families, nor lend to a company in which bank executives hold more than 30 percent of equity, thus limiting interaffiliate services.

The maximum amount of loans that a finance company may extend to any one person is 30 percent of capital funds; guarantees to any one person are limited to 40 percent. The sum of loans to individual persons collectively is restricted to 40 percent of capital funds, and guarantees to this group may not exceed 200 percent of capital funds. Finance companies may not invest in other finance companies; their investments in securities firms are limited to 60 percent of their capital funds; and their investments in other limited companies are restricted to 10 percent of the company's shares.

The liquidity reserve ratio is 7 percent. Of this amount, banks must hold at least 2 percent of their liquid assets in no-interest deposits with the BOT, at most 2.5 percent as cash, and the remainder in eligible securities.

In 1991, banks were allowed to substitute other securities for government securities as the government had not issued bonds since 1988 because of fiscal surpluses. Finance companies must place at least 0.5 percent of their liquid assets with the BOT, at most 5.5 percent in unobligated bonds and debentures guaranteed by the government, and the remainder in deposits or call loans with commercial banks.

All financial institutions have been required since 1995 to hold a 100 percent provision against assets classified as doubtful. Following the 1997 banking crisis, the government began to require banks to hold an additional 15 percent against loans classified as substandard and finance and credit foncier companies to hold 20 percent provisions for the same purposes.

The capital funds to risk asset ratio is limited to 8 percent for banks and 6 percent for finance companies. In the case of banks, this implies that total credits may not exceed 12.5 times the capital base. The calculation of risk assets was changed to the risk-weighted system required by BIS regulations in 1993. In order to allow banks to adjust to this new system, the capital funds to risk assets ratio was lowered to 7 percent in 1993, then raised to 7.5 percent in 1994 and 8 percent in 1995.[12] Finance companies were required to hold capital required according to the BIS standards equal to 7 percent of total capital by 1994.

The government has since established higher standards for the 58 finance companies that were suspended following the Asian currency crisis. Finance companies that wish to reopen are required to have capital adequacy ratios of 15 percent, unless it merges with a bank or one of the 33 remaining finance companies, in which case a capital adequacy ratio of 12 percent is needed.

In addition to the reserve requirements, finance companies must have registered paid-in capital of at least 60 million baht. Life insurance companies must have capital funds of at least 5 million baht and they are required to deposit a minimum portion of insurance reserves with the official insurance registrar. Furthermore, they must make a security deposit of at least 2 million baht.[13] In 1992, revisions to the Insurance Act

---

12. The new system of calculating risk assets explains why many commercial banks and finance companies are diversifying into mortgage lending. According to BIS guidelines, there is very little risk attached to mortgage lending.

13. These insurance company regulations are strict compared to those of other countries in the region.

increased the capital requirements, besides improving supervisory measures and ensuring better qualification for insurance agents and brokers.

Regulations on foreign exchange exposure for banks limit foreign exchange liabilities to 20 percent and foreign exchange assets to 25 percent of capital account.

Rehabilitating the financial sector is a main component of Thailand's 1997 IMF economic program. As such, it includes measures to tighten prudential controls over and increase transparency in the financial sector. Financial institutions are required to strengthen loan classification guidelines and provisioning rules to align them with international standards by the year 2000. Plans for a deposit insurance scheme—to replace a blanket guarantee implemented after the crisis—are to be introduced by 31 December 1998. Finally, the government has also agreed to clarify disclosure and auditing requirements by the end of 1998.

Foreign Participation

When the MOF ceased in 1978 to grant licenses to more banks, there were 14 foreign banks in Thailand. By 1993, these held 7 percent of the country's total financial sector assets (US Treasury 1994, 477). With the 1964 prohibition against the expansion of foreign banks, each bank (with one exception) was allowed to operate only one additional branch, so the 14 foreign banks together had 15 branches.

Generally, foreign banks are permitted to engage in the same activities as domestic banks. They face restrictions, however, on branching, and since ATMs are considered branches, foreign banks have had difficulty accessing the ATM pool. Although they are now permitted to join local ATM networks, they must receive the approval of ATM pool members before they can join the national ATM network.

In prudential regulations, foreign banks are treated somewhat differently from their domestic counterparts. They face a reserve requirement of 125 million baht, which must be invested in low-yielding government securities. They are also restricted in the number of expatriate management personnel, which is a problem as there is a lack of qualified Thai nationals. Because of their different capital structure, foreign banks' capital funds to risk asset ratio was 6.25 percent in 1993; this rate was raised to 6.5 percent in 1994, and to 6.75 percent in 1995. Finally, foreign banks are not subject to the same directed credit requirements that apply to domestic banks.

In 1993, 12 of the 14 foreign banks and 22 of the 43 banks with representative offices in Thailand were granted the right to operate offshore banking units under the BIBF. They generated 47 percent of onshore lending of foreign exchange and 80 percent of international lending in the BIBF (US Treasury 1994). The monetary authorities have considered allowing foreign banks that participate in the BIBF to open two offices outside of Bangkok. By November 1996, authorities had granted 37 foreign banks permission to establish provincial international bank facilities on the offshore market, through which they are permitted to conduct baht transactions (USTR 1997, 366).

In joint venture insurance companies, foreign ownership is restricted to 25 percent of total shares. The 1992 revision of the Insurance Act allowed the Minister of Commerce to grant licenses to foreign companies without obtaining cabinet approval, but until 1995 it was not the government's policy to do so. While Thailand has stated that it will open its markets, as required by GATT/WTO rules, its offer in the 1997 WTO financial services agreement did not significantly increase access for foreign insurance providers. In the agreement, Thailand bound the 25 percent equity ownership limit for foreign insurance firms in the life and nonlife sectors. Subsidiaries in auxiliary insurance services can be 49 percent foreign owned, although the government did not schedule commitments on market access for the pension subsector of the insurance industry.

Foreigners are not allowed to jointly hold more than 49 percent of a company's stocks,[14] although in some instances this level is further reduced. For example, before the 1997 banking crisis, foreign ownership in Thai banks and finance companies was limited to 25 percent—the same as in the insurance sector. Liberalization of foreign equity investment in the financial sector is a crucial part of Thailand's IMF economic program. To help recapitalize the financial system, Thailand has removed restrictions on foreign ownership in banks and financial companies for 10 years, after which new investment will be restricted to 49 percent ownership. Under the terms of Thailand's IMF agreement and WTO financial services offer, the absolute amount of investments by foreign financial institutions that enter the market during the 10-year window will be permanently grandfathered.

Foreigners face no ownership restrictions when purchasing onshore mutual funds but they cannot exercise voting rights, nor are they allowed to be brokers or subbrokers. Despite these restrictions, foreign investment in the stock exchange has increased rapidly. In 1982, foreign trading turnover on the SET was 2.05 percent of total turnover; by 1993, this share had increased to 18.1 percent.

Remaining Obstacles

There remain a number of obstacles to open and efficient financial markets in Thailand. The recent financial crisis revealed the weak regulatory system as a weak link. Inadequate regulation is associated with the uncontrolled proliferation of small finance, securities, and mortgage com-

---

14. This restriction applies to securities companies as well.

panies, many of which were not closed down in the mid-1980s financial crisis. Also of importance are the frequent government bailouts, which create a moral hazard and hinder the development of more responsible risk taking by financial institutions. A deposit insurance mechanism, for which plans are due by 31 December 1998, is seen to be necessary to help strengthen the financial system and support ongoing regulatory reform in this sector.

Another obstacle is the oligopolistic structure of the banking sector, which is responsible for both a wide gap between lending and deposit rates and resistance to foreign as well as additional domestic entry. Deregulation of the financial sector has benefited large customers in that it has provided more opportunities to borrow abroad and to use a wider range of financial instruments in the capital market. Small businesses do not have these options, however, and are more reliant on the oligopolistic banking sector.

Yet another concern is that several types of financial institutions are not controlled by either the BOT or the MOF. This lack of oversight has led to inconsistencies and loopholes in the financial system.

Since the 1997 financial crisis, the government has removed ceilings on foreign ownership of banks and finance companies to help recapitalize the financial system. However, mergers and acquisitions in the financial sector have not proceeded at a rapid pace, in part because of antiquated bankruptcy laws that leave little recourse for bankers when corporate customers do not pay their debts (14 January 1998). The government agreed, as part of the IMF economic program, to revamp bankruptcy laws and to clarify and enforce disclosure and auditing requirements for financial institutions. The implementation of such reforms, scheduled for 1998, will complement financial market liberalization and efforts to stabilize it.

Foreign participation continues to be heavily restricted, although the changes noted above are expected to reduce these obstacles in the future.

References

Frankel, Jeffrey A. 1995. Recent Changes in the Financial Systems of Asian and Pacific Countries. In *Financial Stability in a Changing Environment*, ed. by Kuniho Sawamoto, Zenta Nakajima, and Hiroo Taguchi. New York: MacMillan Press.

Lamble, Peter, and Robin Low. 1995. *The Asia Pacific Insurance Handbook*. Sydney, NWT: Coopers & Lybrand.

Takahashi, Yuichi. 1994. *Financial Sector Reform in the Asia Pacific Countries*. Photocopy.

US Department of the Treasury. 1994. *National Treatment Study*. Washington: Government Printing Office.

US Trade Representative (USTR). 1997. *1997 National Trade Estimate Report on Foreign Trade Barriers*. Washington: Government Printing Office.

Vichyanond, Pakorn. 1995. Financial Sector Development in Thailand. In *Financial Sector Development in Asia: Country Studies*, ed. by Shahid N. Zahid. Hong Kong: Oxford University Press for Asian Development Bank.

References

Ahnlid, Anders. 1996. Comparing GATT and GATS: Regime Creation under and after Hegemony. *Review of International Political Economy* 3, no. 1 (Spring).

Arndt, H. W. 1984. Measuring Trade in Financial Services. *Banca Nazionale del Lavoro Quarterly Review,* no. 149 (June): 197-213.

Arndt, H. W. 1988. Comparative Advantage in Trade in Financial Services. *Banca Nazionale del Lavoro Quarterly Review,* no. 164 (March): 61-78.

Asian Development Bank. 1995. *Asian Development Outlook: 1995 and 1996.* New York: Oxford University Press.

Atiyas, Izak. 1992. Financial Reform and Investment Behavior in Korea: Evidence from Panel Data. Washington: World Bank. Photocopy.

Atje, Raymond, and Boyan Jovanovic. 1993. Stock Markets and Development. *European Economic Review* 37: 632-40.

Babbel, D. F. 1985. Price Elasticity of Demand for Whole Life Insurance. *Journal of Finance* 40, no. 1: 225-239.

Bank for International Settlements. 1996. Central Bank Survey of Foreign Exchange and Derivatives Market Activity, 1995. Basle: Bank for International Settlements.

Bank for International Settlements. 1997. *Bank for International Settlements: 67th Annual Report.* Basle: Bank for International Settlements.

Barfield, Claude E. 1996. *International Financial Markets: Harmonization versus Competition.* Washington: American Enterprise Institute Press.

Barth, James R., Daniel E. Nolle, and Tara N. Rice. 1997. *Commercial Banking Structure, Regulation and Performance: An International Comparison.* Economics Working Papers 97-6 (March). Washington: Office of the Comptroller of the Currency.

Beaurain, Claude. 1996. Les Services Financiers au sein de l'Organisation Mondiale du Commerce (OMC). Paper prepared for a conference on L'Organisation Mondiale du Commerce, Deux Ans Après: Bilan et perspectives avant la conférence de Singapour, sponsored by the Université de Paris-Dauphine, Paris (25 September).

Bencivenga, Valerie R., and Bruce D. Smith. 1991. Financial Intermediation and Endogenous Growth. *Review of Economic Studies* 58 (April): 195-209.

Berger, Allen N., William C. Hunter, and Stephen G. Timme. 1993. The Efficiency of Financial Institutions: A Review and Preview of Research Past, Present, and Future. *Journal of Banking and Finance* 17: 221-49.

Beviglia Zampetti, Americo, and Pierre Sauvé. 1996. Onwards to Singapore: The International Contestability of Markets and the New Trade Agenda. *The World Economy* 19, no. 3 (May): 333-343.

Bhagwati, Jagdish N., and Douglas A. Irwin. 1987. The Return of the Reciprocitarians— US Trade Policy Today. *The World Economy* 10, no. 2 (June): 109-130.

Blommestein, Hans J., and Michael G. Spencer. 1994. In *Building Sound Finance in Emerging Market Economies*, ed. by Gerard Caprio, David Folkerts-Landau, and Timothy D. Lance. Washington: International Monetary Fund and the World Bank.

Bofinger, Peter. 1993. *A Comment on Bernhard Fischer=s Paper*. In Reisen and Fischer (1993).

Bosworth, Barry. 1996. *United States Economic Policy in Asia*. Tokyo Club Papers 9. Tokyo: Tokyo Club Foundation for Global Studies.

Broadman, Harry G. 1994. GATS: The Uruguay Round Accord on International Trade and Investment in Services. *The World Economy* 17, no. 3 (May): 281-292.

Bryant, Ralph C. 1987. *International Financial Intermediation*. Washington: Brookings Institution.

Canada, Department of Finance, Financial Sector Policy Branch. 1995. *The General Agreement on Trade in Services: The Financial Services Sector*. Ottawa.

Caprio, Gerard, Jr. 1996. Banking on Financial Reform? A Case of Sensitive Dependence on Initial Conditions. In Caprio, Atiyas, and Hanson (1996).

Caprio, Gerard, Jr., Izak Atiyas, and James A. Hanson. 1996. *Financial Reform: Theory and Experience*. Cambridge, United Kingdom: Cambridge University Press.

Caprio, Gerard, and Daniela Klingebiel. 1996. Bank Insolvencies: Cross Country Experience. Policy Research Department, Finance and Private Sector Development Division, World Bank, Washington. Photocopy.

Cardoso, Eliana, and A. Helwege. 1992. *Latin America=s Economy: Diversity, Trends, and Conflicts*. Cambridge: MIT Press.

Cecchini, P. 1988. *The European Challenge in 1992: The Benefits of a Single Market*. Aldershot: Gower.

Chant, John. 1997. New Directions in Canadian Financial Policy. In *Reforming the Canadian Financial Sector*, ed. by Thomas J. Courchene and Edwin Neave. Kingston: John Deutsch Institute of Economic Policy.

Claessens, Stijn, Michael P. Dooley, and Andre Warner. 1995. Portfolio Capital Flows: Hot or Cold? *World Bank Economic Review* 9, no. 1 (January): 153-174.

Claessens, Stijn, and Tom Glaessner. 1997. Internationalization of Financial Services in Asia. Washington: World Bank. Photocopy.

Claessens, Stijn, and Tom Glaessner. 1997. *Are Financial Sector Weaknesses Undermining the East Asian Miracle?* Directions in Development series. Washington: World Bank.

DeGregorio, Jose, and Pablo E. Guidotti. 1992. Financial Development and Economic Growth. International Monetary Fund, Washington. Photocopy.

Deloitte & Touche Consulting Group. 1995. *The Future of Retail Banking: A Global Perspective*. Washington: Deloitte Touche Tohmatsu International.

Deutsch, Karl W. 1978. *The Analysis of International Relations*, 2nd ed. Englewood Cliffs, NJ: Prentice-Hall.

Economic Research Europe Ltd., in collaboration with Public & Corporate Economic Consultants (PACEC) and the Institute of European Finance. 1997. Single Market Review 1996: Impact on Services, Credit Institutions and Banking. European Commission, Brussels. Photocopy.

Edey, Malcom, and Ketil Hviding. 1995. *An Assessment of Financial Reform in OECD Countries*. Economics Department Working Papers 154. Paris: Organization for Economic Cooperation and Development.

Edwards, Sebastian. 1984. The Order of Liberalization of the External Sector in Developing Countries. *Princeton Essays in International Finance* 156. Princeton, NJ: Princeton University.

Elyasiani, Elyas, and Seyed Mehdian. 1995. The Comparative Efficiency Performance of

Small and Large US Commercial Banks in the Pre- and Post-Deregulation Era. *Applied Economics* 27: 1069-79 (November).

Employee Benefit Research Institute. 1994. *The Impact of Market Access and Investment Restrictions on Japanese Pension Funds.* EBRI Special Reports SR-26. Washington: Employee Benefit Research Institute (November).

Fernandez-Arias, Eduardo, and Peter J. Montiel. 1996. The Surge in Capital Inflows to Developing Countries: An Analytical Overview. *World Bank Economic Review* 10, no. 1: 51-77.

Financial Leaders Group. 1997. *Barriers to Trade in Financial Services: Case Studies.* London: Barclays.

Fortune 1000 Ranked Within Industries. 1997. *Fortune: The Fortune 500* 135, no. 8: F44-F66.

Frankel, Jeffrey A. 1995. Recent Changes in the Financial Systems of Asian and Pacific Countries. In Sawamoto, Nakajima, and Takaguchi (1995).

Freeman, H. 1997. A Pioneer's View of Financial Services Negotiations in the World Trade Organisation: 16 Years of Work for Something or Nothing? In *Papers from the 12th PROGRES Seminar, Vol. II: Services and Insurance in the International Scene.* Etudes et Dossiers 204. Geneva: Association Internationale pour l'Etude de l'Economie de l'Assurance.

Fry, Maxwell. 1981. Inflation and Economic Growth in Pacific Basin Developing Economies. *Economic Review: Federal Reserve Bank of San Francisco* (Fall): 9-10.

Fry, Maxwell J. 1995. *Money, Interest and Banking in Economic Development.* Baltimore: Johns Hopkins University Press.

Fry, Maxwell J. 1997. In Favour of Financial Liberalisation. *Economic Journal* 107: 754-77.

Fry, Maxwell, Charles A. C. Goodhart, and Alvaro Almeida. 1996. *Central Banking in Developing Countries: Objectives, Activities, and Independence.* London: Routledge.

Fukuyama, Hirofumi. 1993. Technical and Scale Efficiency of Japanese Commercial Banks: A Nonparametric Approach. *Applied Economics* 25: 1101-12.

Gardener, Edward P. M., and Jonathan. L. Tepett. 1995. A Select Replication of the Cecchini Microeconomic Methodology on the EFTA Financial Services Sectors: A Note and Critique. *Services Industry Journal* 15, no. 1 (January):74-89.

Garten, Jeffrey E. 1995. Is America Abandoning Multilateral Trade? *Foreign Affairs* (November/December).

GATT Secretariat. 1994. *Résultats des Négociations Commerciales Multilaterales du Cycle d'Uruguay. Accès aux Marchés pour les Marchandises et les Services: Aperçu des Résultats.* Geneva (November).

Gelb, Alan H. 1989. *Financial Policies, Growth and Efficiency.* Working Papers 202. Washington: World Bank.

Gertler, Mark, and Andrew Rose. 1996. Finance, Public policy, and Growth. In Caprio, Atiyas, and Hansen (1996): 13-48.

Giovannini, Alberto, and Martha De Melo. 1993. Government Revenue from Financial Repression. *American Economic Review* 83, no. 4 (September): 953-963.

Goeltom, Miranda S. 1995. *Indonesia's Financial Liberalization.* Singapore: Institute of Southeast Asian Studies.

Goldsmith, Raymond W. 1969. *Financial Structure and Development.* New Haven, CT: Yale University Press.

Goldstein, Morris. 1997. *The Case for an International Banking Standard.* POLICY ANALYSES IN INTERNATIONAL ECONOMICS 47. Washington: Institute for International Economics.

Goldstein, Morris, and Philip Turner. 1996. *Banking Crises in Emerging Economies: Origins and Policy Options.* Basle: Bank for International Settlements.

Greenwood, Jeremy, and Boyan Jovanovic. 1990. Financial Development, Growth and the Distribution of Income. *Journal of Political Economy* 98 (October): 1076-1107.

Gurley, John G., and E. S. Shaw. 1955. Financial Aspects of Economic Development. *American Economic Review* 45, no. 4: 515-38.

Haggard, Stephan, and Silvia Maxfield. 1993. The Political Economy of Capital Account Liberalisation. In Reisen and Fischer (1993).

Haggard, Stephan, and Silvia Maxfield. 1996. The Political Economy of Financial Internationalization in the Developing World. *International Organization* 50, no. 1 (Winter): 35-68.

Hale, David. 1997. Is Asia's High Growth Era Over? *Kemper Financial.* Chicago. Photocopy.

Harwood, A. 1997. Financial Reform in Developing Countries. In *Sequencing? Financial Strategies for Developing Countries,* ed. by A. Harwood and B. L. R. Smith. Washington: Brookings Institution.

Herring, Richard F., and Robert E. Litan. 1995. *Financial Regulation in the Global Economy.* Washington: Brookings Institution.

Hindley, Brian. 1994. Two Cheers for the Uruguay Round. In *Trade Policy Review,* ed. by Brian Hindley and Deepak Lal. London: Trade Policy Unit of the Center for Policy Studies: 9-28.

Hoekman, Bernard, and Pierre Sauvé. 1994. Regional and Multilateral Liberalization of Services Markets: Complements or Substitutes? *Journal of Common Market Studies* 32, no. 3 (September): 283-317.

Holzmann, R. 1997. Pension Reform, Financial Market Development, and Economic Growth: Preliminary Evidence from Chile. *IMF Staff Papers* 44, no. 2: 149-78.

Hufbauer, Gary C., and Jeffrey R. Schott. 1993. *NAFTA: An Assessment.* Washington: Institute for International Economics.

Institute of International Bankers. 1997. *Economic Benefits to the United States from the activities of International Banks: Financial Services in a Global Economy.* New York: Institute of International Banks.

International Monetary Fund (IMF). 1997. *World Economic Outlook: Interim Assessment.* Washington: International Monetary Fund (December).

Japelli, Tullio, and Marco Pagano. 1994. Saving, Growth and Liquidity Constraints. *Quarterly Journal of Economics* 109, no. 1: 83-109.

Jaramillo, Fidel, Fabio Schiantarelli, and Andrew Weiss. 1996. Capital Market Imperfections, Financial Constraints and Investment: Econometric Evidence from Panel Data from Ecuador. *Journal of Development Economics* 51, no. 2: 367-86.

Jayaratne, Jith, and Philip E. Strahan. 1996. The Finance-Growth Nexus: Evidence from Bank Branch Deregulation. *Quarterly Journal of Economics* 111, no. 3: 639-70.

Johnston, R. Barry, and Ceyla Pazarbasioglu. 1995. *Linkages between Financial Variables, Financial Sector Reform and Economic Growth and Efficiency.* IMF Working Paper WP/95/103. Washington: International Monetary Fund.

Kaminsky, Graciela, and Carmen Reinhart. 1995. The Twin Crises: The Causes of Banking and Balance of Payments Problems. Board of Governors of the Federal Reserve System and International Monetary Fund, Washington. Photocopy.

Key, Sydney J. 1997. *Financial Services in the Uruguay Round and the WTO.* Group of Thirty Occasional Papers 54. Washington: Group of Thirty. .

King, Robert G., and Ross Levine. 1993a. Finance and Growth: Schumpeter May Be Right. *Quarterly Journal of Economics* 108: 717-37.

King, Robert G., and Ross Levine. 1993b. Finance, Entrepreneurship and Growth: Theory and Evidence. *Journal of Monetary Economics* 32: 513-42.

King, Robert G., and Ross Levine. 1993c. Financial Intermediation and Economic Growth. In *Capital Markets and Financial Intermediation,* ed. by C. Mayer and X. Vives: 156-89. Cambridge, United Kingdom: Cambridge University Press for the Centre for Economic Policy Research: 156-89.

Knapp, Ursula. 1994. *L'Accord Général sur le Commerce des Services (GATS): Une Analyse.* Documents de Travail de l'OCDE, vol. II, no. 85. Paris: Organization for Economic Cooperation and Development.

Krugman, Paul. 1994. The Myth of Asia's Miracle. *Foreign Affairs* (November/December): 62-78.

Levine, Ross. 1996. Foreign Banks, Financial Development, and Economic Growth. In

International Financial Markets, ed. by Claude Barfield. Washington: American Enterprise Institute Press.

Levine, Ross. 1997. Financial Development and Economic Growth: Views and Agenda. *Journal of Economic Literature* 35, no. 2: 688-726.

Lindgren, Carl-Johan, Gillian Garcia, and Matthew I. Saal. 1996. *Bank Soundness and Macroeconomic Policy.* Washington: International Monetary Fund.

McCulloch, Rachel. 1987. *International Competition in Services.* NBER Working Papers 2235. Cambridge, MA: National Bureau of Economic Research (May).

McCulloch, Rachel. 1990. Services and the Uruguay Round. *The World Economy* 13, no. 3 (September).

McFadden, Catherine. 1994. Foreign Banks in Australia. Washington: World Bank. Photocopy.

McKinnon, Ronald I. 1973. *Money and Capital in Economic Development.* Washington: Brookings Institution.

McKinnon, Ronald I. 1982. The Order of Economic Liberalisation: Lessons from Chile and Argentina. In *Economic Policy in a World of Change,* ed. by K. Brunner and A. Meltzer. Carnegie Rochester Conference Series. Amsterdam: North Holland: 159-86.

McKinnon, Ronald I. 1991. The Order of Economic Liberalization: Financial Control in the Transition to a Market Economy. Baltimore: Johns Hopkins University Press.

Messerlin, Patrick. 1995. *La Nouvelle Organisation Mondiale du Commerce.* Paris: Institut Français des Relations Internationales and Dunod.

Mishkin, Frederic. 1996. Asymmetric Information and Financial Crisis: A Developing Country Perspective. *International Monetary Fund Seminar Series* 1996-11 (March): 1-61.

Mishkin, Frederic S. 1997. Understanding Financial Crises: A Developing Country Perspective. In *Annual Conference on Development Economics 1996,* ed. by Michael Bruno and Boris Pleskovic. Washington: World Bank.

Molyneux, Philip, Yener Altunbas, and Edward Gardener. 1996. *Efficiency in European Banking.* London: John Wiley.

Moshirian, Fariborz. 1994. Trade in Financial Services. *The World Economy* 17, no. 3 (May): 347-63.

Noland, Marcus. 1996. *Restructuring Korea's Financial Sector for Greater Competitiveness.* Working Paper Series on Asia Pacific Economic Cooperation 96-14. Washington: Institute for International Economics.

Obstfeld, Maurice, and Alan M. Taylor. 1997. *The Great Depression as a Watershed: International Capital Mobility over the Long Run.* NBER Working Paper 5960. Cambridge, MA: National Bureau of Economic Research (March).

Office of Industries. 1995. *Industry Trade and Technology Review.* Publication 2942. Washington: US International Trade Commission (December).

Organization for Economic Cooperation and Development (OECD). 1995. *The New Financial Landscape: Forces Shaping the Revolution in Banking, Risk Management and Capital Markets.* Paris. Organization for Economic Cooperation and Development.

Pagano, Marco. 1993. Financial Markets and Growth: An Overview. *European Economic Review* 37: 613-22.

Pollin, Jean-Paul, and Anne-Gaël Vaubourg. 1996. Architecture Optimale des Systèmes Financiers dans les Pays Emergents. Paper presented at a symposium sponsored by the Caisse des Dépôts et Consignations and the Centre d'économie et de finances internacionales (CEFI) of the Université de Méditerranée (aix-Marseille II) on Stratégie de Croissance et Marchés Emergents in Ho Chi Minh City, Vietnam, (12-13 November).

Price Waterhouse International Economic Consultants. 1988. *The "Cost of Non-Europe" in Financial Services. Research on the "Cost of Non-Europe." Basic Findings,* vol. 9. Brussels: Commission of the European Communities.

Quirk, Peter J., Owen Evans, and IMF Staff Team. 1995. Capital Account Covertibility: Review of Experience and Implications for IMF Policies. *IMF Occasional Paper,* no. 131. Washington: International Monetary Fund.

Rea, John. 1995. U.S. Emerging Market Funds: Hot Money or Stable Source of Investment Capital? *Investment Company Institute Perspective* 2, no. 6.

Reisen, Helmut, and Bernhard Fischer. 1993. *Financial Opening: Policy Issues and Experiences in Developing Countries.* Paris: Organization for Economic Cooperation and Development.

Roubini, Nouriel, and Xavier Sala-i-Martin. 1992. *Financial Development, the Trade Regime, and Economic Growth.* NBER Working Paper 4062. Cambridge, MA: National Bureau of Economic Research.

Royal Bank Financial Group. 1996. *Three Cs of Canadian Banking: Conduct, Competition, Concentration.* Toronto: Royal Bank.

Rubin, Robert E. 1997. Remarks by Treasury Secretary Robert E. Rubin to the Exchequer Club. www.ustreas.gov/treasury/press/pr052197.html (21 May).

Ryan, Cillian. 1990. Trade Liberalization and Financial Services. *The World Economy* 13, no. 3 (September): 349-66.

Sachs, Jeffrey D., Aaron Tornell, and Andrés Velasco. 1996. Financial Crises in Emerging Markets: The Lessons from 1995. *Brookings Papers on Economic Activity* 1: 147-216.

Saint-Paul, Gilles. 1992. Technological Choice, Financial Markets and Economic Growth. *European Economic Review* 36: 763-81.

Salomon Brothers. 1996 . *Asia-Pacific Equity Research* (various issues).

Salomon Brothers. 1997. Foreign Banks in Latin America. *Latin America Equity Research* (19 June).

Sampson, Gary, and Richard Snape. 1985. Identifying the Issues in Trade in Services. *The World Economy* 8, no. 2 (June): 171-182.

Sapir, Andre. 1985. North-South Issues in Trade in Services. *The World Economy* 8, no. 1 (March): 27-42.

Saunders, A., and I. Walter. 1994. *Universal Banking in the United States: What Could We Gain? What Could We Lose?* New York: Oxford University Press.

Sauvé, Pierre. 1990. Trade in Financial Services and the Uruguay Round: The Current State of Play. *European Affairs* Special Issue on the European Finance Symposium.

Sauvé, Pierre. 1995. Rules of the Game—Financial Services. Organization for Economic Cooperation and Development, Paris. Photocopy (23 March).

Sauvé, Pierre. 1996. Regional vs. Multilateral Approaches to Services and Investment Liberalization: Anything to Worry About? Paper presented at a Conference on Regional Trade Agreements after the Uruguay Round: Convergence, Divergence and Interaction, organized by the Institut d'Etudes Juridiques Fernand Dehousse, University of Liège, Belgium (3 October).

Sauvé, Pierre, and Brenda Gonzalez-Hermosillo. 1993. Implications of the NAFTA for Canadian Financial Institutions. The NAFTA Papers. *C. D. Howe Institute Commentary* 44 (April).

Sawamoto, Kuniho, Zenta Nakajima, and Hiroo Takaguchi, eds.. 1995. *Financial Stability in a Changing Environment.* Tokyo: Macmillan Press.

Schott, Jeffrey J., and Johanna W. Buurman. 1994. The Uruguay Round: An Assessment. Washington: Institute for International Economics.

Securities Industry Association (SIA). 1997 Asian Capital Markets: Market Access Restrictions Facing US Securities Firms in Selected Asian Markets. SIA (January).

Schumpeter, Joseph A. 1911. *The Theory of Economic Development.* Cambridge, MA: Harvard University Press.

Shaw, Edward S. 1973. *Financial Deepening in Economic Development.* New York: Oxford University Press.

Skipper, Harold D. 1996. International Trade in Insurance. In *International Financial Markets,* ed. by Claude Barfield. Washington: American Enterprise Institute Press.

Skipper, Harold D. 1997. *Foreign Insurers in Emerging Markets: Issues and Concerns.* IIF Occasional Paper 1. Washington: International Insurance Foundation.

Snape, Richard H., and Malcolm Bosworth. 1996. Advancing Services Negotiations. Paper prepared for a conference on The World Trading System: Challenges Ahead, sponsored by the Institute for International Economics, Washington (24-25 June).

Stiglitz, J. E. 1994. The Role of the State in Financial Markets. In *Proceedings of the World Bank Annual Bank Conference on Development Economics 1993*, ed. by Michael Bruno and Boris Pleskovic. Washington: World Bank: 19-52.

Stiglitz, Joseph, and Marilou Uy. 1996. Financial Markets, Public Policy, and the East Asian Miracle. *World Bank Research Observer* 11, no. 2 (August): 249-76.

Summers, Lawrence H. 1997. Building a Global Financial System for the 21st Century. Speech delivered at the Congressional Economic Leadership Council on 12 August 1997. Treasury News RR-1879. Washington: Department of the Treasury.

Sundarajan, Vasudevan, and Tomas J. T. Balino, eds. 1991. *Banking Crises: Cases and Issues.* Washington: International Monetary Fund.

Tesar, Linda L., and Ingrid M. Werner. 1995. U.S. Equity Investment in Emerging Stock Markets. *World Bank Economic Review* 9, no. 1 (January): 109-130.

Tressel, T. 1996. Finance et Développement. Ecole des Hautes Etudes en Sciences Sociales, Paris. Photocopy.

Turner, Philip, and Jozef van't dack. 1996. Changing Financial Systems in Open Economies: An Overview. In *Policy Papers* no. 1: 5-61. Basle: Bank for International Settlements.

United Nations Conference on Trade and Development (UNCTAD). 1996. *World Investment Report.* Geneva and New York: United Nations.

Vesala, J. 1995. *Banking Industry Performance in Europe: Trends and Issues.* Chapter 3 in Organization for Economic Cooperation and Development (1995).

Vittas, Dimitri. 1991. *Measuring Commercial Bank Efficiency: Use and Misuse of Bank Operating Ratios.* Working Papers 806. Washington: World Bank.

Vittas, Dimitri. 1995. Free Trade Issues in Banking and Insurance. World Bank, Washington. Photocopy.

Walter, Ingo. 1993. *High Performance Financial Systems.* Singapore: Institute of Southeast Asian Studies.

White, Lawrence J. 1995. An Analytical Framework. In Zahid (1995).

White, William R. 1996. Pitfalls and Policy Options Particular to the Financial Systems of Emerging Markets. Bank for International Settlements, Basle. Photocopy.

Williamson, John. 1996. The Crawling Band as an Exchange Rate Regime: Lessons from Chile, Colombia, and Israel. Washington: Institute for International Economics.

Williamson, John. 1994. The Political Economy of Policy Reform. Washington: Institute for International Economics

Williamson, John. 1993. A Cost-Benefit Analysis of Capital Account Liberalisation. In Reisen and Fischer (1993).

Wolf, Charles, Jr. 1991. *Markets or Governments: Choosing between Imperfect Alternatives,* 4th ed. Cambridge, MA: MIT Press.

Woodrow, R. Brian. 1997. The World Trade Organisation and the Liberalization of Trade in Insurance Services. In *Papers from the 12th PROGRES Seminar, Vol. II: Services and Insurance in the International Scene.* Etudes et Dossiers 204. Geneva: Association Internationale pour l'Etude de l'Economie de l'Assurance.

Woolcock, S. 1997. *Liberalization of Financial Services.* London: European Policy Forum.

World Bank. 1995a. *Financial Sector Development in Asia: Country Studies.* Hong Kong: Oxford University Press for the Asian Development Bank.

World Bank. 1995b. *Infrastructure Development in East Asia and Pacific.* Washington: World Bank.

World Bank. 1996a. *Global Economic Prospects and the Developing Countries.* Washington: World Bank.

World Bank. 1996b. *World Development Report 1996: From Plan to Market.* Washington: Oxford University Press.

World Bank. 1997a. *Global Development Finance.* Washington: World Bank.

World Bank. 1997b. *World Development Indicators 1997*. Washington: World Bank.

World Trade Organization (WTO). 1995 *International Trade 1995: Trends and Statistics*. Geneva.

World Trade Organization (WTO). 1997. *Opening Markets in Financial Services and the Role of the GATS*. Special Studies. Geneva.

World Trade Organization (WTO). Various years. *International Trade*. Geneva.

Zahid, Shahid N. 1995. *Financial Sector Development in Asia*. Hong Kong: Oxford University Press for Asian Development Bank.

Index

accounting systems. *see also* prudential regulation
  role in liberalization, 28, 117, 122
ADRs. *see* American Depository Receipts
adverse selection, information asymmetry effect on, 52
Aetna. *see also* insurance market
  Brazil, 148
  Chile, 161
aging population. *see also* pension funds; savings
  in Asian economies, 117, 118-19
Agricultural Bank of China, 168
AIG. *see* American International Group
Allianz Versicherung-Aktien Gesellschaft (Chile), 161
American Depository Receipts (ADRs)
  Argentina, 133
  Brazil, 147
  Chile, 159
  Mexico, 276
American Express Company, 70-71
American International Group (AIG), 71, 84
APEC. *see* Asia Pacific Economic Cooperation Forum
APROC. *see* Asia Pacific Regional Operations Center plan
Argentina
  Bank of the Republic of Argentina (BCRA), 128-29
  banking crisis, 32, 34
  banking industry indicators, 110*t*
  case study
    direct finance, 133

    financial institutions, 129-33, 132*t*
    financial intermediaries, 130-32
    foreign participation, 135-36
    introduction, 127-28
    prudential regulation, 133-35
    regulatory framework, 128-29
    remaining obstacles, 136-37
  Convertibility Plan, 128, 129-30
  Deposit Guarantee Fund (DGF), 134
  equity market, 272
  Financial Entities Law (FEL), 128-29, 134
  financial sector characteristics, 54*t*, 67
  foreign banking assets, 46
  Foreign Institutions Law, 128
  insurance market, 129-30, 131-32, 136, 137
  market access in financial services, 91*t*, 93*t*, 122
  National Securities Commission (CNV), 129
ASEAN. *see* Association of Southeast Asian Nations
Asia Pacific Economic Cooperation (APEC) Forum, 87, 98, 102
  discussed, 88
Asia Pacific Regional Operations Center (APROC) plan, 300, 308
Asian economic crisis. *see also specific countries*
  after-shocks, 107-8, 210
  discussed, 3, 48-52
  preconditions associated with, 9-11, 13, 14, 29-30, 43, 48, 66, 84-85
Asian economies. *see also specific countries*
  banking industry indicators, 110*t*
  deregulation and capital account opening, 5
  financial sector characteristics, 54-61*t*

Asian economies (*Cont.*)
  IMF agreement, 67
  infrastructure development in, 88, 117
  market capitalization, 117-18
  pension funds, 118-19
  performance indicators for banks, 21*t*
  role in MFN-based multilateral agreement,
    81-82
  selected economic indicators, 49*t*
Asian financial institutions. *see also* financial
    institutions
  role in economic crisis, 3
Association of Southeast Asian Nations
    (ASEAN). *see also specific countries*
  economic crisis preconditions in, 9-11
ATMs. *see* automated teller machines
Australia
  domestic- and foreign-owned financial
    institutions performance, 44
  restrictions reduction, effect on interest
    rates, 28
automated teller machines (ATMs), 23-24, 140,
  149, 263, 265, 284, 296, 324

Banco Bamerindus do Brasil (Brazil), 146
Banco de Bilbao Vizcaya (Argentina), 135
Banco de Brasil (Brazil), 143
Banco de Comercio Exterior (Bancomext)
    (Mexico), 271
Banco de Credito (Argentina), 135
Banco de Galicia (Argentina), 133, 135
Banco de Santiago (Chile), 162
Banco del Estado (Chile), 157, 161
Banco Economico (Brazil), 141
Banco Geral de Comércio (Brazil), 146-47
Banco O'Higgins (Chile), 158
Banco Orsono (Chile), 158
Banco Rio de la Plata (Argentina), 133, 135
Banco Roberts (Argentina), 135
Banco Santander
  Argentina, 135
  Brazil, 146
  Chile, 158
Banco Sogeral (Brazil), 147
Bank for Agriculture and Agricultural
    Cooperatives (BAAC) (Thailand), 313, 316
Bank of America, India, 195
Bank of China, 168
Bank of China (Hong Kong), 178
Bank of Communications (China), 169
Bank Indonesia, 201, 203
Bank for International Settlements, 101-2, 113
Bank of Japan (BOJ), 214
Bank of Korea, 241
Bank of Mexico, 270
Bank Negara Malaysia, 257, 259
bank regulatory agencies. *see also* prudential
    regulation; regulation
  efficiency in, 6

Bank of the Republic of Argentina (BCRA),
    128-29
banking
  market access in selected countries, 93*t*
  WTO jurisdiction over, 89
banking crisis. *see also* economic crisis
  associated with internationalization, 8-12,
    109
  Brazil, 141
  Chile, 32, 34, 43, 64, 154, 154-55, 159
  Hong Kong, 11, 177-78, 182
  Indonesia, 207-8
  Japan, 9, 217, 218
  Philippines, 281-82
banks. *see also* financial institutions; *specific
    banks*
  China, regulation of, 53
  commercial. *see* commercial banks
  deposit. *see* deposit money banks
  East Asian, performance indicators for,
    21*t*
  efficiency in, 6, 23, 110
  fee-based products, 23, 110
  government bailout of. *see* government
  merchant. *see* merchant banks
  multipurpose, 142-43
  response to competition, 109-10
  retail, 23-24
  role in economic reform, 63
  role in financial sector, 109-11
  role in monetary policy, 44-46, 71-72, 107
  state-owned, 4, 116, 117, 121, 130-31, 144,
    153, 157
    China, 164-65, 168-70
    India, 121, 185, 189, 190
    Indonesia, 200, 201, 204, 208
    Malaysia, 258
    Mexico, 267
    South Korea, 243
    Taiwan, 302, 303-4
  unit, 19
  universal. *see* universal banks
bilateral agreements. *see also* multilateral
    agreements; negotiations
  for financial reform, 87, 95
Bolivia, FSA offer, 89
bond market
  China, 171-72
  in developing countries, 3, 117
  Indonesia, 206-7
  Japan, 215, 222, 226-27
  Malaysia, 261
  Mexico, 271
  net international financing in, 113-14*t*
  Philippines, 285-86
  Singapore, 291, 293
  South Korea, 246, 247, 250
  Taiwan, 306
  Thailand, 320-21
bonds, bank purchase of, 109, 111

borrowers. *see also* users
  benefits to of financial reform, 16-18
Brazil. *see also* Latin America
  banking crisis, 32
  banking industry indicators, 110*t*
  case study
    direct finance, 144-45
    financial institutions, 142-45
    financial intermediaries, 143-44
    foreign participation, 46, 146-48
    introduction, 139-41
    prudential regulation, 145-46
    regulatory framework, 141-42
    remaining obstacles, 148-49
  Central Bank, 141-42, 148
  Complementary Pension Secretariat (SPC),
    141
  equity market, 272
  financial sector characteristics, 54-55*t*
  insurance market, 141, 144, 147-48, 149
  market access in financial services, 91*t*, 93*t*
  market capitalization, 130, 189
  market opening restrictions, 35-36*t*, 122
  National Economic and Social Development
    Bank (BNDES), 143-44
  National Monetary Council (CMN), 141
  Private Insurance Superintendency
    (SUSEP), 141
  Real Plan, 139-40
  Securities and Exchange Commission
    (CVM), 141
Brock, Bill, 70
brokerage firms. *see also* securities market;
  stock exchange
  Chile, 161
  Japan, 216
  Mexico, 274, 276-77
  operations of, 109
businesses. *see also* firms
  benefits to from financial reform, 17-18
  financial services cost reductions for, 5-6, 11
  financial services use by, 108

Canada
  government-supported financial reforms, 15
  Mexico NAFTA agreement, 275-76
capital, social marginal productivity of, 26
capital account liberalization
  Chile, 64, 155
  definition of term, 4
  European Union, 64
  India, 186, 196-97
  Indonesia, 64-65
capital account opening
  financial liberalization as, 3
  interaction with foreign entry, 33-34, 43
  prerequisite for, 4
capital account restrictions
  in Asian countries, 4-5, 53-54

effect on financial services access, 34
  in emerging markets, 122
  removal of to enhance internationalization,
    9
capital accumulation, speed of, financial
  market development effecting, 2
capital allocation. *see also* investment; savings
  efficiencies in, 26
capital flow
  cross-border, among APEC countries, 88
  in economic crisis, 10, 33-34, 135
  foreign, 3
  as outcome of financial repression, 94-95
  preconditions for, 62-63
  to developing countries, 116, 118*t*
capital flow reversal risk, associated with
  financial reform, 4, 33-34, 63
carve-out provisions, GATS prudential
  regulations for, 5, 34, 76-77, 85
Cecchini Commission Report, 6, 17
Central Bank of China (CBC) (Taiwan), 300,
  307
Chase Manhattan Bank, Singapore, 296
Chibor, China money market, 172
chicken game, negotiation process as, 69-70, 85
Chile
  banking crisis, 32, 34, 43, 64, 154-55, 159
  banking industry indicators, 110*t*
  brokerage firms, 161
  capital account liberalization, 64
  case study
    direct finance, 159
    financial institutions, 156-59, 157*t*
    financial intermediaries, 157-58
    foreign participation, 156, 160-61, 162
    introduction, 151-55
    prudential regulation, 153, 159-60
    regulatory framework, 155-56
    remaining obstacles, 161-62
  Central Bank, 154-55
  encaje system, 152, 161-62
  equity market, 157, 272
  financial sector characteristics, 55*t*, 67
  financial services, 151-52
  foreign banking assets, 46
  foreign entry restrictions, 84*n*
  FSA offers, 89
  insurance market, 155-56, 158, 159, 160, 161,
    162, 273
  market access in financial services, 91*t*, 93*t*
  market capitalization, 190
  market opening restrictions, 36*t*, 122
  nonbank financial institutions (NBFIs), 153,
    157, 158
  pension funds, 152, 156, 157, 158, 159, 162
  Superintendency of Banks and Financial
    Institutions (SBIF), 155
  Superintendency of Securities and
    Insurance (SVS), 155-56
  WTO agreement, 162

China
  Agricultural Bank of China, 168, 169
  Asian financial crisis effecting, 53-54
  Bank of China, 168
  Bank of Communications, 169
  capital flow into, 5, 116
  case study
    direct finance, 170-72
    financial institutions, 168-72, 173-74
    financial intermediaries, 168-70
    foreign participation, 172-74
    introduction, 164-66
    regulatory framework, 166-68
    remaining obstacles, 175-76
  Chibor, 172
  China International Trust and Investment
      Corporation (CITIC), 168
  China Investment Bank (CIB), 168
  Chinese Securities Regulatory Commission
      (CSRC), 167-68
  closed capital account and foreign
      restrictions, 5, 53-62, 121, 122
  credit market, 19, 165, 169-70
  Export-Import Bank, 169
  financial sector characteristics, 55-56t, 67
  Financial Supervision and Regulation
      Department (FSRD), 167
  foreign exchange certificates (FECs), 165-66,
      172
  Industrial and Commercial Bank of China,
      166, 168
  insurance market, 166, 167, 176
  market opening restrictions, 36-37t, 122-23
  money market, 172
  nonbank financial institutions (NBFIs), 169-
      70
  People's Bank of China (PBOC), 166
  People's Construction Bank of China, 168
  People's Insurance Company, 166, 170
  securities market, 53-62, 167-68, 174
  selected economic indicators, 49t
  special economic zones (SEZ), 164
  State Council Securities Policy Commission
      (SCSPC), 167
  State Development Bank, 169
  state-owned enterprises (SOE), 164, 175
  trust and investment companies (TICs), 166
China Development Corp. (Taiwan), 305n
China Investment Bank (CIB), 168
Cigna, in Brazil, 148
Citibank Corp.
  foreign retail banking services, 45-46
  Mexico, 270n
  Singapore, 296
  South Korea, 249
Citizens National Bank (South Korea), 243
Colombia
  banking crisis, 43
  banking industry indicators, 110t
  FSA offer, 89

commercial banks. see also banks; financial
      institutions
  East Asia, expense-asset/expense-income
      ratios, 21-22, 22t
  as financial intermediary, 108-9
  Japan, 221
  lending by, developing country interest in,
      3
  Mexico, 271
  Philippines, 283
  Singapore, 292
  South Korea, 239, 247
  Taiwan, 303
  Thailand, 313-15, 322
commodity exchange. see also stock exchange
  Malaysia, 262
competition
  among regulatory systems, 76
  benefits to users, 6-7, 11, 16-18, 22, 24, 28,
      29-30
  concerns about, 31, 34
  currency appreciation effecting, 63
  effect on transaction costs, 26
  for financial institutions, 107
  relation to saving, 27
connected lending. see also lending
  in United States, intrastate banking
      deregulation effects on, 16
consensus. see also cooperation; politics
  for financial reform, 88
consumption, relation to investment, 33-34
consumption smoothing, relation to saving
      rate, 27
cooperation. see also negotiations; reciprocity
  in APEC, 88
  for financial reform, 87, 101-3
  game-theoretic approach to, 69n
  as strategy for market opening, 14
Cooperative Bank (Taiwan), 303-4
corporate governance. see also risk minimiza-
      tion
  effect on of financial market development,
      2-3
  financial systems effect on, 15
Costa Rica, FSA offer, 89
cost indicators, foreign entry effect on, 22
cost reductions. see also efficiency
  as benefit of financial reform, 5-7t, 16,
      17
covered interest parity, in international
      finance, 115
crawling peg exchange regime. see also
      exchange rate
  discussed, 152n, 154
credit card
  access opportunities to, 6, 24
  multipurpose stored value cards, 179
credit company, as financial intermediary,
      108-9
credit foncier companies, Thailand, 317

credit growth
associated with banking crisis, 33
associated with financial deregulation, 4
credit market
Argentina, 131
Brazil, 143-44
Chile, 153, 158
China, 19, 165, 169-70
costs of, domestic vs. foreign, 17-18, 47
effect of on saving rate, 27
Hong Kong, 18-19, 179
India, 189
Indonesia, 207
Japan, 223
Malaysia, 256, 257, 259
with nonbank financial institutions, 153
Philippines, 281-82, 284
for small and medium-sized firms, 17-18, 44
South Korea, 18-19, 243-44, 247
Taiwan, 303-4, 306
Thailand, 317
credit unions
efficiency in, 6, 20, 22
Japan, 223
South Korea, 243*n*
cross-border trade. *see also* trade
and international financial integration, 112-15
restrictions easement for, 76, 77
WTO negotiations for, 5, 99
cross-sectoral activities, 4
currency, economic crisis effecting, 50-51
currency appreciation
financial reform effecting, 63
relation to capital outflow, 34-43
currency depreciation
effect on exchange rate peg, 9, 153-54
financial reform effecting, 62-63
relation to banking crisis, 33, 43

D'Amato, Sen. Alphonse, 85
demand deposits, economies of scale effecting, 19
deposit insurance, 109, 112. *see also* savings
Argentina, 134
Brazil, 145
Indonesia, 209, 212
Japan, 217, 219, 223
Philippines, 285, 287
South Korea, 247-48
Taiwan, 301, 306
Thailand, 326
deposit money banks. *see also* banks
Malaysia, 256, 260
Mexico, 271
South Korea, 241-42
deposit rate. *see also* interest rate
effect on economic growth, 25

deregulation. *see also* liberalization
economic crisis associated with, 8-12, 32-43
objections to, 8-12
in United States, 4-5, 16
derivatives, international financing in, 113-14
developing countries. *see also* emerging markets
banking industry indicators, 110*t*
economic integration time frame determinations, 2
financial indicators effecting growth, 25
financial services imports and exports, 114-15
foreign entry approaches, 77-78
governments of. *see* government
immature financial systems in, 44
net private capital flow to, 118*t*
objectives of, compared to industrialized countries, 77-78, 96-97
relation to industrialized countries, 115-16
role in MFN-based agreement, 81-83
Development Bank of Singapore, 292
diplomatic pressure. *see* politics
direct finance
Argentina, 133
Brazil, 144-45
Chile, 159
China, 170-72
Hong Kong, 180
India, 190-91
Indonesia, 206-7
Japan, 226-29
Malaysia, 261-62
Mexico, 271-73
Philippines, 285-86
Singapore, 293-95
South Korea, 245-46
Taiwan, 301, 304-6
Thailand, 319-22
discrimination. *see also* nondiscrimination
in China foreign entry, 173
relative to standstill commitment, 75-76
domestic financial reform. *see also* financial reform
definition of term, 3

Economic Cooperation and Development (OECD) countries. *see also* industrialized countries
access commitments by, 2, 3
GATS agreements, 75
Multilateral Agreement on Investment (MAI), 100
South Korea entry to, 237-39, 249
economic crisis. *see also* banking crisis
Argentina, 128
financial reform associated with, 8-12, 32-43, 51

economic growth. *see also* trade
  as benefit of financial reform, 5, 24-29, 98
  effect on of trade in services, 71
  financial market development effecting, 2, 3, 11, 12
  financial systems effect on, 15
  "immiserizing," 63
  in United States, 16
economic indicators, Asian economies, 49*t*
economies of scale. *see also* efficiency
  effect on efficiency, 20
  relation to unit costs, 6, 17, 19
Ecuador, small firms credit access, 18
efficiency
  improved by foreign entry, 2, 11, 22, 24-27, 51
  managerial, 6, 17, 19-20
Egypt
  financial reform conditions, 64
  FSA offer, 89
emerging markets. *see also* developing countries
  capital flow reversal risk to, 4, 34-43
  efficiency potentials in, 22
  financial institution efficiency in, 20
  financial reform conditions, 120-23
  importance of, 79-80, 115-20
  investment in, 45-46
  status quo commitments by, 90
entrepreneurship
  credit access effect on, 24
  promotion of by financial systems, 15, 26
environmental regulations, Mexico, insurance products for, 23
equity market
  Argentina, 272
  boom-bust cycle in, 4
  Brazil, 272
  Chile, 157, 272
  Mexico, 271-72
  Taiwan, 305
Eurobonds, demand for, 112
Euronote, net international financing in, 113*t*
Europe. *see also* industrialized countries
  bank efficiency studies, 19
  Cecchini Commission Report predictions, 6
European Union
  financial integration, 16, 17, 64
  mutual recognition principle, 28, 76
  negotiating agenda, compared to United States, 79, 83-84
  net international financing in, 113*t*
  Second Banking Directive, 76
  single market initiative, 64, 76
  Solvency Ratio and Own Funds Directives, 17
exchange rate pegs. *see also* foreign exchange
  crawling peg, 152*n*, 154
  currency devaluation effect on, 9

determination of, relation to financial reform, 43, 152
exchange rate volatility. *see also* foreign exchange
  associated with internationalization, 9-10
  relation to banking crisis, 33
  expense-asset/expense-income ratios, East Asian banks, 21-22, 22*t*
Export-Import Bank (China), 169

factor accumulation, compared to resource allocation, 94
FDI. *see* foreign direct investment
Federal Reserve Bank, efficiency comparisons within, 20
finance companies. *see also* credit market
  Malaysia, 117, 118, 259-60
  Philippines, 282, 284
  Singapore, 292-93
  South Korea, 243*n*
  Taiwan, 305
  Thailand, 314, 316-17, 318-19, 322-23
financial deregulation. *see* deregulation
financial institutions. *see also* banks
  Argentina, 129-33, 132*t*
  in banking crisis, 10-11, 32, 43
  Brazil, 142-45
  Chile, 156-59, 157*t*
  China, 168-72, 173-74
  competitors for, 107
  domestic protections for, 11
  financial services provided by, 108-12
  Hong Kong, 179-81
  India, 188-91
  Indonesia, 203-7
  Japan, 219-29, 220*t*
  Malaysia, 257-62, 258*t*
  Mexico, 270-73
  Philippines, 283-86
  role in negotiation, 79-80
  Singapore, 292-95, 293*t*
  skilled labor development for, 29
  South Korea, 241-46, 242*t*
  Taiwan, 301-6, 302*t*
  Thailand, 313-22, 313*t*
financial integration
  and cross-border activity, 112-15
  in European Union, 16, 17, 64
financial intermediaries
  Argentina, 130-32
  Brazil, 143-44
  Chile, 157-58
  China, 168-70
  financial services provided by, 108-12
  Hong Kong, 180-81
  India, 189-90
  Indonesia, 204-6
  Japan, 221-26
  Malaysia, 258-61

Mexico, 270-71
Philippines, 283-85
Singapore, 292-93
South Korea, 241-45
Taiwan, 302-4
Thailand, 314-19
types of, 108-9
Financial Leaders Group (FLG)
    FSA evaluations by, 89
    role in negotiation process, 84
financial market development
    effect on economic growth, 25-27
    effecting economic growth, 2
    Financial Services Agreement effecting, 3, 5
financial reform
    Argentina, 127-28
    associated with economic crisis, 8-12, 32-43,
        51
    associated with internationalization, 8-12, 9,
        13, 28, 30
    benefits to users, 5, 6-7t
    "big-bang" reform, 15, 18, 47, 65, 120, 216-
        17, 222n, 228-29, 231, 233
    Brazil, 139-41
    Chile, 151-55
    definition of term, 3-4
    domestic
        foreign entry impact on, 78
        processes for, 98-99, 117
    emerging markets conditions for, 120-23
    forces operating for, 87-89
    GATS/WTO role in, 95-99
    Hong Kong, 177-78
    India, 185-87
    Indonesia, 199-202
    ingredients, 52-62
    Japan, 214-17
    Malaysia, 255-56
    Mexico, 267-69
    Philippines, 281-82
    political economy of, 11, 46-47
    prerequisites, 9, 32-43, 47-48
    sequencing and pacing, 62-65
    Singapore, 290-91
    South Korea, 235-39
    Taiwan, 299-301
    Thailand, 310-12
financial repression. see also government
    benefits of to government, 47
    capital outflow under, 94-95
    effect on economic growth, 24-29
    resources misallocation under, 93-94,
        235-36
financial sector
    foreign entry benefits to, 11
    government regulation of, 107-8
    players in, 108-12
    strategic nature of, 8, 44-46
    strengthening of to enhance liberalization,
        4, 10-11, 17, 32, 51-52, 117

financial services
    Chile, 151-52
    domestic, deregulation of (definition), 3-4
    GATS definition, 73
    home-country vs. host-country regulation
        of, 31
    imports and exports of, 46-47, 114-15
    India, 189
    international, requirements for, 34
    market access (by country), 91-92t
    Uruguay Round negotiations for, 70-72,
        80-81
    WTO jurisdiction over, 96
Financial Services Agreement (FSA)
    acceptance and ratification timeframe, 99
    agreements conclusion process, 69-70
    assessment of, 89-95
    compared to status quo, 91-92t
    components of, 1-2, 5, 34
    effect on financial market development, 3,
        13
    Protocol on Financial Services, 83
financial stability, domestic, foreign entry
        impact on, 78
financial systems, services provided by, 15
firms. see also businesses
    financial services use by, 108
    role in negotiation process, 79-80, 84, 111
    small, benefits to from financial reform,
        17-18
    unproductive, 31, 62
fiscal retrenchment, associated with economic
        crisis, 43
FLG. see Financial Leaders Group
foreign direct investment (FDI). see also
        investment
    China, 5
    to developing countries, 116, 118t
    GATS negotiations for, 100
    growth of, 3, 115
    India, 193
    Taiwan, 299
foreign entry. see also market opening
    Argentina, 135-36
    associated with economic crisis, 32
    benefits of to financial sector, 11, 29-30
    Brazil, 141, 145, 146-48
    Chile, 156, 160-61, 162
    China, 172-74
    financial liberalization allowance for, 3
    Hong Kong, 182-83
    India, 193-96
    Indonesia, 200, 209-11
    interaction with capital account opening,
        33-34
    Japan, 231-32
    Malaysia, 262-64
    Mexico, 274-78
    national treatment requirements for, 72, 75-
        76, 77, 99, 122

foreign direct investment (FDI) (*Cont.*)
Philippines, 287-88
relation to cost indicators and profitability, 22
Singapore, 296-97
South Korea, 236, 248-51
standstill commitments for, 75-76, 83
Taiwan, 307-8
Thailand, 324-25
WTO negotiations for, 5
foreign exchange. *see also* exchange rate
debt liabilities in, 48
financial systems effect on, 15
net international financing in, 113-14*t*
foreign exchange depreciation. *see* currency depreciation
foreign exchange reserves, relation to capital outflows, 43
free riding. *see also* negotiations
in MFN multilateral agreements, 81

game-theoretic approach, to international conflict, 69*n*
GATS. *see* General Agreement on Trade in Services
GATT. *see* General Agreement on Tariffs and Trade
GDRs. *see* Global Depository Receipts
General Agreement on Tariffs and Trade (GATT)
Mexico agreement, 267-68
negotiation agreements, 70, 71, 97
regime creation under, 99
General Agreement on Trade in Services (GATS)
Annex on Financial Services, 76-77
"built-in agenda," 73, 99
carve-out provisions, 5, 34, 76-77, 85
core agreement and annexes, 72-73
Financial Services Agreement relation to, 1, 5
linkages/tradeoffs potential, 97
"memorandum of agreement," 73
objectives, 72, 99-103
obligations and disciplines, 73-74
overview, 14, 72-75, 115
prudential regulation (carve-out) provisions, 5, 34, 76-77, 85
role in financial reform, 95-99
schedules of commitments, 72
"positive"/"negative" lists, 74-75, 96
trade in services definition, 73
Germany. *see also* Europe
bank efficiency studies, 19
banking industry indicators, 110*t*
tax policies, 112
Global Depository Receipts (GDRs), India, 195
gold market, Singapore, 290
Goldman Sachs, India, 195

Government Housing Bank (Thailand), 313, 316
Government Savings Bank (Thailand), 313, 316, 319
governments. *see also* politics
attitudes to financial reform, 8, 11-12, 30, 32, 34, 44, 46, 64-66
East Asia, 50-51, 54-62
emerging markets, 2-3, 90
Indonesia, 65
Malaysia, 50
Thailand, 48-51, 64
financial reforms introduction by, 15, 28, 107, 120-21
financial repression benefits to, 47
financial sector regulation by, 11, 53, 107-9, 112-13, 152, 175, 212, 214, 235-36, 251-52, 299-300
financial services use by, 5-6, 108
intervention of
addressed by trade negotiations, 71
effect on economic growth, 3-4, 8, 25, 31, 116-17, 119-20
in lending practices, 9-11, 19, 22, 31, 121, 165, 185, 214, 251-52, 281
political economy of, 11, 46-47, 53, 66
grandfathering, of standstill commitments, 75-76, 77, 84, 99, 137

Hang Seng Bank (Hong Kong), 180
high-income countries. *see also* industrialized countries
quality improvement welfare gains for, 7-8
Hong Kong
Bank of China, 178
banking crisis, 11, 177-78, 182
banking industry indicators, 110*t*
Banking Ordinance, 177, 178-79, 181
Basic Law of the Hong Kong Special Administrative Region, 177-78
case study
direct finance, 180
financial institutions, 179-81
financial intermediaries, 180-81
foreign participation, 182-83, 184
introduction, 177-78
prudential regulation, 181-82
regulatory framework, 177, 178-79
remaining obstacles, 183-84
contagion effects on currency, 50
credit market, 18-19, 179
expense-asset/expense-income ratios, 21-22, 22*t*
Hong Kong Association of Banks (HKAB), 178
Hong Kong Monetary Authority (HKMA), 178, 179
Hongkong Shanghai Bank, 178, 179, 180
insurance market, 183, 184

performance indicators for banks, 21*t*
Securities and Futures Commission (SFC), 178
Securities (Insider Dealing) Ordinance, 182
securities market, 182-83
selected economic indicators, 49*t*, 122
Standard Chartered Bank, 178
Hongkong Bank, Singapore, 296
Hongkong Shanghai Bank, 178, 179, 180
Hong Kong and Shanghai Banking Corp. (HBSC)
    Argentina, 135
    Brazil, 146
households
    factors effecting saving by, 27
    financial services cost reductions for, 5-6, 11, 30
    financial services use by, 108

IMF. *see* International Monetary Fund
India
    banking industry indicators, 110*t*
    Board of Financial Supervision (BFS), 187
    case study
        direct finance, 190-91
        financial institutions, 188-91
        financial intermediaries, 189-90
        foreign participation, 193-96
        introduction, 185-87
        prudential regulation, 190, 191-93
        regulatory framework, 187-88
        remaining obstacles, 196-98
    credit market, 189
    financial sector characteristics, 56-57*t*, 67
    foreign institutional investors (FIIs), 193-95
    Foreign Investment Promotion Board (FIPB), 188, 193
    FSA offer, 89
    General Insurance Company, 190
    insurance market, 44, 189-90, 197-98
    interest rate administration, 121
    Life Insurance Corporation of India (LIC), 190
    market access in financial services, 91*t*, 93*t*
    market capitalization, 130
    market opening restrictions, 37*t*, 123
    mutual funds, 189, 190, 195
    nonbank financial institutions (NBFIs), 187-88, 189, 195
    nonresident Indians (NRIs), 195-96
    overseas corporate bodies (OCBs), 195-96
    pension funds, 190, 198
    Reserve Bank of India (RBI), 187, 191, 192, 194-95
    Securities and Exchange Board of India (SEBI), 188, 193, 195
    securities market, 190-91, 192
    selected economic indicators, 49*t*

state-owned banks, 121, 185, 189, 190
stock exchange, 188, 190-91, 193, 195
Unit Trust of India (UTI), 190
Indonesia
    Act on Banking Principles, 202
    Bank Indonesia, 201, 203, 207
    banking industry indicators, 110*t*
    case study
        direct finance, 206-7
        financial institutions, 203-7, 204*t*
        financial intermediaries, 204-6
        foreign participation, 200, 209-11
        introduction, 199-202
        prudential regulation, 207-9, 212
        regulatory framework, 202-3
        remaining obstacles, 211-13
    central bank certificates (SBIs), 201, 207
    credit market, 207
    economic crisis
        government response to, 50-51, 64-65, 66
        Pakto reforms, 65, 200-1, 204, 209
        preconditions associated with, 9-10
        reverse sequencing, 64-65
        Sumarlin shocks, 201
    financial sector characteristics, 67
    foreign exchange bank (FOREX), 200
    IMF agreement, 50, 90, 122, 202, 203, 208-9, 212
    Indonesia Bank Restructuring Agency (IBRA), 203
    insurance market, 203, 205-6, 208, 210
    manufacturing firms, financial reform benefits to, 17-18
    market access in financial services, 91*t*, 93*t*, 122
    market capitalization, 189
    market opening restrictions, 37-38*t*
    Ministry of Finance (MOF), 202-3
    money market, 117, 207
    mutual funds, 207
    nonbank financial institutions (NBFIs), 203-4, 205
    nonperforming loans, 201, 207-8
    pension funds, 203, 205
    restrictions reduction, effect on interest rates, 28
    rupiah currency alignment, 199-200, 201-2
    securities market, 204-5, 210-11
    selected economic indicators, 49*t*
    skilled banking labor development in, 29
    state-owned banks, 121, 204
    stock exchange, 204, 206, 211
    WTO agreement, 202, 209, 210
Industrial Bank of Korea, 243
Industrial and Commercial Bank of China, 166, 168
Industrial Finance Corp. of Thailand (IFCT), 313, 318-19
Industrial Revolution, 94

industrialized countries. *see also* high-income
    countries
  banking industry indicators, 110*t*
  deregulation aspects in, 4, 13-14
  financial sector efficiency in, 19
  foreign bank activity in, 46
  internationalization effects in, 5-6
  liberalization in, 94
  objectives of
    compared to developing countries, 77-78
    domestic lobbies effect on, 78-80
    relation to developing countries, 115-16
inefficiencies. *see also* efficiency
  of input, compared to output, 20
inflation. *see also* exchange rate
  capital flow affecting, 10, 43
information asymmetry
  reduction of by financial institutions, 2
  role in economic crisis, 52, 107
information resources
  financial systems effect on, 15, 26, 28, 111,
    117, 119-20
  WTO jurisdiction over, 89
information technology industry, 1
information technology revolution, 94
insurance, effect of on saving rate, 27
insurance industry
  efficiency within, 20, 22, 23, 111
  trade policy agenda, 71, 80, 90
  WTO jurisdiction over, 89
insurance market
  Argentina, 129-30, 131-32, 136, 137
  Brazil, 141, 144, 147-48, 149
  Chile, 155-56, 158, 159, 160, 161, 162, 273
  China, 53, 166, 167, 170, 176
  Hong Kong, 183, 184
  India, 44, 189-90, 197-98
  Indonesia, 203, 205-6, 208, 210
  Japan, 47, 216, 219, 220, 221, 224, 225, 231
  Malaysia, 257, 260-61, 262, 264, 265
  market access in selected countries, 93*t*, 122
  Mexico, 23, 272-73, 277, 278
  Philippines, 29, 282-83, 285, 288
  Singapore, 293, 296, 297
  South Korea, 239, 240, 244, 250-51
  Taiwan, 301, 304
  Thailand, 318-19, 324, 325
insurers, efficiency improvement benefits for,
    6
integration. *see* financial integration
interest rate
  effect on economic growth, 25
  in emerging markets, 116, 117
  enhanced by internationalization, 5-6, 33
  freeing of, 4
  government intervention effecting, 47, 52,
    65, 121, 165, 235, 281
  relation to economic crisis, 33, 64
  relation to saving, 27
interest spread, in emerging markets, 20, 22

International Association of Insurance
    Supervisors, 102
international conflict, game-theoretic
    approach, 69*n*
international financing, activity in, 113*t*-14*t*
International Monetary Fund (IMF)
  Asian countries agreements, 67, 122
  Balance of Payments Statistics, 114
  banking problems among member
    countries, 110
  Indonesia agreement, 50, 90, 122, 202, 203,
    208-9, 212
  Philippines agreement, 282
  South Korea agreement, 5, 50-51, 67, 90,
    122, 238-39, 247, 250, 251
  Thailand agreement, 48-50, 311-13, 325
internationalization. *see also* financial reform;
    liberalization
  definition of term, 3
  economic crisis associated with, 8-12, 32-43
  effects in industrialized countries, 5-6
intrastate banking deregulation, United States,
    5, 16
investment. *see also* foreign direct investment;
    lending
  in emerging markets, 45-46, 94-95, 116-17
  relation to consumption, 33-34
  role in financial development, 25-26, 28-29
investment company, as financial intermedi-
    ary, 108-9
investment trusts. *see also* mutual funds
  Japan, 217, 222, 227-28, 232
investor, benefits to of financial market
    development, 2-3, 6
Islamic bank, Malaysia, 258-59
Italy, bank efficiency studies, 19

Japan
  bank efficiency studies, 19
  Bank of Japan (BOJ), 214, 218
  "big-bang" financial reforms, 47, 120, 216-17,
    222*n*, 228-29, 231, 233
  banking crisis, 9, 217, 218
  banking industry indicators, 110*t*
  Banking Inspection Department, 217-18
  bond market, 215, 222, 226-27
  brokerage firms, 216
  case study
    direct finance, 226-29
    financial institutions, 219-29, 220*t*
    financial intermediaries, 221-26
    foreign participation, 231-32
    introduction, 214-17
    prudential regulation, 229-30
    regulatory framework, 217-19
    remaining obstacles, 233
  competition in consumer lending, 28*n*
  Cooperative Credit Purchasing Corporation,
    223

credit market, 223
financial sector characteristics, 57t, 67
Financial System Reform Act (FSRA), 215-16
GATS agreements, 75
insurance market, 216, 219, 220, 221, 224, 225, 231
keiretsu system, 221-22, 224-25, 227, 231-32, 233
market access in financial services, 91t, 93t
market opening restrictions, 38t
money market, 219, 227
mutual funds, 217, 222, 227, 232
nonbank financial institutions (NBFIs), 221
opening of financial markets, 82
pension funds, 119, 222, 228, 231
postal savings system, 219, 220, 225
Securities and Exchange Surveillance Commission (SESC), 218
securities market, 216-17, 218, 219, 220, 222, 224-25, 232
selected economic indicators, 49t
sogo banks, 222
stock exchange, 218, 226, 227
tax policies, 112
Temporary Interest Rate Adjustment Law (TIRAL), 214-15, 218
WTO agreement, 228

Korean Housing Bank, 243
Kotak Magindra (India), 195

labor costs, in emerging markets, relation to efficiency, 20
labor force
development of by foreign entry, 29
in financial institutions, 144, 173, 263-64, 314, 324
government protection for, 185
in state-owned enterprises, 62
Latin America. *see also specific countries*
bank operating costs, 130
banking industry indicators, 110t
financial reform practices in, 62-64
foreign bank activity in, 46
insurance market, 132
leasing company, as financial intermediary, 108-9
leasing market
credit market costs in, 19
Malaysia, 256
legal systems. *see also* regulation; supervision
role in liberalization, 28, 117, 175, 211
lending. *see also* investment; nonperforming loans
by commercial banks, developing country interest in, 3
connected, 16

consumer, foreign competition effect on, 28n
government-directed, 9-11, 19, 22, 31, 121, 165, 185, 214, 251-52, 281
net international financing in, 113-14t
relation to savings practices, 25-26, 28-29, 33-34
liabilities, of financial intermediaries, 109
liberalization. *see also* financial reform; internationalization
association with banking crisis, 8-12
consistency for, 96
definition of term, 3
domestic reform requirements for, 65-66
in industrialized countries, 94
of trade, 62-63
liquidity risk. *see also* risk management
reduction in, 26
low-income countries. *see also* developing countries
quality improvement welfare gains for, 7-8

M2, relation to capital outflows, 43
macroeconomic conditions
IMF-agreement requirements for, 50-51
relation to financial reform, 9, 32-33, 47, 62-64, 66-67
macroeconomic policy
effect on economic crisis, 10-11, 32-33
as prerequisite for financial reform, 47-48, 66-67, 102
MAI. *see* Multilateral Agreement on Investment
Malaysia
Bank Negara Malaysia, 257, 259
banking industry indicators, 110t
bond market, 261
case study
direct finance, 261-62
financial institutions, 257-62, 258t
financial intermediaries, 258-61
foreign participation, 262-64
introduction, 255-56
prudential regulation, 262
regulatory framework, 256, 257-62
remaining obstacles, 265
commodity exchange, 262
credit market, 256, 257, 259-60
economic crisis, 50, 66, 255-56
Employee Provident Fund (EPF), 260-62
expense-asset/expense-income ratios, 21-22, 22t
finance companies, 117, 118, 259-60
financial sector characteristics, 59t, 67, 122
foreign entry restrictions, 84
FSA offer, 89, 99
government-supported financial reforms, 15
insurance market, 257, 260-61, 262, 264, 265
Islamic bank, 258-59

Malaysia (*Cont.*)
  Labuan Offshore Financial Services
      Authority, 257
  market access in financial services, 92*t*, 93*t*
  market opening restrictions, 39-40*t*
  nonbank financial institutions (NBFIs), 260
  nonresident controlled companies (NRCCs),
      263
  pension funds, 119, 260-62
  performance indicators for banks, 21*t*
  securities market, 258, 261-62, 263
  selected economic indicators, 49*t*
  stock exchange, 257, 261-62
  WTO agreement, 264
Malaysian Bank, Singapore, 296
managerial efficiency. *see* efficiency
Manila Action Plan, among APEC countries,
      88
maritime services, Uruguay Round negotia-
      tions, 80-81
market capitalization
  Argentina, 130, 133, 190
  Brazil, 130, 189, 190
  Chile, 190
  India, 188-89, 190
  Indonesia, 189
  Mexico, 130, 190
market discipline, effect on economic crisis,
      10-11
market failures
  analysis of, 52
  information imperfections effect on, 107
market forces, role in financial reform, 87-89
market opening. *see also* foreign entry
  international cooperation effecting, 14
  objections to, 8-12
  relation to domestic reform, 78
  restrictions on, 35-42*t*
  WTO contribution to, 96
Mauritius, FSA offer, 89
merchant banks
  Malaysia, 260
  Singapore, 292
Mexico
  AFORE/SIEFORE, 270, 272, 274
  Banco de Comercio Exterior (Bancomext),
      271
  Bank of Mexico, 270, 272
  banking industry indicators, 110*t*
  bond market, 271
  brokerage firms, 274, 276-77
  case study
    direct finance, 271-73
    financial institutions, 270-73
    financial intermediaries, 270-71
    foreign participation, 274-78
    introduction, 267-69
    prudential regulation, 268, 273-74
    regulatory framework, 269-70
  CONSAR, 270, 274

equity market, 271-72
  financial sector characteristics, 59, 67
  foreign banking assets in, 46
  FSA offer, 89
  GATS agreement, 75
  GATT agreement, 267-68
  insurance market, 23, 272-73, 277, 278
  market access in financial services, 92*t*, 93*t*,
      122
  market capitalization, 130, 190
  market opening restrictions, 40*t*
  Ministry of Finance and Public Credit
      (SCHP), 269
  Nacional Financiera (Nafin), 271
  NAFTA agreement, 23, 274-78
  National Banking and Securities Commis-
      sion (CNBV), 269
  nonperforming loans, 268-69, 273, 273-74
  pension funds, 270, 272, 277-78
  peso crisis, 32, 33-34, 63, 77, 271-72, 273
    effects in Latin America, 130-34, 151
  securities market, 272, 274
  state-owned banks, 121
  stock exchange, 271-72, 276-77
MFN. *see* most favored nation
middle-income countries. *see also* emerging
      markets
  quality improvement welfare gains for, 7-8
monetary policy, financial institutions role in,
      44-46, 71-72, 107
money market
  China, 172
  in emerging markets, 116-17
  Indonesia, 117, 207
  Japan, 219, 227
  Philippines, 286
  Taiwan, 117, 306
  Thailand, 117, 321
moral hazard
  deregulation effect on, 112
  information asymmetry effect on, 52
  in mandated lending quotas, 165
Morgan Stanley, India, 195
mortgage loans, economies of scale effect on,
      19
most favored nation (MFN) status
  among APEC countries, 88
  denial of, as punishment, 80
  GATS obligations for, 73-74, 75, 77
  multilateral agreements for, 72, 81-83, 99
Multilateral Agreement on Investment (MAI),
      among OECD countries, 100
multilateral agreements. *see also* negotiations
  between developing/industrialized
      countries, 81, 97-99
  between United States and Japan, 82
  for financial reform, 87, 95-99, 102
  objectives for, 72
multipurpose bank, Brazil, 142-43
multipurpose stored value cards, 179

mutual funds
India, 189, 190, 195
Indonesia, 207
insurance market offerings for, 23
Japan, 217, 222, 227, 232
Philippines, 29, 286
South Korea, 253
Taiwan, 304-5
Thailand, 321
United States, 118
mutual funds company, as financial
intermediary, 108-9
"mutual recognition" principle, European
Union, 28

Nacional Financiera (Nafin) (Mexico),
271
NAFTA. *see* North American Free Trade
Agreement
National Agricultural Cooperative (South
Korea), 243
national bank regulatory agency, efficiency
within, 6, 22
National Economic and Social Development
Bank (BNDES) (Brazil), 143-44
national treatment. *see also* foreign entry
among APEC countries, 88
Argentina, 136
Chile, 162
emerging markets restrictions on, 122
India, 196
Japan, 231
Mexico, 274-78
as requirement for foreign entry, 72, 77
South Korea, 238
standstill commitment for, 75-76
natural persons movements. *see also* labor
force
Uruguay Round negotiations for, 80-81,
99
NBFIs. *see* nonbank financial institutions
negotiations. *see also* multilateral agreements
as chicken game, 69-70, 85
for financial reform, 87, 95
for Financial Services Agreement, 69-70
for General Agreement on Trade in
Services, 72-75
for services in Uruguay Round, 70-72
standstill commitments, 75-76, 83
WTO discussions, 80-85
nonbank financial institutions (NBFIs)
Argentina, 130
Chile, 153, 157, 158
China, 169-70
India, 187-88, 189, 195
Indonesia, 203-5
Japan, 221
Malaysia, 260
South Korea, 241

nondiscrimination principles. *see also*
discrimination
GATS obligations for, 73
for multilateral rule, 72
not a feature of FSA, 93
nonperforming loans. *see also* investment;
lending
Brazil, 141
Chile, 154-55, 159
China, 175
currency devaluation effecting, 10
East Asian, 50
government bailout for, 53
India, 191
Indonesia, 201, 207-8
interest rate increase effecting, 9-10, 64
Japan, 223
Malaysia, 255-56
Mexico, 268-69, 273-74
offshore, 46
South Korea, 238, 247
in United States, intrastate banking
deregulation effects on, 16
nontariff barriers, addressed by trade
negotiations, 71
Norin-chukin Bank (Japan), 223
North American Free Trade Agreement
(NAFTA)
Mexico agreement, 23, 274-78
role in economic reform, 87

OECD. *see* Economic Cooperation and
Development countries
oligopolistic market structure. *see also*
government
competition effect on, 17
effect on interest margins, 22
on-line banking, 23-24
operating ratios, in emerging markets, 20
Overseas China Bank (Singapore), 292
Overseas Union Bank (Singapore), 292

pacing, for financial reform, 62-65, 67
Pakistan, FSA offer, 89
pawnbrokers
Malaysia, 256
Philippines, 282
pension funds. *see also* aging population
Argentina, 129, 131
in Asian economies, 118-19
Brazil, 141, 144
Chile, 27, 152, 156, 157, 158, 159, 162
India, 190, 198
Indonesia, 203, 205
Japan, 119, 222, 228, 231
Malaysia, 119, 260-61
Mexico, 23, 270, 272, 277-78
Singapore, 119, 291

pension funds (*Cont.*)
  Taiwan, 304
  Thailand, 322
People's Bank of China (PBOC), 166
People's Construction Bank of China, 168
Philippines
  bond market, 285-86
  case study
    direct finance, 285-86
    financial institutions, 283-86
    financial intermediaries, 283-85
    foreign participation, 287-88
    introduction, 281-82
    prudential regulation, 286-87
    regulatory framework, 282-83
    remaining obstacles, 288-89
  contagion effects on currency, 50
  credit market, 281-82, 284
  finance companies, 282, 284
  financial sector characteristics, 60t, 67
  FSA offer, 89
  IMF agreement, 282
  insurance market, 29, 282-83, 285, 288
  market access in financial services, 92t, 93t
  market opening restrictions, 41t
  money market, 286
  mutual funds, 29, 286
  Offshore Banking Units (OBU), 288
  Philippine Central Bank (BSP), 282
  Philippine National Bank (PNB), 283
  securities market, 282, 284, 287
  selected economic indicators, 49t
  stock exchange, 282, 285
  WTO agreement, 288, 289
Poland, GATS agreement, 75
political economy. *see also* government
  of financial reform, 11, 46-47, 66
politics. *see also* government
  of diplomatic pressure, 11-12, 80
  effect on firms' credit access, 17-18
  effect on negotiating process, 69-70
  of government intervention, 8, 31, 111
  of industrialized countries negotiating
    objectives, 78-79, 82
  role in financial reform, 87-89, 93, 95, 98-99,
    101
portfolio flows. *see also* capital flow
  to developing countries, 3, 116
postal savings system
  Japan, 219, 220
  Singapore, 291
  South Korea, 243n
  Taiwan, 304
poverty, relation to economic growth, 185-86
private saving rate. *see also* savings
  role in financial development, 26
profits
  foreign entry effect on, 17, 22
  potential, lost to inefficiency, 20, 22
  restructuring effect on, 140-41

property market speculation. *see also* lending
  associated with deregulation, 4, 10, 33, 66
prudential regulation. *see also* regulation
  Argentina, 133-35
  Brazil, 145-46
  Chile, 153, 159-60
  GATS carve-out provision for, 5, 34, 76-77,
    85
  Hong Kong, 181-82
  India, 190, 191-93
  Indonesia, 207-9, 212
  Malaysia, 262
  Mexico, 268, 273-74
  Philippines, 286-87
  as prerequisite for financial reform, 48, 111,
    122
  Singapore, 295-96
  South Korea, 246-48
  Taiwan, 306-7
  Thailand, 322-24

Quad. *see also* industrialized countries
  role in financial services negotiations, 84,
    100
quality improvements, foreign entry effect
  on, 23-24, 28

reciprocity. *see also* cooperation
  in financial services negotiations, 96-97,
    99
reform. *see* financial reform
regime creation, under GATT, 99
regulation. *see also* prudential regulation;
    supervision
  effect on financial institutions, 111-12
  effect on foreign-owned retail banking,
    44-45
  home-country vs. host-country, 31
  role in economic crisis, 52-53
  role in liberalization, 28, 31, 63-64, 71
  transparency requirements, 4, 28, 72
regulatory framework
  Argentina, 128-29
  Brazil, 141-42
  Chile, 155-56
  Hong Kong, 177, 178-79
  India, 187-88
  Indonesia, 202-3
  Japan, 217-19
  Malaysia, 256, 257-62
  Mexico, 269-70
  Philippines, 282-83
  Singapore, 291
  South Korea, 239-41
  Taiwan, 301
  Thailand, 312-13
regulatory systems, competition among, 76
Reserve Bank of India (RBI), 187

resource allocation, compared to factor
accumulation, 94
retail banking, efforts for, compared to
wholesale banking, 44-45
retail banks. *see also* banks
services diversification by, 23-24
risk diversification
benefits to users of, 6-7
effects of, 27, 33
risk management
financial systems effect on, 15, 26
reduction of by financial institutions, 2
relation to economic crisis, 10, 13, 51
risk minimization
with fee-based products, 23
in financial reform and internationalization,
8-9
Rubin, Robert E., 18

Samsung Corp., South Korea, 244*n*, 249
savers. *see also* users
benefits to of financial market development, 2-3, 6, 45
benefits to of financial reform, 16-18
saving rate, domestic, financial intermediation
effect on, 26-27
savings. *see also* interest rate
interest rate effect on, 25
relation to investment, 25-26, 28-29, 33-34,
116-17
as role of financial systems, 15
under financial repression, 94-95
savings institution, as financial intermediary,
108-9
savings and loan associations
Japan, 222
Philippines, 283
Taiwan, 303
securities
issued by governments and corporations,
23, 108
portfolio risk-diversification through, 27
securities firms, operations of, 109
securities market
access in selected countries, 93*t*, 121-22
Argentina, 129, 133
Brazil, 145
Chile, 155-56, 161
China, 53-62, 167-68, 174
Hong Kong, 182-83
India, 190-191, 92
Indonesia, 204-5, 210-11
Japan, 216-17, 218, 219, 220, 222, 224-25
Malaysia, 258, 261-62, 263
Mexico, 272, 274
net international financing in, 113-14*t*
Philippines, 282, 284, 287
Singapore, 293-95
South Korea, 239-40, 245, 245-46, 249-51, 253

Taiwan, 304-6, 308
Thailand, 323
WTO jurisdiction over, 89
semiconductors, 10
Senegal, FSA offer, 89
sequencing, for financial reform, 62-65
service improvements, foreign entry effect on,
23-24, 44
Shanghai. *see also* China
credit market in, 19
foreign bank entry, 173
Pudong New Area, 173
stock exchange, 170-72
Shoku-chukin Bank (Japan), 223
short-term debt/equity flow, capital inflow as,
3
Singapore
banking industry indicators, 110*t*
bond market, 291, 293
case study
direct finance, 293-95
financial institutions, 292-95, 293*t*
financial intermediaries, 292-93
foreign participation, 296-97
introduction, 290-91
prudential regulation, 295-96
regulatory framework, 291
remaining obstacles, 297
Central Provident Fund (CPF), 119
Development Bank of Singapore, 292
economic crisis, 11, 53, 66
expense-asset/expense-income ratios, 21-22,
22*t*
finance companies, 292-93
financial sector characteristics, 67, 122
FSA offer, 89
insurance market, 293, 296, 297
Monetary Authority of Singapore (MAS),
291
Overseas China Bank, 292
Overseas Union Bank, 292
pension funds, 119, 291
performance indicators for banks, 21*t*
postal savings system, 291
securities market, 293-95
selected economic indicators, 49*t*
stock exchange, 293-95
United Overseas Bank, 292
Small Industry Finance Corp. of Thailand
(SIFCT), 316
Société Générale (Brazil), 147
South America. *see* Latin America; *specific
countries*
South Korea
Bank of Korea, 241
banking industry indicators, 110*t*
bond market, 246, 247, 250
case study
direct finance, 245-46
financial institutions, 241-46, 242*t*

South Korea (*Cont.*)
  case study (*Cont.*)
    financial intermediaries, 241-45
    foreign participation, 236, 248-51
    introduction, 235-39
    prudential regulation, 246-48
    regulatory framework, 239-41
    remaining obstacles, 251-54
  chaebols, 244
  Citizens National Bank, 243
  credit market, 18-19, 243-44, 247
  economic crisis
    government response to, 50-51, 66
    preconditions associated with, 9, 10-11
  exchange rate volatility in, 9-10
  expense-asset/expense-income ratios, 21-22, 22*t*
  financial sector characteristics, 58*t*, 67
  Foreign Direct Investment Liberalization Plan, 251
  Foreign Exchange Control Act (FECA), 236-37
  FSA offer, 89
  GATS agreement, 75
  Heavy Chemical and Industrial Drive (HCI), 235
  IMF agreement, 5, 50-51, 67, 90, 122, 238-39, 247, 250, 251
  Industrial Bank of Korea, 243
  insurance market, 239, 240, 244, 250-51
  interest rate administration, 121
  Korean Housing Bank, 243
  market access in financial services, 91*t*, 93*t*
  market opening restrictions, 39*t*, 122
  money markets growth, 117
  mutual funds, 253
  National Agricultural Cooperative, 243
  nonbank financial institutions (NBFIs), 241
  OECD entry, 237-39, 249
  performance indicators for banks, 21*t*
  Real Name System law, 247-48
  restrictions removal agreement, 5
  Samsung Corp., 244n9
  securities market, 239-40, 245-46, 253
  selected economic indicators, 49*t*
  small firms, credit market improvements for, 18
  stock exchange, 240, 245, 249
  WTO agreement, 238-39, 249-51
speculation
  role in Asian financial crisis, 50
  role in banking crisis, 4, 10, 33, 66
Sri Lanka, FSA offer, 89
stabilization, relation to trade reform, 63-64
Standard Chartered Bank (Hong Kong), 178
Standard Chartered Bank, Singapore, 296
standstill commitments, reconciliation of, 75-76, 83
State Development Bank (China), 169
state-owned banks. *see* banks, state-owned

status quo
  compared to FSA commitment, 91-92*t*, 93*t*, 102-3
  in emerging markets, 120-21
  and financial markets openness, 35-42*t*, 89-90
sterilization, associated with economic crisis, 43
stock exchange
  Argentina, 129, 133
  Brazil, 144-45, 147
  Chile, 159-60, 161
  China, 170-72, 176
  Hong Kong, 179, 180-81, 183
  India, 188, 190-91, 193, 195
  Indonesia, 204, 206, 211
  Japan, 218, 226, 227
  Malaysia, 257
  Mexico, 271-72, 276
  Philippines, 282, 285
  Singapore, 293-95
  South Korea, 240, 245, 249
  Taiwan, 304-5
  Thailand, 319-20
stock market decline, associated with internationalization, 9
supervision. *see also* regulation
  role in economic crisis, 43, 51, 52
  role in liberalization, 10-11, 28, 31, 71, 101, 117, 119-20

Taiwan
  APROC plan, 300, 308
  banking industry
    deregulation and internationalization effects, 24
    indicators, 110*t*
  bond market, 306
  case study
    direct finance, 301, 304-6
    financial institutions, 301-6, 302*t*
    financial intermediaries, 302-4
    foreign participation, 307-8
    introduction, 299-301
    prudential regulation, 306-7
    regulatory framework, 301
    remaining obstacles, 308-9
  Central Bank of China (CBC), 300, 308
  China Development Corp., 305*n*
  Cooperative Bank, 303-4
  credit market, 303-4, 307
  currency depreciation, 10
  deregulation in, 4-5
  equity market, 305
  finance companies, 305
  financial sector characteristics, 60-61*t*, 67
  insurance market, 301, 304
  market opening restrictions, 41-42*t*, 122
  money market, 117, 306

pension funds, 304
postal savings system, 304
securities market, 304-6, 308
selected economic indicators, 49t
state-owned banks, 121
stock exchange, 304-5
WTO agreement, 308-9
technology, financial institution use of, 6, 19, 22, 23-24, 112, 140
telecommunications industry, 1
telecommunications services
    relation to financial services, 107
    Uruguay Round negotiations for, 80-81, 97
Telmex (Mexico), 271
tequila effect, 32
Thailand
    Asset Management Company (AMC), 313
    baht currency alignment, 9, 48, 84, 201, 282, 310-11
    Bangkok International Banking Facility (BIBF), 312, 315
    Bank for Agriculture and Agricultural Cooperatives (BAAC), 313, 316
    banking industry indicators, 110t
    bond market, 320-21
    case study
        direct finance, 319-22
        financial institutions, 313-22, 313t
        financial intermediaries, 314-19
        foreign participation, 324-25
        introduction, 310-12
        prudential regulation, 322-24
        regulatory framework, 312-13
        remaining obstacles, 325-26
    credit market, 317
    economic crisis
        government response to, 50, 51, 64, 66
        preconditions associated with, 9-10, 48-49
    expense-asset/expense-income ratios, 21-22, 22t
    finance companies, 314, 316-17, 318-19, 322-23
    Financial Restructuring Agency (FRA), 313
    financial sector characteristics, 61t, 67
    GATT offer, 325
    Government Housing Bank, 313, 316
    Government Savings Bank, 313, 316, 319
    IMF agreement, 48-50, 122, 311-13, 325
    Industrial Finance Corp of Thailand (IFCT), 313, 318-19
    insurance market, 318-19, 324, 325
    Lifeboat Scheme, 315, 317
    market access in financial services, 92t, 93t, 122
    market opening restrictions, 42t
    money market, 117, 321
    pension funds, 322
    performance indicators for banks, 21t
    selected economic indicators, 49t

Small Industry Finance Corp. of Thailand (SIFCT), 316
    stock exchange, 319-20
    WTO offer, 312, 325
thrifts
    efficiency improvement benefits for, 6, 20
    Philippines, 283-84, 287
trade. see also cross-border trade; economic growth
    capital flow effect on, 43
    financial systems effect on, 15
    government protection for, 185
    relation to banking crisis, 33
    in services, 46-47, 71
        GATS definitions for, 73
trade liberalization. see also liberalization
    role in financial reform, 62-63
transaction costs, relation to investment opportunity, 26
transparency of oversight. see also regulation
    GATS obligations for, 73-75
    as requirement for foreign entry, 4, 28, 72, 76, 122, 175
trust banks
    Japan, 220, 222, 228
    Philippines, 282
    South Korea, 248-49
Turkey
    bank efficiency studies, 19
    restrictions reduction, effect on interest rates, 28

unilateralism
    among APEC countries, 88
    United States tendency to, 79
unit banks, economies of scale effect on, 19
unit costs. see also cost indicators
    economies of scale effect on, 6, 17
unit trust company, as financial intermediary, 108-9
United Kingdom
    bank efficiency studies, 19
    "big-bang" financial reforms, 15, 65
    financial markets development, 94
United Overseas Bank (Singapore), 292
United States. see also industrialized countries
    bank efficiency studies, 19
    banking industry indicators, 110t
    "big-bang" financial reforms, 15, 18
    financial markets development, 94
    financial services market, 96-97
    GATS negotiating approach, 75
    intrastate banking deregulation
        effects of, 16
        effect on growth rates, 5
    multilateral agreement with Japan, 82
    reciprocal access commitments, 2
    savings and loan crisis, 8-9

United States (*Cont.*)
 trade policy agenda, financial services, 70-71, 78-79, 82-85, 96-97, 99
universal banks
 Mexico, 269
 Philippines, 283, 287
Uruguay Round agreement. *see also* General Agreement on Trade in Services
 financial services in, 70-72
 foreign entry management provisions, 11
 negotiation process for, 70, 80, 101
users. *see also* borrowers; savers
 benefits to of competition, 6-7, 11, 16-18, 22-24, 121
 of financial services, 108
utility companies, privatization of, Argentina, 133

Venezuela
 foreign bank activity in, 46
 FSA offer, 89

welfare gains, generated by cost savings, 7
wholesale banking, efforts for, compared to retail banking, 44-45
window guidance, Japan, 214-15
World Bank, 102
World Trade Organization (WTO)
 "Agenda 2000," 95
 financial services negotiations history, 80-85
 role in financial reform, 5, 87-89, 95-99
WTO. *see* World Trade Organization

X-inefficiencies. *see* efficiency, managerial

Other Publications from the
Institute for International Economics

POLICY ANALYSES IN INTERNATIONAL ECONOMICS Series

1 The Lending Policies of the International Monetary Fund
   John Williamson/*August 1982*
                     ISBN paper 0-88132-000-5   72 pp.

2 "Reciprocity": A New Approach to World Trade Policy?
   William R. Cline/*September 1982*
                     ISBN paper 0-88132-001-3   41 pp.

3 Trade Policy in the 1980s
   C. Fred Bergsten and William R. Cline/*November 1982*
   (out of print)   ISBN paper 0-88132-002-1   84 pp.
   Partially reproduced in the book *Trade Policy in the 1980s.*

4 International Debt and the Stability of the World Economy
   William R. Cline/*September 1983*
                     ISBN paper 0-88132-010-2   134 pp.

5 The Exchange Rate System, Second Edition
   John Williamson/*September 1983, rev. June 1985*
   (out of print)   ISBN paper 0-88132-034-X   61 pp.

6 Economic Sanctions in Support of Foreign Policy Goals
   Gary Clyde Hufbauer and Jeffrey J. Schott/*October 1983*
                     ISBN paper 0-88132-014-5   109 pp.

7 A New SDR Allocation?
   John Williamson/*March 1984*
                     ISBN paper 0-88132-028-5   61 pp.

8 An International Standard for Monetary Stabilization
   Ronald I. McKinnon/*March 1984*
   (out of print)   ISBN paper 0-88132-018-8   108 pp.

9 The Yen/Dollar Agreement: Liberalizing Japanese Capital Markets
   Jeffrey A. Frankel/*December 1984*
                     ISBN paper 0-88132-035-8   86 pp.

10 Bank Lending to Developing Countries: The Policy Alternatives
    C. Fred Bergsten, William R. Cline, and John Williamson/*April 1985*
                     ISBN paper 0-88132-032-3   221 pp.

11 Trading for Growth: The Next Round of Trade Negotiations
    Gary Clyde Hufbauer and Jeffrey J. Schott/*September 1985*
    (out of print)   ISBN paper 0-88132-033-1   109 pp.

12 Financial Intermediation Beyond the Debt Crisis
    Donald R. Lessard and John Williamson/*September 1985*
    (out of print)   ISBN paper 0-88132-021-8   130 pp.

13 The United States-Japan Economic Problem
    C. Fred Bergsten and William R. Cline/*October 1985, 2d ed. January 1987*
    (out of print)   ISBN paper 0-88132-060-9   180 pp.

14 Deficits and the Dollar: The World Economy at Risk
    Stephen Marris/*December 1985, 2d ed. November 1987*
    (out of print)   ISBN paper 0-88132-067-6   415 pp.

15 Trade Policy for Troubled Industries
    Gary Clyde Hufbauer and Howard F. Rosen/*March 1986*
                     ISBN paper 0-88132-020-X   111 pp.

16 The United States and Canada: The Quest for Free Trade
    Paul Wonnacott, with an Appendix by John Williamson/*March 1987*
                     ISBN paper 0-88132-056-0   188 pp.

17 Adjusting to Success: Balance of Payments Policy
    in the East Asian NICs
    Bela Balassa and John Williamson/*June 1987, rev. April 1990*
                     ISBN paper 0-88132-101-X   160 pp.

18 Mobilizing Bank Lending to Debtor Countries
    William R. Cline/*June 1987*
                     ISBN paper 0-88132-062-5   100 pp.

19 **Auction Quotas and United States Trade Policy**
C. Fred Bergsten, Kimberly Ann Elliott, Jeffrey J. Schott, and
Wendy E. Takacs/ *September 1987*
ISBN paper 0-88132-050-1   254 pp.

20 **Agriculture and the GATT: Rewriting the Rules**
Dale E. Hathaway/ *September 1987*
ISBN paper 0-88132-052-8   169 pp.

21 **Anti-Protection: Changing Forces in United States Trade Politics**
I. M. Destler and John S. Odell/ *September 1987*
ISBN paper 0-88132-043-9   220 pp.

22 **Targets and Indicators: A Blueprint for the International
Coordination of Economic Policy**
John Williamson and Marcus H. Miller/ *September 1987*
ISBN paper 0-88132-051-X   118 pp.

23 **Capital Flight: The Problem and Policy Responses**
Donald R. Lessard and John Williamson/ *December 1987*
(out of print)   ISBN paper 0-88132-059-5   80 pp.

24 **United States-Canada Free Trade: An Evaluation of the Agreement**
Jeffrey J. Schott/ *April 1988*
ISBN paper 0-88132-072-2   48 pp.

25 **Voluntary Approaches to Debt Relief**
John Williamson/ *September 1988, rev. May 1989*
ISBN paper 0-88132-098-6   80 pp.

26 **American Trade Adjustment: The Global Impact**
William R. Cline/ *March 1989*
ISBN paper 0-88132-095-1   98 pp.

27 **More Free Trade Areas?**
Jeffrey J. Schott/ *May 1989*   ISBN paper 0-88132-085-4   88 pp.

28 **The Progress of Policy Reform in Latin America**
John Williamson/ *January 1990*
ISBN paper 0-88132-100-1   106 pp.

29 **The Global Trade Negotiations: What Can Be Achieved?**
Jeffrey J. Schott/ *September 1990*
ISBN paper 0-88132-137-0   72 pp.

30 **Economic Policy Coordination: Requiem or Prologue?**
Wendy Dobson/ *April 1991*
ISBN paper 0-88132-102-8   162 pp.

31 **The Economic Opening of Eastern Europe**
John Williamson/ *May 1991*
ISBN paper 0-88132-186-9   92 pp.

32 **Eastern Europe and the Soviet Union in the World Economy**
Susan M. Collins and Dani Rodrik/ *May 1991*
ISBN paper 0-88132-157-5   152 pp.

33 **African Economic Reform: The External Dimension**
Carol Lancaster/ *June 1991*
ISBN paper 0-88132-096-X   82 pp.

34 **Has the Adjustment Process Worked?**
Paul R. Krugman/ *October 1991*
ISBN paper 0-88132-116-8   80 pp.

35 **From Soviet disUnion to Eastern Economic Community?**
Oleh Havrylyshyn and John Williamson/ *October 1991*
ISBN paper 0-88132-192-3   84 pp.

36 **Global Warming: The Economic Stakes**
William R. Cline/ *May 1992*
ISBN paper 0-88132-172-9   128 pp.

37 **Trade and Payments After Soviet Disintegration**
John Williamson/ *June 1992*
ISBN paper 0-88132-173-7   96 pp.

38 **Trade and Migration: NAFTA and Agriculture**
Philip L. Martin/ *October 1993*
ISBN paper 0-88132-201-6   160 pp.

39 **The Exchange Rate System and the IMF: A Modest Agenda**
Morris Goldstein/ *June 1995*
ISBN paper 0-88132-219-9   104 pp.

40 **What Role for Currency Boards?**
John Williamson/ *September 1995*
ISBN paper 0-88132-222-9   64 pp.

41 **Predicting External Imbalances for the United States and Japan**
William R. Cline/ *September 1995*
ISBN paper 0-88132-220-2   104 pp.

42 **Standards and APEC: An Action Agenda**
John S. Wilson/ *October 1995*
ISBN paper 0-88132-223-7   176 pp.

43 **Fundamental Tax Reform and Border Tax Adjustments**
Gary Clyde Hufbauer assisted by Carol Gabyzon/ *January 1996*
ISBN paper 0-88132-225-3   108 pp.

44 **Global Telecom Talks: A Trillion Dollar Deal**
Ben A. Petrazzini/ *June 1996*
ISBN paper 0-88132-230-X   128 pp.

45 **WTO 2000: Setting the Course for World Trade**
Jeffrey J. Schott/ *September 1996*
ISBN paper 0-88132-234-2   72 pp.

46 **The National Economic Council: A Work in Progress**
I. M. Destler/ *November 1996*
ISBN paper 0-88132-239-3   90 pp.

47 **The Case for an International Banking Standard**
Morris Goldstein/ *April 1997*
ISBN paper 0-88132-244-X   128 pp.

48 **Transatlantic Trade: A Strategic Agenda**
Ellen L. Frost/ *May 1997*
ISBN paper 0-88132-228-8   136 pp.

49 **Cooperating with Europe's Monetary Union**
C. Randall Henning/ *May 1997*
ISBN paper 0-88132-245-8   104 pp.

50 **Renewing Fast-Track Legislation**
I.M.Destler/ *September 1997*
ISBN paper 0-88132-252-0   72 pp.

51 **Competition Policies for the Global Economy**
Edward M. Graham and J. David Richardson/ *November 1997*
ISBN paper 0-88132-249-0   96 pp.

52 **Improving Trade Policy Reviews in the World Trade Organization**
Donald Keesing/ *April 1998*
ISBN paper 0-88132-251-2   104 pp.

53 **Agricultural Trade Policy: Completing the Reform**
Timothy Josling/ *April 1998*
ISBN paper 0-88132-256-3   152 pp.

54 **Real Exchange Rates for the Year 2000**
Simon Wren-Lewis and Rebecca Driver/ *April 1998*
ISBN paper 0-88132-253-9   188 pp.

55 **The Asian Financial Crisis: Causes, Cures, and Systemic Implications**
Morris Goldstein/ *June 1998*
ISBN paper 0-88132-261-X   100 pp.

BOOKS

IMF Conditionality
John Williamson, editor/ *1983*   ISBN cloth 0-88132-006-4   695 pp.

Trade Policy in the 1980s
William R. Cline, editor/ *1983*
(out of print)   ISBN paper 0-88132-031-5   810 pp.

Subsidies in International Trade
Gary Clyde Hufbauer and Joanna Shelton Erb/ *1984*
ISBN cloth 0-88132-004-8   299 pp.

International Debt: Systemic Risk and Policy Response
William R. Cline/ *1984*   ISBN cloth 0-88132-015-3   336 pp.

Trade Protection in the United States: 31 Case Studies
Gary Clyde Hufbauer, Diane E. Berliner, and Kimberly Ann Elliott/ *1986*
(out of print)   ISBN paper 0-88132-040-4   371 pp.

Toward Renewed Economic Growth in Latin America
Bela Balassa, Gerardo M. Bueno, Pedro-Pablo Kuczynski,
and Mario Henrique Simonsen/*1986*
(out of stock)　　　　　　ISBN paper 0-88132-045-5　　　　　　205 pp.

Capital Flight and Third World Debt
Donald R. Lessard and John Williamson, editors/*1987*
(out of print)　　　　　　ISBN paper 0-88132-053-6　　　　　　270 pp.

The Canada-United States Free Trade Agreement: The Global Impact
Jeffrey J. Schott and Murray G. Smith, editors/*1988*
　　　　　　ISBN paper 0-88132-073-0　　　　　　211 pp.

World Agricultural Trade: Building a Consensus
William M. Miner and Dale E. Hathaway, editors/*1988*
　　　　　　ISBN paper 0-88132-071-3　　　　　　226 pp.

Japan in the World Economy
Bela Balassa and Marcus Noland/*1988*
　　　　　　ISBN paper 0-88132-041-2　　　　　　306 pp.

America in the World Economy: A Strategy for the 1990s
C. Fred Bergsten/*1988*　　　　ISBN cloth 0-88132-089-7　　　　235 pp.
　　　　　　ISBN paper 0-88132-082-X　　　　　　235 pp.

Managing the Dollar: From the Plaza to the Louvre
Yoichi Funabashi/*1988, 2d ed. 1989*
　　　　　　ISBN paper 0-88132-097-8　　　　　　307 pp.

United States External Adjustment and the World Economy
William R. Cline/*May 1989*　　　ISBN paper 0-88132-048-X　　　　392 pp.

Free Trade Areas and U.S. Trade Policy
Jeffrey J. Schott, editor/*May 1989*
　　　　　　ISBN paper 0-88132-094-3　　　　　　400 pp.

Dollar Politics: Exchange Rate Policymaking in the United States
I. M. Destler and C. Randall Henning/*September 1989*
(out of print)　　　　　　ISBN paper 0-88132-079-X　　　　　　192 pp.

Latin American Adjustment: How Much Has Happened?
John Williamson, editor/*April 1990*
　　　　　　ISBN paper 0-88132-125-7　　　　　　480 pp.

The Future of World Trade in Textiles and Apparel
William R. Cline/*1987, 2d ed. June 1990*
　　　　　　ISBN paper 0-88132-110-9　　　　　　344 pp.

**Completing the Uruguay Round: A Results-Oriented Approach
to the GATT Trade Negotiations**
Jeffrey J. Schott, editor/*September 1990*
　　　　　　ISBN paper 0-88132-130-3　　　　　　256 pp.

Economic Sanctions Reconsidered (in two volumes)
Economic Sanctions Reconsidered: Supplemental Case Histories
Gary Clyde Hufbauer, Jeffrey J. Schott, and Kimberly Ann Elliott/*1985, 2d ed. December 1990*
　　　　　　ISBN cloth 0-88132-115-X　　　　928 pp.
　　　　　　ISBN paper 0-88132-105-2　　　　928 pp.

Economic Sanctions Reconsidered: History and Current Policy
Gary Clyde Hufbauer, Jeffrey J. Schott, and Kimberly Ann Elliott/*December 1990*
　　　　　　ISBN cloth 0-88132-136-2　　　　288 pp.
　　　　　　ISBN paper 0-88132-140-0　　　　288 pp.

Pacific Basin Developing Countries: Prospects for the Future
Marcus Noland/*January 1991*　　ISBN cloth 0-88132-141-9　　　250 pp.
(out of print)　　　　　　ISBN paper 0-88132-081-1　　　　　　250 pp.

Currency Convertibility in Eastern Europe
John Williamson, editor/*October 1991*
　　　　　　ISBN paper 0-88132-128-1　　　　　　396 pp.

International Adjustment and Financing: The Lessons of 1985-1991
C. Fred Bergsten, editor/*January 1992*
　　　　　　ISBN paper 0-88132-112-5　　　　　　336 pp.

North American Free Trade: Issues and Recommendations
Gary Clyde Hufbauer and Jeffrey J. Schott/*April 1992*
　　　　　　ISBN paper 0-88132-120-6　　　　　　392 pp.

Narrowing the U.S. Current Account Deficit
Allen J. Lenz/*June 1992*
(out of print)　　　　　　ISBN paper 0-88132-103-6　　　　　　640 pp.

The Economics of Global Warming
William R. Cline/*June 1992*   ISBN paper 0-88132-132-X   416 pp.

U.S. Taxation of International Income: Blueprint for Reform
Gary Clyde Hufbauer, assisted by Joanna M. van Rooij/*October 1992*
                                   ISBN cloth 0-88132-178-8   304 pp.
                                   ISBN paper 0-88132-134-6   304 pp.

Who's Bashing Whom? Trade Conflict in High-Technology Industries
Laura D'Andrea Tyson/*November 1992*
                                   ISBN paper 0-88132-106-0   352 pp.

Korea in the World Economy
Il SaKong/*January 1993*   ISBN paper 0-88132-106-0   328 pp.

Pacific Dynamism and the International Economic System
C. Fred Bergsten and Marcus Noland, editors/*May 1993*
                                   ISBN paper 0-88132-196-6   424 pp.

Economic Consequences of Soviet Disintegration
John Williamson, editor/*May 1993*
                                   ISBN paper 0-88132-190-7   664 pp.

Reconcilable Differences? United States-Japan Economic Conflict
C. Fred Bergsten and Marcus Noland/*June 1993*
                                   ISBN paper 0-88132-129-X   296 pp.

Does Foreign Exchange Intervention Work?
Kathryn M. Dominguez and Jeffrey A. Frankel/*September 1993*
                                   ISBN paper 0-88132-104-4   192 pp.

Sizing Up U.S. Export Disincentives
J. David Richardson/*September 1993*
                                   ISBN paper 0-88132-107-9   192 pp.

NAFTA: An Assessment
Gary Clyde Hufbauer and Jeffrey J. Schott/*rev. ed. October 1993*
                                   ISBN paper 0-88132-199-0   216 pp.

Adjusting to Volatile Energy Prices
Philip K. Verleger, Jr./*November 1993*
                                   ISBN paper 0-88132-069-2   288 pp.

The Political Economy of Policy Reform
John Williamson, editor/*January 1994*
                                   ISBN paper 0-88132-195-8   624 pp.

Measuring the Costs of Protection in the United States
Gary Clyde Hufbauer and Kimberly Ann Elliott/*January 1994*
                                   ISBN paper 0-88132-108-7   144 pp.

The Dynamics of Korean Economic Development
Cho Soon/*March 1994*
                                   ISBN paper 0-88132-162-1   272 pp.

Reviving the European Union
C. Randall Henning, Eduard Hochreiter and Gary Clyde Hufbauer, editors/*April 1994*
                                   ISBN paper 0-88132-208-3   192 pp.

China in the World Economy
Nicholas R. Lardy/*April 1994*
                                   ISBN paper 0-88132-200-8   176 pp.

Greening the GATT: Trade, Environment, and the Future
Daniel C. Esty/*July 1994*
                                   ISBN paper 0-88132-205-9   344 pp.

Western Hemisphere Economic Integration
Gary Clyde Hufbauer and Jeffrey J. Schott/*July 1994*
                                   ISBN paper 0-88132-159-1   304 pp.

Currencies and Politics in the United States, Germany, and Japan
C. Randall Henning/*September 1994*
                                   ISBN paper 0-88132-127-3   432 pp.

Estimating Equilibrium Exchange Rates
John Williamson, editor/*September 1994*
                                   ISBN paper 0-88132-076-5   320 pp.

Managing the World Economy: Fifty Years After Bretton Woods
Peter B. Kenen, editor/*September 1994*
                                   ISBN paper 0-88132-212-1   448 pp.

Reciprocity and Retaliation in U.S. Trade Policy
Thomas O. Bayard and Kimberly Ann Elliott/*September 1994*
                                   ISBN paper 0-88132-084-6   528 pp.

The Uruguay Round: An Assessment
Jeffrey J. Schott, assisted by Johanna W. Buurman/*November 1994*
                ISBN paper 0-88132-206-7   240 pp.

Measuring the Costs of Protection in Japan
Yoko Sazanami, Shujiro Urata, and Hiroki Kawai/*January 1995*
                ISBN paper 0-88132-211-3   96 pp.

Foreign Direct Investment in the United States, Third Edition
Edward M. Graham and Paul R. Krugman/*January 1995*
                ISBN paper 0-88132-204-0   232 pp.

The Political Economy of Korea-United States Cooperation
C. Fred Bergsten and Il SaKong, editors/*February 1995*
                ISBN paper 0-88132-213-X   128 pp.

International Debt Reexamined
William R. Cline/*February 1995*
                ISBN paper 0-88132-083-8   560 pp.

American Trade Politics, Third Edition
I. M. Destler/*April 1995*   ISBN paper 0-88132-215-6   360 pp.

Managing Official Export Credits: The Quest for a Global Regime
John E. Ray/*July 1995*   ISBN paper 0-88132-207-5   344 pp.

Asia Pacific Fusion: Japan's Role in APEC
Yoichi Funabashi/*October 1995*
                ISBN paper 0-88132-224-5   312 pp.

Korea-United States Cooperation in the New World Order
C. Fred Bergsten and Il SaKong, editors/*February 1996*
                ISBN paper 0-88132-226-1   144 pp.

Why Exports Really Matter!   ISBN paper 0-88132-221-0   34 pp.
Why Exports Matter More!   ISBN paper 0-88132-229-6   36 pp.
J. David Richardson and Karin Rindal/*July 1995; February 1996*

Global Corporations and National Governments
Edward M. Graham/*May 1996*
                ISBN paper 0-88132-111-7   168 pp.

Global Economic Leadership and the Group of Seven
C. Fred Bergsten and C. Randall Henning/*May 1996*
                ISBN paper 0-88132-218-0   192 pp.

The Trading System After the Uruguay Round
John Whalley and Colleen Hamilton/*July 1996*
                ISBN paper 0-88132-131-1   224 pp.

Private Capital Flows to Emerging Markets After the Mexican Crisis
Guillermo A. Calvo, Morris Goldstein, and Eduard Hochreiter/*September 1996*
                ISBN paper 0-88132-232-6   352 pp.

The Crawling Band as an Exchange Rate Regime:
Lessons from Chile, Colombia, and Israel
John Williamson/*September 1996*
                ISBN paper 0-88132-231-8   192 pp.

Flying High: Civil Aviation in the Asia Pacific
Gary Clyde Hufbauer and Christopher Findlay/*November 1996*
                ISBN paper 0-88132-231-8   232 pp.

Measuring the Costs of Visible Protection in Korea
Namdoo Kim/*November 1996*
                ISBN paper 0-88132-236-9   112 pp.

The World Trading System: Challenges Ahead
Jeffrey J. Schott/*December 1996*
                ISBN paper 0-88132-235-0   350 pp.

Has Globalization Gone Too Far?
Dani Rodrik/*March 1997*   ISBN cloth 0-88132-243-1   128 pp.

Korea-United States Economic Relationship
C. Fred Bergsten and Il SaKong, editors/*March 1997*
                ISBN paper 0-88132-240-7   152 pp.

Summitry in the Americas: A Progress Report
Richard E. Feinberg/*April 1997*
                ISBN paper 0-88132-242-3   272 pp.

Corruption and the Global Economy
Kimberly Ann Elliott/*June 1997*
                ISBN paper 0-88132-233-4   256 pp.

Regional Trading Blocs in the World Economic System
Jeffrey A. Frankel/*October 1997*

ISBN paper 0-88132-202-4   346 pp.

Sustaining the Asia Pacific Miracle: Environmental Protection and Economic Integration
André Dua and Daniel C. Esty/*October 1997*

ISBN paper 0-88132-250-4   232 pp.

Trade and Income Distribution
William R. Cline/*November1997*

ISBN paper 0-88132-216-4   296 pp.

Global Competition Policy
Edward M. Graham and J. David Richardson/*December 1997*

ISBN paper 0-88132-166-4   616 pp.

Unfinished Business: Telecommunications after the Uruguay Round
Gary Clyde Hufbauer and Erika Wada/*December 1997*

ISBN paper 0-88132-257-1   272 pp.

Financial Services Liberalization in the WTO
Wendy Dobson and Pierre Jacquet /*June 1998*

ISBN paper 0-88132-254-7   376 pp.

SPECIAL REPORTS

1   **Promoting World Recovery: A Statement on Global Economic Strategy by Twenty-six Economists from Fourteen Countries/***December 1982*
    (out of print)   ISBN paper 0-88132-013-7   45 pp.
2   **Prospects for Adjustment in Argentina, Brazil, and Mexico: Responding to the Debt Crisis**   (out of print)
    John Williamson, editor/*June 1983*
    ISBN paper 0-88132-016-1   71 pp.
3   **Inflation and Indexation: Argentina, Brazil, and Israel**
    John Williamson, editor/*March 1985*
    ISBN paper 0-88132-037-4   191 pp.
4   **Global Economic Imbalances**
    C. Fred Bergsten, editor/*March 1986*
    ISBN cloth 0-88132-038-2   126 pp.
    ISBN paper 0-88132-042-0   126 pp.
5   **African Debt and Financing**
    Carol Lancaster and John Williamson, editors/*May 1986*
    (out of print)   ISBN paper 0-88132-044-7   229 pp.
6   **Resolving the Global Economic Crisis: After Wall Street**
    Thirty-three Economists from Thirteen Countries/*December 1987*
    ISBN paper 0-88132-070-6   30 pp.
7   **World Economic Problems**
    Kimberly Ann Elliott and John Williamson, editors/*April 1988*
    ISBN paper 0-88132-055-2   298 pp.
    Reforming World Agricultural Trade
    Twenty-nine Professionals from Seventeen Countries/*1988*
    ISBN paper 0-88132-088-9   42 pp.
8   **Economic Relations Between the United States and Korea: Conflict or Cooperation?**
    Thomas O. Bayard and Soo-Gil Young, editors/*January 1989*
    ISBN paper 0-88132-068-4   192 pp.
9   **Whither APEC? The Progress to Date and Agenda for the Future**
    C. Fred Bergsten, editor/*October 1997*
    ISBN paper 0-88132-248-2   272 pp.
10 **Economic Integration of the Korean Peninsula**
    Marcus Noland, editor/*January 1998*
    ISBN paper 0-88132-255-5   250 pp.
11 **Restarting Fast Track**
    Jeffrey J. Schott, editor/*April 1998*
    ISBN paper 0-88132-259-8   250 pp.

WORKS IN PROGRESS

The US - Japan Economic Relationship
C. Fred Bergsten, Marcus Noland, and Takatoshi Ito
China's Entry to the World Economy
Richard N. Cooper
Economic Sanctions After the Cold War
Kimberly Ann Elliott, Gary C. Hufbauer and Jeffrey J. Schott

Trade and Labor Standards
Kimberly Ann Elliott and Richard Freeman
Leading Indicators of Financial Crises in the Emerging Economies
Morris Goldstein and Carmen Reinhart
Prospects for Western Hemisphere Free Trade
Gary Clyde Hufbauer and Jeffrey J. Schott
The Future of US Foreign Aid
Carol Lancaster
The Asian Financial Crisis and Global Adjustment
Li-Gang Liu, Marcus Noland, Sherman Robinson, and Zhi Wang
The Economics of Korean Unification
Marcus Noland
International Lender of Last Resort
Catherine L. Mann
A Primer on US External Balance
Catherine L. Mann
Foreign Direct Investment and Development:
The New Policy Agenda for Developing Countries and Economies in Transition
Theodore Moran
How Much is Enough for Japan?
Adam Posen
Globalization, the NAIRU, and Monetary Policy
Adam Posen
Foreign Enterprises in the Chinese Marketplace
Daniel Rosen
Measuring the Costs of Protection in China
Zhang Shuguang, Zhang Yansheng, and Wan Zhongxin

DISTRIBUTORS OUTSIDE THE UNITED STATES

Canada
RENOUF BOOKSTORE
5369 Canotek Road, Unit 1,
Ottawa, Ontario K1J 9J3, Canada
(tel: (613) 745-2665
fax: (613) 745-7660)
http://www.renoufbooks.com/

Caribbean
SYSTEMATICS STUDIES LIMITED
St. Augustine Shopping Centre
Eastern Main Road, St. Augustine
Trinidad and Tobago, West Indies
(tel: 868-645-8466; fax: 868-645-8467)
email: tobe@trinidad.net

Japan
UNITED PUBLISHERS SERVICES, LTD.
Kenkyu-Sha Bldg.
9, Kanda Surugadai 2-Chome
Chiyoda-Ku, Tokyo 101, Japan
(tel: 81-3-3291-4541; fax: 81-3-3292-8610)
email: saito@ups.co.jp

Visit our website at:
http://www.iie.com

E-mail orders to:
iiecon@pmds.com